S0-AAA-951

1 8 6 6 - 1 9 9 1
125th
ANNIVERSARY

Language
Maven
Strikes
Again

BOOKS BY WILLIAM SAFIRE

Language

You Could Look It Up
Take My Word for It
I Stand Corrected
What's the Good Word?
On Language

Politics

Safire's Washington
Before the Fall
Safire's Political Dictionary
Plunging into Politics
The Relations Explosion

Anthologies
(with Leonard Safir)

Leadership
Words of Wisdom
Good Advice

Fiction

Freedom
Full Disclosure

WILLIAM

 AN OWL BOOK

SAFIRE

Language Maven Strikes Again

HENRY HOLT AND COMPANY   NEW YORK

Copyright © 1990 by The Cobbett Corporation
All essays originally appeared in *The New York Times*.
Copyright © 1984–1988 by The New York Times Company.
Reprinted by permission.
All rights reserved, including the right to reproduce
this book or portions thereof in any form.
Published by Henry Holt and Company, Inc.,
115 West 18th Street, New York, New York 10011.
Published in Canada by Fitzhenry & Whiteside Limited,
195 Allstate Parkway, Markham, Ontario L3R 4T8.

Library of Congress Cataloging-in-Publication Data
Safire, William.
Language maven strikes again / William Safire.
p.   cm.
1st Owl Book ed.
A collection of the author's weekly columns "On language" from the
New York Times Magazine.
"First published in hardcover by Doubleday and Co. in 1990"—T.p.
verso.
"An Owl book."
Includes index.
1. English language—Usage.   2. English language—Style.   I. New
York Times Magazine.   II. Title
[PE1421.S225   1991]
428—dc20   91–23085
                                                              CIP
ISBN 0-8050-1766-6 (An Owl Book: pbk.)

Henry Holt books are available at special dicounts
for bulk purchases for sales promotions, premiums,
fund-raising, or educational use. Special editions
or book excerpts can also be created to specification.
For details contact:
Special Sales Director, Henry Holt and Company, Inc.,
115 West 18th Street, New York, New York 10011.

First published in hardcover by
Doubleday and Co. in 1990.

First Owl Book Edition—1991

Printed in the United States of America
Recognizing the importance of preserving the written word,
Henry Holt and Company, Inc., by policy, prints all of its
first editions on acid-free paper. ∞

10   9   8   7   6   5   4   3   2   1

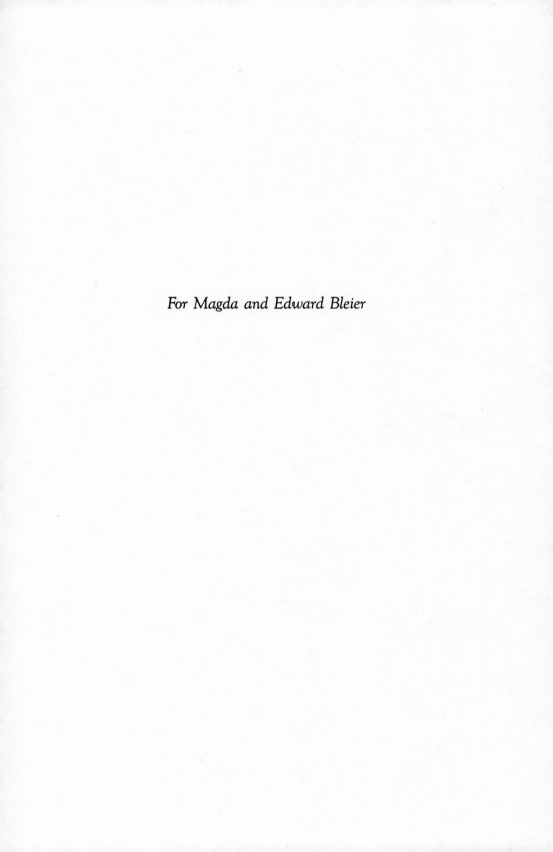

For Magda and Edward Bleier

Foreword

"Eureka!" cried A. M. Rosenthal, then editor of *The New York Times*, explaining to his colleagues that the Greek word meant "I've found it." His inspiration: "Safire will do a language column."

It was OK with me (or OK *by* me, as they say in New York). I had written a hefty political dictionary, contributed an annual "Vogue Word Watch" to the *Times Magazine* and fiddled with words all my working life. Why not become English-Speaking World Usage Dictator? So what if I hadn't finished college, or even studied Latin? In the language dodge, I figured, a cat could look at a king. Maybe the series could be strung out for a year.

That was in 1979. I have been riding this tiger ever since and am afraid to get off. This is the sixth compilation of "On Language" columns and, as always, it is enlivened by the roars, hisses, applause and emendations of the Lexicographic Irregulars—the legion of language-lovers who seize upon this outlet for their frustrations (*"Prioritize?* Ugly!") and questioning ("How many words end in *gry?"*). In the newspaper column, I don't have the space to let my readers expound; in books, however, I can let them blaze away.

This outlet for the literate led beyond usage and word games (*prioritize* is bureaucratic, but has as much right to live as *finalize*, and you don't need to know the words beyond *angry* and *hungry*) to the seamy side of semiotics: How do you address a letter in the post-"Gentlemen" era? Where is the graveyard of forgotten words like *knickers* and *sink stopper*? Which of the nonce words will stay with us beyond the nonce—the nuts-based *nerd* (nah) or the whimper-based *wimp*?

I used to feel like a jerk when a correspondent pointed out an obvious mistake. Now I'm with Mayor Fiorello La Guardia—"When I make a mistake," he would say, "it's a beaut"—and when I make a linguistic misstep, it's grist for a column.

Some people, probably conspiracy theorists, think that I make mistakes deliberately, as a mail-pull. Good; let them think that. It enhances respect for authority.

A note about Authority: In these pages, you will be given The Word about The Words. Here is what I think about what is correct and constructive, what is imprecise and destructive. You may disagree, as many of my articulate and scholarly (or plain ornery) readers do. It's your language, too, buddy; if you want to abuse it and muddle it up, you will do that for yourself, not for me. If, on the other hand, you are willing to think about how we communicate, and consider the words and the forms of grammar, then you are automatically a member of the Authority, entitled to a ring and a secret handshake and the thrill of membership. A word of warning: If you get hooked on the study of the language, you're in that sorority, or fraternity, for life.

You'll be watching, as I am now, for the word that encompasses *sorority* and *fraternity*, that turns sisterhood and brotherhood into familyhood. I don't know what that word is, but not to worry—some reader will find it or coin it and send it in.

Introduction
Watch My Style

S tyle, in the literary sense, is the way we use words to express what we think or feel. Too often, grammarians and less self-conscious writers limit the meaning of the word to the rules of spelling, punctuation or usage that can be found in a *style book* (or, as some style books direct, *stylebook*); but the elements of style, to use the name of the best-selling little book on that subject, include not merely the agreed-upon conventions of the writing trade, but encompass the strength, precision, grace and honesty—or lack of those virtues—that characterize the way we communicate.

The paragraph above is not written in my style. Readers of dictums in this space have come to expect a grabber of a lead—a quotation with some egregious misuse of *masterful* for *masterly* and other such solecisms in vogue, or a shout of outrage from some big shot cut down to medium shot—followed by a deluge of erudition that sugarcoats a grammatical pronunciamento or pinpricks some political orator's trial balloon. These readers know that I would die before lining myself up before the memorandums of the Squad Squad with a redundancy like *agreed-upon convention*.

Why, then, have I reverted to the soporific kind of lead that you can read in any how-to book on writing for success, or dressing for writing, or writing and dressing to seduce impressionable young literary agents and take down megabucks? Nobody but a pedant, a professional esthete or a language-book author would begin any article or chapter with "Style, in the literary sense. . . ."

Such a la-di-da ringing of the belles-lettres, haughtily presenting such unasked-for information, causes the sensible reader to demand: "Why do I need to know this? Why is this man lecturing at me?" and to turn the page with the knuckle-to-the-lips satisfaction of an adult videogoer fast-forwarding past the tape's opening credits to get right to the hard-core pornography.

My purpose in beginning with a let-go lead, opposite of a grabber, is to limit my readership to people who are really hung up on the subject of style, surface-variety. That means we are in no great lecture hall; we're in a tight little seminar of the sort of elitists who grimly stick to *dicta, encomia* and *memoranda* despite the general preference for *-ums*. First comes the assignment of books for outside reading.

Publishers of language books have crowned me the Great Pooh-Bah of Plugsville because I happily blurb for books on how to write. I have been reduced to such encomiums as "Even this book of pedagogic pettifoggery may help." For years, I have held that any decent book on plain writing will help the reader improve his style, because most people don't pay any attention to style at all, and, as a result, banal words and stereotypes are chosen, sentences with passive constructions mar the literary skyline and paragraphs lurch on the page without benefit of topic sentences.

However, I have in my hand a letter from Alistair Cooke. A longtime social and political commentator who interprets America to the mother country on the BBC, he is familiar to many Americans as a man who sits in an easy chair in front of a fireplace and gives meaning and perspective to episodes of television series. Everyone can understand what he is saying because he is a life-long student of language who works hard on his writing and speaks the words easily but with care. He is the epitome of urbane renewal.

Mr. Cooke's letter chides my American-English bias in a recent piece on mnemonics—I wrote of a way to remember the musical treble clef with "Every Good Boy Does Fine" while Britons say "Deserves Favor"—and he asks for the origin of the expression "start from scratch," which I will look up when I get the itch.* Then he writes:

* To scratch the itch: in racing, one who starts from a mark scratched in the ground is without special advantages, in contrast to one who races with a designated handicap.

"As for books that say—keep your sentences short, cut out all adjectives and adverbs, don't use dashes—I simply ignore them."

Now that is breathtaking iconoclasm. Down the midway of the twentieth century, authors from Hemingway to Doctorow have championed the short, simple declarative sentence. The most memorable American literary sentence of the nineteenth century, precursor to the modern style, was Herman Melville's "Call me Ishmael."

Every book on writing you can find these days says essentially the same thing: keep it short. Take it a bite at a time. Dispense with the adjectival frills. Put the punch in the verb and not the adverb (he added weakly). Edit, edit, edit, and avoid repetition. Less is more, spare is fair. Our taste in style matches our taste in corned beef: lean is keen.

Maybe we are going overboard. The burst of the business memo, the snap-and-spit of the television news "bite," the mincing sentences of post-Hemingway novelists—all have led to the canonization of brevity. Introduce it, lay it out, sum it up. The dash is dead. It is not for nothing, as the Communists say, that the hottest word in communication is *briefing.*

I decry this trend. (*Decry* is a word used only in newspaper headlines; it is shorter than *disparage, denounce* or *complain about,* and editors are more interested in its length than the plain fact that the word is not used in the spoken language. Try it: "Don't decry, dear." You never heard that anywhere; the vestigial verb's presence on front pages is a triumph of briefmanship.)

This is not to call for a return to long-windedness or a plea for studding sentences with redundancies and festooning them with modifying clauses, but I suggest this: You don't have to be flowery to love adjectives, and your judicious use of words ending in *-ly* adds color and nuance to the stark action of your trendiest verbs; although short sentences have punch—"I decry this trend" makes the point mightily, if I may be permitted an adverb —too many crisp declarations leave the reader punch-drunk, reeling from incessant short shots, wondering where he can find a writer who can drop brevity's bludgeon and bedazzle with fancy footwork; in this regard, cadence counts (your corporal was right), and while the sort of Churchillian prose that sweeps the reader rhythmically along may have no place in news reports or the bulletins of avant-guardhouse poets, it must not be lost to the arsenal of the artist or historian—lest we bend our knee to the staccato style book that barks "Be brief!" and orders us to come to a full stop before we have finished saying all we have to say in just the way we want to say it.

Stop thinking about writing style as an outer garment with which to dress your thoughts. Style, in the sense I have in mind, is not the synonym of "form," the antonym of "substance," a fashion to be adopted and set aside. Style is not a mask, an image or a persona: upon his admission to the French Academy in 1753, Comte Georges-Louis de Leclerc Buffon said, "Style is the man himself," arguing that style is essence. The way you write reflects the way you think, and the way you think is the mark of the kind of person you are.

In the second paragraph of this introductory discourse (no need to turn back the page, I rarely misquote myself), I dumped on the first paragraph as not being in my style. You took that to mean "not the way I usually write," an assumption quickly reinforced by a comparison of grabber and let-go leads. (Better go back.) But that was a trick; you were misled by my seeming acceptance of the most common current meaning of the word *style*. What I really meant was more profound than "that's not the way I write"; it was also "that's not how I think," and when you keep peeling that onion until you're down where the tears are, "that is not the sort of person I am."

You want to fix up your writing, parse your sentences, use the right words? Fine, pick up the little books, learn to avoid mistakes, revere taut prose and revile tautology. But do not flatter yourself that you have significantly changed your style. First, straighten out yourself so that you can then think straight and soon afterward write straight. Your writing style is yourself in the process of thinking and the act of writing, and you cannot buy that in a bookstore or fix it up in a seminar.

Language
Maven
Strikes
Again

Access Gaining

My son the hacker, trained at the knee of the superhacker Andrew Glass of Cox Newspapers, reconfigured the files in my personal computer—and for a frightening moment I didn't know where anything was.

"How do I get at the 'On Language' column?" I asked.

"You mean," he replied coolly, speaking in a language he calls "Basic," "how do you *access* it?"

That's the new magic word. Now that all the world's information has been "inputted," the trick is to get at it, and the operative verb is *to access.* This is the shortened form of the old phrase *to gain access to,* and it has gained wide acceptance, much as *to make contact with* became *to contact* a couple of generations ago. Don't fight the verbifying: to make a withdrawal from your grammar-friendly data bank, you must adopt the necessary lingo. If you don't use *access,* you won't get in anywhere.

That is also the message in the new vogue for the word as a noun. In Washington, for many years people in the lobbying business sold *influence.*

This word gained a pejorative connotation in 1949, when a "five percenter" testified to Congress that "I have nothing to sell but influence." Objection to this line of work led to the wide use of the phrase *influence peddler*, and now no opinion-respecting consultant in your nation's capital sells that word anymore. (The predecessor word, *pull*, derived from *wire-puller*, long ago fell into disuse.)

Today, what lobbyists like to say they sell is *access*—that is, an open door or telephone line to the people in power. In an article in *Washington Dossier* magazine titled "Playing the Access Game," Dom Bonafede writes: "Access —the very word is lovingly caressed simply in its saying by those who have it—is like a fragrant lubricant smoothing the way for political and social acceptance."

Presumably, this *access* merely ensures a client a prompt and fair hearing, which the unintroduced citizen is less likely to get. The word is intended to strip from the activity the connotation of favoritism implicit in the noun and verb *influence*.

And yet, *access*, the insider's noun, is formed from the verb *accede*, based on the Latin *cedere*, "to yield." That's what the government official is supposed to be doing, and it is the ability to induce such sweet surrender that the sellers of *access* are selling.

Acronym Sought

What's in an acronym? Plenty. In areas of great public controversy, propagandists seek to get a message into the name of the product or program, and when they are successful the "sell" appears every time the subject comes up.

We are not talking here of the old "Lux Radio Theater," which plugged the soap sponsor every time the program appeared in the newspaper listings. (The newspapers got wise and soon started calling it just "Radio Theater." I still miss the soothing sound of Cecil B. De Mille's saying "Good night from Holly-w-o-o-d.")

A good example of built-in message delivery is "right-to-work laws." Who can be against the right to work? Organized labor was, of course, because the laws, when passed, struck down the union shop; labor soon began referring to the legislation as "union-busting laws."

A more subtle escalation of the technique appeared in the controversy over abortion. Anti-abortion forces did not want to put themselves in the position of campaigning for a negative, and chose "pro-life"; pro-abortion forces did not like to be identified with encouraging abortion, which is a harsh word, and countered with "pro-choice." That produced a "slogan-ary" standoff: what are you for, life or choice?

The Reagan Administration was alert in its early days to the need for a "fresh start" in arms-control negotiations and was aware that Mr. Reagan had campaigned against the second strategic arms limitation talks (SALT) treaty as "fatally flawed" (which many people still think is a description of improperly installed linoleum). They came up with a fresh acronym to replace SALT: the strategic arms reduction talks, acronamed Start. (When an acronym exceeds four letters, capitalize only the first letter.)

The trick in acronaming, by the way, is to find a series of initial letters that spell out a pronounceable word. M.B.F.R., the interminable negotia-tions in Vienna about Mutual and Balanced Force Reduction (which right-wingers remember in derision as "More Better for Russia"), is not an acro-nym. M.B.F.R. is pronounced as a series of letters, not a word, and these talks will not be immortalized in a word until someone starts calling them "Mubalfor" or some such.

Acronyms applied after the fact of naming an organization or program can ridicule the activity named. I was particularly sensitive to this in my political days, and closely examined the name of the Committee to Re-elect the President in 1972 for possible backfiring. C.T.R.T.P.? Comrep? Crepres? Safe enough, I decided; and so what later became famous as Creep was born. In the same way, the Law of the Sea Treaty advocates did not recognize the time bomb ticking in the treaty's name; when the se-lected initials came out LOST, the opponents who considered it all to be a power-grab by the third world had a handy weapon. (The ratification of the treaty by the United States was sunk in what Washington wags called "scuttle diplomacy.")

Imagine the chagrin of the Reagan people, so sensitive to the nuances of implanting "sell" in program titles, when the President announced his idea for a defense in space against incoming missiles and the notion was head-lined immediately as "Reagan's Star Wars Proposal." The application of the movie title to the futuristic defense was buttressed by the President's earlier use of the phrase "evil empire" to describe the Soviet Union's imperialism, which seemed identical to the "empire" lined up against the good guys in the George Lucas film.

Grimly, Pentacrats jettisoned the phrase that had been used by the pro-gram's early defenders—High Frontier—which comes down to the acronymic Hifron, no competition for Star Wars. Instead, bureaucrats, in what can be charitably called a holding action, described the idea as Strategic Defense Initiative, or S.D.I.; this phrase has not really caught on, and the initials do not form an acronym. Some thought has been given to changing the countername to Strategic Initiative for Defense, so that it could be called SID (remembering that the Pentagon is on Shirley Highway) but this acronym has a nebbishistic ring.

What to do? The critics of the defense idea were having a field day with the built-in derision of Star Wars. The President complained: "I wish whoever coined that expression would take it back again, because it gives a false impression of what it is we're talking about." In his second Inaugural Address, he came up with a lame substitute: a "security shield," which, like "security guard," is redundant. The "shield" image was useful—a global, or planetary, shield describes the unaggressive weapon—but some of the President's advisers thought it promised too much. One of them bitterly complained that they were "up the laser river."

In this linguistic pickle, the Administration, on deep background, is outreaching desperately. It is looking for suggestions for the antidote to the poison in the name Star Wars, which is what Andrei Gromyko, who has never even seen the movie, delights in calling our mind-boggling new idea.

It is in the tradition of *The New York Times* that a great institution turn to its public for help of this kind. Almost ninety years ago, when "All the News That's Fit to Print" was first suggested for *The Times*'s slogan, a contest was conducted to come up with a better idea. Thousands of entries were submitted. The winning slogan was "All the World News, but not a School for Scandal," a play on the title of Richard Brinsley Sheridan's 1777 comedy. As it happened, the publisher kept the original suggestion, so the motto is still "All the News That's Fit to Print," but the involvement of the public always gives a nice sense of participation.

In that spirit, the Lexicographic Irregulars are called upon now to help the Administration find a suitable and catchy name for what, let's face it, everybody calls the Star Wars program. Here is the current state of play: the President is down for "security shield," no acronym. The Pentagon has its chips on the Strategic Defense Initiative, initials S.D.I. I like "global shield," no acronym. The Charles River gang, up at Harvard and the Massachusetts Institute of Technology, which pooh-poohs the program, prefers to stick with Star Wars. (They are also stuck with MAD, the acronym for Mutual Assured Destruction, which describes their strategic deterrence. They now realize that MAD is even worse than LOST and almost as bad as Creep.)

Arms-control types within the Administration, who call themselves arms-*reduction* specialists, are toying with such ideas as the low-key Study of Protection (acronym: STOP) and the strained Security Assured for Each (SAFE). In a *New York Times* interview, the President floated out a play on MAD: "Why don't we have MAS instead—Mutual Assured Security." (MAS may not fly—it sounds vaguely Marxist and looks like an incomplete version of "M*A*S*H.")

Here is one submitted even as this copy is being filed: ZYD, a legitimate acronym (because the Y can be a vowel sound) standing for Zap! You're Dead. Come on, now—no more of those. Space defense is serious business.

Your column triggered thoughts about what you term "built-in message delivery." New York's Welfare Law provides that a recipient is entitled to a "fair hearing" under certain circumstances, before benefits can be terminated. The Welfare Department, in creating a unit to implement this provision, entitled it "The Fair Hearing" office. Who can possibly complain of the decision issued by a "Fair Hearing Officer"?

Similarly, parents who disagree with the Board of Education about the services offered to a handicapped child are entitled to be heard by an "Impartial Hearing Officer."

The massage is the message.

> *Paul L. Klein*
> *Judge of the Housing Court*
> *New York, New York*

Your column brought back to mind my years as a Confidential Assistant to five presidential appointment level bosses in D.C.

Seemed everything was either written, spoken or not-pronounced. For instance you would never pronounce the Civil Aeronautics Board (CAB). You said it. But most other things were pronounced. Even Federal Telephone and Telegraph, which is FFFtttt.

However, I stopped with one phone call—the changing of our military to the National Military Establishment. The minute I saw it in the *Aviation Daily* I called Stu Symington's office—got his aide Grant Mason on the wire and said, "You can't call it the National Military Establishment." He wanted to know why, of course, so I told him to write down the initials and he would see that he was working for the NME—enemy. He howled into the telephone, slammed it down, and now we have the Department of Defense—or DOD to us all.

Thought you'd get a kick out of this true story.

> *Helene du Toit*
> *West Hempstead, New York*

I was a bit startled to see your rather simplistic explanation of the terms used in the current abortion debate. The crux of that debate has never been whether one is "for" or "against" abortion, but rather whether one is for or against *legal restrictions* on abortion. Those who favoured the repeal of Prohibition are not "pro-alcohol"; those who would like fewer legal encumbrances on divorce are not "pro-divorce"; those who oppose censorship are not "pro-pornography." Why do you insist that those who favour a woman's right to choose (or not to choose) abortion are "pro-abortion"?

The pro-choice majority (no shudder quotes, please) have anti-abortionists in their ranks. Their view is that abortion is a problem, and that the solution to that problem lies in better, more available contraception, contraceptive information and sex education. Whether this non-coercive approach will in fact eliminate abortion may be open to question: but it hardly qualifies as a "pro-abortion" stance.

I agree with you about the use of "pro-life" to describe those anti-abortion forces who are also anti-choice. I'm pro-life. Also pro-choice.

John Baglow
Ottawa, Ontario

New Name for "Star Wars"

We are a nation of acronymaniacs. A piece in this space pointing to the President's unhappiness with the derisive nickname "Star Wars" and asking for suggestions of a new name for the global shield he intends to protect us from incoming missiles has elicited six hundred responses—not all signed "Best, Mirv."

Many entries from opponents of the strategic defense system were uncalled-for personal attacks on the President. The "Governmental Inter-Planetary Program for Effective Response," or Gipper, was the brainchild of Harold Emanuel of Morris Plains, New Jersey; several irate citizens suggested "Ballistic Offense Neutralization Zone" or "Bulwark Order Negating Zealous Offensive" to come up with Bonzo, the name of a chimpanzee in an early Ronald Reagan movie. A subtler dig is Susan Rasky's "Research Aimed at Yielding Greater Universal Nuclear Security," Rayguns, which would quickly be remembered as "Ronald's Rayguns."

I refuse to send these along to the White House and have also censored the "Defensive Umbrella," DUMB, as well as "Shield to Ultimately Provide International Defense," Stupid; "Wistful Attempts to Circumvent

Killing Ourselves," or Wacko. Such stridency stems from the old "Mutual Assured Destruction," MAD, and triggered the ripostumous "Nuclear Universal Tactical Systems," NUTS. It makes no sense to forward "Reagan's Expensive Space Toys Involving Nuclear Proliferation and Evading Arms Control Enactments" (Rest in Peace) and "Fly Little Intergalactic Missiles for Love and Money" (Flimflam), which are overly long; "Western Intercontinental Missile Protection" (WIMP) is at least crisp. The derogation most frequently submitted is PITS, for "Pie In the Sky."

Not all opponents of the plan chose acronymic abuse: to label it as a scandal, Christian Starpoli of Poughkeepsie puts forward "Heaven's Gate," which would probably be written "Heavensgate," a celestial rip-off (and the most original *-gate* construction since the condemnation of an expense-account fraud as "Doublebillingsgate"). But most correspondents, like Stuart Sheedy of Syosset, Long Island, stuck to words formed from initials: "Positive Interception of Far-Flung Lethal Engines," Piffle, and "Incoming Missile Barrier Employing Concentrated Intense Laser Energy," or Imbecile. The scandal angle can be covered with "Strategic Counter Against Missiles," SCAM.

Other suggestions were flippant without being abusive. Combinations of letters using the undesired "Star Wars" will of course not be accepted, but that did not stop those who offered "Star Wars Aerial Technology," SWAT, or "Star Wars Anti-Missile Program," Swamp; one colleague, whom I will identify only as Jonathan Frankel's father, offers "Send the Arms Race Winging Around Rarefied Space," and another writer likes "Stop the Arms Race, We Are Reasonably Sane," both of which come out to Star Wars.

Timothy Perry of Syracuse, muttering "dee-fense," suggests "Nuclear Intercept Capability Keeping Extraterrestrial Leverage," explaining: "As any red-blooded football fan knows, the term 'nickel defense' was coined to describe the deployment of a fifth, or nickel, defensive back into the secondary to guard against the long pass, or 'bomb.' "

Of the foreign-language acronyms, I liked "Allied Defense Initiative for Outer Space," or Adios, but the other Spanish entry, "Militarily Advanced Ceiling High Overhead," Macho won't fly.

All right, now, let's get serious. The Administration needs a name, and its "Strategic Defense Initiative"—the S.D.I., or "Stradefi"—is a nonstarter.

"Assured Independent Survival" is the suggestion of Lindsay Naythons of Hollywood, who cannot resist adding, "How about ACNE for 'Arms Control Negotiations'?" His AIS, pronounced "ace," is countered by "Defense of Upper Space," or DEUS, which might be pronounced "deuce," from Albert Fener of Bellingham, Massachusetts. Nope.

Lots of entries on SANE. " 'Way back in 1983," writes William Rusher, publisher of *National Review,* "I began trying to get General Dan Graham to promote the name Security Against Nuclear Extinction, with the acronym SANE. He passed the idea along to the White House, which apparently vetoed it because they feared confusion with the old Committee for a Sane Nuclear Policy. . . . It didn't take hold, so here I am, trying again."

SANE, with its evident opposition to MAD, has also been used by proponents of "Strategic Anti-Nuclear Experimentation," "Spacial Anti-Nuclear Effort," "Shield Against Nuclear Encroachment" (a football fan offside there), and "Strategic Arms Neutralization Endeavor." When Jim Guirard Jr. of Washington suggested his variant, "Shield Against Nuclear Extermination," to Lieut. Gen. James Abrahamson, director of the Strategic Defense Initiative Organization at the Pentagon, the harassed general replied: "We endeavor to correct the misconception generated by the inappropriate name 'Star Wars' at almost every speaking engagement. . . . I see considerable merit in promoting Government use of an additional program description."

Naturally, where there's SANE, there's SAFE: "Shield Against Fatal Encounter" and "Shield America From Everything." Those strain too hard; Jorio Dauster of London prefers the plain "Defense in Space Against Russian Missiles," Disarm, and Lansing Lamont of New York offers the simple "High Altitude Laser Targeting," HALT. An acronym that is not already a word, sent in by three people independently, is DANA: "Defense Against Nuclear Attack"; that's a possibility.

HOPE springs eternal: from "Hostile Projectile Elimination" to "High Orbit Protection Echelon" to "Humanity Offers to Prevent Extinction." DOME is a good image, but its suggested words, "Defense Oriented Missile Employment" and "Defense of Mankind Everywhere," are easily penetrable by criticism.

A word from the Greek that merits consideration is *aegis,* which was the name of the shield, or breastplate, of Zeus and Athena. A half-dozen letters came in with this: Michael Wilson of Hoboken shapes it into "Atmospheric Engagement and Global Intelligence System" (adding, "although I still like 'Star Wars' ") and Dave Limebrook of Van Nuys, California, suggests "End Game Intercept System" or "American Earth Guard in Space," also adding, "Frankly, I think 'Star Wars' says it all."

The word *aegis* means "protection," with a more modern meaning of "auspices, sponsorship"; maybe it needs no backup phraseology at all. Who says our space defense must have an acronym?

Maybe just a name is needed, like "Sam." (No, that's an acronym for "surface-to-air missile.") Or a simple image: *shell* is out because it could be twisted into *shell game,* and *carapace*—the outer shell of a turtle, metaphorically projected to a hard covering for anything—calls for too much explanation.

There is one word that people keep coming back to: *shield.* Do we really need to fit it out with words to make it an acronym? If we have Stealth technology, why not Shield technology? I push "global shield" (already the name of an annual exercise of the Strategic Air Command) while the President tentatively mentions "security shield" (which Paul Lambert of New York thinks is "secshi")—but could it be that the name is staring at us, needing no adjective or artificial devices?

The White House ought to take a hard look at Earth's sweet-flowing breastplate. If we are to pay for protection in space, we might as well buy the word that describes the first military defense against the sword: the shield.

I intend to place all the letters received on this subject into a large wastepaper basket and carry it over to the Arms Control and Disarmament Agency. These letters represent the Voice of the People, at least the phrase-coining people, and as the old doggerel goes, "You tell 'em, *populi,* you got the *vox.*"

"Star Wars" is going to be as hard for Mr. Reagan to shake as "West Bank" was for Mr. Begin. But if he wants to try, my shield file is all his. The deadline for entries is past; send additional suggestions to the White House direct. The motto of my office is "Everybody Now Undo Followups," ENUF!

May I suggest the following: "Space-based Anti-missile Defense," or SAD.

> *Victor Wouk*
> *New York, New York*

Global Shield? Why, that's Glosh—a blend-word of golly and gosh. I say bosh! (I'm sure you realize it's an acronym for Ballistic & Orbital Systems Hegemony.)

> *Stephen Patterson*
> *La Jolla, California*

All Engines Full Retronym!

A retronym is a noun fitted with an adjective that it never used to need but now cannot do without. It is a throwback-compound, the new adjective substituting for an adjective that formerly brought the noun up to date.

For example, a *watch* used to be a *watch*. It had hands that went around its face. Then along came the *digital watch*, with numbers displayed; when that became the way most watches were, an adjective had to be affixed to the old watches with hands: hence, *analog watch*, the retronym. Similarly, when *baseball* largely became *night baseball*, the retronym was *day baseball*; when a *guitar* was replaced by an *electric guitar*, the old originals became known as *acoustic guitars*. This linguistic concept, and its name, was conceived and coined by Frank Mankiewicz, and is of greater significance to language students than his father's "Rosebud."

A recent retronym shows what sex has done to us. Daniel Schorr, just chosen in *On Cable* magazine's survey of cableniks as "favorite news personality of the year" (*cable television* has not yet spawned the retronym *broadcast television*), was perusing the classified ads in *The Washington Weekly*. What caused the CNN correspondent to turn to this reading matter I do not know and am not asking. He sent me the page that is headed "Massage," with its subhead: "Advertisements in this section are for therapeutic massage only."

"Since the word *massage* has taken on the connotation of a sexual act," writes Mr. Schorr, "it now becomes necessary to speak of a *therapeutic massage* to mean what plain old *massage* used to mean." This is a special classification of retronym, in which the adjective replaces an unwritten but newly understood adjective. That is what you hear when a Times Square sharpie hails you with "Check it out" and hands you a flier for what he calls a (heh-heh) "massage."

From Georgetown, Massachusetts, comes this topper from John Riordan, enclosing an advertisement from *Retail Technology* magazine. The Pitney Bowes Company offers this label printer: "Monarch's new Pathfinder portable (cordless), electronically controlled label printer produces UPC or EAN bar codes and/or human-readable information."

Presumably, this retronym began with the old *readable*, which has been modified for the last few years with the mind-boggling *machine-readable* or *computer-readable*. All your supermarket items have markings that are *machine-readable* and make the cash register at the checkout counter go "Beep!" if the checkout clerk bangs an item down on the counter hard enough or runs it back and forth a few times over some cyclopic beam shooting up through the floor—before cursing and asking the manager how much he's charging that week for a can of corn.

"Human-readable takes the retronym thing a bit too far," says Mr. Riordan. "Unless, that is, the copy was written by an ad-agency robot."

Re: retronyms and "cable television has not yet spawned the retronym *broadcast television.*"

Oh, yes, it has. Just see page 2 of "The Guide" section in *The Times* every Sunday. It's been there for quite a while.

I can only conclude that you don't have time for much television. Or you don't read *The Times.*

Marcia C. Spires
New York, New York

"Natural Language" is used by a branch of artificial intelligence to refer to that which you and I write and speak. I first encountered the term while on sabbatical at the Naval Research Lab several years ago and was quite baffled when I first heard it.

Michael Gaynor
Professor of Psychology
Bloomsburg University
Bloomsburg, Pennsylvania

I particularly enjoyed your article on "retronyms," as I had been searching for the word ever since "ice hockey" came to Southern California!

Janet P. Brown
Temple City, California

The digital watch, whose days may be numbered, makes me wonder if the day of the newspaper photo-caption direction *clockwise* may be numbered as well. Too, a new word is needed to describe the act of "dialing" a push-button telephone. "Punching" or "index-fingering" or even "digiting" doesn't seem appropriate.

A couple of "phony" words need to be coined.

Jerome Agel
New York, New York

I would like to retrofit an addendum on your lucid and engaging piece on retronyms. The first portable chronometers fit into small pockets. They were simply called *watches* (a noun formed from the verb *to watch*). The watch worn strapped to the wrist came many years later, so it was necessary to dub it a *wrist watch*, to distinguish it from its more old-fashioned precursor. As wrist watches became more common, the term *pocket watch* was devised to distinguish it from the newer style of timepiece. So the process of retronymic specification started even before the age of digital watches.

Phil Nicolaides
Springfield, Virginia

When I glanced at the theater listings in last week's *L.A. Times,* I could not help but think of your recent article on retrofitting words. I call your attention to Pacific Theatre's need to distinguish their indoor theaters by the epithet "Walk-in Theatres." This distresses me, as it has always seemed obvious that it would be hard to get an automobile through the doors of most of our local cinemas. Too much sun, I suppose, blinds the population to this truth.

Christine M. Rose
Visiting Lecturer in English and History
University of California
Santa Barbara, California

Retronyms, from my classes in non-fiction writing:
reel-to-reel tape recorder
non-filter cigarette
flat iron
manual transmission
horse-drawn carriage
steam locomotive
hardcover book
copper penny
tin foil
tin can
straight razor

silent movie
one-speed bicycle
legitimate theater

And my own contribution to the list:
conventional war.

Tom Miller
Visiting Lecturer
University of Arizona
Tucson, Arizona

The University of California at Berkeley's computing services news-letter contains what I think is a previously unchronicled retronym, "paper mail." This is a true retronym, like "analog watch" or "acoustic guitar," arising from the fact that the program by which one sends messages to another "user" on a computer network is usually called "mail" and is "invoked" with the command, "mail." (What a lot of jargon we seem to have here!) In a computer environment (everywhere?) the unmarked term is thus taken to be the electronic version of mail and a new marker is prepended to indicate non-electronic (i.e. "paper") mail. Paper mail presumably includes any non-electronic delivery of text, and thus telegrams, mailgrams and the like, though transmitted electronically at one stage, would count as paper mail rather than mail.

Daniel F. Melia
Associate Professor, Rhetoric
Associate Dean, Graduate Division
University of California
Berkeley, California

Perhaps thought should be given to the reverse construction—dropping modifiers and thereby narrowing the meaning of formerly broad-gauge words.

For example, you write for the "media," which are no longer distinguished as mass communications media. What has happened to media of exchange, media of transportation, media of expression?

Purists lament this pre-emption of the term, and also the fact that the word is used only in the plural. The *Podunk Gazette* is "the media," not a medium.

Sometimes it is the noun that is improperly dropped, not the adjective. Thus when transistor radios were introduced they quickly and improperly were called "transistors."

Some modifiers are dropped, Victorian-style, to euphemize female bodily functions: a woman's period does not refer to her period of meditation, period of activity, etc. A woman's "change" is not a change of community, husband or lifestyle.

Sex begets other truncated modifiers. Intercourse not further defined now has only one meaning. What happened to social intercourse? Intercourse's awkward synonym "to have sex" no longer is used to identify plants and animals with separate genders.

The latest example I've encountered is the program to stamp "Explicit" on labels of audio tapes with dirty lyrics. Explicit now means only sexually explicit.

You are waging a magnificent and no doubt losing battle to protect our language. Keep fighting.

Warren R. Dix
Athens, Greece

A toast to you for your article on retronyms. Bartender, a gin martini straight-up, please.

Ed Quinn
Pinole, California

Arcane Brown Bag

People who carry bottles of wine into restaurants that do not have liquor licenses are known as *brown-baggers*. When the New York State Liquor Authority decided to crack down on this widespread and not-all-that-nefarious practice, the teetotaling legislation introduced in the State Legislature was promptly dubbed "the anti-brown-bag law."

Mayor Koch sided with the hordes of brown-baggers, where both the winos and the voters are. He denounced the state ban in these adjectives: "It's archaic, it's arcane, it's stupid."

Most of us know that *archaic* means "antiquated, no longer used" and that nobody who reads this column is *stupid*, but the meaning of *arcane* is often hidden. Elizabeth S. Stone of Rancho Palos Verdes, California, where the local wine is readily available in restaurants, circled the Mayor's use of *arcane* and demanded an explanation.

I forwarded her complaint to Mr. Koch and received this reply: "My reference to that 'anti-brown-bag law' as *archaic, arcane* and *stupid* was intended to convey that the law is outmoded, obscure and mysterious in its origin and without question idiotic. I still brown-bag it!"

This example of civil disobedience is worthy of Henry David Thoreau, and we all look forward to that picture of the Mayor brandishing a brown bag behind bars, his acceptance of incarceration giving meaning to his beliefs, but the Koch definition of *arcane* deserves closer scrutiny.

Hizzoner uses *archaic* to mean "outmoded," which is correct, and finds *stupid* synonymous with "idiotic," which is only slightly excessive, and defines *arcane* as "obscure and mysterious in its origin."

He's not wrong about *arcane*—some dictionaries will agree with him—but he's not quite right. *Arcane* means "hidden, concealed, secret," which can be stretched to "mysterious, obscure." The origin is in the Latin *arcanum*, something hidden, as stuck deep into a chest or an ark; the philosophers' stone was an *arcanum*, the secret by which base metals could be turned into gold.

But precise, he's not: *arcane* means "secret," and to use it to mean "hard to fathom" is a few degrees off. The Koch usage, I think, had more to do with rhyme than reason: *archaic, arcane* has a lilt to it, and I am the last to become a nattering nabob of negativism about alliteration or assonance.

Now to *brown-bagging*. One meaning, taken from the noun form spotted by Merriam-Webster in 1950, is "one who carries his lunch to work in a brown bag," thereby exhibiting frugality toward both money and time. The citation is from a piece on campus slang in *Time* magazine: "The deskbound undergraduate has been variously damned as a *swot*, a *brown-bagger*, or a *mug*." (We used to say *grind*; current campus slang for the genuinely studious is *wonk*, or "know" spelled backward.)

Those hard-working, studious *brown-baggers* soon turned the noun into the verb *to brown-bag*, and it has now become bargain-hunter chic: Bloomingdale's year-round shopping bags are imprinted with "Big Brown Bag," and a weekly staff luncheon at *The New York Times*'s Washington bureau presided over by the bureau chief, Bill Kovach (big sport), is called "the brown-bag lunch." In the metaphor of the modern worker, the brown bag has replaced the lunch pail.

Meanwhile, the same phrase has spawned a distinctly different meaning, which is curious in slang, in which the dominant meaning of a phrase usually wins out early.

"Brown-bagging is the genteel disguise," wrote Harry Golden in *The Satur-*

day Review in 1967, "adopted by a patron to furnish his own liquor when he dines at the local restaurant." That second meaning— "mock conceal-ment of a bottle to satisfy the provisions of a liquor law"—is expressed in "New York's anti-brown-bag law."

The laborious exegesis of "brown-bagging" is disappointingly, un-characteristically out of touch with life as she is lived. Simply put: (1) a brown bag is what a bottle *comes* in when one stops off at a liquor store on the way to a license-less restaurant (a rare vintage from one's own cellar schleppe nicht in a bag, though if Abercrombie were still on Madison you might be able to order up a smart little leather case for the purpose labeled, say, Le Porte-vin); (2) Harry Golden's rather euphuistic "genteel disguise" is, moreover, naïve and unintentionally ironic given the circumstances of brown-bagging's *usual* provenance— the Bowery bum's way of hiding his pint of cheap muscatel, in a doorway or on a curb, from the eyes of the law. "Genteel" my, er, foot.

Oskar Anderson
East Quogue, New York

More than thirty years ago when I was a student at MIT, excessively studious students were called brown-baggers because they always car-ried their books with them, often in a shapeless brown bag which actually was sold at Harvard, our Charles River rivals. They also car-ried slide rules, which were a quaint precursor of the computer. When the MIT bookstore began selling a book bag it was identical to the Harvard one except it was green. So the grinds became green-brown-baggers.

I've recently gone back to school, at laid-back University of Califor-nia at Santa Cruz. We carry our books in stylish backpacks, which make the entire student body look like an overage Boy Scout troop.

Charles B. Johnson
Santa Cruz, California

You originate *arcane* from the Latin *arcanum*. I'm not familiar with a Latin *arcanum*. *Arcana*, yes, as in: *arcana imperii* or *arcana caelestia*. I thought *arcanum* was more a modern form of *arcana*, already some 2,000 years strong before *arcanum* entered the language. However, be that as it may, you write: "The origin [of *arcane*] is in the Latin *arca-num*." I thought it was in the Latin *arcanus*.

Bob Brody
Los Angeles, California

Back to Tool

The Kremlin may be expert at encrypting missile telemetry, but it is helpless to decipher the latest American college slang. Our own Defense Intelligence Agency, monitoring all calls home for money, is wondering if some pernicious wax has clogged up its all-hearing "Big Ear." Post-teen lingo is changing too fast for this generation of computers, and the harried snoopspooks cannot hack it.

I have broken the code. Thanks to submissions to the Nonce Word Institute from moles on a dozen college campuses, some of the communications between yesterday's *wimps* and today's *squids* can now be analyzed. A new generation's attempt to keep its data from prying older eyes is thus thwarted.

Consider the locution that has stumped code breakers from Langley to Dzerzhinsky Square: *"The rents will pay for the shwench's za."*

The key, or *pony,* supplied to the N.W.I. by Jon Pelson of Dartmouth College, is the elimination of first syllables in post-teen speech, which I refer to as *'guage.* As we learned last year, *'rents* are "parents," with only the vestigial last syllable pronounced. This technique is used on verbal phrases as well as single words, as in the clipping of *parental units* to *units*. (To further clip this phrase to *'nits* would be the work of a louse.)

Let us use the same key to unlock the meaning of *'za*. What is the food most consumed by college students that ends with the syllable *'za*? Pizza, of course, with the *'za* pronounced as "tsuh," somewhat similar to the first sound in "Dzerzhinsky," though bereft of its chicken fricative.

Now we come to *'shwench,* its encryption infinitely more sophisticated. Obviously it is the last syllable of some college word, but there is no English word ending in *shwench.* A quick runthrough of all other languages led nowhere, though Serbo-Croatian looked promising for a time. But try a different tack: Let us assume that *wench* is a current sexist way of making a masculine or neuter noun apply to women. We can hypothesize that *'shwench* is a feminine form of *'shmen.* From this breakthrough, we can then ask: What word used frequently by sophomores has *'shmen* as its last syllable?

Nothing to it: "Freshmen" is that word. (*Frosh* has long departed the campus scene, and is used now infrequently as a verb melding *fress* and *nosh,* meaning "to nibble or graze on junk food," the collegiate form of sustenance.) We may conclude, then, that the feminine form of the noun *'shmen* is *'shwench,* and that the sentence *"The 'rents will pay for the 'shwench's 'za,"* decodes as, "My mother and father will underwrite the cost of providing this Italian pie to this first-year woman student."

I should acknowledge that the men at D.I.A. were close to this breakthrough, their discovery delayed only by the assumption that the word *'tsup* meant "ketchup"; in reality, it should be spelled *T'sup* and means "What's up?" similar to *Zappening?*

Synonyms for earnest students, or "pre-professional *dweebs,"* are proliferating. The student with nose to grindstone was at one time termed a *grind.* Benjamin H. Hall's 1856 *Collection of College Words and Customs* defines *grind* as "an exaction; an oppressive action. Students speak of a very long lesson which they are required to learn, or of any thing which it is very unpleasant or difficult to perform, as a *grind."* This noun, formed from the verb "to grind" in the sense of "to afflict or harass," came in turn to apply to the American student oppressed by studies. By 1897, it is defined in Albert Barrere and C. G. Leland's slang dictionary as "a plodding student who keeps aloof from the usual sports and pastimes."

By 1900, reports the American Dialect Society's "Dialect Notes," the *grind* was also known as a *hot-dog* or, if the student worked hard at exam time, a *cram.* (The verb "to cram" in the sense of "to memorize temporarily in order to pass an exam" is, in fact, contrary to hard study for the sake of real learning; Isaac Watts first pointed out this difference in his 1741 trea- tise *The Improvement of the Mind*: "Endless readers may cram themselves in vain with intellectual food, and without real improvement of their minds, for want of digesting it by proper reflections.")

Yesterday's *grind* is today's *tool.* To give emphasis to these words, college lingo turns to prefixes. *Mega-,* as in *mega-eraser head,* is passé; *power-,* as in *power boot,* is on the decline, while *mondo-* as in *mondo-mindbind,* is boom- ing. The hot-dog student is still a *power tool,* but with the fading of "power" as a prefix, a new phrase has made its appearance: *Black & Decker* is the name of a company that manufactures power tools; consequently, a mid- night-oil-burning scholar is being referred to on some campuses as a *Black and Decker.* (Kremlin codebreakers have been completely put off by this logical leap; they have been exploring the possibility that a "B.&D." has to do with "bondage and discipline," which is completely off the track.)

Other current synonyms for *grind* vary widely. At the University of Michigan, for instance, a *grind* is a *gunner* (a *gun* in 1900, according to "Dialect Notes," was "a student good in any subject"). The *gunner* of Mich- igan is the *weenie* of Yale, the *squid* of Wesleyan in Connecticut, the *super strap* of Bucknell, and the *throat* of Tufts (perhaps derived from the cut- throat competition among grinds). Bill Weiss of Columbia University re- ports the latest synonym: *grub.*

Central to college lingo is the derogation of the weak as well as the studious. If you are still talking in terms of *nerds* and *wimps,* you are hope- lessly *waldo.* To the Department of Health and Human Services, *generic* means "desirably inexpensive"; but on campus, according to Jacqueline Kaplan of Madison, Wisconsin, the slang meaning of *generic* is "dull, stu- pid, ordinary."

Assume you have ducked all difficult courses (called *hardcores, killers,* or *grinders)* and enrolled in *sliders,* which used to be called *guts.* In that nefari- ous way, you can *beat the mean* (come in above average) by *acing the easy* (probably from the old card game easy aces). You are then *chill*—which is now much hotter than *cool*—and can spend your spare time *lurking,* or idly ogling members of the opposite sex, including *untouchables,* who are re- vered as being the most desirable. The seduction game continues to use the metaphor of sport—in my college days, I dreamed of *scoring*—but baseball's *reaching home plate* has recently been eclipsed by football's *getting over.* Hap- pily, a recent term for necking—*sucking face*—is on the decline, replaced by the more romantic *doing face time.* The use of *consenting,* probably from "consenting adults," is on the rise.

Those who fail to attract, or who have rejected or repelled others, are scorned as *grimbo, dork* and *earth pig,* the last a corruption of "earth mother." The strongest competition to *squid* and *grimbo* as successor term to *nerd* is *dexter*, a shortening of *poindexter*, probably based on a cartoon character.

A time-honored preoccupation of students is drinking and throwing up. What used to be called *loaded*, *piffled*, *soused* and *plastered* is now *hammered*, *polluted* and *kraeusened* (perhaps from the beer-fermenting process). In a piece about campus lingo a few years ago, I explained how this activity led to such locutions as *driving the big white bus* or *praying to the porcelain god*; today, such activity is described as *laughing at the carpet*, *talking to Ralph on the big white phone* or—showing the originality and vividness of collegiate phrase-making—*the technicolor yawn*.

The Nonce Word Institute is closing down for the semester. It is better for the kids to keep some locutions secret.

Oh no! The Nonce Word Institute is closing down for the semester, and once again my term paper is late! Here are some additions for your Nonce Word file.

"Hot dog" has come a long way since 1900, and would never be used by any self-respecting college student to mean a "grind." In fact, it means just the opposite: one who does not take anything seriously, or who goofs off much of the time. "Hot dogging" is Southern California lingo for performing intricate tricks on a skateboard (or skis), and *these* hot dogs would be insulted if they thought you were considering them "tools" or "grinds."

A "tool" is much more generic (read *commonplace* or *wide-ranging*) than just one who works hard. It is used by college students to describe anyone who is overly enthusiastic (about class, getting a job, anything), or simply someone who is grating to be around.

Gut courses were called "micks" where I came from (Stanford, '84), derived, methinks, from "Mickey Mouse" classes. Specific courses were the proverbial Underwater Basketweaving, Rocks for Jocks (or, at Stanford, "Physics for Poets," an actual course offering), and my favorite, Clapping for Credit ("Introductory Music Appreciation").

Please give credit where credit is due—"Technicolor Yawn" is not a product of the imagination of American college students, but in fact slang stolen from our friends Down Under. Australians of my parents' vintage (yes, even the old folks!) have used it for years to mean Bowing to the Buddha, Losing Your Lunch, or, more politely, Blowing Chunks.

Luke Cole
Washington, D.C.

I asked my students (University of Massachusetts) to submit examples of current slang that you had *not* mentioned. I thought you might be interested in what they came up with; here are some of them:

TAKE A CHILL PILL—relax. Also CHILL OUT

MASHED—muscular, "built." Also RIPPED (That guy is really ripped.)

CRASH—to sleep (especially after drinking)

SCOPING—checking out the opposite sex

SCAMMING—out looking for a pickup

SCOOPING—actually picking up someone

TOTALLY TUBULAR—cool, attractive; an all-purpose honorific. My student says this is a metaphor from surfing, and I quote her: "The spot at which the wave curls over is known as 'the tube.' If you can surf through this 'tube' and come out alive, you've made it through the tube, and you are thus cool, or 'totally tubular, man!' " (Student's name is Laurie Woolrich.)

JONESIN'—doin' nothin'

PRIME and CHOICE—good-looking men (meat metaphor)

ob shnay—fuck off, up yours, etc.

KNARLEY—outrageous;   both   honorific   and   pejorative. WICKED.

Walker Gibson
Amherst, Massachusetts

When We Popped Scotch
"My great granddad had been a piffled grind,"
I 'guaged the Black and Decker, who was plugged
into a mega-treatise on the whine
of waldo squids in campus seas. My mug
of beer was doing froth time with the earth
pig broomie witch, who'd swept under the sheets
of Dexter's papers all the grimbo mirth
from *Playpork* she'd been troughing. "Don't chop meat
with gunners like my grandpa did," I spun.
"Let's get as plastered as a brandied wall!
The great *White Horse* is in my tinny son
Porsche ofabitchin' van!" That night I crawled
to drive the big white bus. On mondo lawns
grubs peacocked in bright Technicolor yawns.

Ted Yund, M.D.
Gloversville, New York

On the subject of "A's"—I never came across "acing the easy" in conversation but "aced" constantly. I left the U. of Michigan about two years ago so my information is less than current but then, as now, it struck me that "aced" refers to the "A" received. "Acing the easy" might then have arisen from "I aced an easy exam."

> E. Hatton
> *Astoria, New York*

You applaud "the technicolor yawn" as showing "the originality and vividness of collegiate phrase-making." I'm afraid those students were less original than you assumed. For twenty years I have admired a mug which my sister keeps in her London townhouse, on which is printed a song with three or four verses and a refrain. Here is the first verse:

> I was down by Bondi Pier
> Drinking cubes of ice-cold beer
> With a bucket full of prawns upon my knee;
> When I'd swallowed the last prawn
> I had a Technicolor yawn,
> And I chundered in the old Pacific Sea.

The song contains many similar locutions, including "to throw your voice," "to go for the big spit," and "liquid laughs." My sister tells me that it was composed by Barry Humphreys and printed in *Private Eye*, probably in the mid-1960s.

> Eric Walther
> *New York, New York*

You mention a number of ingenious gross-out expressions for vomiting. "Technicolor yawn," "laugh at the carpet" (I quote the second from memory, but "ground" would come to the same thing), etc. I agree with you about the ingenuity. But all of these anti-euphemisms come from the brilliant, irreplaceable cartoon strip "Barry Mackenzie," drawn by Nicholas Garland and written by Barry Humphries, which flourished in the London sheet *Private Eye* between about 1966 and about 1974. The argot is Australian, and absolutely memorable. There is also the excellently figurative Glasgow expression "pavement bolognese." . . .

> Christopher Hitchens
> The Nation
> *New York, New York*

It may be worth noting that in 1983 there was a band in Austin, Texas, called the Technicolor Yawns. They played, and may still, good, witty New Wave music, and one of their members was the son of a member of President Carter's cabinet. We thus have a *terminus ante quem* for the arrival of the phrase from the Antipodes, and some indication of possible lines of work for the offspring of out-of-office politicians.

Lee T. Pearcy
Merion, Pennsylvania

The revelation that in your college days you "scored" is a shocking admission of your extreme youth. In my years (1932–34) at an American school—Yale one year, Harvard the next—"making out" was the operative announcement. But this was exclusively an Eastern prep. school or, perhaps, Ivy League usage. "Making out" to the rest of the population meant simply succeeding (not—as we said at Cambridge, England, in the years 1927–32—in a "sub rosa" sense. The rough translation of "sub rosa" was "between the sheets.") The only laudatory adjective was "swell." Robert Benchley once wrote: "American dramatic criticism is now at the point where a play is either swell or lousy."

A brief note on the going sexual lingo at Cambridge might amuse. We had only two words for scoring: poking and grinding.

On my first transatlantic trip—the *Laconia*, out of Liverpool to Cobh and Boston, September 1932—there was a pretty sixteen-year-old Bostonian. She told us of her dread at going home to her dentist, a fussy type who, as she said, "pokes me here, pokes me there." Need I say that we arriving Commonwealth Fellows—there were five of us on the ship—"fell about." The American college words were quite unknown: e.g. screw, lay, along with the whole mammary language—which, I discovered when I came on the compulsory dirty book *Fanny Hill*, unknown in England, was English eighteenth-century town slang that had passed over to America and expired in Britain: bubs and boobies.

As ever,
Alistair [Cooke]
New York, New York

You blew it regarding the designation "earth pig" for an unattractive female. It has *nothing whatever* to do with "earth mother." Rather, it's an intensive of "pig"—unattractive female—meaning *even uglier* than merely swinish.

The etymology of this phrase is quite interesting. It is a literal trans-lation from Afrikaans (or obsolete Dutch) *aardvark,* as any etymologi-cal dictionary will confirm. Some clever undergraduate happened to know the word *aardvark*'s derivation and invented the intensive. If you've ever seen a picture of one of these critters, you'll agree that they are not just ugly but of *surpassing* ugliness.

> *Richard H. Reis*
> *Professor of English*
> *Southeastern Massachusetts University*
> *North Dartmouth, Massachusetts*

Certainly "acing the easy" must come from tennis, not cards. The neo-prefix "mondo" comes almost certainly from *Mondo Cane,* the first documentary gross-out movie.

> *Jon Carroll*
> San Francisco Chronicle
> *San Francisco, California*

You mention a metaphor for seduction, "getting over." I am famil-iar with this term, but not as a synonym for seduction. In my lexicon, this term refers to successfully evading discovery of something (not quite) illegal and/or avoiding concomitant punishment. I can't use this expression until after I might have expected to receive some bad news. An element in getting over is the other side's intentions. A free meal at a soup kitchen isn't "getting over" because the soup kitchen intends that people should eat there gratis. Another element is your intention. If you willfully cheat, evade, or remain silent when you should speak up, you may be able to "get over." You can also fail to "get over" if someone catches you in your scam.

A situation in which I might use this expression might be: "I wrote off my vacation as a business expense last year; IRS didn't catch me. I really got over!" In this case, I have stretched the truth about ex-penses, and succeeded in convincing IRS that the expenses were legiti-mate. IRS could have rejected my claim for expenses, but didn't. They are injured (I paid insufficient taxes), and I "got over."

> *Richard J. Rodriguez*
> *Second Secretary*
> *American Embassy, Bangkok*

I have fondly read some of your articles titled "The English Lan-guage" in the Indian bi-weekly magazine *Frontline.* You have written about a "Nonce Word Institute." I am eager to find out more about this organization. Would you therefore be so kind to send me its complete address.

Javed Husain
Aligarh, India

Bashful-Bashing

W hen you come up with a zingy locution that will astound your friends and confound your enemies—go for it!

Too many excellent coinages or puns are lost to the English language because creative minds are shy or excessively modest. One way out of the bashfulness bind is taken by Rozanne L. Ridgway, Assistant Secretary of State for European and Canadian Affairs, who studs her briefings with "if you will," an early form of pre-emptive apology, now often replaced with "gimme a break."

Others in the self-effacing Bashfulness Brigade send their offerings to me. They will not take the leap without help, and rely on my addiction to wordplay to see to it that their frissons go rolling along.

For example, Dr. Lawrence A. Dworkin of Portland, Oregon, was explaining the latest medical technical jargon on the subject of coronary artery bypass grafts, which most of us call "triple bypass heart surgery."

"In accordance with my profession's love of terse acronyms," writes Dr. Dworkin, "the coronary artery bypass graft has become shortened to CABG, pronounced 'cabbage.' " The acronym can be used as a noun ("He had his cabbage last Tuesday") or a verb ("He was cabbaged last week").

"Sometimes a CABG will fail," the doctor notes sadly, "becoming totally occluded by blood clot. I have thought of referring to this as a 'stuffed cabbage,' but lacked the moxie."

In a similar vein, one of my secret sources in the *Washington Post* editorial pages reports that the writers there had a daring headline for a piece urging understanding for Bhagwan Shree Rajneesh, arrested before he could leave the country. The headline was never used, owing to a failure of nerve, and is saved for posterity here: "Let Bhagwans Be Bhagwans."

Should a female bhagwan be called a bhaglady? No? Were the Justice
Dept. guys that went after old Rajneesh given the official exhortation
"Bhagwan for me"?

Calvin K. Towle
Brooklyn, New York

Belated Related

I have asked my son, the programmer, to come up with a way for me to
hit a single key on my word processor to see the phrase "And in a
related development" come up on the screen.

For pundits as well as newscasters, life has become a series of related
developments; this familiar phrase has become as necessary to us as the
fabled ASAP is to speedwriters, and as required as a flight attendant's
"check for any belongings you may have brought aboard." ("There are all
kinds of items I *may* have brought aboard," growls Professor Joseph H.
Fichter, S.J., at Loyola University in New Orleans, "but I always leave them
at home.")

A solution has spilled across my desk. A reporter, Robert D. Hershey,
Jr., sends me a note about the misuse of *the lion's share*—it's every bit the
lion wants, not merely the largest part—and attaches that to an observation that too many of us are using *fraction* as a synonym for "small part of,"
when a fraction can be a plurality. That's nice to know, but I covered it a
couple of years ago; what grabbed my attention by the throat was the word
he used to link the two items: *relatedly.*

A lunge to the Merriam-Webster unabridged Third New International
shows that adverb to be alive and well-coined. Just as *in the same way* can be
adverbialized to *similarly*, our old standby *in a related development* can be
shortened to *relatedly.* You will not see the long form here again, because an
adverb can be as quick as a keystroke.

Professors should be careful when they scoff at ordinary people's
usage. It was the flight attendant who was correct and the professor at
Loyola wrong, as are so many people who use 'may' when they mean
'might.' Passengers should certainly check on any belongings they *may*
have brought aboard; they needn't check on those they *might* have

brought if the situation had been otherwise than what it was. We really can't afford to lose this distinction, so please hold the line.

> Hope Hale Davis
> Cambridge, Massachusetts

You mentioned "hitting" a key on your word processor. We technical writers have long struggled with what to do with a key. "Hitting" or "striking" it is a bit extreme, but some writers do resort to the more violent form. Since we are generally writing about hardware our companies manufacture or service, we prefer "pressing" keys as they will last longer. ("Depressing" keys has negative emotional connotations.) I once heard of some writers who prescribed "poking" keys, but that form had sexual connotations in Australian slang.

> John C. Stearns
> Mountain View, California

Benjy Was a Chemist

"A merican officials," wrote diplomatic correspondent Bernard Gwertzman in *The New York Times*, ". . . said the main accomplishment . . . was the 'good chemistry' between King Fahd and Mr. Reagan."

"Chemistry plays a far more crucial role in politics than is usually imagined," wrote Zbigniew Brzezinski in his memoirs, *Power and Principle*.

Cyrus R. Vance, the former Secretary of State who reacted to Mr. Brzezinski the way sodium sulfide reacts when mixed with hydrochloric acid to make hydrogen sulfide (rotten-egg gas), wrote in his memoirs, *Hard Choices*: "The chemistry between Carter and Rabin was poor. . . ."

Something is cooking in the test tube of diplolingo over the bunsen burner of our language. Elliott White, professor of political science at Temple University in Philadelphia, wonders: "Is the shorthand *chemistry* coming to stand for good or poor personal relations?"

At Merriam-Webster, the earliest citation for *personal chemistry* was in a comment to *Time* magazine by an NBC producer, Max Liebman, in 1955, complaining about a Betty Hutton production: "It's a matter of accident whether the personal chemistry works or not."

Fred Mish, editorial director at Merriam-Webster, says that the nonscientific meaning of *chemistry* has been a vogue term since 1967, when it began to be used often to describe relationships. In Webster's Ninth New Collegiate, a third sense of the old (1646) scientific word is "a strong mutual attraction, attachment, or sympathy."

Of late, I detect a neutralization of the term, as if sodium hydroxide had been poured into carbonic acid to render it inert. The new *chemistry* is neither good nor bad, but requires an adjective to describe it.

The new advertising for Chemical Bank and Fidelity Investments, for instance, states, "For mutual funds, the chemistry is *just right* between Chemical and Fidelity." The best operating definition for this sense of *chemistry* comes from daytime television. In a "General Hospital" scene last month written by Robert Guza, Jr., Celia explains her affair with Jimmy Lee to her friend Holly by saying, "I have this *chemistry* with Jimmy Lee." Holly answers, "That's a polite word for *animal attraction.*"

Beyond that, a new sense is being added. M. A. Farber wrote in a *New York Times* article about the Westmoreland case against CBS: ". . . the aplomb of the lawyers and the manner of their witnesses—the 'chemistry' in the courtroom—were important determinants of jury reaction." In this sense, *chemistry* means "a charged atmosphere," the human elements in a room that govern reactions.

If you want to use the idea, but react explosively to vogue terms, try the positive *affinity, sympathy, empathy, harmony, concord* or *compatibility*. For chemistry that runs in the other direction, there are always *animosity, antipathy, hostility, enmity, rancor* and *repellence.*

Who started this? This department does not presume to claim a first-use sighting, but Jeff McQuain, my in-house lexicographer, has come up with the psychologist Carl G. Jung's 1933 observation, in *Modern Man in Search of a Soul* (translated by William Dell and Cary Baynes): "The meeting of two personalities is like the contact of two chemical substances: if there is any reaction, both are transformed."

In Ernst Lubitsch's classic 1939 film, *Ninotchka*, after the White Russian, Leon (Melvyn Douglas), announces to the Bolshevik, Ninotchka (Greta Garbo), that he is falling in love with her, she advises him that "Love is a romantic designation for a most ordinary biological or, shall we say, chemical process" and then goes on, "Chemically, we are already quite sympathetic."

These quotations are taken from *Ernst Lubitsch's Ninotchka*, The Film Classic Library; Richard J. Anobile, editor (Avon Books 1975).

Charles R. Bergoffen
New York, New York

I think I may be able to help you on the matter of "chemistry" as metaphor and on its origins as such. In Chapter Five of Book One of *Brideshead Revisited* (Et in Arcadia Ego), Charles Ryder has begun to notice that his friend Sebastian Flyte drinks not for pleasure but "to escape":

> Julia used to say, "Poor Sebastian. It's something chemical in him."
> That was the cant phrase of the time, derived from heaven knows what misconception of popular science. "There's something chemical between them" was used to explain the over-mastering hate or love of any two people. It was the old concept of determinism in a new form. I do not believe there was anything chemical in my friend.

Waugh was writing during the Second World War, but Brideshead is a careful attempt to re-create the manners and attitudes of the Twenties. One cannot date the action precisely, but the year in question is either 1924 or 1925. This is earlier than the Jungian reference unearthed by your associate, but might not be too early not to be anachronistic, if you see what I mean. (You should have a go at "anachronism" one day —people keep using it to mean outmoded.)

Christopher Hitchens
The Nation
New York, New York

I draw your attention to the following quotation from Shaw's *You Never Can Tell* (1897) for its use of "chemistry" in describing human relationships:

> Gloria: I hope you are not going to be so foolish—so vulgar—as to say love.
> Valentine: No, no, no, no, no. Not love: we know better than that. Let's call it chemistry. You can't deny that there is such a thing as chemical action, chemical affinity, chemical combination: the most irresistible of all natural forces. Well, you're attracting me irresistibly. Chemically.

Ernest Davis
New York, New York

It is unlikely that an alert reader, pouncing upon your query about the earliest use of *chemistry* in describing human relations, has not already brought to your attention Johann Wolfgang von Goethe's delightful apologia for adultery, *Elective Affinities*, an 1809 novel, with the mouth-filling German title, *Die Wahlverwandtschaften*.

Borrowing the term and concept ("elective affinities") from contemporary chemistry, Goethe used it to denote the mutual attraction of two substances, although originally bound chemically to others. These bound substances will subsequently separate and seek to establish a new bond with a kindred of their choice, hence, "elective affinities."

That human passions are like chemical substances in primitive impulses promoted Goethe's view and his novel which were guided by his absorbing interest in chemistry.

Esther K. Labovitz
English Department
Queens College (CUNY)
Flushing, New York

Among romantic writers, animal magnetism was used to express the affinity (sexual and otherwise) between the sexes.

In the "Historical Note" of the Northwestern-Newberry edition of Herman Melville's *Pierre; or, the Ambiguities,* page 374, the commentators speculate that Melville may have been thinking of Goethe's "elective affinity" when he has Isabel, jealous of the intrusion of Lucy into their ménage, tell Pierre that he can "elect" Lucy, the "good angel," or Isabel, the "bad angel." (Book 23, Part III, page 314)

However, Melville uses the idea of "elective [chemical] affinity," more directly, if ironically, in *Mardi; or, a Voyage Thither* (Northwestern-Newberry edition, Chapter 95, page 292) when he establishes a relationship between "jolly" Borabolla and "demure" Jarl by comparing their "affinity" to the "affinity between those chemical opposites chlorine and hydrogen . . . promoted by caloric." Borabolla and Jarl's "affinity" was promoted by the "warmth of the wine they drank."

Collamer M. Abbott
White River Junction, Vermont

I was reading Boswell's *London Journal* at about the same time your article appeared. Here is what Boswell wrote on Sunday, 19 December 1762. It is a dialogue between Boswell and his friend Erskine:

"Erskine," said I, "don't I make your existence pass more cleverly than anybody?" "Yes, you do." "Don't I make you say more good things?" "Yes. You extract more out of me, you are more chemical to me, than anybody." We drank tea at Dempster's.

I thought of chemistry as such a modern word that I never imagined it being used in conversation in 1762.

Stan Spielman
Port Washington, New York

As a retired Chemistry teacher, I respond as follows to your bit of Chemistry. There are two products from the reaction between carbonic acid and sodium hydroxide: water (which of course is neutral) and sodium carbonate which is alkaline. Neither product is inert.

As to the chemistry between two people: This type of language developed probably from the well-known affinity between oppositely charged particles—denoted positive and negative by custom.

However, the attraction between people has sometimes been described as "vibes," which in terms of physics would be "harmonic vibrations" or similar wave lengths. (I am tuned in to your wave length. Or, we are in sync.)

Two people who are enjoying a "meaningful relationship" thus might be described in scientific terms as having Bio Chem Sync to the Max.

Jack B. Hester
Floral Park, New York

I have never been able to determine from your column what the requirements are for membership in that mystical and amorphous group dubbed by you the Lexicographic Irregulars. I am writing you about your usage of the word "inert" in the hope that I may gain at least adjunct membership in the LI's by pointing out usage that rings false to the trained ear, as well as assaulting the scientific sensibilities of most chemistry students of my era, circa 1949.

When I took Freshman chemistry under the late illustrious Dr. Feigenbaum at RPI in 1949, certain unassailable truths were vouchsafed to us freshmen engineering students. One of the most memorable was that the inert gases, Helium, Neon, Argon, Krypton, Xenon and Radon did not react with any other elements and, therefore, were found in nature in their elemental, uncombined state; hence the classification name "inert."

The reaction you allude to—carbonic acid with sodium hydroxide—produces a neutral solution, neither basic nor acidic, in chemical parlance a "pH of 7." It is not rendered "inert," simply "neutral."

"Inert" in chemical usage means specifically and only "non-reactive," i.e., will not combine with any other of the elements of the periodic table under known conditions of temperature and pressure.

Glad to be of service and I know that the ghost of Dr. Feigenbaum is smiling.

J. E. Randall
Summit, New Jersey

Of the various terms you list for positive feelings of persons toward each other, "empathy" really is out of place since it refers to the ability of one person to enter into and understand another without implying a mutual relation. It is a late nineteenth- early twentieth-century coinage, from the German psychologist Lipps' *einfühling*—the English translation—and represents a special sense of merging into the other. The proper use would be the older "sympathy" which implied mutuality. Thus, Mr. Goleman should have spoken of the sympathy between the two, unless he meant to imply that they had a two-sided relationship: attraction of matching "sides" and repulsion of opposing "sides." A Freudian could certainly play around with that metaphor.

Harold L. Orbach
Associate Professor of Sociology
Kansas State University
Manhattan, Kansas

Beware the Junk-Bond Bust-Up Takeover

"The combination of bust-up takeover threats with greenmail has become a national scandal," writes Martin Lipton, a lawyer, in *The New York Law Journal.* He adds, ominously, "The junk-bond bust-up takeover is replacing the two-tier bootstrap bust-up takeover."

"National scandal" is the only phrase I recognize in that burst of tycoon-speak. "The new vocabulary of our business," the investment banker Felix G. Rohatyn has written, reflects a go-go atmosphere in which "two-tier tender offers, Pac-Man and poison-pill defenses, crown-jewel options, greenmail, golden parachutes, self-tenders all have become part of our everyday business."

Let us master that lexicon by considering the individual words and phrases. (This will be a lexical bust-up takeover.) When Brian Fernandez of Normura Securities is quoted in *Newsweek* as saying, "I'm sure I.T.T. has a mine field of poison pills and shark repellent to keep people away," what does he mean?

Shark repellent is the action taken by a company's board of directors to shoo away *raiders*—the "sharks" circling the company and hoping to chew it up. (The much-derogated sharks can be investors wanting virtuously to throw out inefficient management that has been living off the stockholders' backs, but let's look at takeovers from the point of view of the fearful company.)

"One way to repel sharks is to stagger the board of directors," reports Fred R. Bleakley of *The New York Times.* "Instead of having the terms expire for all the board members at the same time, making a takeover easier, the staggering might mean that only one member's term expires at any given time," which might try a shark's patience. Another repellent is a *fair-price amendment* to the company's bylaws, preventing the shark from offering different prices on bids to different stockholders for their shares. Yet another is the *crown-jewel option,* selling off the most profitable segment of the company; this comes from the figurative use of "the jewel in the crown," now the title of a television series having nothing to do with the world of big business.

My favorite repellent is *the poison pill,* taken from the world of espionage, in which the agent is supposed to bite a pellet of cyanide rather than permit torture after capture (the Central Intelligence Agency finds it hard to get agents to do that anymore). To make a stock less attractive to sharks, a new class of stock may be issued: this is "a preferred stock or warrant," Arthur Liman, a lawyer, informs me, "that becomes valuable only if another company acquires control. Because it becomes valuable to the target, it becomes costly to the buyer: when the buyer takes the bite, to follow the metaphor, he has to swallow the poison pill."

A *junk bond* is a high-yield, high-risk security specially designed to finance a takeover; this is supposed to enable the issuer of the bond to get enough bank financing to offer stockholders cash for all the stock in the company. "Following the takeover," writes Mr. Lipton, "the target is busted up to retire part of the takeover financing. Plants are closed, assets are sold, employees are thrown out of work and pension plans are terminated." That's what comes of a *junk-bond bust-up takeover.*

In extremis, a corporate survivor can try *greenmail.* First the shark swims around the company, showing its wicked fin and making menacing splashes; the shark keeps buying stock, but not enough to take over. Then the shark offers the frightened directors on the life raft a deal: use company assets to buy in the shark-held stock at a premium, higher than the market price. Big profit for shark, safe jobs for management, and only the other company stockholders get hurt. This is the sort of thing the labor racketeer Louis (Lepke) Buchalter did for garment-center operators in the good old days: the shark sells protection from shark bites. The essence of *greenmail* is the bonus paid over the market price: "We certainly don't identify it as greenmail," said T. Boone Pickens, Jr., of his withdrawn bid to take over Phillips Petroleum, "because we negotiated substantially the same deal for the stockholders as we got for ourselves."

"*Greenmail* is patterned on *blackmail,* with the green representing *green-backs,*" reports Sol Steinmetz, a lexicographer, of Barnhart Books. "It may have been inspired by the earlier *graymail.*" That is a threat by a defense attorney to force the government to drop an espionage case by demanding the exposure of secrets.

I am not going into *two-tier tender offers* or *Pac-Man defenses* because it is not my intent to steal students from the Harvard Graduate School of Business, but the *golden parachute* deserves etymological examination. This agreement to pay an executive his salary and benefits, even if the company is taken over by somebody who wants to heave him into shark-infested waters, is based on *golden handcuffs,* coined in 1976 to mean "incentives offered executives to keep them from moving to other jobs." In turn, this was based on the British *golden handshake,* a 1960 term for a whopping sum given as severance pay.

You are now prepared for a raid on a medium-size lemonade stand. If in trouble, get yourself a White Knight, which is either a friendly bidder or a washday miracle.

Someone threw you a curve ball on junk bonds. A junk bond *is* "a high-yield, high-risk security." But it does not have to be "specially designed to finance a takeover." Most experts would define a junk bond as a debt instrument that is below "investment grade." In other words, a bond issued by a company that may not be able to honor its obligations. Examples include bonds issued by once healthy firms that have fallen on hard times. New (and therefore unproven) companies also issue junk bonds because they don't have the track record to attract funds at rates that General Motors pays.

Joseph Lisanti
Managing Editor
Fact
New York, New York

A junk bond (non-hyphenated, please) is any debt security that is rated "speculative" by the two major credit rating agencies (below Moody's Baa and Standard & Poor's BBB). Also, they are much more common in non-takeover situations. Since they have high risk, investors do demand a higher yield.

Theodore J. Komosa
New York, New York

The Boffin Speaks

"I n a recent column you said you were seeking a replacement for the word *pundit,*" writes Godfrey Sperling, Jr., of *The Christian Science Monitor.* How about *maven?*" Mr. Sperling, whose newsmaking breakfasts are a Washington institution and whose granddaughter is named Mavyn, adds: "What is the precise English translation of this Yiddish word—or is it Yiddish? Does *expert* do justice to the word?"

I am a language *maven* and a political *pundit.* Those two nouns, one of them relatively new to English, have quite different meanings.

A *maven* is a self-proclaimed expert. When someone says "I am a *maven,*" however, a note of self-mockery is added, as if to say "and if I'm not such an expert, sue me." Just as the Yiddishism *kibitzer,* or "participating onlooker," was adopted by the English-speaking in the last generation, *maven* has made its way into the dictionaries in this yuppier generation. In the synonymy of expertise, a slot has been left open: *connoisseur* connotes a person of exquisitely discriminating taste; *expert* or *authority* has a technocratic or academic ring, and *aficionado* or *enthusiast* carries a meaning of less discrimination and greater devotion. What of somebody who loudly and happily asserts that his love for the subject has made him an expert? He may not wear the ring of authority, and to a connoisseur he's no connoisseur; but to his peers, only when it comes to his special interest, the *maven* has The Word. The phrase closest in meaning, but with bookish overtones, is *opinion leader.*

As can be seen, *maven* is a word I like, and Bud Sperling's granddaughter has a name that augurs a great career; but *pundit,* as a term for "political commentator," is getting tired. The Hindi word for "learned man" was popularized in the United States by Henry R. Luce, founder of *Time* magazine, who applied it to Walter Lippmann, the columnist and full-time sage.

Luce, I always believed, took that word from the Pundits Club, a group of undergraduates at Yale, and carried it with him into the newsmagazine dodge.

However, I am informed by Professor Russell Judkins of New York State University's College of Arts and Science at Geneseo that an earlier Pundit Club was formed in Rochester in 1854 by the anthropologist Lewis Henry Morgan, and an article titled "Reminiscences of the Pundit Club" was published by the Rochester Historical Society in 1923. The notion of a club's using the Hindi word as its name was evidently widely bruited about early in this century.

Further digging in the Oxford English Dictionary shows *pundit* to have been used in this colloquial, mocking sense as far back as 1816: "For English pundets condescend/ Th' observatory to ascend" was in the poem "The Grand Master" by Quiz, a pseudonym probably for William Combe. In 1862, *The Saturday Review* used the word as it is used today: "A point upon which the doctors of etiquette and the pundits of refinement will differ." In 1948, after Henry Luce had made the word known to a wider audience, John Steinbeck, the novelist, used a word that cast aspersions on the characteristics of a pundit: "News has become a matter of punditry. A man sitting at a desk in Washington or New York reads the cables and rearranges them to fit his own mental pattern and his by-line."

Well, yes, that's often how it is done, and it is not hard to bash the damnable media for being what Albert Julius, a London jeweler, called *Kopfverdreher*, "head-twisters," or "mind-turners." But *pundit* just doesn't seem to have any zip left. What other choices are there to describe the "panjandrums of the opinion Mafia" (Arthur Schlesinger, Jr.'s phrase)?

"*Savant* is too precious by far," writes Edward Engberg of Santa Barbara, Calif., dismissing the term for "knowing one." He prefers a coinage like *wisant*. Another *-ant* coinage suggested was *sagant*, but that sounds too much like *sergeant*; several writers like *pedant*, but the teaching profession has that locked up.

Another response to the query for a word between *wise man* and *wise guy* that came in from several readers was *polymath*, a Greek-based word meaning "a person of great learning." I have rejected that because it conjures a vision of a parrot loudly spouting numbers, which limits its use to economic columnists.

Chochem has its legion of supporters. "If the French *savant* is in the running as a replacement for the Sanskrit *pundit,*" writes Miriam Gross of New York, "why not also consider the Yiddish *chochem*? Depending on how it is used, it can mean 'wise man, clever fellow' or, sarcastically, 'wise guy.' " No; with *maven* already in the field, the fricative fricassee of *chochem* is redundant.

Another possibility, from the scientific world, is *bonze*. "Like *pundit*, the word comes from South Asia, in this case I think, Vietnam," writes Dietrick Thomsen of *Science News* in Washington. "It refers to a very senior Buddhist monk, the sort who is always propounding the most inscrutable koans. In past decades it was used by German university students (particularly in physics) to refer to professors whose pronouncements were unassailable. Einstein, Bohr, Pauli, Heisenberg . . . were all bonzen." This is a pretty good word, and bears watching; I wonder what the Heisenberg effect on *bonze* will be.

The most colorful contribution was by Dr. Daniel Hely of Carlisle, Pennsylvania, who found *the hair-ball oracle*, a title of a chapter in Mark Twain's *Adventures of Huckleberry Finn*. "Miss Watson's nigger, Jim," recounts Huck, "had a hair-ball as big as your fist, which had been took out of the fourth stomach of an ox, and he used to do magic with it. He said there was a spirit inside of it, and it knowed everything."

However, *hair-ball oracle* is a tad too pretentious. Portmanteau words like *savantaleck*, *wisdomfont* and *greminence* are off the mark. My favorite is *boffin*.

"For *pundit* try *boffin*," suggests David Sider of the department of classical and Oriental languages at Queens College in New York. "This is a British term of recent coinage that is defined (defining clauses begin with *that*—right?) by the O.E.D. Supplement as referring primarily to scientists with 'back-room' knowledge, but I've heard it applied to experts in general."

The lexicographers at Oxford point out that *boffin*, etymology unknown, was first used by young naval officers about their elders, and later by members of the Royal Air Force about the scientists working on radar. The word has a nice sound to it, and a folk etymology could quickly be fashioned ("from *griffin*, mythical beast with the head of an eagle and the body of a lion, influenced by *buffoon*").

Dear Bill:

I thank you. My granddaughter thanks you. And her parents and my wife thank you.

But "boffin"? I doubt it. After looking over all the alternatives you list, I am even more convinced that "maven" is the word you want. Just keep calling pundits "mavens" and, before long, your usage—

together with the general usage it will help bring about—will make mavens out of them.

My plea: Don't give up on "maven"!

Godfrey Sperling, Jr.
Washington, D.C.

Dear Bill:

Please forgive my *chutzpah* for criticizing your definition of *maven*, but you're a *heimish mensch*, and also a big *chochem*, so I know you won't mind.

A *maven* is not, as you say, a "self-proclaimed expert." All the uses of this word that I have collected (and they're many) show clearly that a *maven* means a good judge of quality (in some specified area), one having a fine appreciation or understanding of something, a knowledgeable person; hence the word is synonymous with *connoisseur* or *cognoscente*, rather than with *expert*, *authority*, and *pundit*, which imply mastery over a particular field or discipline. Because *maven* is synonymous with *connoisseur*, people speak of "a wine maven," "a boxing maven," "a maven on movies," "a Rubik's cube maven." In all such instances the reference is to another person, never to oneself; no one normally proclaims "I am a maven" unless he's joking, just as no one says "I am a connoisseur" unless he's kidding you or himself.

Another important distinction is that in current English use *maven* is highly informal and somewhat humorous, whereas *connoisseur* and *pundit* are standard terms without any suggestion of informality or humor.

Finally, in answer to Mr. Sperling's question about the origin of this word, English *maven* is a borrowing of standard Yiddish *meyvn*, meaning a connoisseur or expert. The Yiddish word, which is neither informal nor humorous, was adapted from Late Hebrew *mēvīn*, literally "understanding," from Hebrew *l'havin* "to understand."

You, Bill, are a language *maven* and a political *pundit* because you are considered a connoisseur of language and an authority on politics, *not* because you're a self-proclaimed expert in language and an acknowledged authority on politics. The essential difference between a maven and a pundit is the same as that between a gourmet cook and a restaurant chef: the former is a skilled amateur while the latter is an expert professional.

Be well (free translation of Yiddish *zay gezunt*).

Sol Steinmetz
Clarence L. Barnhart, Inc.
Bronxville, New York

Dear Bill,

Yes, *maven* and *chochem* are *used* in Yiddish but they are originally Hebrew words which, like many other Hebrew words, have been incorporated into Yiddish.

Maven (correctly, may-veen) is the active participle of a word meaning "to see," and its nominal form can be translated as "discerner."

Chochem is a corruption of *chah-cham,* a wise man. The Sephardic Jews call their rabbis *chachamim,* and a rather good translation of the word is "sage," which might well be another substitute for pundit. To many of us boffin is far from boffo.

> *Rabbi Samuel M. Silver*
> *Delray Beach, Florida*

The word "maven" began to creep into the language sometime in late 1964 when I launched a campaign for Vita Herring with the Beloved Herring Maven as spokesman.

The campaign took root so deeply that last year, when I wrote a batch of new maven commercials, people were under the impression we'd been off the air for just a few years—even though we'd been off since 1969.

A couple of years into the maven campaign, I began to pick up on the usage. Agencies referred to media people as "media mavens." A company advertised in *Women's Wear Daily* as "The Rayon Mavens." Appetizing stores opened up calling themselves "Gourmavens." Candice Bergen wrote an article in *Playboy* in which she confessed she was not a "China Maven." *Time* magazine referred to critic Jay Cocks as their "movie maven." The artist Betty Dodson was referred to in *The Village Voice* as the "masturbation maven." And today's *Adweek* quotes a marketing executive in L.A.: "Pizza lovers can tell the difference between pizza mavens and actors just looking for work."

All along I've figured that I rated at least a footnote in etymology.

> *Martin Solow*
> *New York, New York*

In a paper I wrote in 1966 on "The Political Economy of Efficiency . . ." the following sentence appears on page 64: "The good systems analyst is a *chochem,* a Yiddish word meaning 'wise man,' with overtones of 'wise guy.' "

> *Aaron Wildavsky*
> *Professor of Political Science and Public Policy*
> *University of California*
> *Berkeley, California*

You described *chochem* as a Yiddish term. Actually, it is a fine old Hebrew word. The distinction is significant because Sephardim, whose vernacular is not Yiddish, use the term *Mahem* (softer consonants) to refer to a chief rabbi or great scholar.

James N. Rudolph
New York, New York

May I suggest the title "sachem," which is an American Indian word.

Vincent P. Carr
Mount Vernon, New York

Yiddish has more to offer than *maven*; didn't any of your sources mention *kenner*? That word is practically English already, and while it is plainly German, like most of Yiddish, it is only in a Jewish context, I believe, that it carries the flavor you are looking for.

A maven is a knower, to be sure, but he is also an enthusiast, maybe even a glutton. A kenner, on the other hand, is purely a knower, and (in czarist Poland, at least) a knower of Talmud and Bible. He did not have to be a holy man himself, much less a rabbi, bonze or pundit; just one who *understands* such things, and able to grace a debate with apposite quotations and reasonings.

Sholem Aleichem's Tevye (of *Fiddler on the Roof*) was in part a parody of a kenner, with his ridiculous garbling of learned sayings. There was of course more to the stories of Tevye than this, and even here Tevye was mocking phony kennerism rather than the real thing.

Just as Eskimos are said to have twenty-three—or eighty-three?—words for snow, snow being essentially all they deal in, so Yiddish is, for analogous Eastern European reasons, peculiarly rich in words describing the varieties and degrees of intellectual worth, and of wit.

Ralph A. Raimi
Rochester, New York

Dear Bill:

Apropos of *bonze*, you may want to know that it has long been used in French, even in the feminine (*bonzesse*—in Voltaire). By the turn of the nineteenth century it had acquired the mocking tone, usually in the combination *vieux bonze* = old fuddy-duddy, though once an authority, perhaps.

Jacques [Barzun]
Charles Scribner's Sons, Publishers
New York, New York

Dietrick Thomsen ventured "South Asia, in this case I think, Vietnam" as source of the term *bonze*. But the accepted derivation is as follows:

Chinese scholars transcribed Sanskrit "Brahma" with characters which are read nowadays (in the system of Romanization devised by Y R Chao in collaboration with philosopher Lin Yutang) as *fannmo*. The *fann* portion evolved into a sort of combining form in references to Buddhism; thus, *fannseng*, "Buddhist priest."

On Japanese tongues *fannseng* became *bonzou*. Portuguese missionaries and traders took this over as *bonzo* and, passing into English via French, it became *bonze*.

The latter part of this derivation is traced in the etymology given in Webster II.

Grant Sharman
Hollywood, California

As I am sure many Bonzen from the field of modern German history have already informed you, the word *Bonzen* was a popular pejorative term for political party leaders during the Weimar Republic, carrying the meaning of corrupt party bosses, bigwigs or hacks. The word was especially popular with the extremist parties, in particular the Nazis, as a term of opprobrium for the leaders of the more moderate, pro-Republican parties, above all those of the Social Democratic Party. To my ear the term is still too loaded to be an acceptable replacement for the more neutral "pundit."

James M. Diehl
Associate Professor of History
Indiana University
Bloomington, Indiana

I first ran across this word *Bonzen* when I was interrogating German POWs in World War II. These prisoners used the word to denote big shots, the brass, etc., and it was always used sarcastically and sometimes humorously.

Generally, the word *grosse* precedes *Bonzen* in speech—meaning, of course, the big shots.

William E. Ringel
New York, New York

PLEASE do not accept "bonze." In spite of its origin and its usage by German students for Einstein et al., its current connotation is for high-up officials in government, parties, unions, large organizations of any kind, and is not always meant as a compliment. With quite a fair proportion of the population here knowing German, and the Germans themselves avidly reading American papers and journals, I do not think "bonze" is quite the right replacement for "pundit."

(Mrs.) Lu Fenton
New York, New York

The word *bonze* is of Japanese origin, and has never had any reference to or connection with South Asia, much less Vietnam; the correct etymology is easily available in a number of reference works, e.g. my book *The Japanese Language* (University of Chicago Press, 1967; paperback Midway Reprint 1900), p. 221. Long common in a number of European languages, together with English, *bonze* is, for example, the word for the Buddhist priest in *Madame Butterfly,* and in many other contexts that render a Vietnamese connection out of the question; its phonetic form also fits directly with attested earlier dialect forms of modern standard Japanese *bōzu,* "a Buddhist priest."

Roy Andrew Miller
Professor of Asian Languages and Literature
University of Washington
Seattle, Washington

No! Boffin won't do! A boffin is an unknown back-room planner/engineer/scientist adviser, unknown and unobtrusive; hardly suitable to describe the publicized and recognized authority of a pundit.

Chochem won't do either! A chochem is a know-all.

How about a "policator" or "policant"? You can buy them for the same money with their verbs "to policate" or "to policant."

Monty Platt
Monte Carlo, Monaco

Boffin is pretty good; a little rakish maybe. Would you consider *clerisist?* Coleridge brought out the term *clerisy* to describe the whole world of literati and scholars, not just the clergy.

How about *weisenheimer* or *wisenheimer?* Well, of course, that's a fellow who wants you to think he's pretty smart. I think it's still in the Midwestern vernacular.

One of my favorites is *ghommid.* It means, or I think it means, or I like to think it means, "spook of the jungle" in Dahoman or something.

Eugene Newsom
Bigelow, Arkansas

A boffin may be a British coinage for sure, but I had always supposed it was invented by Dickens in *Our Mutual Friend* to describe that great character Noddy Boffin, the Golden Dustman, hardly a scientific expert.

Mary R. Baker
New York, New York

A word with wide currency in Africa is *fundi* (pronounced foon dee). A Standard Swahili-English Dictionary, Oxford University Press, Nairobi, defines it as: "a person skilled in any art, craft, or profession, and so able to instruct others in it . . ." A Dictionary of English Usage in Southern Africa (Oxford University Press, Cape Town) gives it as an abbreviation of the Zulu word *umfundisi* equivalent to the English words teacher, minister, learned, well-informed. Maybe you will find this a useful addition to your synonymy of expertise.

Warren Garst
Chicago, Illinois

"Fricative" alludes to consonant sounds such as (f), (v), (s), (z), (sh), (zh) and (th), which are produced when a stream of air is pushed through a constricted passage formed between the lips and teeth or tongue and teeth. Since the (ch) sound in question is made at the rear of the mouth and involves different parts of the articulatory anatomy, may I suggest an alternative phrase such as "uvular euphemism."

Rita Braun
Lawrenceville, New Jersey

"Boffin Follow-up"

Because the word *pundit* has become worn out, it was suggested here that *boffin*, a Briticism for "well-intentioned, if fumbling, expert," be used as a synonym.

Lexicographic Irregulars have offered different origins for this useful term. English Professor John Conlon of the University of Massachusetts writes, "You might want to refresh your memory of the great-granddaddy of all boffins, Mr. Nicodemus Boffin, the Golden Dustman in *Our Mutual Friend* by Charles Dickens."

The late Eric Partridge, whose great Dictionary of Slang and Unconventional English has just been updated and reissued by Macmillan, speculated that the word may have been taken from "The Boffin Books," a series for children with an "owlish wisdom" sought by sages through the ages.

J. Brant of Lincoln, Massachusetts, sends me the 1962 book *The Rise of the Boffins,* by Ronald Clark, which quotes a fanciful etymology by Air Vice Marshal G. P. Chamberlain, the first commanding officer of the fighter-interception unit at Tangmere and a man who helped develop radar.

"A puffin, a bird with a mournful cry, got crossed with a Baffin, a mercifully very obsolete Fleet Air Arm aircraft," Mr. Chamberlain said. "Their offspring was a boffin, a bird of astonishingly queer appearance, bursting with weird and sometimes inopportune ideas, but possessed of staggering inventiveness, analytical powers and persistence. Its ideas, like its eggs, were conical and unbreakable. You push the unwanted ones away, and they just roll back."

"Whatever its exact origin," writes Mr. Clark, *"boffin* had become, long before the end of the war, a word for one particular type of scientist—the man who could understand the viewpoint of the services, who worked with them, and who frequently shared their dangers."

Uncle! My day is made.

About a week after I read your last boffin installment, I was taken aback to actually hear the word "boffin" emanate from my television. I was watching *The Safecracker,* a 1958 film about a thief (Ray Milland) who uses his talents to aid the British military during WW II. In return for helping steal a list of German agents (in Britain) from a safe located in a French château, Ray Milland is promised a pardon, to cut his prison sentence short.

Prior to the mission, the other enlisted soldiers on the team are curious and they are prodding him for information. One says, "You're the boffin . . ." meaning, of course, that he is the specialist, the expert they're taking with them, and therefore he should know the plan.

I thought you would be interested to learn of this specific usage of "boffin."

Ian Parmiter
New York, New York

Brooke Shields v. McCall's et al.

I n her book *On Your Own*, actress, model and role model Brooke Shields, now already eighteen, explains why she has refused to have an affair: "Like me, there are plenty of college girls who don't want to be bogged down with demanding involvements. . . . We're more concerned with getting ahead."

Like me, there are plenty of grizzled grammarians who think the best way for kids to get ahead in life is to stop fooling around with awkwardly placed modifiers.

Modifiers, even those clad only in their Calvin Klein jeans, should snuggle up to the word or phrase they modify. The prepositional phrase *like me* belongs next to *girls*, and the sentence would be better cast as "There are plenty of college girls like me who don't want to be bogged down . . ." (Better yet, "Plenty of college girls like me don't . . ." would make the point more strongly, but I want to stick to an example using a relative pronoun like the *who* in *girls who do*. This is not about how to avoid misplaced modifiers, which is kid's stuff, but rather about how to construe relative clauses, which is heavy grammar. Back to the sugarcoating.)

Miss Shields, though perhaps guilty of a *misplaced modifier*, is surely innocent of a *dangling modifier*; a modifier is said to be *dangling* only when the sentence in which it appears has no noun for it to modify, like "Not wanting to be bogged down, involvements can be too demanding."

More important, Miss Shields is pure in construing the verb of her relative clause as plural. A relative clause is a group of words that relates to an antecedent (a noun that has gone before) in the way *who don't want to be bogged down* relates to *college girls*. Correctly, Miss Shields says that college girls like her *don't* (not *doesn't*) want to be bogged down. She is one of the plural *girls*; the girls are not distinguished from *her*. As we shall see, that is no mere theoretical statement. Reputations of great editors and huge communications combines, as well as megabucks approaching gigabucks, ride on an understanding of relative clauses. Here's why:

A slyly plaintive letter has come to me from Robert Stein, editor of *McCall's* magazine. It begins: "This is in the nature of an appeal to the Supreme Court of Current English Usage." I blush but press on: "As you can quickly see from the enclosed letters to *Advertising Age*, ad people are passionately debating the use of a singular rather than a plural verb in our new advertising campaign."

Attached are letters calling attention to the line of copy under pictures of such sophisticated knockouts as Carly Simon, Diane von Furstenberg and Tina Turner, reading: "One of the drab homebodies who reads *Mc-Call's*." Sometimes the equally ironic "boring housewives" is substituted for "drab homebodies" in a campaign designed to put the magazine into closer competition with *Cosmopolitan*, where Helen Gurley Brown has been having it all. Other readers have sent the *McCall's* full-page ads to me, including the recent picture of Cher Bono—in rhinestone earrings that dangle as few participles can—over the caption "One of the typical mothers who reads *McCall's*."

Editor Stein writes: "My understanding is that the use of a singular verb is permissible in informal language, although the plural is correct in formal usage." He then puts it squarely up to me: "Would you care to render your judgment?"

Certiorari granted. (That's the Latin for "to be made more certain," now meaning simply "review." Up here, we call it *cert* for short.)

An amicus, or friend-of-the-court, brief has been submitted by Sue Warga of Hoboken, New Jersey: "Another copywriter lured by the proximity of the plural, alas. I based this judgment on what I thought was the intended meaning of the advertisement, namely, that if the likes of Turner, von Furstenberg, and Simon read *McCall's* magazine, then it's definitely cool for the average woman to read it as well. But if you take the ad as is, what it now says is 'This is one woman who reads *McCall's* magazine, out of all those boring housewives.' This would seem to separate the famous woman from the masses, and one would think that the whole point of this advertisement is to promote identification by the consumer with the rich, powerful and beautiful."

Miss Warga submits a letter to her from the promotion director of *Mc-Call's*, in response to her objection to the way *McCall's* construes the antecedent as singular: "We are referring to the one and only Tina Turner (you may have noticed her name is not mentioned, but everyone knows who she is). The same applies to Carly Simon, Cher and Diane von Furstenberg. Each is a *singular* woman, not to be mistaken for any other. And it is to the singular 'one' we refer."

That makes no grammatical sense to Miss Warga, who has circled the sentence in the *McCall's* letter to her: "Someone has suggested that William Safire settle things in his column and *McCall's* would be content with his judgment." I am beginning to think I am being neatly roped into a good promotion, but up here I cannot be influenced either by irate amici or learned public relations counsel.

When the numeral *One* is followed by a prepositional phrase like *of the drab homebodies*, the question is whether the relative clause—in this case, *who read/reads McCall's*—refers to the singular *One* or the plural *homebodies* as the antecedent. When the clause that follows is true of only the "one," then the clause's verb is singular (only "one who *reads*"); when the clause is true of more than one, the verb must be plural (many "housewives who *read*").

Some of the spectators in the back of the courtroom have just fallen asleep, so the bench will rephrase the issue. Who are we talking about here? Are we talking about *one* of the boring housewives, namely Tina Turner— or are we talking about *the boring housewives*, one of whom is Tina Turner?

The publication's defenders argue that *who* refers to *One*, specifically the luscious, appealing and singular woman whose face graces the page. In this pro-*McCall's* argument, the prepositional phrases *of the boring housewives* and *of the drab homebodies* are modifiers of *One*. Hence, the subject is construed as singular and the verb, to agree, would be *reads*, not *read*.

To test this argument, we may place that prepositional phrase at the beginning of the sentence. If it then said, "Of the drab homebodies, one who reads *McCall's*," the meaning implied is that, of all the drab homebodies in the world, the woman in the picture is the only one who reads *McCall's*. That cannot be the intent of the circulation director.

The Supreme Maven finds in this case that, while proximity to the antecedent is not controlling, the relative clause refers to the many and not the *One*. *One* is not the true antecedent. *One of the typical mothers, One of the boring housewives, One of the drab homebodies* contain plural antecedents with which the relative clause that follows must agree in number: *housewives who read*.

The arbiter has had recent experience with this common error. In zapping New Zealand, I wrote about "one of those little episodes in the relations between nations that illustrates the nature of alliances"; my brother in columny, William Buckley, circled my *illustrates* and wrote a dismayed "Bill!!" on top. He was right: it should have been many *episodes . . . that illustrate*, not the only *one . . . that illustrates*. (On the other hand, he may have been objecting to my use of *illustrate* when I meant *illuminate*; Buckley writes hurried postcards.)

Try it with Brooke Shields: she is one of the many college girls who *don't* want to be bogged down, not the only one of them who *doesn't*. She may misplace her modifier, but she relates well to her antecedents.

Therefore, it is ordered that *McCall's* stop mumbling about informal usage and get right with clarity. I am one of those grammatical nit-pickers who read *McCall's*, or at least who read *McCall's* ads. I am not one of those round-heeled copywriters who sell *McCall's*.

You, up there with the pot of glue and the huge poster—come on down; the whole thing's off.

Dear Bill,

I do not disagree with your answer, but with your question, or rather the content of the question put to you.

The "drab homebodies" phrase should be read *as if* it were in quotation marks; i.e., the "non-sentence sentence" should be read "One of those who **is perceived** to be a 'drab homebody,' but who (obviously if the 'one,' happens to be Tina Turner [uh, who?]) is not, who *reads McCall's.*"

Presumably *McCall's* is not aiming at the honest 'drab homebody,' but at the 'drab homebody' who believes she really isn't a drab homebody, a Tina Turner [who?] in the making. [Oh dear, that sounds like one of *your* puns!]

Therefore, since the thrust of the ad is to invite the potential subscriber to identify with the *class* of "ones" (each singular) only perceived to be "drab homebodies" and said P.S. is to consider herself singular, then the verb must be in the singular.

I mean, would a reader of *McCall's* wish to identify her[him?]self with the plural class of "drab homebodies"?

Michael Brisbane McCrary
Hong Kong BCC

I disagree. "One of the drab homebodies who reads *McCall's*" is a response to an unstated assertion—"Only drab homebodies read *McCall's.*" The response is really saying, "Tina Turner, a drab homebody (? !), reads *McCall's.*"

If the ad copy had read "One of the women who reads *McCall's*" beneath a picture of Carly Simon, your pedantic position would be proper. But in denying the unspoken, for *McCall's* unspeakable premise that only typical mothers or drab housewives peruse the magazine's copy and fall victims to its advertisers, the ad campaign is making the positive statement that each of these clearly atypical, anything but boring, women actually reads the thing. Before you believe that, get affidavits, your honor.

R. Skok Little
Stratford, Connecticut

I happen to be one of those drab homebodies who does not read *McCall's*.

You have, I think, missed the point. Advertising copy is hardly intended to inform, but rather to attract attention. To dramatize the irony of "who! is a drab homebody," *McCall's* did very well to use the singular verb after "one." If the reader notices at all, he may linger longer on just who is (or are!) the subject of the verb.

That proposition should be tested empirically—and the market sample should include some who do not now read *McCall's*, but might aspire to identification with the sophisticates pictured—hopeless, I fear, for the likes of thee and me.

Joshua Lederberg
President, The Rockefeller University
New York, New York

You state: "When the numeral *One* is followed by a prepositional phrase like *of the drab homebodies*, the question is whether the relative clause—in this case, *who read/reads McCall's*—refers to the singular *One* or the plural *homebodies* as the antecedent." And now I must ask my damning question: what relative clause? The sentence we are considering has only one verb, therefore it can have only one clause, the subject of which can only be *One*. Consequently *McCall's* is correct in using the third person singular rather than plural. The phrase *of the drab homebodies* is a complement to the noun *One*, and *who* is there only for stylistic effect and has no grammatical function of its own.

If you don't believe me, try this: dispense with either of the contenders for the function of subject, and see in which of the cases you still have a grammatically correct phrase. If you remove *One* the result is as follows: Of the drab homebodies who read *McCall's*. There is no subject. If you remove *of the drab homebodies* you find: One who reads *McCall's*. Not only is this a complete sentence, but it even makes sense.

However, as a conciliatory gesture, I must add that had we been dealing with a relative clause, if, in other words, there had been a second verb, you would have been correct, e.g. This is one of the drab homebodies who read *McCall's*. I shall also add that I suspect *McCall's* was correct only by accident: had they really known their grammar, they themselves would have offered this explanation, rather than "mumbling about informal usage".

Michael E. Erwin
New York, New York

Gotcha on a veritable whomdinger: "Who are we talking about here?"

> *Steven G. Kellman*
> *Professor of Comparative Literature*
> *The University of Texas*
> *San Antonio, Texas*

Notwithstanding that some grammarians have succumbed to what they call "common usage," I remain a staunch contender for the preservation of that time-honored and very practical pronoun "whom."

> Something in my brain goes Boom!
> When I see a "who" which should be "whom."

Consequently, when I read, in your opinion, the line "who are we talking about here?", the Boom!! was resounding. I trust that I am not being disloyal or seditious in questioning, ever so humbly, the grammar of the Supreme Maven.

> *Michael J. Fasman*
> *Beverly Hills, California*

You refer to "those round-heeled copywriters." Now, Mr. Safire, I was sure you didn't mean to make a slanderous remark in this connection, so I checked with the World Book Encyclopedia, 1976 Edition. Its second definition of the expression, "a promiscuous woman," is the meaning I have always associated with this phrase. However, the first definition is probably what you had in mind, namely, "easily swayed, or unable to resist a particular appeal."

> *Mary Lu Segelberg*
> *Omaha, Nebraska*

I think *Certiorari* means "You [the lower court] shall certify to us the record in this case."
In other words—"Send me the file."

> *Frederic F. Brace, Jr.*
> *Chicago, Illinois*

But It Would Be Wrong

*R*IGHT is not always the right word.

You are in a taxicab. You are familiar with your destination, but the driver is not. He asks, "Make a left at the next corner?" You want him to do that, but the word that leaps to your lips is "right"—you know that is the wrong word, because it may cause him to switch lanes to turn right, causing a great screeching of tires behind you, followed by terrible anguish at Lloyd's of London. So what do you say?

The bookish reader, who has never faced this terrible moment, will suggest serenely that the proper answer in that situation is "yes." That reader does not live in the real world of directions and turns and sudden stops and outraged cursing. If you, the direction-giver, are ready to say "yes," your alternative answer is "no"; and if you want the driver to turn right when he asks if you want him to turn left, "no" is a stupid, inadequate response.

Those of us who like our directions to be crisp and unambiguous are ready with three responses to the query "Make a left?" If left is not the direction desired, answer "Make a right" or "Straight ahead." If left is your way to go, the correct and unconfusing answer is "correct." Whatever your direction, stay away from the word *right*—it causes accidents.

In a similar way, *wrong* is not always the right word.

An Op-Ed page in the *Washington Post* on the subject of aid to the contras in Nicaragua had these headlines: "Kirkpatrick and Krauthammer Are Wrong," "Podhoretz Is Wrong" and—in the only headline that nobody would find objectionable—"The *Post* Is Wrong."

Wrong is a word that editorialists like, because we are by nature opinionated, and *wrong* rings with the voice of judgment. "Virginia," wrote Francis P. Church in the most famous editorial ever, "your little friends are wrong."

So are your little headline writers, Meg. *Wrong* is one of those sweeping words that contain a multitude of charges. When you blast someone for being *wrong*, do you mean what he says is *incorrect, false, inaccurate, imprecise*? Or do you intend the word to convey a charge of venality, that your target is himself *evil, improper, unethical, unrighteous, bad*, perhaps *willfully misleading?* Does your *wrong* carry a deliciously crackbrained connotation so often found in *unwitting dupe,* which so many of us take to mean a combination of *nitwit* and *dope?* Or do you mean merely that your opponent in debate is *mistaken?*

As *right* is akin to the Latin for "straight," *wrong* is rooted in the Old Norse for "twisted." That pair of meanings is simple enough, but *right* and *wrong* have become bifurcated (big word in academic circles, *bifurcated*; try it at the next faculty party as you try to spear a shrimp with a two-pronged fork). *Correct* and *incorrect* now vie with *good* and *bad* in telling *right* and *wrong* from right and wrong.

Example: B. Gallagher of Cleveland Heights, Ohio, sends me a brochure received from the Book-of-the-Month Club selling *A Treasury for Word Lovers,* by Morton S. Freeman, which blurbs: "An invaluable resource for everyone who wants to express themselves correctly. . . ." Back to the recasting couch, copywriter: change the *everyone who wants* to *all who want* or, if you're not afraid of feminists, change the *themselves* to *himself.* That Mistake-of-the-Month is not *wrong*; it's only *incorrect.* To be *mistaken* is not to be *wrong*; a slip of the tongue is not a fall from grammatical grace, nor is a solecism a sin.

Precision in disputation adds to civility in discourse. (Sentences like that make me want to bifurcate.) If your target is evil incarnate, excoriate him for being *in the wrong* and label him a real *wrongo.* Recognize the informality and imprecision of "You're wrong."

Try another formulation that lets you be different in your differing. I was trying to find the origin of *New Deal* for my political dictionary; the phrase was used by Mark Twain, David Lloyd George and Woodrow Wilson, but to get the coiner in the Roosevelt era, I wrote to Judge Samuel I. Rosenman, author of many of Franklin Delano Roosevelt's speeches and the editor of F.D.R.'s papers. He allowed as how he had worked on the peroration to the acceptance speech at the 1932 Democratic National Convention, when the candidate said, "I pledge you, I pledge myself, to a new deal for the American people."

Then I asked another man who worked on F.D.R. speeches, the columnist Raymond Moley, who wrote back: "The expression *new deal* was in the draft which I left at Albany with Roosevelt."

But what of Rosenman's indication that the phrase was his contribution? Was Sammy the Rose wrong and Raymond the Mole right?

Here is how Mr. Moley handled that: "When Rosenman says that he wrote it, he is in error."

In error. Not *wrong*; not even *mistaken*; merely in a state of incorrectness, perhaps not his fault. That's a riposte that shows class.

Dear Bill:

I join your campaign for precision with gladness and alacrity. But there are a couple of difficulties arising out of your precepts about *right* and *wrong*.

When you want us to say "in the wrong," for evil incarnate, you change the distinction that reserves that phrase for excusable moral wrong: "In that dispute, Jones was in the wrong." A murderer is not "in the wrong" or "wrong."

Furthermore, *correct* and *incorrect* only conceal the word *right*, which you want us to be chary of in the common expression "you are right," to which "you are wrong" is a fair counterpart.

And isn't "I am mistaken" another imprecise remark as you use it? "I am mistaken for my twin brother"—yes. But: "I mistake when I get 6 by adding 4 and 4." Yet whom will you get to say "I mistake?"

Jacques [Barzun]
Charles Scribner's Sons, Publishers
New York, New York

When you pointed out the mistake in the blurb for a book on language, you graciously added, "a slip of the tongue is not a fall from grammatical grace. . . ."

The mistake, being written rather than spoken, was not a slip of the tongue *(lapsus linguae)*, but a slip of the pen *(lapsus calami)*, literally, a slip of the reed. It's a nice distinction, rarely made.

Arthur J. Morgan
New York, New York

Lloyds of London is spelled *without* an apostrophe. The name denotes the original family of LLOYDS, not an individual.

Lorene L. Kramer
New York, New York

Buzz Off, Interceptor

"I am outraged!" said the caller.

"And I am Safire," I replied. However, the name of the man on the phone was Sam Donaldson, the irrepressible ABC News reporter and weighty anchorman. Outraged was the name of his state.

The reason for his ire was that he felt he had been linguistically suckered on a story by the White House. "What does the word *intercept* mean to you?"

Colleagues often call me when a dictionary is not handy; my number does not make a bulge in their pockets. I said that the verb *intercept* meant to stop or seize something on its way somewhere.

"And the noun? What's *an intercept?*"

I became cagey; these new nouns derived from verbs, especially when the *-tion* is shunned, can get tricky. I asked for a context, and then held the phone a foot away from my ear, which is how you listen to Donaldson.

"The White House announced there had been an *intercept* of one of our planes by two Libyan jets," he said. "We led the show with it. Then it turns out that the Libyans merely approached our plane in an unmenacing manner, and the press office claims that's what an *intercept* is. I told them the next time one of our missiles intercepts another missile, I hope they're standing on ground zero, not me."

I told Outraged I would noodle it over and render judgment in this space.

The noun *interception* was coined in 1597, and was used two years later by Shakespeare in *Henry V* in a remark about spying on traitors, an act later called counterespionage: "The King hath note of all that they intend/ By interception which they dream not of." That specific meaning of catching information on its way elsewhere is preserved in today's spookspeak by *Elint* and *Sigint*, electronic or signal intelligence gleaned by intercepting messages. In that sense, however, an *intercept* is a message that has been read and copied but not stopped or seized.

So what does *intercept*, both as verb and clipped noun, mean today? The Oxford English Dictionary's supplement, as authoritative a source as anyone can turn to, defines *interception* as "the action of closing in on and trying to destroy an enemy aircraft or missile." When *Aviation Week & Space Technology* wrote in 1978 that "MIG-25 Foxbat interceptors would be used for close-in *intercepts* of cruise missiles," the meaning was "tracking, catching up to and destroying" the missiles.

In fact, the Government's own most frequent use of the term underscores the "seizure" meaning: "Operation Intercept" is an attempt to control smuggling on the Mexican-American border by grabbing as much of the smack, snow and grass (heroin, cocaine and marijuana) as the narcs can. The narcotics agents do not benignly look over the drugs and let them go on their merry way; they glom on to the stuff with great shouts of "Gotcha!" and their meaning of *intercept* is clearly "seize and destroy."

Finally, in football, an *interception*—the word has not yet been penalized for clipping—is a snatching-away of a ball on the flight toward its hoped-for destination. When we hear a coach groan, "Oh, those turnovers," he is not remembering the delicious apple pastries of his youth, but is describing the disasters that befall teams prone to fumbling and throwing passes that are intercepted.

Thus, a strong case can be made that Outraged was right and the White House used a word that was unduly alarming.

Hold on. A call to the Pentagon reaches Major Jan Dalby, an Air Force spokesman described by one of the many people who transferred the call as "the action officer" in these matters.

(No, says Dalby, the presence of an *action officer* does not mean there are *inaction officers* or *deliberation officers* in the Pentagon. *Action officer* strikes me the same as *distinguished professor*; both titles make colleagues seem like sloths or mediocrities.)

Whipping out a copy of the Dictionary of Military and Associated Terms, Dalby reports no listing for the noun *intercept*, but this for *interceptor*: "A manned aircraft utilized for identification and/or engagement of airborne objects." The action-oriented major adds: "*Intercept*, then, would fall somewhere between *surveillance*, which can involve systematic observation, and *engagement*, in case of war." In the same dictionary at his fingertips (Dalby apparently gets calls from his friends with no pockets, same as I do from mine), *engagement* is defined as "an attack with guns or air-to-air missiles by an interceptor aircraft."

"If a Soviet aircraft should stray into our airspace," he adds, "we would scramble interceptors to identify and observe the aircraft. That would be more than *surveillance*, less than *engagement*." Between those two easy-to-define realities falls the shadow of *interception*.

"*Intercept* as a noun goes back to World War II at least," says Brendan M. Greeley, Jr., military editor of *Aviation Week & Space Technology*, "and it usually referred to a 'radar intercept.' These days, there is a *standard intercept*, what we call *intercepting the Bear* on his way from the Soviet Union to Cuba, for instance. We send F-106's out of Massachusetts or F-15's out of Langley, and they may get close enough to smile and wave at the Bear's pilot. The interceptors gather visual information. An *intercept* in that sense is a rendezvous, a kind of joining. It usually involves monitoring and then breaking away. When any firing begins, that's *engagement.*"

In the language of the specialists, then, the White House was correct in calling the *surveillance* short of *engagement* an *intercept*. And yet, and yet—there was probably an element of anger in the surveillance, as if the pursuing jets were sending a message of intimidation. In that case, the *New York Times* headline writer chose the perfect verb to describe the encounter: "Libyan Fighters Buzz U.S. Plane."

In the graphic display of data, the crossing of the line formed on the data points with one of the coordinates on a graph is called the "intercept," as in "The ordinate intercept was positive with a value of X."

Irwin H. Rosenberg, M.D.
Professor of Medicine
University of Chicago
Chicago, Illinois

Two non-parallel lines intersect someplace. When one line is an axis of reference, the location along it where the other line crosses is referred to as the "intercept." Where a line crosses the Y, or vertical, axis on a traditional plane graph, the crossing point is called the "y-intercept." Hundreds of analytical geometers use that noun every day, and the practice goes back many centuries.

In the context of your article, the mathematical use of "intercept" is analogous to a mere crossing of paths on the part of the various aircraft. No collisions and no bullets.

Carl Oppedahl
New York, New York

Intercept as a noun is a century or so old and refers to a step in plotting lines of position from celestial observations. In methods described by two nineteenth-century naval officers—the American Captain Thomas H. Sumner and the French Commander Marc Saint-Hilaire—the difference between the observed altitude (Ho) and computed altitude (Hc) of a celestial body is plotted on a chart on a line towards or away from its apparent position on the earth (GP). A perpendicular through that point is the Line of Position on a Mercator chart. That value is called the *altitude intercept* or the *intercept* (see attached excerpts from the 1958 edition of the *American Practical Navigator*, especially the Glossary definition of *intercept*).

In time, any quantity which determines a line on a plotting chart came to be called the *intercept*. Thus, while there was not an *interception* in the skies over the Mediterranean, there was, no doubt, an *intercept* (and probably dozens of them) on the plotting tables, whether paper or electronic, of both their guys and our guys.

Philip T. Weinstein
Miami, Florida

Canute's Bum Rap

Adam Yarmolinsky, who is located somewhere between Adam Walinsky and Daniel Yankelovich, wrote an Op-Ed piece opposing the President's attempt to reverse the ebb tide of defense spending. Before jumping on this good man for his mangled metaphor, let me hoot at the identification at the bottom of his piece: "professor of policy sciences at the University of Maryland."

Policy sciences? What is it with our great universities that they have to turn every subject into an *art*, every course into a *study* or every department into a *science?* To sign up for courses in English, cooking and welfare cheating, today's student has to traipse from the Institute of Linguistic Arts to the Center for Culinary Studies to the Program in Policy Sciences.

The University of Maryland, a good school too eager to plug into the lingo of nearby think tanks, has grouped its courses about national security, health insurance, unemployment, geriatrics, housing and the like into a terrapin soup called *policy sciences.*

These would-be with-it academics don't quite have the hang of it yet.

Here in the hallowed halls of Safire U., our undistinguished professors are curriculating their courses in finger painting and rock-music appreciation together under *arts sciences,* headed by a ten-yeared chairman of *arts policies studies,* or *arts studies policies,* who will offer our students-for-life their multi-disciplinary graduate degrees in *study policies arts* or *policy arts studies.*

Professor Yarmolinsky cannot be blamed for the pretentious name of the department (or program, or whatever) he has just joined. (As Al Haig replied when asked his political plans for 1988, "It's too soon to start posturing.") However, the professor is responsible for the following lead paragraph: "Ronald Reagan is playing a favorite role: King Canute—but he has the role backward. Though there is wide agreement that the tide has turned on military spending, Mr. Reagan is trying to keep it flowing in the same direction. In fact, he wants to speed up the flow."

This canard about Canute was brought to my attention by Simon Hoggart, Washington bureau chief of *The Observer,* one of London's most literate newspapers.

"King Canute was held up in this article as an example of overweening human pride in believing that Nature's immutable laws can be changed," writes this defender of the ancient royal reputation. "But as every English schoolchild learns (and mysteriously forgets in adulthood), it was not Canute but his courtiers who believed that he could turn back the tide. The King took them to the seashore for a practical demonstration that he had no such power."

When, then, should we use Canute in Op-Ed leads? "The fable is not about vanity but about sycophancy," concludes Mr. Hoggart, "and Canute should be regarded as a hero rather than a fool."

An endowed chaise longue awaits you, sir, at our famed Center for Maritime Metaphor Studies and Policy Arts.

> You state, "The University of Maryland, a good school too eager to plug into the lingo of think tanks . . ." For me, a university has many components, such as buildings, classrooms, people, etc. Perhaps when you were writing about the quality of this institution you were meaning to say something about the "good" that occurs in the education of the students, and perhaps when saying something about the eagerness of the University, you were referring to some of the people associated with the school.
>
> Every day we hear such language as "The White House states that . . . ," when we are fully aware that buildings do not make

statements. Does the common usage of journalists dictate the correctness of the language?

Ed Flowers
Sebastopol, California

The Caplet Solution

Quick, what's a *caplet?*
Some will rush out on the balcony to blurt Juliet's line: "Deny thy father and refuse thy name or . . . I'll no longer be a Capulet." Others will think of chewing gum; still others will find it suggests the name of a Washington hockey team with a puckish goalie.

But *caplet* is the gulp-of-desperation word seized upon by Johnson & Johnson, makers of Tylenol, whose capsules were again tampered with by some unknown killer. A *caplet* is a *tablet* shaped like a *capsule.*

This is an example of a *portmanteau word.* (I do not use *blend word* anymore, because *blenders* are being chopped and sliced to bits by *processors,* and I await the appearance of a *processed word;* meantime, the old *portmanteau* looks better than ever.) *Portmanteau* comes from the French verb *porter,* to carry, and *manteau,* a mantle or cloak: a *portmanteau* is the leather suitcase that opens, like a book, into two sections, allowing you to carry your cloak in one side and your dagger or toothbrush in the other. By metaphoric extension, a *portmanteau word* carries pieces of two words in one bag: slam it shut, and you have one word.

"If you have Tylenol capsules," headlined the full-page ad, "we'll replace them with Tylenol caplets." The copy explained that "the caplet is a solid form" of the pain reliever, which the maker asserted is "the form most preferred by consumers. Unlike tablets, it is specially shaped and coated for easy, comfortable swallowing."

Over at the American Institute of the History of Pharmacy, the *caplet* is not seen as the savior of the industry. "It's just a tablet compressed in the shape of a capsule," says Dr. Gregory Higby, "and is not a standard pharmaceutical term by any means. *Tablet* and *capsule* are standard terms, while *caplet* is more of a bastard term, though the industry has been offering this product shape for decades."

But who first portered the manteau? Fred Mish, editorial director of Merriam-Webster, has an ad from early 1968 for the analgesic Vanquish, which boasts that "the caplet shape makes it easy to swallow." In addition, lexicographer Mish, to whom I turn whenever I have a coinage headache, has found in the 1941 edition of the Modern Drug Encyclopedia, by Jacob Gutman, a glossary entry that reads *"caplet*—capsule-shaped preparation, coated."

That's a good beginning for the hunt for the coiner. The hot new term is at least two generations old and encompasses two qualities: first, a somewhat rectangular shape, the corners smoothed; second, an aqueous coating to make it slip down the gullet like a speeding oyster. The word has another, entirely different meaning: "in the shape of a small cape"; an Associated Press fashion story in 1980 gushed over "those wonderful warm coats . . . that thrilled you in 'Dr. Zhivago,' with their double caplet collars. . . ."

Can a *caplet*, in its pharmaceutical garb, be called a *pill*, which comes from the Latin *pilula*, the diminutive of *pila*, a ball? Purists will say no, insisting that the caplet's rejection of a spherical shape makes it a nonpill; but *tablet*, from the Latin for "small slab," long ago knocked the pill out of shape, and now we even include *capsules* (little Latin boxes) under the *pill* rubric.

The man who coined the phrase *portmanteau word* was Lewis Carroll, creator of Alice in Wonderland; he delighted in putting together *slimy* and *lithe* to produce "the *slithy* toves," and combined a *snort* with a *chuckle* in "Jabberwocky" to have "*chortled* in his joy."

Before that, in 1812, a great political word was coined when the painter Gilbert Stuart looked at political district lines drawn to include certain voters, sketched on a couple of legs and said, "That will do for a salamander." Benjamin Russell of *The Boston Centinel* suggested, "Call it a Gerrymander," after Governor Elbridge Gerry, supposedly the perpetrator of the political serpent, and a Federalist war cry was born. (*Gerrymander* is pronounced with a soft G; Gerry pronounced his name with a hard G, like Gary; fame is fleeting.)

In our time, the great creators of portmanteau words* have been Walter Winchell, whose *cinemactresses* were always *infanticipating*, and the editors of *Time* magazine, who married *cinemoppets* to *admen*, and on a cover coined a new one: "*Televangelist* Pat Robertson."

It's my guesstimate that the frequent use of this technique has not been happenstance; we'll talk it over at brunch, if you can get through the smog.

* For more on this subject, see *port manteau* on p. 300.

I've even heard President Reagan blend his phrases. While talking about his family's relationships, he said that problems had been "blown out of whack." No doubt he meant a combination of "blown out of proportion" and "out of whack."

Stephanie Oddleifson
New Haven, Connecticut

The Case of the President's Case

"To the ramparts!" writes Ethel Hubbard of Williston Park, Long Island. "President Reagan, in his Inaugural Address, said, 'If not *us*, who?' For shame. He should have said, 'If not *we*, who?' "

From Richard Hall at the Lovett School in Atlanta comes this dismayed reaction: "My colleagues and I spend a good bit of energy attending to details such as pronoun case and agreement in students' writing. It bothers me to see such a crass error coming from the President on such an important occasion and, further, to find no one calling him to task on it."

The responsibility devolves upon me, your local grammarian, to do it here, in a column devoted to soft sell of linguistic standards. If not in this space, where? If not me, who?

Or should that be—if not I, whom? If not me, whom? If not I, who?

The President's rhetorical question, which he has been asking since his California Governor days, involves an error in case. Let's get down to cases on *case*.

People hung up on Latin and Greek are case-hardened. You will hear them throwing around words like *nominative, genitive, dative, ablative* and *vocative* as if they still mean something to modern English. They do not. I don't want to be accusative, but the case for *case* in the language we speak today is limited. Useful, but limited, to be defended in a narrow area.

When a young person heavily in touch with his own feelings comes up to an English teacher and says, "What's with this *case* jazz?" the best response is: "Do you believe in relationships?" Of course, today "relationships" is all —no commitment, no hurting, just touch lives and run.

Same with *case*. Grammatical case is the relationship between classes of words to indicate their functions in a sentence. (Means nothing; try again.) *Case* is a word that describes how certain words relate to the words around them. (Better. I hear you.) The doer of an action is in one category and has to relate to the receiver of an action. The doers are subjects, in the *subjec-*

tive case; the receivers are objects, in the *objective* case. These *subjective* and *objective* cases are frequently married in sentences; just as in real life, the words in each case are tempted to have outside affairs, and those relationships of belonging or possessing are done in the sleazy motel rooms of the *possessive* case. (You're on a roll, man; lay it on me.)

What sort of crowd do you find in the *subjective* case? That's the domain of the doers, the assertive big-shot types, *I, we, he, she, they, who*, all looking out for Number One.

On the other hand, if you go to a disco for *objective* cases, you get a lot of slow dancing and meek acceptances from the likes of *me, us, him, her, them* and *whom*.

When the two cases get together, you have clear relationships: *I* hit *her*. *We* clobbered *him*. *They* sued *us*. When the two cases branch out to impose their ownership or lust to be possessed, they relate to the *possessive* case: *I* got *mine*. *He's* got *his*. *They* got *their* or *theirs*. *Who* got *whose*.

Let's play a little game to show how happy we can all be when we stick within our case-assigned relationships: *subjective* gets *possessive* for the *objective*. Here goes: *I* got *mine* for *me*. *We* got *ours* for *us*. *He* or *she* got *his* or *hers* for *him* or *her*. *They* got *theirs* for *them*. *Who* got *whose* for *whom*.

That is the state of relationships in the perfect world, with every word knowing its case the way Victorians knew their places. Now that we have steeped ourselves in the meaning of case and accepted its simple and orderly scheme, I have troubling news: we live in an imperfect world.

One of the linguistic problems of the real world stems from our tendency to take verbal shortcuts. We leap from peak to peak and expect the listener to fill in the valleys. When we speak or write and omit words that we expect to be understood, we are engaging in *elliptical construction*, and that's where much of the confusion about case takes place.

Take, for example, the President's catchy question: "If not us, who?" Let's assume he meant "If *we* do not make the hard decision, then *who* will?" In that case (using *case* in two meanings), what he meant to say was "If not *we*, *who*?"

But wait. What if his elliptical construction were built this way: "If hard decisions are not made by *us*, then by *whom* will they be made?" In that case, he meant "If not *us*, *whom*?"

The trick is to be consistent within the case: if he goes *subjective*, it should be *we/who*; if he goes *objective* case, it should be *us/whom*.

"The President's question represents a clear failure in pronoun-case agreement," charges Mr. Hall. He is correct; Mr. Reagan, to agree with himself, should have said either, "If not we, who?" or "If not us, whom?"

Now—who is going to walk up to el Presidente and accuse him of corrupting the grammar of the nation's youth?

Not me.

Why not? Haven't I fearlessly corrected his pronunciation of *liaison* (he used to say "lay-i-zon," but has now admitted error and changed his ways). Has he not been castigated in this space for going to the "well" too often? (His press conference answers began: "Well, we're going to stay with the treaties. . . ." "Well, the Treasury plan. . . ." "Well, remove it in the sense of its present structure. . . ." "Well, what I'm saying is. . . ." "Well, I was actually speaking to some clergymen. . . ." and six more "wells." I may go to a press conference to ask, "How are you feeling, Mr. President?" just to let him use the word in a substantive sense.)

The reason for today's timorousness is my own use of the natural-sounding "Not *me*" just above. The correct answer was "Not I," because that is my ellipsis for "I am not the one" or "The one to do it is not I." But I would not say "Not I" because I am a native speaker passionately in love with Norma Loquendi, and she wouldn't be caught dead saying the snooty-sounding, pedantic "Not I."

In the same way, if Norma and I were holding hands outside the Oval Office and the President called out "Whozat?" we would reply "It's us." If we were to reply with the formally correct "It is we," the President would think he was being approached by a couple of reactionary linguistic kooks.

In the real world, case has been taking a bit of a buffeting in the last couple of generations. Today it is pedantry to insist on the subjective case (*I, he, we*) when the objective case falls more naturally on the ear. The English teacher who hears such permissiveness from a language maven need not be dismayed: "*Us* Tareyton smokers" and "*them* guys" still sound as unschooled as "*Me* Tarzan, you Jane," and "between you and *I*" is still incorrect. Their students should be taught why such constructions make the speakers appear to be straining to be members of the underworld or make writers seem condescending or illiterate. (The use of *their* at the beginning of that sentence, referring back to "the English teacher" in the previous sentence, though not so obvious a blunder, is a misuse of the possessive case, which, had it not been picked up by an astute rewriter, would have been the source of great embarrassment. Next week: pronoun-antecedent agreement.)

A good case can be made for the consistent use of case—in most cases. Similarly, a neat and logical argument can be put forward for clarity in personal relationships, with married people, and single people living together, and happy hermits all by themselves—but some mixing of categories is definitely taking place.

The great question is: should case-crossing—the breakdown of absolute consistency in grammatical case rules—be furiously resisted, quietly tolerated, openly condoned, or actively encouraged?

Put me down for quiet toleration in formal writing, open condonement in speech. When it comes to usage, President Reagan is a rhetorical roundheels, as befits a politician seeking empathy with his audience. He is the McGovern of pronoun-case agreement, an accommodationist of the first order.

He was fully aware that, even in an Inaugural Address, the formal "If not we, who?" or "If not us, whom?" would have seemed laughably stilted. He chose the comfortable "If not us, who?" and Norma Loquendi wriggled in enthusiastic agreement, which is why, in this matter, the legion of the rampart-dwellers would do well to get off his case.

Dear Bill,

Your column contains a distressingly large number of errors of the worst kind, namely errors that most knowledgeable persons think not to be errors.

(i) Your statement that *"Case* is a word that describes how certain words relate to the words around them" confuses the distinct but related notions of "case" and "grammatical relation." The connection between the two notions is that in a language that has distinct cases, each case will correspond to one or more grammatical relations that it is used to express. The correspondence between cases and grammatical relations is rather loose in several respects: all languages have grammatical relations, though many languages do not have cases; it is common for a single case to serve as an expression of several different grammatical relations (e.g. the English accusative case [I'll stick with the Latinate terminology that I'm used to and eschew terms like 'objective'] is used for direct objects, indirect objects, objects of prepositions, and subjects of certain non-finite clauses, as in *For us to quit now would be unthinkable*—if you want arguments that *us* in that is not the object of *for*, I'll happily provide some—and as you point out yourself, in colloquial English it has still other uses, such as for predicate noun phrases *(It's us)*. Cases are inflectional forms, not grammatical relations.

(ii) One or three sentences later (depending on whether you count the parenthesized sentences, though that seems to subvert the function of parentheses), you confuse grammatical relations (such as "subject" and "direct object") with such semantic relations as "agent" and "patient." Sufficiently many thousands of teachers have drilled into their pupils' heads the fairy tale that a verb denotes an action, its subject the "doer" of the action, and its object the "receiver" that it won't be easy to stamp out that piece of misinformation, but before you repeat it again, I urge you to ponder the fact that many verbs denote something other than an action (e.g. *resemble, imply, contain*) and thus are not combined with any "doer" or "receiver" (in *John resembles a gorilla,* John is not represented as doing anything, nor a gorilla as receiving anything), as well as the fact that there are many verbs whose subjects denote "receivers" of actions mentioned in the verb or the object (as in *John received a warning* or *Mary underwent surgery*). The popularity of the fairy tale about actions, doers, and receivers can be attributed to the fact that the most obvious example sentences conform to the fairy tale (if someone wants an example of a simple sentence, he's more likely to come up with *Brutus stabbed Caesar* than with *John resembles a gorilla*), combined with the fact that teachers of grammar are rarely trained to seek out examples that will test the grammatical propositions that they propound.

(iii) You give one absolutely bizarre example: "They got *their* or *theirs."* I presume that you do not mean to say that *They got their* is normal English (that's an error that turns up in elementary-level English-as-a-second-language classes and is duly corrected). I trust that there was supposed to be a noun after *their* and that it somehow got omitted. It would have done your readers some good, though, if you had pointed out that English has not just a single series of possessive pronouns but both a strong series (*mine, yours,* . . .) and a weak series (*my, your,* . . .), with the strong series used in predicate position (*This is mine*) or when the modified noun is omitted (*Take mine*) and the weak series used when there is an overt modified noun (*Take my car*). (*His* serves as both strong and weak form, and the weak form *its* has no corresponding strong form, which makes for some odd gaps in the language, e.g. you can't say *This is its*, meaning, say, 'This is the company's').

(iv) In bringing up *them guys,* you speak as if it had an inappropriately chosen case. Surely you aren't recommending that your readers say sentences like *They guys bother me*, a use of *they* that is abnormal in most varieties of English, though it is found in some Scottish dialects. *Them guys* (and *they guys,* for those dialects that have it) is an extension to the third person of a combination that in most dialects of English is available only in the first and second person plural: combinations of (nonpossessive) pronoun and plural noun such as *we linguists* and *you columnists.* There is no consensus as to the syntactic structure of those expressions: they have often been described as appositions, but there is a minority (to which I belong) who maintain that the pronoun here functions as an article. Note that if it is treated as an apposition there is something peculiar about it, since a noun without an article is normally not possible as the second part of an apposition: *those persons linguists* (cf. *those persons, the linguists*).

James D. McCawley
Professor of Linguistics
University of Chicago
Chicago, Illinois

Don't bother teaching grammar,
That stuff is for the birds.
There aren't no parts of speech no more,
They're just so many words.
Just leave the kids talk like they want,
They're going to, anyhow.
'Twon't make no odds to you and I
A hundred years from now.

Frances E. Holmes
Montpelier, Vermont

Your references to types of modern living are an excellent way to explain cases and such.

Having lived in the era when I had four years of Latin in high school and a couple in college I now see the start of return to classic background studies of English. The tide is turning.

Knowing cases and declensions and the like helps us understand English, as you know. Moreover, schools are beginning *again*, thank goodness, to teach foreign languages—and require them. How much easier it would be for a student to learn foreign languages after the nitty-gritty study of Latin. Your sugar-coated method won't be necessary for long!

Fairlee T. Hersey
Norton, Massachusetts

It seems to me that one of the reasons why object pronouns (me, him, etc.) are so commonly used where subject forms are, strictly speaking, correct is that English lacks so-called disjunctive pronouns. French, for example, has three first-person pronouns: *je* (subject), *me* (object), and *moi* (disjunctive). Disjunctive forms are used in one-word responses (*"Qui a fait cette erreur?"*/*"Moi"*), after prepositions (*"Venez avec moi"*), in phrases like *"C'est moi"* and in other positions where the pronoun is stressed. In both English and French, the object pronoun is not normally stressed (He sees me; *Il me voit*). In French the disjunctive can be used for any case.

Most English speakers have merely compensated for the lack of such forms by using object pronouns. In my opinion, this practice should be made standard, especially since it is so prevalent in the language of a wide range of speakers of diverse educational and socio-economic backgrounds.

Richard A. Schutz
Philadelphia, Pennsylvania

You think you're being permissive, but in fact you are too hard on those who say, "If not us, who?" In their case, the ellipsis may signify: "If hard decisions are not made by *us*, then *who* will make them?"

Leonard Rubin
New York, New York

You make an equation between "If *we* do not make the hard decision, then *who* will?" and "If hard decisions are not made by *us*, then by *whom* will they be made?" To connect these two hypothetical questions, you write: "But wait. What if his elliptical construction were built this way:" It is about your use of "were" that I am writing to you. You are presumably making the point that either of the two possible sentences which President Reagan could have made could be correct, that they are two equal sentences, that neither one was right or wrong, and that neither was impossible nor unlikely. If there ever *was* an example where "was" was correct, this is it.

M. Vernon Ordiway, M.D.
Ridgway, Pennsylvania

So a native speaker passionately devoted to Norma Loquendi wouldn't say, "Not I"?

What about all those undeniably native speakers, the cow, the dog and whatnot, who repeatedly answered, "Not I," when the Little Red Hen asked them to help her grind the grain, knead the flour and bake the bread?

Or was that grade-school fable, which I always took to be designed for ethical uplift, really a subversion of native speech?

Bill Branche
New York, New York

I was delighted, amused and enlightened by "The Case Of the President's Case." However, I was disappointed that there was not even *sotto voce* mention of the source of the President's undeniably great exhortation to social responsibility. Surely, "If not us, who? If not now, when?" might rank President Reagan in the same class with President Kennedy, whose "Ask not what your country can do for you . . ." touched similar emotions in listeners, were it not for the fact that President Reagan's words are "borrowed" from the first century B.C. Rabbi Hillel's "Ethics of the Fathers."

The problem with President Reagan's "case" developed because he has not (nor has anyone at "The Times") credited the great Hebrew scholar and said that the thought, translated with attendant grammatical difficulties from Hillel's Hebrew, is as valid today as when Hillel expressed it many centuries ago. Case closed?

Paul Rosenfeld
Professor, Music & Art
Bronx Community College (CUNY)
Bronx, New York

How could you possibly devote a column to "If not we, who?" without reference to its obvious springboard—Hillel [30 B.C.–10 A.D.]:

"If I am not for myself, then who am I for?
If I am for myself alone, then what am I?
And if not now, when?"

Obviously, your early childhood readings were sadly neglected! Or in the wrong pew.

Bernard Gould
Hackensack, New Jersey

In one of the languages that has had a very profound effect on ours, the language of the Norman conquerors of 1066, there is a case which exists almost solely for the purpose of handling the problem you bring up in your article. I am referring to the French use of the *emphatic* forms of the personal pronouns: *moi, toi, lui,* etc. Some grammarians call these the "disjunctive pronouns," but I prefer to think of them as a different case rather than as a whole new series of words.

For the purpose of my argument, let's take as our test sentence your first-person variation on the President's mistake, "Not me." In French, as you probably know, that would be: *"Pas moi,"* which rolls very naturally off the tongue, and which would be perfectly acceptable to your friend Norma if she were French. By saying "Not me," I suggest that you are merely following the natural trend of English-speaking people to drift toward the better-sounding French way of dealing with the problem.

I would like to suggest that we take a cue from our Gallic cousins and coin our own versions of the emphatic personal pronouns: me, you, him, her, us, you, and them. Not as distinctive as the French, but they have the advantage of being already in majority use. And think how elated the French will be to see an example of a possible reversal in the growing tide of English encroachment into their glorious tongue, a small backcurrent against the wave of "Franglais." Perhaps as a champion of living language you should push for the adoption of these or other English versions of the personal pronouns. If not you, who?

John Boylan
Los Angeles, California

You say that the President was aware that he was committing a grammatical error (to be immortalized in history) but chose to do so because its sound was more acceptable to the listening ears of the hoi-polloi.

Was this merely a matter of politics? I don't think so. I can't help thinking that neither he, though he has had a lifetime of familiarity with language, nor his speech-writers recognized the error. Had they done so, all they had to do was express the thought in another way. They used that phrase because they just didn't know any better. And that is the tragedy and the shame.

The President said, "If not us, who?" The implied sentence is, "If we are not the people to take this action, who will?" Could he possibly have said, "If us are not the people . . ."? The subject of the sentence is "we" in apposition to [the understood] "it." The case is, and can only be, the nominative. No choice.

Syntax has been established over thousands of years for the single purpose of clarity of expression. It exists not only in English, but in all other languages. It's not open to change, like words. It's part and parcel of the language itself.

Our humanity is in our language. Our intellectual history is in our language. English happens to be the most eminent in the world today, containing more words than any other, providing us with the means of expressing complex and subtle ideas. Now there are those who want to suit syntax to their lack of knowledge.

"It is I" is correct. How can proper English have become "stilted"? Rather, it's been corrupted by careless use, inadequate education, and the undermining of standards. There is a dearth of standard-bearers, of whom you, dear Bill, are one.

As such you cannot abdicate your responsibility by quibbling, making excuses, or stooping to using man-in-the-street gibberish.

Ethel Hubbard
Williston Park, New York

Caviar, General?

A couple of heavyweight professors were sparring on the "CBS Morning News" about the wisdom of the nuclear shield called Star Wars. I was in bed in a hotel room, getting a second reprieve from a snooze alarm, when I heard the voice of Arthur M. Schlesinger, Jr., a Distinguished Professor of the City University of New York (who happens also to be a distinguished professor, uncapitalized, in real life). He was knocking the President's plan, which did not interrupt my reverie, but then he said something about "not helping the *sclerotic economy.*"

Moments later, Professor Richard E. Pipes of Harvard, a Star Wars enthusiast, picked up the word, perhaps ironically, and talked of "the *sclerotic economy* of the Soviet Union." I sat up, smacked the snooze alarm again (*snooze* strikes me as a marriage of *snore* and *doze*, but the word has been drifting off since 1788) and waited for the interviewer to ask "Wait a minute—what does *sclerotic* mean?"

She did not. Maria Shriver, an intelligent reporter, is not yet secure enough to admit ignorance of a word. Come to think of it, I have never heard any commentator or reporter say, "That's an interesting word—what does it mean?" The interviewer is either ashamed at appearing ignorant or worried that the guest will not know the answer and come apart in chagrin on the air.

In any event, the two professors went on with their verbal auto-scleroticism and I did not know the meaning of their favorite word, and in a hotel room the Gideons do not provide a dictionary. (Why doesn't some hotel chain lay in a stock of dictionaries, placed lovingly on the pillow, instead of a fattening chocolate? I would gladly forgo a bottle of fabric rinse, whatever that is, for a vest-pocket dictionary in the bathroom.)

Noodling it around, I asked myself "What is *arteriosclerosis?*" and answered, "It's a high-priced specialist's way of saying 'hardening of the arteries.' " From that, I puzzled out that the adjective *sclerotic* had been formed from the noun *sclerosis,* which meant that the professors were talking about a hardening, or stiffening, or dangerous aging of an economy in stagnation. *Sclerotic,* then, means "inelastic, brittle."

Satisfied, I grabbed ten more minutes from the snooze alarm, which vies with the rye bagel as a major technological contribution to people's mornings. But dozing was denied: why did Arthur, eager to make a serious point with a wide audience, use a word that most viewers did not know? Why did Dick Pipes repeat it? I know both those guys, and neither has need to show off his erudition. Either they could not think of a simple word like "aging," or they were willing to sacrifice immediate understanding by asking their audience to reach up for an unfamiliar word.

That poses a big question: Should you use a ring-a-ding word, smack on the button of your meaning, when your listener or reader is not likely to understand? Dilemma: Do you settle for a more generally understood term, thereby pandering to your audience's ignorance—or do you use the unfamiliar word, thereby failing to communicate and appearing to be a showoff? Is your job to communicate or to educate?

Another example: Peregrine Worsthorne, the tower of Kiplingesque conservatism at *The Sunday Telegraph* in London, has taken to zapping his American neo-conservative cousins on the subject of hawkishness in foreign policy. Stung, our neo-cons have responded: in *Contentions,* a sprightly eight-page viewsletter published monthly by the Committee for the Free World, Neal Kozodoy described Perry's occasional Diary in London's *Spectator* accurately as "divagating with clubby ease and amiability on political events, on the virtues of the marmalade to be had in Vence . . . and 'Why do I find almost all women journalists who write about public affairs so tiresome?' "

Neo-con Kozodoy quotes tradi-con Worsthorne on terrorism in this way: "What is 'remarkable,' Mr. Worsthorne apodictically confides, 'is not that Westerners are terrorized so much as that they are terrorized so little.' "

Quick, now: do you ever find yourself *divagating* with ease, clubby or otherwise, or confiding *apodictically?* I took the best advice of a James Thurber character ("You could look it up") and discovered that to *divagate* is "to wander from a course or stray from a subject," a synonym for "to digress." *Divagate* is a dangerous verb to use, because listeners may assume you mean *divaricate,* "to diverge," similar but not the same.

Apodictically, with a Greek root meaning "demonstrate," means "with absolute certainty." I can say *apodictically* that you will get blank looks when you accuse somebody of *divagating.*

Back to the question: Should you ever use a word that you know most of your audience will not know?

My answer: Fly over everybody's head only when your purpose is to teach or to tease. In a political column, I wrote that Vice President Bush was "the Gus Lesnevich of American politics." I knew that few readers would readily recall Mr. Lesnevich, but enough would ask around to find out, and the allusion would gain impact in that way for really devoted readers who had a slow day. I also was quite apodictic that Mr. Bush would call up Richard Moore, his canny old adviser, to find out what the hell I meant, and that Mr. Moore would surely remember that Gus Lesnevich was the light-heavyweight champion of the world, virtually unbeatable in his class, but in the era of Joe Louis never able to win the heavyweight crown.

Admittedly, this was an inside derogation, a kind of infra dig: I was soon scratching my head from a message left by William F. Gavin, in the House minority leader's office, asking, "Does this mean that Jack Kemp is the Chuck Davey of American politics?" Thumbing through yellowed clips, I found that Chuck Davey was a well-educated welterweight of great promise who was stopped just as he entered the big time.

These are rifle shots in the shotgun blasts of mass communication, playful and permissible if done rarely; the reader is told, "If you want to know, go look it up."

Overhead flying is also allowed, in my view, when the writer or speaker is dealing with an elite audience that will appreciate arcana and consider unfamiliar words and obscure allusions to be delicious inside stuff, caviar for the general. Thus, in *Contentions*, where such writers as Mr. Kozodoy and Dorothy Rabinowitz sparkle, big words find a congenial home. Too few readers take the trouble to look them up, but more should, and more will as soon as we get dictionaries in hotel rooms, instead of packages of needle and thread that are sealed too tightly to open. But I divagate.

I would not, however, use big words to a mass audience when my primary aim is to persuade rather than to educate. Lay off *sclerotic*, fellas, lest frustrated viewers become choleric.

The best system, for those who want to educate while persuading, is to do vocabulary tricks in a context that makes meanings plain. For example, a few paragraphs up, I slipped in "caviar for the general," predefining it as "delicious inside stuff."

Most people don't know that allusion; most who do think it means "that expensive food appreciated by big shots," but they are wrong. The phrase was coined in *Hamlet*, as he told the players that "the play . . . pleas'd not the million, 'twas caviary to the general." The "general" was not some gourmet leader of troops, but the general public, which thought caviar was a mess of foul-smelling fish eggs and did not appreciate the delicacy. The phrase has been twisted into meaning "a delicacy appreciated by the General."

In using it above, I adopted the current meaning, and defined it in passing, so that you couldn't taste the medicine going down. That is fairer to the reader, even the highly educated readership that tends to forget, and is equivalent to a few rounds with Gus Lesnevich.

Is there a gap in your knowledge? I'm beginning to think you're the Leon Spinks of the word mavens.

I don't consider myself highly intellectual but I know the meaning of apodictic and I wouldn't grudge Mr. Kozodoy the use of divagation when it slides so neatly into his prose.

I work in the theater where the precise use of language is of passionate concern. I would have thought you were one of us, someone who would have argued until the sun went down about the necessity for *le mot propre*. I wanted you to say: "If it's accurate, if it's precise, if it's evocative, *use it!* If some don't get it at first glance, well, what are dictionaries for?" But you didn't.

I like "sclerotic." It has a certain salivary eloquence that feels nice and diseased as it rolls off the tongue. It made you take notice, didn't it? Isn't that the crucial point—good words in good order make you sit up and take notice—to really hear. Coleridge didn't say "good words in general usage," he said "good words," period.

I know you have this bizarre infatuation with Jeane Kirkpatrick but I always forgot all that when you wrote about language with such redeeming wit and eloquence. I always thought you could be counted on to inspire us to higher standards of speech but now . . .

Say it isn't so.

Edward Payson Call
New York, New York

Thank you for your explanation of "apodictally." Without your help, I would have been intimidated by Berton Roueché's "Profiles— A New Kind of City" in *The New Yorker*. In this complimentary (and rightfully so) article about my hometown, Mr. Roueché writes, "The smallest park in Portland is called Mill Ends Park, and it is also (one would imagine) the smallest park in the world. That seems to be apodictic." Apodictic is hot stuff this month, that's for sure!

Lawrence A. Dworkin, M.D.
Portland, Oregon

I think you missed your correspondent's real point when he asked whether Jack Kemp might be "the Chuck Davey of American politics."

True, as you pointed out, Davey was "a well-educated welterweight of great promise who was stopped just as he entered the big time."

But he was also a carefully groomed media personality whose manufactured reputation exceeded his ability. Those were the days (the early 1950s) when the boxing game was trying to disassociate itself from smelly, smoke-filled, mob-frequented arenas and adopt a refined image that would spell success on TV.

Davey, a clean-cut, blond-haired Midwestern schoolteacher, was deliberately chosen to personify this image. He starred in a series of a half-dozen or so well-hyped TV bouts against substandard opponents before meeting up with a less telegenic but more able boxer who knocked him out.

Frank McNeirney
Arlington, Virginia

I was interested in your observation that *"Snooze* strikes me as a marriage of *snore* and *doze."*

While you are quite right that many colloquialisms originate as blends (such as *brunch* from *breakfast* and *lunch*), the vowel seems wrong here. From a simple blend, one would expect either *snawze* or—more likely—*snoze.*

My suggestion is that we are dealing here with a form of colloquial vowel-substitution that I have christened "ooglification." (See the enclosed offprint "Ooglification in American English Slang," *Verbatim,* Essex, CT, February 1977.) An example of the replacement of "long" o by "double" o is the slang form *oof* for standard *oaf.*

The replacement of r by z may be, as you suggest, a partial blend. But it may also be a case of the colloquial consonant-substitution that I have elsewhere termed "zazzification" (in "Zazzification in American English Slang," *Forum Linguisticum,* Lake Bluff, IL, December 1978, pp. 185–87). An example would be the by-form *huzza* of the cheer *hurrah.*

Since these two forms of sound-substitution are both common, it is hardly surprising that they co-occur, as in the slang noun *foozle,* "elderly person," from *fossil.* In a forthcoming publication, I intend to refer to the combination of ooglification and zazzification as (not surprisingly) "zoozification."

Apropos of the form *snooze,* are you familiar with its use as a mock-preterit of *sneeze,* as in the following quatrain, cited (but not, I believe, composed) by Bennett Cerf?

I sneezed a sneeze into the air:
It fell to earth, I know not where.
But hard and froze were the looks of those
In whose vicinity I snoze.

Roger W. Wescott
Professor of Linguistics
Anthropology Department
Drew University
Madison, New Jersey

Codswallop, Poppycock and Horsefeathers

Faced with a charge by Sir Fred Hoyle, astronomer, and Chandra Wickramasinghe, an astrophysicist, that the fossil known as archaeopteryx—whose reptilian bones adorned with beautifully preserved feathers suggest a link between reptiles and birds—is a fake, Alan J. Charig of the British Museum of Natural History, in London, told *New Scientist* magazine: "We think the suggestion that it's a fake is a load of *codswallop*."

(That is a classic lead sentence. They're just not writing leads like that anymore. Savor it; as the eulogists say, we shall not soon see its like again.)

The clipping on the archaeopteryx (say "arky op-terix"—the name means "ancient wing") controversy was sent to me by John Noble Wilford, a science correspondent of *The New York Times* and possessor of the classiest name in journalism today. My colleague asked: " 'A load of codswallop.' I have a clear enough picture of the meaning intended, but Merriam-Webster's Third Unabridged does not acknowledge the existence of such a colorful expression. Can you? Or is it not 'fit to print'?"

The Economist, a magazine not noted for its salaciousness, uses it all the time. Assessing a Turkish argument for refusing concessions on Cyprus, a special *Economist* correspondent in New York wrote in 1975: "The Greeks . . . regard all this as codswallop." A year later, in a piece on the individualism of the Australian, the magazine asked, "A load of generalised sociological codswallop?"

The word, meaning "nonsense," is British English: as a slang synonym for *rubbish, bosh, humbug, hogwash, tommyrot, tripe* and *drivel,* the newer *cods-*

wallop was observed in *The Radio Times* in 1963. The Supplement to the Oxford English Dictionary published in 1972 tosses in an etymological sponge with a despairing "Origin unknown."

Poppycock! James McDonald, in his 1984 book *Wordly Wise,* writes that in the nineteenth century "an inventor called Hiram Codd patented a new type of bottle with a glass marble in its neck. Mineral waters were sold in such bottles and, *wallop* being a slang term for fizzy ale, the contents became known as *Codd's Wallop.*" An alternative etymology is suggested by Farmer and Henley's slang dictionary, completed in 1904, which describes *cods* as a term of venery. In Norman W. Schur's *English English,* the noun *codswallop,* defined as "hot air," follows a slang verb, *cod,* meaning "to horse around."

Poppycock, an older term for *codswallop* (though not as old as the seventeenth-century *balderdash,* a silly mixture of liquids like milk and ale), comes in lots rather than loads. When told *The London Observer* had reported that President Reagan had postponed a colonoscopy because of the 1984 election campaign, the White House spokesman Larry Speakes said, "That's not true, that's poppycock, as the British would say."

So would Americans. The O.E.D. labels *poppycock* as originally United States slang, and Burchfield's Brigade has recently unearthed a use by Charles Farrar Browne, the humorist who went by the name of Artemus Ward, in 1865: "You won't be able to find such another pack of poppycock gabblers as the present Congress of the United States," a statement that we might expect to hear today from a White House spokesman.

In *Horsefeathers,* by Charles Earle Funk, an etymology is put forward for *poppycock* based on the Dutch scatological word *pappekak,* but the Artemus Ward usage suggests an imitative origin in the gabbling of a goose, similar to a rooster's *cock-a-doodle-doo.*

Horsefeathers—like *poppycock, balderdash,* and *tommyrot*—is a three-syllable explosion of derision usually followed by an exclamation point when standing alone. *Horsefeathers* had an early building-trade use referring to the tapered boards laid to provide a flat surface for asphalt roof shingles, also called "feathering strips." But this word's use as a euphemism for a barnyard epithet was coined in the 1920s by the cartoonist William De Beck, creator of Barney Google and Snuffy Smith, and later became the title of a popular song.

Therefore, those of us who believe in the plumed reptile named Arky Opterix, as we fervently believe in the existence of Tinker Bell, can clap our hands and shout derisively at the doubting Sir Fred and Miss Wickramasinghe: *Lizardfeathers!*

My wife, knowing of my interest in the outlandish and sometimes brilliant views of Fred Hoyle and colleagues at the U. of Cambridge, looked up from the paper last Sunday morning and asked "Did you know that Wickramasinghe is a woman?" "No," I answered, somewhat astonished, in view of Cambridge's reputation for being a male bastion. "Safire says so," she said. A quick check with Who's Who at the library, of course, bore me out. His full name is Nalin Chandra Wickramasinghe, and it's Ceylonese. Usually he is referred to as N. C. Wickramasinghe, and so appears in the just-published *The New York Times Guide to the Return of Halley's Comet* (p. 134). That *Guide*, following the convention of most scientific writing, gives no clue as to sex of most scientists, by the device of giving only initials and surname. The case of Sir Fred is a rare exception.

Philip P. Jones
Bethesda, Maryland

You mentioned an etymology by Farmer and Henley describing *cods* "as a term of venery." Stumped by the last word, I found two separate entries, both archaic, in my Concise Oxford Dictionary:

venery[1]: Hunting.
venery[2]: Sexual indulgence.

Please let me know which was meant, and whether you copied F. and H.'s word or chose it yourself. I look forward to your response.

Corey Miller
Cambridge, Massachusetts

Note from W.S.: The second.

Codswallop is the kind of word you'd expect to find in judicial opinions because it simultaneously expresses disapproval and (because almost nobody has ever heard the word before) erudition. There is, however, only one judicial use of the word in reported decisions of courts in the United States. In United States v. William Valencia, the United States Court of Appeals for the Second Circuit at first announced a new rule in entrapment cases and sent the case back to the trial court, but when the case returned for a second time to the Court of Appeals one of the judges believed that the new rule had been abandoned by the two other members of the original tribunal.

Thus, the dissenting opinion of James L. Oakes, filed on April 22, 1982, states, "As it is, our first opinion was an exercise in futility—

what we said so much codswallop—though it has gained some commentary support. Note, Entrapment Through Unsuspecting Middlemen, 95 Harv. L. Rev. 1122, 1127–28 n.39, 1140 (1982)."

I was the lawyer for Mr. Valencia in the case. When the opinion arrived neither I nor any of my colleagues in the Federal Defender Appeals Unit knew exactly what the word meant though we certainly understood what was being said. After exhausting our research possibilities we learned about the word from one of the judge's clerks.

David Seth Michaels
New York, New York

"Codswallop" is a word that is quite frequently used in Australia and I agree with all you have said about it, including your statement that it is a slang term for fizzy ale in the U.K.

The reason for my letter is that I visited a friend in Nether Wallop in 1976 and discovered that there are two adjacent villages named Middle Wallop and Upper Wallop. All three are only a few miles east of Salisbury in southern England.

Therefore I was most interested to read an article on the subject in the Travel section of *The New York Times.* Your correspondent stated that the word came into the language after the success of a reprisal raid on France by an Admiral Wallop during the reign of Queen Elizabeth I. History apparently records that the good admiral razed some twenty-nine French villages and on his return it was stated that he had walloped the French.

Bill Mollard
South Melbourne, Australia

The expression "horsefeathers": I have used this word for years, and have always been under the impression that it is a polite expression for "horse s__t," used in the sense of disbelief, or even of contempt. I have heard "bull feathers" used in the same way, but less often.

Robin Leech
Edmonton, Alberta

Colon's Other Meaning

At one time, if you asked someone in the language dodge what a *colon* was, you would get this answer: "one dot above another, the punctuation mark following *to wit,*" or, if you asked any good pedant, "grammatical discontinuity more prolonged than that marked by a semicolon but not as complete as that indicated by a period."

Since President Reagan's operation, however, the first meaning that comes to everyone's mind is "the large intestine, from the cecum to the rectum."

Is there any linguistic connection? The root of both, *kolon,* is a transliteration of ancient Greek. With no mark over the first *o,* the word means "food, meat, or the place in the belly where it goes"; with a mark over the first syllable, however, the meaning becomes "limb, member, portion," which took Greek grammarians into using *kolon* for independent clauses and then applying that word to the mark between some clauses.

Now to a word that used to be whispered, and even now is often spoken with dread: *cancer.* The surgeon who briefed the press after the operation at Bethesda Naval Hospital opened with a matter-of-fact stunner: "The President has cancer." In that sense, the word denotes a disease marked by growth of malignant cells. When laymen ask surgeons, "Did you get it all out?" the implication is that cancer—*a* cancer—can be removed, and the patient thus cured. Many cancer specialists (who call themselves *oncologists,* from the Greek *onkos,* "mass," for the branch of medicine dealing with tumors) think of cancer as a continuing threat that can be *arrested;* they hesitate to use the word *cured,* preferring *remission,* or, to remove that term's connotation of temporariness, *permanent remission.*

Strictly speaking, an oncologist is a tumor specialist, not a cancer specialist, because not all tumors are cancerous. A tumor may be *benign* or *malignant;* although the adjectives *benignant* and *malign* exist, and you would think that parallel construction would call for *benign* vs. *malign,* that's not the way the language goes in this case.

What's the connection between the disease and the sign of the zodiac? *Cancer* is the Latin and Greek word for "crab"; the disease, according to the Greek physician Galen, was named for the resemblance of the swollen veins surrounding a tumor to the legs of a crab. (*Canker* has the same origin, but came to mean "ulcer.") The fourth sign of the zodiac is named *Cancer* for a constellation supposedly shaped like a crab. "Since the 1960s," says Sol Steinmetz of Barnhart Books, "many people born under that sign have not wanted the ominous connotation of the disease and refer to themselves as *moon children* because of the supposed influence of the moon on the house of Cancer."

While we're at it—and I guess we should cover the rest of it—*polyp*, the name for the type of tumor in the President's colon, comes from "many-footed," named for the shape projecting from the membrane. (Wags promptly called Mr. Reagan's Cabinet "the Polyp-buro," which caused some forced smiles but no great thigh-slapping.)

The most worrisome word in this vocabulary is *metastasize*, Greek for "to change from one place to another"; in cancer, such metastasis takes place if cancer cells are transferred from a tumor through the bloodstream to other parts of the body.

"He's *champing at the bit*," said the White House spokesman during Mr. Reagan's hospital stay, indicating a healthy desire to get back to work; the phrase was quoted in *The New York Times* headline.

To champ means "to munch, chew vigorously, bite down on something hard." The first application to a horse was in Thomas Phaer's 1558 translation of Virgil's *Aeneid:* "The palfrey . . . on the fomy bit of gold with teeth he champes." William Makepeace Thackeray, in 1852, immortalized "Horses . . . champing at the bit."

On the newscasts I was monitoring, that verb was pronounced *chomping*. In Britain, *champ* is standard and *chomp* is dialect; in the United States, *champ* is less often used to describe chewing than *chomp*, a Southernism frequently employed by the cartoonist Al Capp in his "Li'l Abner" strip. Thus, to spell it *champing at the bit* when most people would say *chomping at the bit* is to slavishly follow outdated dictionary preferences. The word is imitative, so it should imitate the sound that most people use to imitate loud chewing. Who would say "General Grant champed on his cigar"?

Chew that over, lexicographers (chomp, chomp).

About Greek *kolon:* your "With no mark over the first *o* . . . ; with a mark over the first syllable" is baby talk. The distinction is between *omicron* and *omega*, not between typesetting/printing devices containing or lacking the macron. Rewrite: "With omicron (short *o*) in the first syllable . . . ; with omega (long *o*)" and so forth.

William Doyle
Everett, Massachusetts

A prominent Australian man of letters, on being told he would have to have Mr. Reagan's operation, said, "Better a semi-colon than a full stop."

This was in the Sydney paper one day about a year ago. Wish I had cut it out so I could tell you who he was.

Tony Randall
New York, New York

Come As You Are

A "reminder that you are expected" card came in the other day, which struck me as a more sensible memory-jogger than a repeat of the original engraved invitation with a "To Remind" written in the corner.

The reminderman was John Sargent of Doubleday, who takes me to the opera every year to find out, in an elegantly indirect way, when I am going to deliver a novel begun when Puccini was a pup. The time, date and place were briskly and neatly laid out, and then, in the corner, a mysterious instruction about dress: *"Not Black Tie."*

What is that supposed to mean? Perhaps it is a way of saying, "I know that you, a traditionalist, always wear black tie to the opera, but just this once the rest of us are dressing like slobs and I'm telling you this so you won't feel out of place." Or, "Look, I'm aware of how time-consuming it is to go hire a soup-and-fish just for this occasion—time which would be much more productively spent on all our behalfs at your word processor— so the rest of us will dress your way, like a pack of ragamuffins, this time."

Profound motives aside, does *not black tie* mean *business suit,* which is what it says on the Turkish Embassy's invitation to a reception? Taking it a step further (not *farther,* I'm being figurative), does that mean today's American Uniform (blue blazer, beige pants) is out? Does *not black tie* mean "any old tie," or even "no tie at all"?

Indeed, does *formal* mean *black tie* or *white tie?* Does *informal* on an invitation mean that no ties are permitted? Does *casual* mean shoeless, bare midriff and gold chains? The language of engraved invitations, once a bastion of tradition, seems to be slipping its moorings, and the yacht is drifting out to sea.

Mr. and Mrs. Reader are cordially invited to re-examine . . . no. You and your spouse are . . . no. You and a guest (what the hell, let's swing a little) are cordially invited to a reassessment of social semantics.

For guidance, I have turned to Judith Martin, foremost living expert on etiquette, author of *Miss Manners' Guide to Excruciatingly Correct Behavior* and *Miss Manners' Guide to Rearing Perfect Children*. I knew Miss Manners back when she was a feature writer named Judy, in an era when I could misspell a word and the Gotcha! Gang would not turn out in force (and who were most recently stupefied by my misspelling, "stupify," which was really stuped). These days, Miss Manners and I have a lock on both ends of the correctness dodge; thanks to a tradition known as "columnists' courtesy," I can call on her to find an alibi for my gaffes and blunders on the cocktail-party circuit and she can get me to justify her errors in English.

"The term *informal* changes its meaning," says Miss Manners, "depending on the particular age, geographical location and set of people using the word. We now live in a time of chaos." (C'mon, Judy, help the people.) "Guests who really care to know what the invitation means have learned to question closely. The best definition of *informal* I've heard recently came from Meg Greenfield, the editorialist, when I asked about an 'informal' party she was giving. She told me, 'Wear something that no one will remember the next day.' "

What is *formal?* Miss Manners explains: "At one time, *formal* meant 'white tie'; a gentleman wore a tailcoat, a stiff shirt, a white waistcoat, and literally a white tie for a formal evening. At that time, *informal* meant 'black tie'—but nowadays, *black tie* is used to denote 'formal, but not white tie.' "

For women, *formal* means "long dress," according to Peter Murray, editor of *The Green Book,* Washington's social list. He adds: "Sometimes cocktail dresses that are shorter may be worn. It is acceptable practice to call the hostess if you are a woman who is uncomfortable about wearing a shorter dress." *White tie,* because it means *formal,* also means "long dress." What does *black tie* mean to women, because not many will take that literally? "It usually means a long dinner dress," opines Miss Manners, "although shorter dresses are occasionally worn."

Business attire? "Again, depends on the group. It might mean a suit and tie for men, maybe a dark suit in Washington, D.C., and a dress or suit for women." But I have these two different blazers that look, with a pair of beige pants and a pair of gray pants, like a whole wardrobe. "In some circles, it might mean a blazer," Miss Manners says, sighing. (In return, let me point out that *excruciatingly,* in current tongue-in-cheek usage, correctly conveys the impression of serious mock-seriousness.)

Turning to the dictionaries, I find that *formal* meant *white tie* until the 1930s. "Till some time after 1914," wrote historian R. C. K. Ensor in 1936, "there was no rigorous division between a white-tie and a black-tie *ensemble*, such as now compels gentlemen to keep two sets of evening dress." In the '30s, *black tie* became dominant in men's evening fashion, and in the early 1950s, *white tie* was coined to mean "especially formal, specifically, tails."

Tuxedo, a dark suit with satin lapels and matching trousers, worn with a black tie and fancy shirt, was named after a country club near Tuxedo Lake, New York (*Tuxedo* was a Lenape Indian word that has been translated as "He has a round foot," denoting a wolf; etymology goes deeper than etiquette.) The term is rarely used these days; *dinner jacket* is preferred, which can be white in summer or some other color worn with a black tie or a bow tie of a different color. An alternative to a waistcoat is a *cummerbund*, from the Hindi *kamarband*, a "loin band" that became a sash worn round the waist.

The hostess who writes the all-embracing *evening dress* on an invitation is not being helpful at all. She would be better advised to write the jocular *monkey suit*, meaning black tie with matching pants, or *soup-and-fish*, for white tie and tails (and if a member of the Lexicographic Irregulars has an early citation for the derivation of that, I'll help him with his stud behind his neck).

In my set, *formal* means *black tie*, and *white tie* must be specified if a tailcoat is desired. *Business attire* means any kind of suit and tie. *Informal* means "not black tie," which in turn means "dark suit in the evening," and is the way most people now think is proper to go to the opera. Watch out for *informal*, though—it slops over in meaning to *casual*, which means "no tie needed"; I have seen *very casual*, which means jeans and carefully tattered garments, and is sometimes accompanied by a welcome *bring a bathing suit*. I think *very casual*, in my peer group, is the equivalent of *semiformal* in a younger set, but suspect that *semiformal* may mean "jacket and shoes, no tie but no T-shirt" to most teenagers.

"The only term I really despise is *semiformal*," says Miss Manners. "It is a despicable term that deserves to be eliminated. Sounds as if the pants are not to match the jacket."

In California we have some different terms for attire. In Southern California a dinner jacket is something you get when one walks into L'Hermitage for dinner without a jacket—some time ago someone did an entire article on "dinner jackets" in different Los Angeles restaurants! In Marin County "semiformal" means that women may wear dresses, but means nothing for men. "Very casual" means bring your own pot, and the hot tub is available. I'm not sure about "informal" as yet, since I've only been out here seven years, but I think it means cross-dressing is permitted.

> *Harold Kocin*
> *Tiburon, California*

Semiformal has a clear and specific meaning. An afternoon semiformal means come with your truck washed. An evening semiformal means that the drivers are to wear ties.

Semiformals are for semitough people.

> *Larry Beinhart*
> *New York, New York*

In 1971, when I coordinated the grand opening of the Hyatt Regency Acapulco Hotel, we had a different reservation card for each of the many functions. Each card indicated time, place and dress suggested. A. N. Pritzker, the patriarch of the Pritzker family—owners of Hyatt Hotels—asked me the difference between "informal" and "casual." I advised him that "informal" meant he had to wear shoes. He complimented me and went off to find a pair.

I agree with Miss Manners and her dislike of "semiformal." To me it means "Come in Your Prom Dress." Awful.

> *Georgia Beach*
> *Director of Public Relations/New York*
> *Hyatt International Hotels*
> *New York, New York*

Formal attire in the military means miniature medals will be worn.

> *Henry Untermeyer*
> *Palm Springs, California*

Back in the '20s and '30s, in my family, if Granny said to Gramps, "We're dining at the Wilsons' tonight, so it's the *soup-and-fish* for you, my boy," it was perfectly understood by all that Mrs. Wilson's dinners were always Formal-formal, i.e., they consisted of a *soup* course, a *fish* course, a roast (meat) course, a salad course and a dessert course, thus making them a more formal dinner than one omitting the *soup and fish*, and thus requiring a more formal dress, namely, white tie and tails.

So, having placed my fork and knife (blade toward oneself, of

course) transverse my plate to signify I am through . . . I am
through.

Robert O. Vaughn
West New York, New Jersey

You wrote, ". . . time which would be much more productively
spent on all our behalfs at your word processor." Wouldn't it have
been more productive to have said "spent on behalf of all concerned"
or perhaps "spent on everyone's behalf"? I am unable to find "behalfs" in any dictionary; did you coin it recently? I don't believe that
this is a correct locution, since the plural of the base word "half" is
"halves," not "halfs." I am afraid that the paragraph in question is
based upon a half-baked sentence.

Sally P. Davis
Los Angeles, California

You failed to mention the problems that one can encounter when
one takes the engraved words of an invitation too literally, as was the
case when I arrived at a party the invitation announced as being
"Black Tie Only."

(Mr.) Jamie Elliott
Richmond, Virginia

Crispy Crunchy

I used the adjective *crispy* to describe a brittle covering for egg rolls and to
raise hackles.

Dorothy Reynolds of New York wrote to complain of a picture caption
in *The New York Times* that read: "a sunny day with crispy temperatures."

"*Crispy!* What is wrong with *crisp?* I don't mind 'Rice Krispies' as a cereal
trade name, but is there not some way to stamp out *crispy* in general
usage?"

The Latin *crispus* meant "curled"; that meaning is preserved in *munchies*
like potato chips, which are called *crisps* in Britain; the English use *chips* to
denote what Americans call *french fries*, which are usually too soggy to rate
the term *crisp*.

Snow and frost curl around landscapes and windows, and the cold can curl your fingers and toes: one sense of *crisp* transferred to the weather, perhaps influenced by *brisk*, and *crisp* came to mean *bracing*, like a welcome slap in the face by a fragrant scruffing lotion that I intend to return because scruffiness is for hippies.

Crisp is a splendid word, blessed with a great etymological pedigree that runs parallel to its onomatopoeia: the word's sound helps evoke its meaning. *Crispy* is an itsy-pooism. It's OK to say *crunchy*, because the imitative noun, *crunch*, needs a *y* to turn it into an adjective, but *crisp* is an adjective that later was used by English potato-chip makers as a noun. One of the senses of *crisp* is *short*; surely this adjective needs no lengthening. Stick with crisp; resist itsy-pooisms.

"Crispy" is a correct usage and it has nothing to do with food. It refers to someone who is burnt out (usually from overindulgent drug use)—whose mind is "fried" to the point of losing connection to reality. The usage is not new.

> *Betty Dawson*
> *Hensdale, Illinois*

"It is important to insist upon . . . a relatively strict interpretation of the term onomatopoeia . . . for it is very easy for an unwary critic to attribute to onomatopoeia effects that arise from other causes" (p. 534 of *Understanding Poetry,* by Cleanth Brooks and Robert Penn Warren; Holt, Rinehart and Winston, 1976).

I will gladly call you slim, but I will also call you incorrect. In my high school poetry class I learned from the aforementioned book that the term onomatopoeia refers only to those words that are imitative of a sound. When snow falls it makes no sound. Potato chips, when eaten, make the sound "crunch." I can think of no object, animate or inanimate, that makes the sound "crisp." The word *crisp* is not an onomatopoeia. Its effect, however, is mimetic; it is imitative of the quality, or object, it describes. Blubber-guts is also mimetic, I believe.

> *Winifred T. Gordon*
> *Willimantic, Connecticut*

You object to "crispy" and state that "Crisp is an adjective that later was used by English potato-chip [hyphen?] makers as a noun." That may well be, but what about the very American dessert Apple Crisp? A crisp in home bakers' language is a very real noun, denoting sliced fruit (usually apples) baked under a topping of oats, shortening and sweetener, until *crisp*.

Susan Asanovic
Wilton, Connecticut

Y oh Y have you joined the critics of that traditional and useful adjectival suffix -y?

Crisp may be "blessed with a great etymological pedigree"—but so is *crispy*. The O.E.D. traces it to the fourteenth century, and cites among other users Thomas Kyd and William Morris, neither of them usually considered itsy-poo.

And if you are going to oppose adding -y to adjectives, shouldn't you be opposed to words like *lanky* (seventeenth c), *stilly* (eighteenth c, among users Coleridge, Shelley, Tennyson, and George "Oft in the Stilly Night" Moore), *vasty* (probably introduced by Shakespeare in 1596, when Owen Glendower, striving to be impressive as possible, says "I can call spirits from the vasty deep," in *Henry IV, Part One*), and most common of all, *chilly* (sixteenth c, used by Southey, Dickens, Keats and Browning, and countless idiomatic speakers who find the adjective *chill* just not shivery enough to describe a chilly day).

William Carlos Williams, a master of American speech rhythms, uses -y as both a title and a kind of repeated refrain in what is surely one of the greatest of his late poems, *Asphodel, That Greeny Flower*. *Crispy* is not only rich in history, it is in excellent literary and vernacular company. So I can't see why anyone would want to "stamp out crispy." If your correspondents have some idiosyncratic distaste for the word, they should of course not use it. And of course they should leave the rest of us alone with our literature and the traditions of the English language.

Jim Quinn
Philadelphia, Pennsylvania

DARE Is Here!

What you mean sometimes depends on where you are.

If you're in Louisiana, singing along with Linda Ronstadt's recording of "Blue Bayou," the word *bayou* means "sluggish stream, lazy-flowing creek." But if you head west, and sing along in neighboring Texas, the meaning of the word can be different: "a deep ravine," or a watercourse that is usually dry. Up North, from the Appalachians to the Rockies, a *bayou* is usually "a stretch of still water off to the side of a river," or a lake's armlet, though people in Oklahoma, Indiana and Mississippi often define the word simply as a lake or pond.

Pronunciation differs, too: in Arkansas, it's *BY-oo*, changing to *BY-oh* in Tennessee, *BAH-oh* in Texas and *BY-uh* in Wisconsin.

How can I be sure of this? Because I have glommed onto the long-awaited first volume of the Dictionary of American Regional English (DARE), 903 pages covering the letters A through C, in which *bayou* is one of the many thousands of words and phrases that have been explored, mapped and meticulously recorded.

Remember when I hazarded a guess that a phrase headlined in *The New York Times* as *champing at the bit* should have been spelled *chomping?* I had no underpinning for such a linguistic leap, but here, look, on page 647 of DARE: *"champ* is now generally less common than *chomp* in U.S.: responses to DARE . . . include 3 instances of *champ* as against 45 of *chomp."*

The responses to DARE so often referred to in the definitions are the answers given by Americans in a thousand communities over the last two decades to a couple of thousand questions about the local dialect. For example, an interviewer would say, "What joking expressions do you have around here about snoring?" A respondent—not just a "respondent," but a real person in Pennsylvania, whose husband sawed wood all night— would reply, "I'd say, *he's blowing Z's."* This bit of folklore would be entered in the dictionary as "blow Z's, v phr joc"—a verbal phrase, jocular— defined as "to sleep or snore."

What's so important about this? For the first time, we have a picture of the way Americans speak English to one another at home, relaxed, when nobody's *airish.* No word in this dictionary is standard; when the work is completed, we will have five volumes of entries, with DARE treading in that *terra incognita* beyond the domain of most other dictionaries.

This work builds on others: Eric Partridge's Dictionary of Slang and Unconventional English was a vast undertaking for one man; and in America, Stuart Berg Flexner's Dictionary of American Slang caught much of our folk language; Mitford M. Mathews's Dictionary of Americanisms laid the groundwork for some of this study, as did Raven I. McDavid's Linguistic Atlas of the Middle and South Atlantic States, and Hans Kurath's Linguistic Atlas of New England. But not since the six-volume English Dialect Dictionary was published, in 1905 has there been such a concerted drive to understand ourselves in the language used locally. And never—not even with the monumental Oxford English Dictionary and its Supplements —has there been such a reaching-out by lexicographers to find words in local, mostly spoken, use. DARE was not content with words recorded in print; it sent people into the field to find out what words native speakers were using to describe the things and events in their lives.

Airish is the answer given by many, asked for a word to describe a woman who puts on airs. (Other answers include *stuck-up, highfalutin', uppity, high-hat* and *snooty,* which we will see in subsequent volumes.) A different meaning of *airish* is "chilly, cool," a meaning that DARE says is still current in Scottish English, but obsolete in standard English.

Look up *Adam,* the archetypal man. In the dialects of Americans, one meaning is "a person one does not know." To complete the sentence, "I wouldn't know him from _____" the response is *Adam*, or *Adam's off-ox*, with Southerners saying "from *Adam's house cat*" or "from *Adam's pet monkey*" (along with other terms unprintable here, but unblushingly presented in DARE). Another meaning is "from time immemorial," responding to "The first time I heard that one—": *Adam was a pup* or *Adam wore short pants*. (See also *Hector*, in the next volume.) A third meaning is "ignorance of the obvious," completing "He doesn't know from _____" with *Adam*, along with alliterative alternatives. Finally, there is the meaning of nakedness: "They went in swimming _____?" posed the interviewers, and heard "dressed like Adam" from the skinny-dipping set.

The average American, leafing through this book, can find himself an instant expert and critic—not often, but once in a while. Sticking with *Adam*: for *Adam-and-Eve*, the meaning given is "putty-root," a plant with a bulbous root (Adam) connected to another bulb (Eve); in Kentucky, it is the name of a "small white flower like last-of-the-summer." But in Maine, *Adam-and-Eve-in-the-bower* is the name for the common monkshood.

A short-order cook will look at that entry, shrug off the flowers, and cry: "Cassidy! What about *Adam-and-Eve-on-a-raft?*" DARE has not asked everything: that reference to "poached eggs on toast" is missing. The mail that is headed to DARE, at the University of Wisconsin at Madison, is sure to be irate, expert and enthusiastic, because everyone is an expert in his own dialect or jargon.

The Cassidy who is certain to be beset by legions of *carrot-eaters*, *mackerel-snappers* and *bubelehs* (Mormons, Catholics and Jewish babies) is Professor Frederic G. Cassidy, America's answer to England's Sir James A. H. Murray, the guiding spirit who was behind the Oxford English Dictionary.

Cassidy is on my list of Ten Greatest Living Americans. Born in Jamaica, he prepared himself for his life's great work by first writing the Dictionary of Jamaican English; for twenty-one years, he has been pushing along his dream of a nonstandard dictionary that would help Americans discover one another through an understanding of their ways of talking. He has been wheedling grants out of foundations, schools and governments to pay for interviewers and editors, which has taken time from his own editorial work, but he keeps pushing on. Perhaps now, with his first volume as a sample, he can get the funds needed for the rest of the project. The book is published by the Belknap Press of Harvard University Press, at $60, and the first edition will be selling for a bundle a hundred years from now. Let's face it, the price is steep; if you cannot afford one, go to your library and demand that it be stocked. If you're a foundation, climb on board; you will not be treated as Samuel Johnson treated the late-coming Lord Chesterfield.

I have been unabashedly touting the man from DARE in this space for years, ever since we had lunch and I ordered a bibb lettuce salad, and he said, "I wonder who Bibb was?" That's my kind of mind. (Major John Bibb was the nineteenth-century horticulturist big on leafy vegetables; now I'm ready, but nobody asks.)

He asks the right questions. The questionnaire, printed in the front of the first volume, evokes thoughts of words that lie beneath the surface of our written discourse. For example: "When somebody takes too long about coming to a decision, you might say, 'I wish he'd quit_____.' " (Among the 212 different responses were *stalling, hemming and hawing, sitting on the fence* and the Southern *beating the devil around the stump.*) Or: "What joking names do you have for an out-of-the-way place . . . ?" *(The sticks, wide place in the road, hicktown, podunk,* etc.) The interviewers sought the name for "a small shelf hanging on the wall with small decorative articles on it." *(Whatnot, knickknack shelf, shadow box, dustcatcher,* etc.) And: "If a man asks a woman to marry him and she refuses, you'd say she _____." *(Turned him down, jilted him, stood him up,* or *shot him down.)*

Cassidy, DARE's chief editor, oversees a staff of sixteen. He became eighty-one in 1989 and is lively, articulate and helpful as ever: "I'm in a race with this dictionary, to see who finishes first." We can hope that Cassidy is recognized and aided, and DARE finishes first.

As a resident of Texas for seventy-five of my nearly eighty years I never have heard bayou pronounced ba-oh. Before writing you I consulted Dr. George Williams, Professor Emeritus of English at Rice University, and the news directors of the three television stations. All agreed that the pronunciations Texans use are Buy'-oo or Buy-o with the former preferred.

Perhaps in such barbarian sections of Texas as Dallas or Amarillo, ba-oh is heard but not in the more civilized Gulf Coast contiguous to Louisiana where the word began as far as the United States is concerned.

Victor Emanuel, Sr.
Houston, Texas

"Airish" in New England when I was a child meant chilly: time to put that sweater on. This same definition is given in Webster's Third.

Richard Seinfeld
Houston, Texas

Delicious Delicto

An oddly named cast of characters domiciles itself in the attic of my mind. The leading lady is Norma Loquendi, a sassy modern woman with the common touch who levels every hoity-toity suitor with her street smarts. She has a serious-minded sister with less of an attic shape named Licentia, a member of the media who shoves microphones in people's faces. Both women are menaced by N. Flagrante Delicto, a big guy in a white suit who looks like an easily catchable Sydney Greenstreet, and are in love with Lex Terrae, played by Tarzan.

These names, of course, are derived from Latin phrases: *norma loquendi* is "everyday speaking," or common usage; *licentia loquendi* is "liberty of speaking," or free speech; *lex terrae* is "law of the land," and *in flagrante delicto* is the Latin term for "caught in the act"—literally, "while the crime is blazing," presumably coined when an arsonist was caught with lighted Roman candle in hand.

In flagrante delicto is rarely used by Norma and the rest of us because it has acquired a lightheartedly leering connotation, perhaps from use in cases when someone surprises a spouse in bed having a guilty party. The melodramatic overtone has been influenced by the overuse of *in flagrante delicto* by mystery writers too enamored of the smoking gun.

Tass, the Soviet news and propaganda agency, used the phrase the other day with a straight face, betraying a lack of understanding of the arched eyebrow and mock shock associated with the phrase in the American idiom. According to Tass, a second secretary at the United States Embassy "was detained . . . *in flagrante delicto* as he was having a meeting with a Soviet citizen recruited by the United States intelligence." (Tass meant "apprehended *in flagrante delicto*," and detained later, but I'll let that go.) The Tass translator can be forgiven for his decision to use Latin because he could not readily use the common English expression, *red-handed.*

Peppering one's speech and writing with Latin phrases is affectation, but if done with good humor or a special aptness it can be condoned or even appreciated. When *The Times* of London wrote an obituary for the vituperative journalist William Cobbett in 1835, it said, *"Nitor in adversum* was a motto to which none could lay equal claim." Readers then did not have to break their heads to figure out the double meaning: "struggle in adversity" and "shine in opposition," both of which applied to the born-aginner.

In my dusty trek through the Great Used-Book Stores of America, I discovered—in University Place Bookshop, way upstairs on Twelfth Street and Broadway in New York, now run by William French—a disbound translation of the foreign quotations in Blackstone's *Commentaries*. Therein lies a store of useful observations, like the compassionate *Furiosus furore solum punitur*, "A nut is punished by his own nuttiness" (my translation), and *de bene esse*, a must for any political dealmaker or oil-company purchaser: "to be accepted for the time being, subject to change if somebody comes along with a better deal."

Continuando, people who have had it with acrimony can say *Interest reipublicae ut sit finis litium*, or "For the public good, let there be an end to contention." Pundits can proudly say *scribere est agere*, "to write is to act," and a self-righteous soul can identify himself as *custos morum*, "keeper of the morals," while those diplomatically selling out brave allies can exhume *salvo pundore*, "decency being observed."

Copy these and keep them in your wallet; a little Latin goes a long way, as they say at Tass. And all you Latin Looies out there, don't threaten to sue me for getting any of these a little bit wrong: *De minimis non curat lex* ("The law cannot be concerned with trifles").

I was amused to see a reference to our wonderful legal aphorism *De minimus non curat lex*, "The law does not care about trifles." I cannot avoid the temptation to send you this limerick:

> There once was a lawyer named Tex
> Who was sadly deficient in sex.
> When arraigned for exposure
> He remarked with composure
> *De minimus non curat lex.*

One subject you did not discuss which I think bears some discussion is that of the great gap in the term *index*. In medicine, the plural of index is correctly indicated as *indices* while in financial news or in other non-medical contexts they are routinely called *indexes*.

Sidney P. Kadish, M.D.
Worcester, Massachusetts

The Derogator

Ⓘn this movie I have in mind, to star Arnold Schwarzenegger or somebody with more spectral pectorals, the central character is dreaded throughout the linguistic world as "The Derogator."

He knocks people over the head with words. No weak, used-up derogations for him—you won't hear him use the archaic *jerk, simp, dumb bunny* or *chowderhead.* The put-downs of the 1970s are scorned as well—all the sting has gone out of *wimp* (derived from *whimper,* influenced by the cartoon character Wimpy), and only the teen-aging use *nerd* (from *nerts,* a variation of *nuts,* influenced by a rhyming scatological word). *Turkey* is as out-of-date as *geek,* the old carny term.

Today's nyah-nyah set prefers original, sometimes ephemeral, slams in the teeth. For example, when the President of the United States turned to his crack speech-writing team for a suitable term to disparage certain other world leaders, he was provided with the devastating *Looney Tunes.* Probably mindful of the Churchillian *pumpernickel principalities* blast at the Nazis, Mr. Reagan sallied forth with "we are especially not going to tolerate these attacks from outlaw states run by the strangest collection of misfits, Looney Tunes and squalid criminals . . ."

Although some analysts confused Mr. Reagan's reference with the stuttered "Th-th-that's all, folks" at the end of each cartoon in the series called Merry Melodies, the President and his derogation helpers had in mind another series of Warner Brothers cartoons developed by Hugh Harman and Rudolf Ising in 1930. The two men, who liked to point out that their last names formed "harmanising," concocted the name Looney Tunes as a play on Walt Disney's Silly Symphonies. (Dutch newspapers, unaware of the phrase's film etymology, translated Mr. Reagan's blast as *stripfiguren,* "comic-strip figures.")

According to a presidential speechwriter with a lifetime interest in crimebusting, the title *Looney Tunes* is in current use in law-enforcement circles as an adjectival phrase: "He's *Looney Tunes*" is a policeman's way of describing a subject as crazed, similar to the British "He's *bonkers*" (from the sound imitative of a knock on the head) or the nautical "He's *only got one oar in the water*" (which should properly be "He's *got only* one oar in the water," but there can be no arguing with idiom). *Looney*, of course, is from *lunatic*, meaning "moonstruck."

A second hot detraction used at the highest levels of the American military is *ballistic*. General John A. Wickham, Jr., Army Chief of Staff, favors light-infantry divisions, but budget-cutters have removed all chances of the charge of an American light brigade. George C. Wilson in the *Washington Post* reported one Pentagon source's description of the general's reaction: "Wickham went *ballistic* when he heard about the recommendation."

Apparently *ballistic* has replaced *bananas* in Pentagon use. The word is more apt than *bananas*, since it includes the connotation of a missile blazing skyward. In the synonymy of this special branch of derogation, *bonkers* is crazy, out of one's mind, around the bend; *bananas* can be either *bonkers* or enraged to the point of flipping one's lid; *ballistic* is driven up the wall in frustration, but not quite *bananas*.

Sometimes a derogation becomes dormant for a generation and then makes a comeback. Referring to preliminary findings by a disciplinary panel of lawyers, the attorney Roy M. Cohn said: "It's not my nature to be intimidated or frightened by this bunch of *yo-yos*."

The yo-yo, a toy made of a spool on a string, was invented in the Philippines and imported to the United States soon after World War I. The Tagalog name was soon applied derisively to anyone whose mood or opinion or support went up and down like the toy, then changed from "variable" to "stupid" and went into decline, although it has apparently been reborn in New York legal circles. (The only other Tagalog word I can think of in current English is *boonies*, from *boondocks*, the word in the Philippine language for mountains. Manila envelopes on this subject will be welcomed.)

A rock group named Dire Straits, whose name subtly asserts its members' urgent heterosexuality, has a current hit about greed and envy called "Money for Nothing" that begins "Look at them yo-yos," with "them yo-yos" referring to other rock stars.

Another group of them yo-yos called Wham!, in a song titled "Wake Me Up Before You Go-Go," sings (or "goes") "Don't leave me hanging on/ Like a yo-yo," returning to the toy metaphor and equating a spurned lover to a spinning spool hanging from a swinging string. (For these up-to-date citations, I am indebted to Ann Elise Rubin, who is thinking of starting a group of her own called The Usual Suspects. I can hear the harried talent agent now, saying, "See if you can round up . . .")

The Derogator, in whose presence The Terminator and The Liquidator tremble, has recently added a new detraction to his arsenal: *zod*. This was spotted by *Time* magazine in a 1982 article by Michael Demarest on the language of California Valley Girls: "People'd look at you and just go, 'Ew, she's a zod,' like get away."

At Random House, the dictionary department's editor in chief Stuart Berg Flexner says that *zod* might be a variation of *zob*, a predecessor of *jerk* used about 1900. He also suggests, "It may be our version of the British *sod*, for someone who is not a gentleman." Let us dare indelicacy: in Britain, a *sod* is now any kind of sap, but the origin is in a shortening of *sodomist*. The new word's popularity may have been influenced by Izod, the trade name for a shirt with a little alligator on the front; also, in the 1980 Superman movie, one of the villains was a General Zod.

We come now to the most controversial word in The Derogator's arsenal, *dweeb*, which is the subject of intense study at the Nonce Word Institute, where it defies neologic. A couple of months ago, I attributed this new term to computer lingo and defined it as a synonym for *nerd*, which drew this response from Arthur M. Miller of New York, who used to be an associate in the tax department of Richard Nixon's old law firm.

"The term *dweeb* has been used in that department since at least 1980," reports Mr. Miller, "and at first meant any associate, without differentiation as to class. A corruption of the word changed the meaning to 'underling, subordinate,' e.g., junior partners are *dweebs* to senior partners. However, a *dweeb* is not necessarily a *nerd*. Synonyms for *dweeb* are *flunky* and *stiff*; however, those words have pejorative overtones that do not convey the paternalistic attitudes of partners for *dweebs*."

Lexicographer Flexner, true to the profession, has found an etymon in the Scottish word *dwble*, which some of us pronounce "dweeble," a centuries-old term meaning "feeble, shaky."

Which is appropriate. When The Derogator strikes, the rest of us go all Looney Tunes and turn into dweebs.

RE "Going Ballistic": As Army slang for excited anger, you got it exactly backwards. The term comes from smallish tactical missiles, ok, but not blazing skyward (your term, not mine). When such a missile is no longer guided, it is said to have "gone ballistic"; it is out of control and apt to go anywhere. It is the twentieth-century equivalent of the "loose cannon"—sort of.

Howard R. Pyle
Waukegan, Illinois

I don't read "went ballistic" as "went mad," but "got mad."

Indoors, it implies (as a consequence) "hit the ceiling." Outdoors, it is implied (as a consequence) by "flew off the handle."

Since the locale is indoors, particularly in the Pentagon, the former image was probably the one intended.

Martin B. Brilliant
Holmdel, New Jersey

You used the term "ballistic", and implied that it meant (almost) "bananas," etc. I think you have misunderstood; if a "Pentagon source" used the term, they would probably mean acting the way a ballistic missile acts on reentry; i.e., *unguided.* The sense is that any errors earlier cannot be corrected, and might result in impact at any place at all. Therefore, when "Wickersham went ballistic," he was, presumably, striking out (verbally, I hope) randomly at any target around.

Eugene Edelstein
Hicksville, New York

When a missile, usually one fired from an airplane but also a surface-to-air missile, does not follow its assigned course to a target but simply flies straight like a bullet, pilots say that it went "ballistic"—which, in this case, means "out of control." Thus the officer in your column who went ballistic flew out of control.

Zalin Grant
Asnières, France

Several years ago, when the Western world put on its new-tech sneakers and went jogging, a crucial aspect of the ritual was the "warm-up," by means of which the body is given warning of impending abuse. The approved style was the slow, careful, incremental stretch, and the non-approved, derogated warm-up was the "ballistic stretch," which involved bouncing the weight of the body against the limits of its natural range of movement.

This latter technique, while it can give the illusion of useful function, actually results in overreactions and shortening of the muscles involved, and possible damage to connective tissues.

Another ballistic exercise is the classic "side-straddle hop," a truly vivid example of dramatic, wasteful expenditure of energy.

So you can see that in the minds of many of us, the term "ballistic" is perhaps a little less elevated than a ". . . missile blazing skyward," and more like the born-again "yo-yo" of the next paragraph in your column: a tantrum, as opposed to a launch.

Frank Sheffield
San Diego, California

When something "goes ballistic," it becomes a missile, and its course or trajectory will be independent of any influence other than the laws of physics. A bullet, for example, goes ballistic as soon as it leaves a gun's barrel. Any bomb, except a smart bomb, with special fins or rockets attached, is ballistic when dropped.

The phrase is used increasingly often now that there are missiles such as the Exocet, which goes ballistic after its motor and radar guidance system shut down. Once one has gone ballistic, it can not be defeated (i.e., lured off course) by countermeasures, only destroyed by a missile or shell. I have also seen the term used retroactively to describe Kamikaze planes in World War II. One of the problems with the Navy's 20mm and 40mm anti-aircraft guns was that they were not powerful enough to destroy a Kamikaze plane after it had gone ballistic. Such a plane, at the end of its dive, would continue on its course to hit its target even if the pilot were dead and the plane on fire. The only remedy was guns big enough to blow such planes out of the sky, and the Navy was planning to replace the 20s and 40s with 3-inch guns in 1945.

Jonathan D. Beard
New York, New York

When a guided missile is functioning properly, it appears to fly in a straight line towards the impact point with its target. If the target maneuvers, the missile can be observed to respond almost instantaneously with its own compensating maneuver. When the guidance system fails (which, on rare occasions, has been known to occur), the moving missile becomes subject to only the natural forces of gravity and aerodynamics. It behaves like a thrown rock, or an unguided bullet, and is said to follow a "ballistic" trajectory.

In the jargon of the military-industry complex, when a guided missile is observed to fail during its flight, one often says: "it went ballistic," meaning a sudden transition from carefully guided flight to completely uncontrolled (and essentially unpredictable) flight. The nuances of applying this terminology, with all that it implies (of which the above brief dissertation is only the most cursory outline), to a sudden change in a person's behavior, particularly that of someone of

significant military authority, are, I believe, far richer than those described by you.

Charles H. Bonesteel
Boston, Massachusetts

Your statement "Although some analysts confused Mr. Reagan's
reference with the stuttered 'Th-th-that's all, folks' at the end of each
cartoon in the series called Merry [sic] Melodies . . ." is quite misleading. In point of fact, the phrase in question *never* appeared at the
end of a Merrie Melodies cartoon. The phrase was originally "So long,
folks," and was heard at the end of each Looney Tunes until Porky Pig
came to prominence. At that point, Porky's stutter gave rise to the
famous "Th-th-that's all, folks" format and was delivered by Porky as
he burst through a drum.

The Looney Tunes series was done in black and white and featured
"name" players, whereas the Merrie Melodies were mostly one-shot
cartoons and were done in color (after 1934). Both had different
theme songs and different closings. The ending to a Merrie Melodies
was a series of concentric circles with the "Th-th-that's-all, folks" being written across the screen in script format.

Allan Greenfield
New York, New York

With regard to the etymology of "Looney Tunes," used deroga-
tively, the obvious base reference is to the Warner Brothers cartoon
series, but I'm surprised that none of your fellow journalists have
written to remind you that Looney Tunes was a common description
of the Mourabitoun militia among American reporters, photographers, embassy personnel and military observers in Beirut, from '79 to
the present. The derivation is not unlike Cockney rhyming slang. The
President may well have picked up this locution in a briefing, or simply by osmosis.

David Gates
Provincetown, Massachusetts

On *Looney Tunes,* I refer you to Philip Caputo's very fine novel,
DelCorso's Gallery, which is about a photojournalist in Vietnam and
later Lebanon. Looney Tunes was the name applied by foreign journalists in Lebanon to the factional group known as Mourabitoun (which
means "ambusher" in Arabic). "The vicious excesses of the Looney
Tunes were legend even in Beirut, where vicious excesses had become
commonplace," Mr. Caputo writes. I believe Mr. Caputo was at one

time a foreign correspondent in Lebanon, and I suspect that this derogation of the Mourabitoun may be factual—and well deserved.

Leah Robinson
New York, New York

If there is a word spelled *dwble,* I am sure it is the Welsh form of the
Scottish *dwaible,* meaning "weak." The Welsh word would be pronounced about like "DOO-bleh," Welsh being the only language I
know of to use the letter "w" for the vowel of "who," "pool," and
"rude."

L. Sprague de Camp
Villanova, Pennsylvania

The word "dweeb" is most likely one of the many variations of the
ancient derogation "plebeian," shortened in English to plebe rather
than pleb and best known for putting in their place underlings at
military academies.

One other variation of "plebe" that was especially popular in my
college days for its variety of entendres, was "pube" or someone from
a public school, who, at certain universities swarming with neologists,
were considered beneath private school boys like me.

Robert Wechsler
Highland Park, New Jersey

You suggest that "wimp" derives from "whimper." Are you sure? I
have a different idea.

I have heard reruns on public radio of the "Fibber McGee and
Molly" series. A helpless, henpecked character on that program went
by the name Wallace Wimple. Fibber called him "Wimp" for short.

I've always thought the word entered the language that way.

Eric Ringham
Minneapolis, Minnesota

I was struck by your mention of the word "sod." It reminded me,
for some reason, of a piece of doggerel that I have heard was popular
around Cambridge University after the turn of the century and probably related to a certain Mr. Wilde, now buried in Père La Chaise
Cemetery in Paris. The little poem went:

Here lies Oscar,
Gone to God,

Not earth to earth,
But sod to sod.

Alan G. Branigan
Nutley, New Jersey

The Village Voice has been filled with ads over the last few months for a band called The Usual Suspects. John Kruth, a poet from Brooklyn, routinely invited musicians from the audience to back him on stage at his shows, calling for a "roundup of the usual suspects." Eventually he formed a full-time group known as The Usual Suspects and they are currently performing around New York.

Heikki Hamalainen
New York, New York

You expressed an interest in Tagalog words in current English usage. Leo Rosten's book *Hooray for Yiddish,* in a footnote about borrowed words on page 10, shows the word "taffy" as having come from Tagalog.

Robert M. Rubin
Tampa, Florida

"He's got only one oar in the water" is acceptable if a little naïve. Us (or is it we) deep-water mariners prefer "He's carrying a little left rudder."

Peter M. Coope
North Stonington, Connecticut

In the same class as "He's only got one oar in the water" is "His elevator doesn't go all the way to the top."

Or perhaps you will like my own creation, "His set doesn't get all the channels."

Sydney Michael Rogers, Jr.
Larchmont, New York

Discussing Discussants

"The word *discussant* . . . does not appear in my dictionary," writes Allen R. Kramer, an architect in St. Michaels, Maryland, attaching a Baltimore film-forum program that lists *moderator* and *discussant* after each movie to be shown. "I fear it is the kind of word which *[sic]* will quickly spread to TV forums and assorted groups devoted to talking about up-lifting subjects. Perhaps some comments from you can prevent an epi-demic."

My advice to Mr. Kramer is to get a new dictionary. *Discussant* can be found in the current Random House, Webster's New World, and Merriam-Webster's Ninth New Collegiate dictionaries, and is defined as meaning "one who participates in a symposium or formal discussion." Anyone who tries to deal with today's neologisms using an old dictionary is like an architect plotting a cantilevered aerie with a blunt pair of calipers. (I will get letters from irate Fountainheaders on that: who uses calipers anymore?)

The point to remember about *discussant,* which has been in use since 1927, is: this person who is putting the entire audience to sleep by going on and on about that fellow's paper, which was dull enough by itself, is not just casually shooting the breeze. The *discussant* has come prepared to dis-cuss a paper he has usually been allowed to peruse in advance. He is not supposed to be as disputatious as the *respondent,* who is expected to begin his response with "What a waste of time!" or some other expostulation or riposte. (The program for the Modern Language Association's convention in Chicago last December lists no *discussants,* only *respondents;* that must have been lively, unless they thought of themselves as *panelists.*)

Discussant won out over *discusser,* in use for almost four centuries, for no special reason: I would speculate that a *discusser* sounded too much like one who hurls "discures." *Discutant* had a crack at it, on the analogy of *dispu-tant,* but was shouted down, as was *discussionist,* which sounded too much like the kid with the new set of drums upstairs driving everybody in the apartment house crazy.

All these words we've been discussing are rooted in the Latin *discutere,* Latin for "agitate," or more accurately, "to shake to pieces," which is what discussants would really like to do to the papers they serenely address.

Respondent, curiously, is rooted in *spondere,* "to promise, to betroth, as in the word *spouse*"; a *co-respondent* is someone with whom you have been making embarrassing promises, and to *correspond* is to agree; a *correspondent* was one who communicated agreeably, or stayed in touch secretly, but that's all changed now.

Panelist, in a free-association test, would bring forth "Kitty Carlisle" by a young generation that would not recognize the song "June in January." Originally, a *panellist*—two *l*'s—was one of a group of doctors working together under the National Insurance Act of 1913. It has since become an occupation, like *celebrity,* and is probably rooted in the Latin *pannus,* "cloth," from which one strips a piece in a kind of rip-off.

Do you ever wonder about good words that get crowded out? One who mulled things over was called a *deliberant* by Thomas Jefferson; I'd like to see that come back (and not *deliberator,* a role that would be played by Arnold Schwarzenegger.) You don't agree? You want to argue? Be a *controverter.*

When the critic John Simon appeared on my radio program, an irate listener wrote, "If that Nazi can't pronounce the letter "r" any better than he does, he should stop being a dramatic critic."

I showed the postcard to John and asked if he planned any career change. "Tell that listener," he said, "that I will, indeed, give up dchramatic kchriticism, and become, instead, a Play Discussant."

> *Jean Bach*
> *New York, New York*

Indeed I do wonder about good words that get crowded out!

Take, for example, the first cousin of "anywhere" and "anyhow." That pair we encounter with a frequency that makes one wonder why "anywhen" just never made it.

The sadly forgotten book reviewer and novelist Isabel Paterson used it to advantage in *The Road of the Gods.* Instead of writing "not then or subsequently" at the book's conclusion, she chose to say "not then or anywhen," which seems to me infinitely more graceful.

> *Thomas G. Morgansen*
> *Jackson Heights, New York*

Dishing the Full Plate

S tressed out? Overworked? Wrapped too tightly? In this condition, you no longer use the simile "busy as a one-armed paperhanger"; the phrase died out because of overuse or because it is now viewed as a slur against the handicapped. Instead, we have embraced, or swallowed, the metaphor of the *full plate.*

"I find myself with a very full plate," reports the actress Linda Hunt, featured in the movie *Eleni,* a film sniffed at by anti-anti-Communists and hailed by full-plated conservatives.

Israel "has a full plate" in dealing with its economic problems, said Senator Richard G. Lugar of Indiana, precluding wider agreements.

The metaphor has spawned a malapropism: "They might as well wrap this up if they can," said Richard L. Armitage, assistant secretary of defense for international security affairs, "because it's just not going to pass from their plate." Craig R. Whitney, an assistant managing editor of *The New York Times,* called *full plates* to my attention: "This is probably a confusion with Matthew 26:39, 'If it be possible, let this cup pass from me.'" (An additional source of confusion in the Pentagon is "my cup runneth over," from the 23d Psalm, now no longer used in connection with defense budgets.)

Whence this vogue trope? The *full dinner pail* has been tracked to Theodore Roosevelt, in 1894, and was the slogan of the 1900 McKinley campaign, but in those days the word *full* was something to be desired. In the 1920s, however, the adjective gained a connotation of *that's enough, already,* and the word-picture appeared in a 1928 *Daily Express* article quoting one Elton Pace as saying: "I cannot say. I have a lot on my plate . . . a lot of worry, my lord."

The expression has been crowding the platter ever since, overriding *overloaded, surfeited* and *up to here.* Writers who use it regularly are urged to go on a diet.

In a related development, a verb based on an old English plate has been resuscitated in America. When Dan Rather and Walter Cronkite protested against a film about the patron saint of CBS News, Edward R. Murrow, the president of Home Box Office, Michael Fuchs, said: "We have no reason to do an anti-CBS film. There's no dishin' going on here."

To *dish* is English slang for "to defeat, cheat, circumvent or baffle," which probably comes from the notion of food's being done, finished cooking and dished up, or placed in a dish; Eric Partridge dates it to the mid-1700s and associates it with *to cook one's goose* or *to settle one's hash*.

The most famous use of the term is attributed to Lord Derby, who with the aid of Benjamin Disraeli passed a reform bill long advocated by the Whig opposition and cried gleefully, "Don't you see we've dished the Whigs?"

The use of the term is slowly growing in the United States, where sports headline writers, whose plate is never too full, need a good short verb to substitute for *crush, rip, dump, flatten* and *trounce*.

You neglected to discuss the most common definition for the current slang term "to dish." As anyone who works in Hollywood can tell you, "to dish" means to gossip (usually maliciously). The term is a shortened form of "to dish the dirt"; one can get together with another to dish in a general way, or one can dish a person. One can even be known for "giving good dish."

Judith Boasberg
Los Angeles, California

As to the verb "dish," it has long been in use in Gay slang to mean to gossip or to make disparaging remarks with bitchy motives. Compare the line "Won't dish the dirt with the rest of the girls" from "The Lady Is a Tramp" by Cole Porter.

To dish in the presence of the victim is to "trash"; to trash when the statements are basically true is to "read," "read [one] out," or "read [one's] beads."

Paul G. Stack
New York, New York

Downer

A company that was a takeover target was faced, according to *The New York Times*, with a large debt and "with the prospect of shrinking its business to help pay down that burden."

"Why pay *down?*" writes Mark Pearson of San Francisco. "Because pay *off* has taken on sinister connotations?"

In a debt-ridden world, in which payment is made to service interest rather than reduce the principal of loans, the word *down* is coming up. It all began in 1926 with *down payment*, the first money put up; more recently, a subsidy paid to a homebuyer by a builder to make monthly payments less in the first few years of a mortgage, thereby permitting the buyer to qualify for a loan, is called a *buy-down*.

Why not use the simple *repay*, if *pay off* seems sinister? The reason is that the new usage is more sophisticated than it seems: *begin to repay* implies a plan to repay in full, and *pay down* implies nothing more than the beginning of a reduction in the money owed. How many of us pay down our loans to nothing, compared to those who refinance, or roll over, or go sedately bankrupt, or skip town? The language reflects the practice in subtle ways: we have differentiated between *pay out, pay off, pay up* and *pay down*.

"We have differentiated between *pay out, pay off, pay up* and *pay down*. . . ." Among you and me, I think you have it wrong.

Spencer Dvorkin
Scarsdale, New York

Draco Lives

"**O**fficials have described the spending reductions needed," went the front-page story in *The New York Times*, ". . . as Draconian."

A few days later, Senator Richard G. Lugar of Indiana picked up on Washington's vogue word: "In a year when draconian measures are being taken on the overall budget, foreign aid will not be immune."

Studying these stories, political observers wondered (1) who was this Draco, and what election did he win, and (2) more important, do you capitalize the eponymous adjective or not?

Draco was a no-nonsense kind of lawgiver. In ancient Athens, about six centuries B.C., he was one of the thesmothetes, or Stockman-type officials, assigned by the archon to record and codify the laws that had been strewed around on little scraps of papyrus, or whatever. (Aristotle disputes this, but I go with my source.)

Draco delivered what remains today as the easiest-to-remember criminal-punishment code in all history: For murder, death. For stealing a piece of fruit, death. For spitting on the marble sidewalk, death. No coddling, no turn-'em-loose-Bruce judges; thanks to Draco, the lawbreaker knew where he stood, and the prisons of Athens were not overcrowded.

However, some Athenian bleeding hearts, probably on Thesmothete's Day, called on another legislator to mitigate the severity of the Draconian code on all crimes except homicide. That was Solon, and to this day softy politicians are called solons, with a small *s.* (In an election campaign in the United States today, Draco would whip Solon hands down.)

Draconian edged out *Draconic* as the adjective, and the word has long meant "severe, cruel, harsh." However, as used in Washington today, *draconian* means "sweeping, dramatic, cathartic," a less pejorative connotation.

So do you capitalize it or not? If you are talking specifically about Draco and his set of laws, as some will be doing in discussing the plans of Edwin Meese 3d as Attorney General, you capitalize. If you are using the word more generally, to apply to any harsh or sweeping budget cut, use a small *d.*

I have a plan for the economy: balance the budget tomorrow morning; stop printing paper money, cut inflation to zero with unemployment. It's called *Draconomics.*

Why dracon*ian* and not dracon*ic*?

When speaking of Plato it's always a simple *platonic*, not platonian. (Platonian sounds too dangerous anyway, like the stuff that bombs are made of.)

Lizann R. Bradshaw
Kingston, New Jersey

I propose the noun and adjective *draconic* (small d), now that the original adjective is draconian anyway, on analogy with mnemonic (small m), a tool for remembering, akin to Mnemosyne, the mother of the muses and Draco's own goddess of memory. A draconic device is a specific kind of mnemonic, one that stays in the mind because of its dramatically harsh nature: a demonic mnemonic, if you will.

(Ms.) Merle Berk
Philadelphia, Pennsylvania

Drudgery It Ain't

"This is a historic occasion," pronounced Daniel Boorstin, historian, Librarian of Congress and author of *The Discoverers*, a bestselling history of the world. The occasion was a gathering at the library of renowned scholars, including a babble of wordsmen, to mark the two-hundredth anniversary of the death of Samuel Johnson—poet, essayist, novelist, critic and, above all, lexicographer.

I was about to salute Dr. Boorstin for saying *a* historic, using the naturally aspirant *h* rather than what Fowler's *Modern English Usage* characterizes disdainfully by suggesting that *an* historic "lingers curiously." But Senator Charles McC. Mathias, Jr., of Maryland gently corrected the host: "With deference to the spirit of the man we honor today, I think we should call this a *historical* occasion."

Senator Mathias likes to pose as a cracker-barrel country lawyer, but he is a closet intellectual; we have crossed swords before on the spelling and pronunciation of *snollygoster*, the mythical bird he insists is a *snallygaster*, but I refrain from zapping him and his atrophying wing of liberal Republicans, because he calls me "Dictionary Safire."

The senator was right: An occasion that makes history is *historic*; an occasion that deals with history is *historical*. Perhaps the Librarian meant both—an assembly of historians can be historic as well as historical, if they do something memorable—but he did not challenge the correction of one of the solons who oversee the library's budget. Dan Boorstin did, however, challenge Samuel Johnson's definition of a lexicographer as "a harmless drudge," a phrase that clings to the writers of dictionaries. "As we celebrate the vagaries of language," said Dr. Boorstin, "we share the delight of the drudgery of doing what you want to do."

You could feel the electricity in the room: the Librarian had pronounced *vagaries* vuh-GAIR-ies, and all of us who have been saying VAY-geries wondered if he had erred or if we have been making oafs of ourselves for all these years by mispronouncing the word whose meaning wanders between "caprices" and "oddities." (After the meeting, in a mad dash for the dictionaries, it was found that vuh-GAIR-ies or the similar vuh-GER-ies is the first pronunciation listed in Random House and Webster's New World. An additional listing is VAY-geries. Most people, I think, say VAY-geries, and the word has the same root as *vague*. The dictionaries should get with it; in pronunciation and ultimately in usage, when enough of us are wrong, we're right.)

A British diplomat rose to say that all the anti-American sentiments uttered by Dr. Johnson during the Revolution did not really make him anti-American, but this tongue-in-cheek effort to smooth over past differences went nowhere. Robert Burchfield, editor of the Oxford English Dictionary and a world-class lexie, observed that Dr. Johnson had a bias against Americanisms: a word like *skunk*, for example, with which Dr. Johnson was probably familiar, did not make his 1755 dictionary.

Burchfield, a New Zealander who thinks that lexicography includes a stiff belt of drudgery and who plans next to write a grammar, pointed out later that the human element was one of the charms of Johnson's dictionary: "He was not above putting in a word for a friend." In the definition of *magazine*, Johnson put first the common meaning, "storehouse, commonly an arsenal or armory." In what is now known as an unabashed plug, he then added a second meaning that must have delighted an associate and editor: "Of late this word has signified a miscellaneous pamphlet, from a periodical miscellany named the *Gentleman's Magazine*, by Edward Cave."

"Most people" don't say VAYgeries, or even vuhGAIRies. Most people don't use the word, or else have only a vague idea of what it means. I should suspect that most of the people who gathered at the Library of Congress on the occasion you describe in your column were accustomed to hearing the word properly pronounced, especially by people like Dr. Boorstin. "All of you" (six people? eight?) who had been mispronouncing it have indeed been making oafs of yourselves for all these years.

Donald W. Chilton
Huntington, New York

No one who is acquainted with *Iolanthe* could possibly have insisted, as you did, that we agree henceforth to pronounce vagary with an accent on the vay. And certainly no one who has ever *sung* the part of the Lord Chancellor, in this exchange with the Fairy Queen:

> Chancellor unWARy, it's highly necesSARy
> Your tongue to teach respectful speech,
> Your attitude to VARy;
> Your badinage so AIRy, your manner arbiTRARy,
> Are out of place when face to face
> With an in-flu-ential FAIRy.

Here is his response:

> A plague on this vaGARy, I'm in a nice quanDARy,
> Of hasty tone with dames unknown
> I ought to be more CHARy;
> It seems that she's a FAIRy, from Andersen's liBRARy,
> And I took her for the proprietor
> Of a la-dy's se-mi-NARY.

I've already proved too much: I do *not*, in ordinary conversation, pronounce it "quanDARy."

Alfred E. Kahn
Ithaca, New York

I am curious about the construction of a sentence in your column on "vagaries":

> After the meeting, in a mad dash for the dictionaries, it was found that vuh-GAIR-ies or the similar vuh-GER-ies is the first pronunciation listed in Random House and Webster's New World.

What does "in a mad dash for the dictionaries" modify? After such an introductory phrase, readers (or at least I) expect to find the agent of the dashing as the subject of the sentence. Since your writing shows your broad knowledge of grammar and usage, I was surprised to find what grammarians call a dangling prepositional phrase in this sentence. Even if one justifies the construction on the basis that "in a mad dash for the dictionaries" modifies the entire main clause (which I would reject), the passive is awkward and seems unnecessary here.

Lois DeBakey
Professor of Scientific Communication
Baylor College of Medicine
Houston, Texas

Drunk Again

The euphemism used to be *inebriated* or *intoxicated.* Ladies and gentlemen who drank too much were said to be *tipsy* or *high;* those more seriously concerned about others habituated to the overuse of alcohol called them *alcoholics.*

Not so much anymore. In a salutary reaction against the use of euphemism, the word now used without self-consciousness or fear of condemnation is the noun that is also the past participle of *drink:* "Not being a drunk is the only way I'm going to stay alive," Elizabeth Taylor told a reporter last month. "Drunk is a hard word, but I've had to be hard with myself to face it. A drunk is a drunk. . . . There's no polite way of saying it."

After two months in a rehabilitation center, Miss Taylor felt the need to use the blunt word to demonstrate her willingness to face the consequences of compulsive drinking. The shock in the word is treated as an awakener to be valued rather than an insult to be avoided.

"We use *alcoholics* in our group's name," says a spokesman for Alcoholics Anonymous, which by its nature prefers its spokesmen to remain unidentified, "but one of our co-founders very often would use *drunks* in meetings. He always referred to himself as *a drunk* even though he had not gotten drunk for a long while."

Isn't *drunk* pejorative? "Certainly *drunk* is the stronger word," says the spokesman, "though not quite as strong as *lush* or *souse. Alcoholic* has more of a clinical tone, more specific than *drunk.* We think of alcoholism as a disease, so far incurable. I haven't had a drink in eighteen years, but I am still an alcoholic."

The word *drunk* has not yet made it to New York State legal statutes; according to John O'Connor, a lawyer, lawmakers still prefer *intoxicated* or *under the influence of alcohol.* Black's Law Dictionary, 1968 edition, finds *drunk* and *intoxicated* to be synonymous, defining a person who is *drunk* partly as "so far under the influence of liquor that his passions are visibly excited or his judgment impaired. . . ." A *drunkard* is defined as one "whose ebriety has become habitual," and Black's properly finds "habitual drunkard" redundant.

The new popularity of the harsh word—used almost as if a dysphemism were being sought—can be partly attributed to the effective campaign by MADD, Mothers Against Drunk Drivers. Curiously, now that their use of the word as a kind of prepunishment is being widely adopted in more formal speech, MADD has second thoughts. Anne Seymour, a MADD media contact (sorry, that's how she is identified), says: "In spite of *drunk's* being in our organization's name, we are moving away from using either *drunk* or *alcoholic* in our vocabulary. The word we are using now is *impaired.* That's because we are equally concerned with eliminating driving by someone who may not be drunk, but is under the influence of other drugs."

Although MADD (whose members are not to be confused with the strategic nuclear concept acronymed MAD, for Mutual Assured Destruction) is seeking to extend strictures against those driving while *hopped up* or *spaced out* as well as drunk, the organization has not yet reached the point of dropping *drunk* from its name. The title is being changed slightly, but not in a way that affects the acronym: from Mothers Against Drunk Drivers to Mothers Against Drunk Driving. Apparently it wants to inveigh against the activity rather than the practitioners.

Impaired probably will not get off the ground as a substitute for "influenced by drugs, including alcohol," and not only because Mothers Against Impaired Driving would offer a less suitable acronym. *Impaired* may be used in law to describe drunk or hopped-up driving, but in the general language *impaired* is being used widely to modify or more accurately describe what used to be called *blind* or *deaf*. People who are not wholly blind or deaf are called *sight-impaired* or *hearing-impaired*, and if it helps them get jobs or feel better, anti-euphemists should not take offense. In other contexts, *impaired* is used as a euphemism for *retarded*, itself a euphemism now losing its gentle connotation. Because *impaired* is a kind vogue word, it is unlikely to be widely applied to an activity to be condemned, such as endangering lives while driving drunk.

I think that's good: *drunk* is a word that has more jocular slang synonyms than almost any other, from *blotto* to *pickled* to *pifflicated* to *three sheets to the wind*, but is less than ever a laughing matter or one to be soothed by kind words. The emergence of *drunk* into formal discourse signifies the wide public recognition of a problem; I suggest Mothers Against Drunk and/or Drugged Drivers (MADDD).

What ever happened to good ol' dipsomania?

E. Fulton Caldwell
Redding, Connecticut

The way out of your difficulty with "impaired" is a bit of Phillips Exeter Academy slang: "modified," meaning under the influence of any drug, including alcohol. E.g., "Hey man, let's get *modified.*"

Kenneth J. Sheridan
Balliol College
Oxford, England

The Effect Effect

I n political writing, nothing beats the application of a scientific phrase to the murky art of politics.

Immediately after the first Reagan-Mondale debate, some polls showed a 10-point victory for the challenger; after the commentators and opinion leaders had their say, this spread increased to an overwhelming 50-point decision for Mondale. I fully expected some public-opinion savant to cite this as an example of Lazarsfeld's Theory of Two-Step Communication, but I was mistaken; something more esoteric was in the works.

"This seemed to be a political application," wrote George Church in *Time* magazine, "of what in physics is known as the Heisenberg uncertainty principle: the very act of measuring a phenomenon changes the phenomenon being measured in such a way as to make future readings unpredictable." One week later, Sidney Blumenthal wrote in *The New Republic* about the Bush-Ferraro debate: "And the polls, partly reflecting the Heisenberg effect of media influence, showed Bush a slight winner."

Who is Heisenberg, and what is he doing to warp the views of the people being buttonholed by pollsters?

Werner Karl Heisenberg, a German physicist and quantum mechanic who died in 1976, saw his "uncertainty principle" stolen from physics in 1970: "There is the possibility," wrote *The Times* of London, "of a Heisenberg effect: the act of trying to outguess market psychology itself becomes a factor in the psychology and may invalidate the conclusion."

Richard Reeves, the columnist who introduced the popcorn diet to his fellow pundits, is probably responsible for importing this phrase onto the United States political scene. Writing about President Jimmy Carter in *The New York Times* in 1977, Reeves observed: "No one does or can do the same things onstage that he does unobserved. It's the popularized Heisenberg effect: the act of observing inevitably changes the process under observation."

This effect is similar to *the Hawthorne effect*. In the 1920s, at the Western Electric Company's Hawthorne Works in Cicero, Illinois, experiments to improve worker performance yielded an odd result: the fact that management paid such attention to worker conditions in itself raised morale and productivity. Lights were turned up, productivity rose; then lights were lowered, productivity rose again, its cause having less to do with the lighting than the fun of being part of an experiment.

I asked Sol Steinmetz of Barnhart Books to run a fast check through the last effects, and he reports: "The first *effect* I found was *the halo effect*, a psychological term from 1928, defined as 'a bias whereby one fundamental characteristic of an individual (such as friendliness) influences the overall judgment of his character.' Others include *effects* named for some person, such as *the Einstein effect*, or some thing, such as *the Hawthorne effect*. Lately, we've had *the echo effect, the ratchet effect* and *the ripple effect*. Recently, scientific naming has received general application by analogy."

We can expect more furrowed-brow use of scientists like Heisenberg, making all our commentary sound like the titles of Robert Ludlum novels. What about Austria's physicist Christian Doppler? In *the Doppler effect* on frequencies, the closer you get, the higher they sound; this has yet to be applied to a politician talking about the deficit.

But all is not lost: if this study of the vogue use of *effect* in nonscientific parlance makes analogists self-conscious about using the term, we will be witnessing *the Heisenberg effect* on *the Heisenberg effect*.

Sorry, you misstated the Doppler effect. It has nothing to do with *closer*; it has to do with *faster*. The faster you approach the source of the sound, the higher the pitch; and the faster you retreat from it, the lower the pitch.

The effect also works on waves other than sound, e.g., light. It is used to explain a phenomenon known as the red shift, in which spectrograms of light from distant galaxies show a frequency shift to the red (lower frequency) end of the visible spectrum. The galaxies are believed to be moving away from us at a high speed, hence the Doppler shift to the red.

We must be thankful that the term *red shift* has never been appropriated by the Right to describe a liberal moving rapidly to the Left.

G.J.A. O'Toole
Mount Vernon, New York

As a popularizer of science *(vulgarisateur* to the French, a term which conveys a more accurate impression of the enterprise to some) I cannot let your description of the Doppler effect pass without comment. You stated: "In the Doppler effect on frequencies, the closer you get, the higher they sound." The Doppler effect depends not upon distance, but upon speed. A correct statement would be: "The faster you approach the source of sound (or *it* approaches *you*), the higher the frequency.

Suppose someone stands still and fires peanuts at you at the rate of ten per second. If you now run toward the firer—who is still firing ten per second, so that the spacing between peanuts remains the same— you will be *hit* at a higher frequency than ten per second because each peanut has a shorter distance to travel than its predecessor before hitting you. The interval between hits has been reduced by your running toward the firer. If you run *away* from your peanut firer, you *reduce* the frequency of hits by increasing the distance successive peanuts must travel to reach you.

The remainder of your sentence, on politicians and the deficit, made me think of an early (1842) test of the mathematical expression for the Doppler effect. A locomotive pulled a flatcar loaded with trumpeters back and forth at different speeds before a group of musicians blessed with absolute pitch. You must admit that trumpeting from behind a locomotive does have political overtones.

Grace Marmor Spruch
Professor of Physics
Newark College of Arts and Sciences
Newark, New Jersey

You say that Richard Reeves was the columnist who introduced the Heisenberg effect, or Heisenberg principle of uncertainty to the general public in 1977. Unfortunately he probably picked it up from me, for I wrote about it nearly a decade earlier, calling it by its proper name of the Heisenberg Principle of Indeterminancy, in my article for *New York* magazine (September 16, 1968) on "If You Saw It on TV, Is It Really What Happened?"

So far as I know this Rule of Heisenberg's had not been applied to anything but physics before my article, and both my (then) husband David Burnham and myself were enchanted by the wide applications of the Rule to almost everything in our everyday lives. I am sure that David talked about it at the *Times* (and indeed Richard, being no dope, undoubtedly read that two-part cover story in *New York* and remembered the Principle, perhaps, although forgetting, as we tend to do, over the course of the next eight or nine years where he got the idea).

There was once a time when in college I made a real true brilliant philosophical discovery—and then discovered that Plato had said it first. I was greatly discouraged, but in this case feel a modest obligation to say, at least this time, *me first!*

Sophy Burnham
Washington, D.C.

I fear you have been led astray by other authors referring to Heisenberg's uncertainty *principle* as Heisenberg's *effect*. Heisenberg discovered the uncertainty principle in the course of mathematical studies connected with the establishment of quantum mechanics (which was often referred to in those days as "wave mechanics"). He showed that there is a fundamental limit on the precision with which a measurement could be made; specifically if one tried to measure the position of an atom (or electron) very precisely, one could not simultaneously know the particle's momentum.

To the best of my knowledge nobody has demonstrated this experimentally, so it should not be called an "effect." A well-known "gedanken experiment" due, I think, to Einstein, points out that to measure an atomic particle's position you would have to use light whose wavelength would be short compared to the particle's radius. This would require use of an X ray, and the energy carried by an X-ray photon is great enough to give a lot of momentum to the particle.

Thus the principle rests on a firm base in theory, even though the effect is far too small to observe.

Don't forget that a "quantum leap" or the emission or absorption of one quantum is the *smallest* amount by which the energy of an atom (or molecule) can change, by whatever process is under consideration.

J. B. Horner Kuper
Setauket, New York

I am familiar with the words *quantum mechanics* (noun) and *quantum-mechanical* (adjective), but your use of the word *quantum mechanic* stumped me. A specialist in *kinetics* is referred to as a *kineticist*. I know of no word for a specialist in quantum mechanics. However, in the absence of a dictionary entry, wouldn't the word *quantum mechanicist* better describe Werner Heisenberg?

David I. Loewus
Frankfurt, Federal Republic of Germany

As to Werner Karl Heisenberg: his *field* involved quantum mechanics. This, however does *not* make him a "quantum mechanic." Your reference to him as such is tantamount to calling Neils Bohr a nuclear physic!

Leonard Rutstein
Swartswood, New Jersey

You listed Heisenberg, halo, Hawthorne, and other effects. That made me wonder about named phenomena as Phi Phenomenon. Phi is the one that designates apparent motion where there is no actual motion. Movies, for example, being made of a series of still photos, appear to have motion. I wonder if there are other Greek letter phenomena. I'd love to see such a list with explanations!

Daniel S. Lirones
President, Film Central Ltd.
Saline, Michigan

Did you mean: "all is not lost" or "not all is lost"?

Camillo A. Orso
Summit, New Jersey

Doppler's Defenders

Christian Doppler, you are not forgotten. In a piece on the widening use of *effect*—from ripples and halos to Hawthorne and Heisenberg—I described *the Doppler effect* on frequencies as "the closer you get, the higher they sound."

That is a nefarious perversion of Doppler's contribution to science, as a legion of his students have pointed out. "Barring a Heisenberg effect on the Doppler effect," writes Donald Morrison of Chicago, "perceived frequencies depend on whether you are coming or going, and how fast, not on how close you are. It's the intensity of the sound that depends on distance, not the frequency."

A physics professor, Mark Snyder of Wellesley College in Massachusetts, puts it this way: "If an object emitting sound is moving toward you, the frequency of the sound will be higher than if the object were at rest . . . the change in frequency is a result of the object's motion with respect to you, not of your distance from the object."

"The classic example of the Doppler effect," writes Dr. Allan Greenberg of New York, whose practice is limited to endodontics, "is the speeding freight train emitting a constant-frequency horn blast. The apparent tone (as opposed to volume) changes from high to low because of changes not in relative position but in relative velocity (first toward, then away from, the listener)."

OK; why? "Sound waves are thought of as peaks and valleys of air compression," explains Irving Seideman of Lawrenceville, New Jersey. "The number of these that reach your ear at a given time determine the frequency (or pitch) of the tone you hear. If you run toward the source of sound, your ear intercepts a few more of the peaks and valleys than it would if you were standing still. As a result, the pitch that you hear goes higher. It is the speed, not the distance. . . ."

"The frequencies can be those of light as well as sound," contributes Steve Lang of Denver. "This is well known to astronomers, who use the Doppler effect to measure the speed at which celestial objects are moving away from the Earth. This is known as 'red shift.' "

"I will ascribe your gratuitous Doppeltalk to the Deadline Effect," beats Bruce Bush of Highland Park, New Jersey. Thank you. The next reference to the comings and goings of the Doppler effect will be defined quickly as "the faster you approach, the higher the apparent tone."

An *endodontist*, by the way, is not a person who goes around predicting the accelerating approach of Armageddon (which sounds higher as it gets nearer). It is a dentist specializing in root-canal work. Supply-side economists like Jude Wanniski deride traditionalists who preach austerity and suffer recessions for their "root-canal economics"; that can now be shortened to *endonomics.*

Dear Bill—
Have to admit I don't deserve credit for "deep-root-canal" endonomics. Bob Novak is the guy. (I did start the use of "schmooze,"

combining the Yiddish usage and Al Capp's schmoo, which is now common parlance on the political circuit.)

Jude [Wanniski]
Morristown, New Jersey

The '88 Rhetorical Watch

As a presidential campaign approaches, great rhetorical and metaphoric strain is placed on the language. Candidates, spokesmen and even thinksmen are tempted to scale heights of hyperbole and word-configuration that are never attempted in pursuit of less exalted office.

Lest this abusage corrupt the young, this department instituted (I started) the scrupulously bipartisan 1988 Hyperbolic and Metaphoric Watch. It was to include Sensitivity Citations for creative use of euphemism to avoid offense to any voting group and Misspokesmanship Awards for skillful cover-ups. Let us begin. (That is a quotation remembered by Kennedyites; it was followed by Lyndon B. Johnson's use of "Let us continue," pronounced "continya," in what is known in political phrasemaking as "boosting." Other examples of this technique are *Bamboo Curtain* boosting on *Iron Curtain,* and all the *-gate* constructions that followed *Watergate,* the best of which was a term exposing a minor expense-account scandal, *Doublebillingsgate.* Boosting is one of the many devices to be closely observed in this revolving *tour d'horizon.*)

The first item spotted in the '88 Watch involves a counterpunch to one's own head. Gary Hart, the leading Democratic contender, came bounding out of his corner to touch gloves with President Reagan, who had said he wanted America's defenses to be like those of Jack Dempsey, a heavyweight champion so tough that nobody dared insult him.

"Now, Jack Dempsey was big, all right," said Senator Hart, setting the President up for a metaphoric right cross. "But in arguing for a 'Jack Dempsey military,' the President forgot about another boxer, Gene Tunney. Tunney was smaller, swifter and better trained—and he beat Dempsey twice."

This undercutting uppercut depended for its efficacy on the relative size of the two heavyweights: the ponderous big guy was contrasted to the swift little guy, making the rhetorical point about a muscle-bound military versus a smaller, reformed defense establishment.

But let us look at the facts. On September 23, 1926, Jack Dempsey climbed into the ring in Philadelphia weighing 190 pounds. The challenger, Gene Tunney, weighed in at 189.5 pounds. Had Dempsey spit out his chewing gum, the two men would have weighed exactly the same.

Height? Dempsey was six feet three-quarters of an inch; Tunney was six feet one-half inch. That is about as close as you can get to equal height. The notion that Tunney was "smaller" does not hold up. (Hart partisans will say: "Aha, what about the return match?" Dempsey put on two pounds. Big deal.)

Although Tunney was surely the more intellectual of the two men, the politician from Troublesome Gulch was in error in suggesting Tunney could use trope-a-dope against a larger Manassa Mauler. Better dance away from pugilistic figures of speech, Gary; in every political crowd, there is at least one of the world's experts on whatever sports metaphor you use to jab an opponent, and he is ready to throw a record book at the man on the podium.

Now to the '88 Watch's first egregious misuse of a foreign phrase. Representative Jack Kemp of New York, after impressing a gathering of Republicans in Nashville with a brilliant survey of the issues facing the nation, said, "I've given you a grand *tour de force.*"

A *tour de force*, from the French "feat of strength," is a breathtaking performance, masterly production or stunning creation. Kemp is not a braggart and thus could not have meant that.

He probably meant *tour d'horizon*, planted a few paragraphs above, meaning "circuit of the horizon," a metaphor for a general survey. In its pronunciation, unlike *tour de force*—which sounds similar in both languages—*tour d'horizon* should sound like "toor dor-ee-ZOHN." If the pronunciation of *horizon* is Anglicized, the whole phrase should be in English: *tour of the horizon*.

Kemp's intention could be read in his whole phrase, *grand tour de force*; the *grand tour* was a visit to the capital cities of Europe, especially London, Paris and Rome. (In politics, the new grand tour is a visit to Ireland, Italy and Israel, sometimes called the "Three-I League," named after the minor baseball league made up of teams in Indiana, Illinois and Iowa.) In the case of this speech, candidate Kemp was making his own grand tour of the issues, and though his supporters claim his performance was a *tour de force*, it could be modestly self-described only as a *tour d'horizon*, and to a yuppie-scorning political audience, as a "tour of the horizon."

(A digression: Yuppese will be a category to consider in the '88 Watch, but I am not yet prepared to deal with Vice President Bush's remark that the recent friendliness of Chinese officials toward Americans would, a decade ago, have placed those officials "in *deep doo-doo.*" This has the advantage of being alliterative, and I am the last to knock that technique, but the phrase has no other advantage at all.)

Although President Reagan is not a candidate, his rhetoric will surely be eligible for watching, especially in the clarifying. (*Clarify,* in its political meaning, does not mean "make clear"; it is closer to the meaning in cookery. Clarified butter is made by melting butter and letting casein and other nonfats drop out; the clear liquid that remains has less flavor but a higher burning point. A clarified statement also has less flavor and is less incendiary.)

Recently, White House aides put out the word that we were to expect a *full-court press* on military aid to the Nicaraguan contras. I received a phone call immediately from Tom Brokaw of NBC News, who used to play basketball: "I won't use that on the air," said this slam-dunk broadcaster, "because they mean they plan to go on the offensive. But a *full-court press* is a defensive maneuver."

However, the White House staff is not always that rhetorically off-the-rim. When reporters were ushered out of a room where the President was speaking, Mr. Reagan was heard over a live microphone to mutter, "sons of bitches." Because the Reagan words were recorded, as sometimes still happens in the White House, this posed a problem in what spookspeak calls "plausible denial."

Into this difficult spot sailed the White House spokesman, Larry Speakes, with the President's answer to questions from those you-know-whats among my colleagues: "He doesn't recall saying it." That is called in the trade a *round denial,* which is smoother and more effervescent than a *flat denial:* the President may have said what the tape shows he said, but he does not "recall" it, because he has put the matter out of his mind. (Spokesmen are expected to offer denials both round and flat.)

Mr. Speakes went on, however, to apply a light touch that earns him the first Misspokesmanship Award of the campaign of '88. "If he said anything," he added, "he said, 'it's sunny, and you're rich.' "

Never before in politics has a euphemistic homophone so accurately stated a political figure's political outlook.

Mr. Brokaw's precipitate putdown of the White House aides and their use of "full-court press" was itself somewhat in error. Mr. Brokaw may have played basketball but I still play the sport and a full-court press is only a *defensive* maneuver in the same sense that a punt in football is an *offensive* maneuver because it is executed by the team on offense.

In fact, with the occasional recourse to a quick-kick noted as an exception, a punt is really a defensive maneuver; if the team on offense doesn't kick the ball away it may have to yield possession under markedly inferior circumstances. In the same way, while utilized by the team on defense, a full-court press is a very offensively minded tactic. It is intended to wear down another team, force turnovers and otherwise create offensive opportunities.

Donald O. Souden
New Canaan, Connecticut

Tour d'horizon much better, certainly, but hardly used. Perhaps *coup d'oeil générale* for survey.

Günter Steuer
Huntington Beach, California

Emphasis on Stress

You have two minutes and thirty seconds to read and fully comprehend this piece. (Snap to it, and better not miss anything because you will be savagely tested and cruelly graded.)

"I once had *anxiety,*" says a scrawny, straggly-haired, self-hugging character in a syndicated strip by the cartoonist Jules Feiffer. "Now I have *stress.*"

When Mr. Feiffer takes note of language change, lexicographers listen. He was the one, in 1967, who caught the political ring-around-the-rosy in the use of *black:* "As a matter of racial pride we want to be called *blacks.* Which has replaced the term *Afro-American.* Which replaced *Negroes.* Which replaced *colored people.* Which replaced *darkies.* Which replaced *blacks.*"

Two years before that, the *Village Voice* cartoonist was the first to grasp the nomenclature of neediness: "I used to think I was *poor.* Then they told me I wasn't *poor,* I was *needy.* They told me it was self-defeating to think of myself as *needy;* I was *deprived.* Then they told me *underprivileged* was overused. I was *disadvantaged.* I still don't have a dime. But I have a great vocabulary."

Accordingly, dictionary makers and language mavens are poring over his analysis of *stress.* "I go to a weekly stress lab . . ." says his character in the wash-and-wear hairdo, her body language shouting out her leaned-on, tugged-at, pushed-around mental state. "And take stress tests and stresser-cise classes. I'm on a stress diet and take stress vitamins. I go out with stress-mates and play stress-games and have stress-sex. *Anxiety* was so iso-lated," she says, finally smiling. "Thank God for *stress.*"

The socialization of stress, and its voguish selection as the root of all modern health evil, has not hitherto been subjected to linguistic examina-tion. (How you doin', reader? Most people your age and social class are about three paragraphs farther on. You're sure you grasped the full import of the academese in the sentence before this parenthetical aside? Your peer group is looking over your shoulder.)

Stress, the noun, is a shortening of *distress*, rooted in the Latin *distringere*, "to hinder, molest." *Stress*, the verb, has another root as well: the Latin *stringere*, "to draw tight, press together," which is related to *strain*. Here is a stringent lesson: The result of *stress* is *strain*.

As a generalized noun, *stress* has come to take its meaning from the verb: the pressure—whether through direct force, tension or torsion—exerted on a person or thing. Specialized meanings abound: People in the language dodge use *stress* to mean *accent* (*accent* changes the syllable stressed when it switches from noun to verb). Orators stress certain points ("Let me empha-size, my stressed-out friends . . ."). But those familiar old *stresses* are not the specific *stress* so much in vogue on analysts' couches and in gatherings of the gaseous glitterati.

The stress that is "in"—trendy stress, swank angst—is the mental-physi-cal ailment that psychiatrists call *the stress syndrome* and gastroenterologists, ears cocked to a proliferation of burbling stomachs, call their ticket to a good life. (Lest we treat the problem too lightly, it is good to remember that emotional reactions can cause physiological tensions, which can lead to disease, as ulcer sufferers know.)

Dr. George A. Engel, in a 1953 study of ego and stress, wrote that "*Psychological stress* refers to all processes, whether originating in the exter-nal environment or within the person, which impose a demand or require-ment upon the organism the resolution or handling of which requires . . . activity of the mental apparatus before any other system is involved or activated." *Stress*, in its psychiatric sense, is what happens when uncon-scious impulses call for action that conflicts with ordinary behavior. That is somewhat more complex than simple, or layman's, stress, which is how you feel when your boss leans on you to put hospital corners on your spread-sheets, or your spouse makes strange new demands, or your language maven reminds you that you should have finished this piece long ago. (Come on, skim the next graph—you're really holding up your whole cohort.) In either the medical or lay notions of stress, you may suddenly get very tired or break out in a rash or hit the panic button.

"*Stress* is now being used as a catchall term for almost any response to anxiety or depression," says Dr. Rex Buxton, a psychiatrist in Potomac, Maryland. "Most often, it is used by people who feel tired, worn out, and are making an analogy to metallurgy—stressed metal is more brittle, more liable to be fractured." Dr. Howard Bogard, a Manhattan psychologist, does not think of the word as a clinical term, but as a word spread by internists asking patients, "Is there stress in your life, your job, your marriage?" to which the answer is always an enthusiastic yes.

Dr. Bruce Dan, senior editor of the *Journal of the American Medical Association*, recalls a "Life Stress Scale" in the early 1970s that listed hard-to-take conditions like divorce and death of a spouse. "The presence of stress causes physical changes that can be measured," says Dr. Dan. "You can observe increases in pulse, respiration, heartbeat, and this stress can lead to more serious physical problems. It's a very useful word. *Anxiety* is not so much a synonym for *stress* as it is a result of stress."

For purists, then, *pressure, tension* and *stress,* which are synonymous in general use, lead to *anxiety* and *strain,* also synonymous. The vogue term, and perhaps that metaphor of metallurgical strain (stressed-out people are sometimes described as *bent),* was presaged by John Locke circa 1698: "Though the faculties of the mind are improved by exercise, yet they must not be put to a stress beyond their strength."

(You finished last. Now you can relax and enjoy the rest of the book. But don't feel bad: Have you ever met a slob who had stress?)

Stress, as presently used, was coined only a few decades ago by Hans Selye who defined it as the "non-specific response of the organism to any demand for change." Selye indicated that he had actually borrowed it from physics where it had been used for centuries to describe the effects of external loads or stresses on tensile materials which produced manifest distortion or strain (Hooke's Law, 1676). He often complained to me that had his knowledge of English been more precise, he would have used the word "strain." Subsequently, it became necessary for him to create a new word "stressor" to refer to those stimuli which elicited the stress response.

This created all sorts of linguistic problems when Selye's theories had to be translated into foreign languages. In 1946 when he was invited to give a series of lectures at the College de France, its academicians could find no suitable word or phrase to translate stress. After a spirited debate, the male chauvinists apparently supervened and "le stress" was born. This was quickly followed by "el stress," "lo stress," "der Stress," and similar neologisms in Japanese, Chinese, and Russian.

Initially, stress was primarily the domain of research scientists who nevertheless continued to confuse cause and effect. One critic, cited in Selye's *1st Annual Report on Stress* (1951), using verbatim citations from Selye's publications, complained that apparently "Stress in addition to being itself and the result of itself, is also the cause of itself."

Paul J. Rosch, M.D., F.A.C.P.
President, The American Institute of Stress
Yonkers, New York

Let us start with the concept of strain which may be described as the deformation due to stress. This gets us to another related concept, elasticity. A perfectly elastic substance may be deformed as a result of stress, but upon removal of the stress will return to its original form. Since there are no perfectly elastic substances or systems, limits to elasticity exist. Should the stress be great enough to result in deformation which exceeds the elastic limit, the deformation becomes permanent.

I believe that these considerations add to the use of these concepts in psychological and sociological analogies, and hope that you might find them of some interest.

John deL. Moomaw
Elkton, Maryland

Being a metallurgist, I never thought that I would be correcting "On Language." In our jargon stress is the intensity of force or pressure. Stressed metal is not more brittle *because* of the stress. Just as the President's operation did not cause his cancer, the brittleness in metals exists; the stress does not cause it, but reveals it.

Our terminology differs from common usage in several other ways. For example, pressure, tension, and stress are not synonymous in metallurgy. However, we conform in that stress results in strain (distortion), and follow John Locke's usage of stress and strength. You might also be interested to learn that we give a number of common words special usage: dislocation, twins, slip, creep, cleavage, and necking are examples.

Alan R. Rosenfield
Columbus, Ohio

In metallurgy, fracture is the response of a solid to stress; without stress there can be no "separation into component parts." It is true however that the stress may be either externally applied or of a more internal origin, and in this sense Dr. Buxton's analogy is well drawn. Internal stresses can arise as a consequence of structural changes within the metal or rapid changes in its environment, again suggesting a fruitful field for metaphor.

And so to brittle, that much misunderstood but in fact very specific metallurgical term. Whether or not your aunt's favorite cup hits the floor, it is nevertheless brittle. To wit, if sufficiently stressed it will become pieces with little detectable deformation (maybe we can glue it back together before she gets home!). The opposite of brittle is tough, the essential difference being the amount of energy consumed while cracking up (now try straightening out the silver fork you just stepped on).

> John D. Meakin
> Metallurgist
> Newark, Delaware

I do not know why you did not include the word *agida* in your stress column, since it is so apropos of what many on the treadmill feel. The Italian use of it means "heartburn." At least in the Northeast, it has come to personify stress, e.g., "You give me agida!" It appears to be a bastardized version of *agita* from *agitare* meaning to disturb or excite emotionally.

> Frank J. Williams
> President, The Lincoln Group of Boston
> Hope Valley, Rhode Island

Your article on "stress" reminded me of a story my late cardiologist, the world-famous Paul Dudley White, told me almost twenty years ago, about a meeting of doctors wherein the question of stress came up. Like all large organizations, they appointed a committee to look into it before the next meeting. The first thing they were told to do was to come up with a definition of stress. The next year the committee came back with the report (and I quote from Dr. White's printed lecture of August 18, 1966): "Stress is life and you had better enjoy it." Wonderful! It has kept me off tranquilizers and enjoying a reasonably balanced head for years.

> William Schwann
> Schwann Record & Tape Guide
> Boston, Massachusetts

Falasha

"No one here can be of help with that word," snaps a voice at the Ethiopian Embassy in Washington, and the line clicks dead. The word—in Amharic, the Semitic language of the Abyssinian plateau that is the official language of Ethiopia—that the diplomats of that nation find so inconvenient to translate is *Falasha*.

The *Falashas* are the black Jews of Ethiopia, thousands of Africans who claim to be descended from King Solomon and the Queen of Sheba and whose Jewishness was officially affirmed by religious authorities in Israel ten years ago. Few historians will certify the union of Solomon and Sheba's queen, but some will identify the people living in the war-torn and famine-ridden totalitarian state as descendants of the tribe of Dan.

In most reports and commentary about the attempt by Israel to remove these Jews from the war zone and airlift them to Israel, the word *Falasha* is interpreted as "stranger." Not so, says Mrs. Julian Kossow of Sarasota, Florida, whose husband taught law in Ethiopia in 1973; the word for "stranger" in Amharic is *feringi,* and *Falasha* is a far more insulting term, meaning "one who is illegitimate, a bastard."

Professor Jordan Gebre-Medhin of Northeastern University in Boston defines the word as "outcast, outsider, alien." The meaning, he agrees, is not as benign as "stranger": *"Falasha* means a lot of things, including the idea of someone who is illegitimate. The negative concept is familiar to any caste society: if you think of the lower caste in the system of India, *Untouchable* would be the same idea as *Falasha."*

The people labeled *Falashas*—the plural usually carries an *s,* but sometimes does not, and the word is capitalized when it refers to the group—call themselves Beth Israel, "House of Israel," not *Falashas.* That should demonstrate (1) that Ethiopia's Jews have long been treated shabbily in their country, and (2) that, even when used by humanitarians trying to call attention to their plight, the word can be an insult.

About the origin of the word *falasha:* the noun is derived from a verb, *fellese,* meaning to uproot, or to emigrate or disperse. (References are Baeteman's *Dictionnaire Amarigna-Français* (1929), or Dr. Wolf Leslau's introduction to *A Falasha Anthology.)* The idea of the Falasha being uprooted makes sense in several ways. It implies that they were originally immigrants to their Ethiopian homeland (which is arguable). They are also, by tradition, landless, making their living as artisans for their Amhara neighbors. Artisans are a despised caste among the Amhara—thus the translation of *falasha* as "outcast."

The plural of *falasha* in Amharic, by the way, would be *falashoch.* But in Amharic using the plural is optional unless there is some reason to be specific, so *falasha* will do for either singular or plural.

I don't know of a good one-word translation of "stranger" in Amharic; the usual word given is *ingida,* a courteous extension of the word for "guest." *Ferenji* is the word for a European, or by extension an American, not for just any outsider. It is derived from the Arabic term for the "Franks," the European crusaders to the Holy Land who brought their *lingua franca* to the eastern Mediterranean. Before the Ethiopian revolution crowds of children used to taunt foreigners by chanting *"ferenj, ferenj"* after them in the streets of Addis Ababa—it happened to me often enough, and I'm sure it did to Mrs. Kossow. Nowadays there are fewer Westerners and tighter controls.

In case you ever need to' consult an expert on Amharic again— which I doubt—there are several Ethiopian linguists now living in the United States. Dr. Hailu Fulass, who was teaching at Howard, is in Bethesda, Maryland, and Dr. Abraham Demoz is in the Department of Linguistics at Northwestern University. Dr. Leslau, who was their teacher, is Professor Emeritus at UCLA and has worked on Falasha materials.

I hope these observations from a *ferenji* who has enjoyed the hospitality of Ethiopians over many years will clarify things for you.

Susan J. Hoben
African Studies Center
Boston University
Boston, Massachusetts

Analogous to the defamatory *Falasha* is the word applied to Spanish Jews whose ancestors converted to Catholicism, but retained the memory of their Jewish origin: *Marranos*.

On a trip to Europe some years ago, I met a man who told me that although his family was Catholic, they remembered their origin as Spanish Jews, and even kept some Jewish traditions.

"Oh," I remarked innocently, "Marranos."

The man reddened. "Please don't use that word," he said. "I'm sure you didn't intend to insult us, but *marrano* means 'pig.' "

"I'm awfully sorry," I apologized; "I didn't know. But how did that word come to be used for families like yours?"

He seemed embarrassed, but finally explained. "In the time of the Inquisition, to keep from being burned at the stake as false converts, as many were, our family and others kept pigs and served pork. Their neighbors, aware of the reasons for this display, called us first 'pig-servers' and then 'pigs.' "

"What would you call yourselves, then?" I inquired.

"Ethnic Jews," he replied.

Arthur J. Morgan
New York, New York

Fiber Bored

For people afflicted with stress who cannot change their lives, many find happiness with *fiber*. Walk down a supermarket aisle; like midshipmen's swords over Flirtation Walk, boxes of products with *fiber* in their title seem to leap out and form a canopy. (That error is implanted to elicit a blast from the Nitpickers' League: "Sir: Flirtation Walk is at West Point, where midshipmen rarely are married . . .")

Fiber is a nutritionist's word that has replaced its popular predecessor: As far back as 1975, Marian Burros was writing in the *Washington Post* about "how little space is devoted to the need for fiber or, as grandmother used to call it, roughage." *Roughage* is no longer used; most people think it is a penalty slapped on overeager linebackers.

Today's lusted-after *fiber* is indigestible material that stimulates peristalsis or, as doctors say briskly, bulks up the stool. But what about *bran?* Next to *fiber*, the word sweeping Madison Avenue is *bran.* The two words are not synonymous: *Bran* is the fibrous portion strictly of grains: the husks or skins of wheat, oats or rye that are left in the strainer after the flour has been sifted. *Fiber*, short for *dietary fiber*, subsumes *bran*—that is, it includes bran but also embraces cellulose, the structural polymers of cell walls, pectin, lignin and other lip-smacking culinary delights.

The essence of the word *fiber*, from the Latin *fibra*, "filament," and perhaps related to *filum*, "thread," is that it is a single strand capable of joining with other strands to produce a substance of flexibility and strength. "Great blunders are often made," wrote Victor Hugo in *Les Misérables* (translated by Charles E. Wilbour), "like large ropes, of a multitude of fibers." The word's connotation—from old-fashioned *moral fiber* to newfangled *fiber optics*—is always upbeat.

Remember those words, ye admen desperate for a different box top, when a creative copywriter comes up with next year's raisin-flecked, frosted-flaked answer to stress in the executive suite: new, improved *roughage.* Right after that, someone will come up with a better idea: a cereal that's flogged as *fiber-free.*

First, Grace

At a high-powered luncheon in the executive offices of a major media empire, a guest picked up a card on which was printed a grace prayer. Instead of "Grace Before Meal," as he expected, the title of the poem by John H. Finley was "Grace Before Meat"; the visitor wondered if a typographical error had made it uncorrected right to the top.

Grace before meals is a common phrase; Ralph Waldo Emerson used it in an 1856 essay on university life. But *grace before meat* dates to Shakespeare's time: "Your soldiers use him," says a character about the general Coriolanus, who was on the tip of all tongues, "as the Grace 'fore meate." In *Measure for Measure*, the same thought is expressed as "thanksgiving before meat."

The use of *meat* to stand for the entire meal is *synecdoche*, pronounced sort of like Schenectady. This is a device that uses a part to describe the whole, such as *head* for cattle, or the other way around, *the law* for a policeman. The device is ancient, and adds a nice touch to modern executive dining rooms. It is also used in modern slang; the visitor who did not find a typo in "Grace Before Meat" was wearing nice threads.

You are, I think, in error to read Mr. Finley's "meat" as a synecdoche for "meal."

"Meat" acquired quite the contrary semantic seasoning over linguistic time. My trusty American Heritage Dictionary, at "meat," serves up "Middle English *mete*, 'food,' meat, Old English *mete*, food." Thus if I con their use of the quotation marks aright, "meat" in its oldest attestations meant "food" and only in the later Middle Ages turned to signify that most substantial of foods.

Mr. Finley, then, was indulging in a bit of poetic archaism, not synecdoche. The O.E.D. defines the primary meaning of "meat" "usually, as solid food, in contradistinction to drink. Now arch. and dial."

Jay F. McKeage
New York, New York

Your closing paragraphs on Grace Before Meat reminded me of the charming "A Child's Grace" by Shakespeare's contemporary, Robert Herrick (1591–1674):

> Here a little child I stand
> Heaving up my either hand;
> Cold as paddocks [frogs] though they be,
> Here I lift them up to Thee,
> For a benison to fall
> On our meat and on us all. Amen.

Maureen Van Horn
Pittsfield, New Hampshire

In defining synecdoche, you said it was "a device that uses a part to describe the whole . . ." But *to describe* something is to offer its major characteristics. Synecdoche does not do that, of course. It uses the part *to refer* to the whole.

Here's what the O.E.D. says of the current sense of *describe:* "To set forth in words, written or spoken, by reference to qualities, recognizable features, or characteristic marks; to give a detailed or graphic account of."

Anyway, thanks for all you've taught me (and my students).

Arthur Edelstein
Pomfret Center, Connecticut

One of your quotations dates *from* or dates *back to*, not "dates to."

Jacques [Barzun]
Charles Scribner's Sons, Publishers
New York, New York

Flakes Will Fall

President Reagan in a news conference called the Libyan leader Muammar el-Qaddafi "flaky."

This is not one of your regular diplomatic terms of art, like *intransigent;* next day, from the highest levels of the White House came this urgent call: "What is the derivation and current meaning of *flaky?*"

Frankly, I had been awaiting a different query: How come there is no *u* after the *Q* in Qaddafi? (Answer, on the back of my tongue: a *Q* without a *u* is intended to represent the velar sound of *k.*)

Although Shakespeare used the adjective in *Richard III* to describe the breaking of dawn—"and flaky darkness breaks within the east"—the word, in its current slang meaning of "off-beat, eccentric," was first reported by Leonard Koppett in *The New York Times* in 1964. Baseball players like Joe Pepitone, Jim Bouton and Phil Linz were said to be *flaky.*

The term appears to have replaced *kook* as a synonym for "nutty," although, as Mr. Reagan pointed out, it is not used to mean "mentally deranged," a more serious affliction. It is sometimes spelled *flakey,* to insure pronunciation with a long *a,* to differentiate it from *flak,* an acronym for *Flieger Abwehr Kanone,* meaning "criticism."

The last time *flaky* was used politically was in derogation of Governor Jerry Brown of California, who responded vigorously by denouncing those in favor of building bigger nuclear power plants: "They are the flakes."

You know, I am sure, that Arabic (like Hebrew) has a script of its own and a number of phonemes not duplicated in European languages. What complicates matters is that Arabic has a "literary" form —sometimes called "standard" or "classical"—which is used only in writing and in formal speech, and which is fairly uniform throughout the Arab world; but it also has a number of regional "colloquials" which differ from the literary idiom and from one another in syntax, in vocabulary, and in the ways the same letter may be pronounced. This has caused endless trouble to people with only partial familiarity with the language, or not particularly concerned with its niceties: when Lawrence's *Seven Pillars of Wisdom* was in the press, he received a letter from his publisher complaining that he had spelled the same place-name in two different ways; he responded by offering another half-dozen alternatives!

To come down to the gentleman who has attracted President Reagan's *flak* (a word which in my soldiering days was applied most specifically to anti-aircraft fire): Most Libyans would, in informal speech, pronounce his name as Gaddāfi, and this was the spelling one encountered most frequently in news reports in the early days of his career. In its literary form, however, the first letter is indeed a velar "k", and nowadays this is transliterated as "q" by most Arabists—but not by all: the authoritative Encyclopaedia of Islam used "ḳ" instead. And the double consonant in the middle is pronounced "d" only in the colloquial: in literary Arabic it ought to be pronounced like "th" in "the." The entire name may therefore be transliterated as al-Ḳadhdhāfī in accordance with the Encyclopaedia of Islam's system, or as al-Qaddāfī if one follows Brockelmann's *Geschichte der Arabischen Litteratur*. The wiseacres who have adopted el-Qaddafi are attempting a compromise between two practices—or falling between two stools.

I use all this heavy ammunition merely to knock down the notion that there is a "correct" or universally accepted way of representing Arabic sounds in Latin script. And valid as the efforts of Arabists may be to achieve some uniformity within their own discipline, these cannot become normative for English orthography as a whole.

Pierre Cachia
Department of Middle East
Languages and Cultures
Columbia University
New York, New York

"Flak" is the acronym for either *Flugabwehrkanone* or *Fliegerabwehrkanone*, both of which mean anti-aircraft gun. Both are compound words, and cannot be split up. You were correct to capitalize German nouns, but not to split up *Fliegerabwehrkanone*. My grandfather, who commanded a *Flak* battery in the Luftwaffe, prefers the term *Flugabwehrkanone* to *Fliegerabwehrkanone*.

Erhard F. Konerding
Government Documents Librarian
Wesleyan University
Middletown, Connecticut

I work in Bell Labs' Department of Linguistics and Artificial Intelligence. A particular piece of software may be called flaky, suggesting a certain amount of inherent instability leading to intermittent failure for no apparent reason. When a person is called flaky, the implication is that s/he, while usually displaying perfectly rational behavior, is subject to brief episodes of incomprehensible behavior. Flaky software is useful but mildly irritating on the occasions when it flakes out; a flaky person is generally pleasant to have around, but confusing when s/he flakes out. Applied to a person, the term implies (within technological subcultures) that the person's unpredictability is amusing, possibly even endearing.

Hank Bromley
Murray Hill, New Jersey

Flaky people have been around much longer than the 1964 citing (sighting?) of baseball oddballs by Leonard Koppett in *The New York Times.* From the 1920s, "flaky" has been used to describe cocaine addicts. And I have here a rather didactic 1945 usage from William J. Spillard's *Needle in a Haystack:* "We couldn't help enjoying the name Flaky Lou. She was named after cocaine, which is flaky in appearance." "Snow" and "Flake" have been street names for cocaine for most of this century.

Hence if the White House is seeking the derivation of modern flakiness, they should look to the narcotics underworld, and not to Shakespeare's flaky sky.

Joan Murray
Buffalo, New York

Flush Right

"Toilet" used to be the word we most often used for a *lavatory*. Then along came American euphemisms such as *restroom* and *comfort station*, along with the British euphemisms *water closet* and *loo*. According to a Dictionary of American Regional English survey, some responses to the question "What do you call an indoor toilet?" were *bathroom, commode, john* and *Mrs. Jones*. It seemed as if *toilet* was falling into disuse.

Along came the charge that the Defense Department had paid $640 for a toilet seat, which critics of defense spending made symbolic of waste and inefficiency in Pentagon procurement. At a televised press conference, a reporter asked the President, ". . . Why did you so strongly denounce the misrepresentation of Secretary Weinberger as being wasteful and the cartooning of him with a toilet seat around his neck . . . ?"

President Reagan replied: ". . . We didn't buy any $600 toilet seat. We bought a $600 molded plastic cover for the entire toilet system."

By focusing on *toilet seat*, for which there was no euphemism, the Pentagon critics (and cartoonist Herblock) stopped the erosion of the word *toilet*; by elevating the toilet seat to part of a modern *entire toilet system*—a proud component of a technological advance in a formerly mechanical process—the President rescued the word for generations to come.

The Pentagon spokesman trained to handle toilet queries is named, through no fault of his own, Glenn Flood. He says: "The original price we were charged was $640, not just for a toilet seat, but for the large molded plastic assembly covering the entire seat, tank and full toilet assembly. The seat itself cost nine dollars and some cents." He adds, "The supplier charged too much, and we had the amount corrected."

It's a relief for taxpayers to know that there is no "$640 toilet seat," but more important, lexicographers on both sides of the Atlantic are flushed with excitement at the de-tabooization of a plain word that started out as a euphemism itself.

A lavatory is not a toilet but a handbasin. The typical bathroom contains a toilet (or water closet), a tub bath or a shower, and a lavatory. The sink belongs in the kitchen, the lavatory in the bathroom. Lavatory comes from the Latin and French and refers to washing.

Alfred Gray Reid
Littlebourne, England

Subjoin the Fun

"It seemed as if *toilet* was falling into disuse," I wrote in a piece on euphemisms, on my way to the *restroom, comfort station, john* or *loo.*

"A few days after your article appeared," responded Thomas E. Freeley of Evanston, Illinois, "Mike Royko used the same verb form in an 'if' clause. In an article in *The New York Times Travel* section, Lewis B. Frumkes did likewise. Whatever happened to the subjunctive mood?"

The subjunctive is alive and well and living in the language. At an Oxford University Press symposium at the Library of Congress, Robert Burchfield, the man who has just finished the four-volume supplement to the Oxford English Dictionary, gave the subjunctive a big plug: "This very useful verbal distinction is not at all tottering toward extinction." He gave as examples of hot, with-it subjunctive terms: *be that as it may, if I were you* and *suffice it to say.*

If it were not for the subjunctive, we would be less able to express desire, supposition, doubt; more important, we would find it hard to set up a situation contrary to fact—a shocker, something ridiculous—to see how we would deal with it. However, the subjunctive mood is getting kicked around and needs a few defenders.

Before we start, let's settle the tangential business of *as if* and *as though.* They are interchangeable. I prefer *if* because it is so clearly iffy; the archaic "if" sense of *though* has atrophied over the centuries, and is preserved only in this phrase, but *as though* is not incorrect; it's not as though it were a big deal.

What is a big grammatical deal is the mood of the verb that follows the *if.* Assume you're setting up a situation that ain't so; the signal you send to the reader not to believe what he sees is the subjunctive mood—not *is* or *was,* but the subjunctive *were.*

More than one close reader of this space had a donnybrook over my use of *was* (the indicative mood) in "It seemed as if *toilet* was falling into disuse." Jeff McQuain, my research associate here in Washington, held that the mood should be subjunctive, *were,* and predicted nitpicking letters if the *if* was followed by the indicative *was.* In New York, the copy editor argued that the situation described was not contrary to fact—that my point was that the word *toilet* was actually going down the drain—which meant that the indicative *was* was correct (just as it is in this sentence's "if the *if* was followed . . ."). We left it as *if* . . . *was* and awaited the nitpicking mail from the hardy breed of subjunctivarians, which blessedly came with Mr. Freeley's missive from Evanston.

Do not allow yourself to slip into a nongrammatical mood like the present depressive, because the distinction between subjunctive mood and indicative mood remains, as the sainted Burchfield and I insist, useful. A law professor testified at a recent Congressional hearing that Senator John C. Danforth's product-liability bill "reads as though it *were* written by James Joyce." Obviously, the bill was not written by the long-dead author of the punctuation-disdaining novel *Ulysses,* which meant that the witness's don't-you-believe-it subjunctive *were* was necessary; if the indicative, here-comes-a-fact *was* had been used, hordes of illiterate legislators would have been led to assume that James Joyce was a Danforth staffer.

Moreover, were it not for the subjunctive, we would have no way of quickly saying, "Look, I've taken liberties here, and my tongue is stuck slightly in my cheek, but you know what I mean—really, old fellow, I don't have to spell out what I mean in exhausting exactitude for someone of your sophistication." That shorthand expression is *as it were,* a use of the subjunctive coined by Chaucer six centuries ago—often with a gentle, self-deprecating cough—so speakers need not fill in the spaces with "as if it were so."

Is the subjunctive mood worth preserving? If I were James Joyce, I would say: Yes you bet it is yes yes yes always use *were* before a phrase contrary to fact yes yes but I always confuse *subjunctive* with *subjective* yes yes then stop using *subjective* and call that case *nominative* yes because *subjunctive* comes from *subjoin* which means "tacked on at the end" and that's what the mood does yes yes

Robert Burchfield's list of "examples of hot, with-it subjunctive terms" provides little evidence that "The subjunctive is alive and well and living in the language," since two of the three items on the list are fixed phrases that contain forms that are no longer used productively: while speakers of modern English do say *be that as it may* and *suffice it to say,* they don't say "*I wonder if that be possible*" or "*I doubt that it suffice to say that you are mistaken.*" Anyway, the uses of *be* and *suffice* in those two phrases are strictly speaking optative rather than subjunctive and have nothing to do with the form that you devote the next few paragraphs to defending.

James D. McCawley
Professor of Linguistics
University of Chicago
Chicago, Illinois

You got involved with the subjunctive over the universally misused "as if." Surely it is a simple conditional. There is an ellipse: "He looks as (he would look) if he *had* a cold." The point is bypassed when you use the past tense (he looked).

Alistair [Cooke]
New York, New York

I agree with your research associate that your sentence "It seemed as if *toilet* was falling into disuse" is in the past indicative and that *was* is correct, but the implication that *were* could have been used to express contrariness-to-fact is misleading. Since the time clearly is in the past (note "seemed"), the appropriate subjunctive form would be not the present subjunctive *were* but the past subjunctive *had been*, as in "If *toilet* had been falling into disuse back then, it would have disappeared by now."

That contrary subjunctive is signaled not so much by the use of *were* instead of *was* (a fine distinction that exists, after all, only in the first and third persons singular of *to be*) as by the use of a verb form more commonly used to shift the action into the past. In the subjunctive, the speaker's substitution of, say, *knew* for *know*, or *had known* for *knew*, leaves the time unchanged and indicates the speaker's disbelief.

Harvey Wachtel
Brooklyn, New York

Your concern that the subjunctive mood may be threatened is truly misplaced. To the contrary, the subjunctive threatens to displace the indicative mood—at least judging from the millions who man cash registers, switchboards, information booths, and reception desks throughout this country.

In the few isolated regions where telephone operators still give out numbers in a real human voice, you are likely to hear, "That number would be . . ." ("were it not disconnected"?). Cashiers at fast-food restaurants and other places where one pays in advance usually announce total tabs with "That would come to . . ." ("were we not closed for the day"?). Police officers, guards, receptionists, and others routinely asked for directions are increasingly likely to respond with something like "That would be about two miles from here . . ." ("were it not burned to the ground"?).

James R. Beniger
Los Angeles, California

Allow me to enter the fray concerning the sentence "It seemed as if *toilet* was falling into disuse."

I accept your rationale in using the indicative in this sentence. You seem to wish to say that the noun *toilet* appears to be falling into disuse; that this is a fact which you have observed.

The problem with the construction is that you have muddled your intention by using the subjunctive *signifier* "as if." The presence of "as if" in the construction as it stands implies an apparent state of affairs which is not in fact true. What you appear to wish to say is that *toilet* is not, emphatically, falling into disuse. And so, the indicative form rings false, and even contradictory.

Allow me to suggest that you use the indicative *signifier* "that." The sentence now reads "It seemed that *toilet* was falling into disuse."

Simple, solid declarative from beginning to end. C. T. Onions would be pleased.

James Cummings
San Francisco, California

Whether the subjunctive is useful or charming has little to do with whether it is a part of our living language. What determines grammatical viability is continued use by living speakers.

The examples you use to illustrate the grace of the subjunctive are petrified phrases that survive through continued idiomatic reinforcement: "If I were you . . . ," "Be that as it may . . ." Try the same constructions using words you've never heard in those constructions, and the subjunctive mood will sound stiff and ungrammatical: "If my aunt arrive by bus . . . ," or "Be he a poet or a truck driver . . ."

We have one construction in modern English in which the subjunctive is alive and well: following a set of verbs that express an indirect command or obligation. Examples:

"The new law requires that every driver wear a seat belt." *Wear* in the imbedded clause must be subjunctive.

"The director demanded that I be at my station early."

Try an indicative *was* or *am* after *I* and you'll hear the need for the subjunctive.

Notice that this use of the subjunctive does not depend on the iffyness of the clauses. Nor is the choice of mood a matter of conscious elegance. These sentences require the subjunctive mood because it is part of our living language.

Neil Daniel
English Professor
Texas Christian University
Fort Worth, Texas

Forget Me Not

Never forget: much can turn on the shadow of a meaning of the commonest of words.

In a New Orleans courtroom, with the Governor of Louisiana on trial on charges of racketeering, the United States Attorney cross-examined the accused. What about his failure to instruct his tax accountant to disclose a profit of $2 million, made between gubernatorial terms, on the sale of state certificates to build hospitals? "So you simply forgot!"

"I didn't *forget,*" Governor Edwin Edwards replied coolly, "because that implies a conscious attempt to remember." He said that the fact simply did not occur to him.

Reputations, sometimes verdicts, can hinge on such distinctions. We're not talking semantics here—we're talking time in the slammer. Does the verb *to forget* imply a conscious attempt to remember?

The etymology of the verb treats the mind as a million hands, each grasping a thought: to *forget* is "to lose one's hold" on one of those thoughts. In its earliest use, in King Alfred's 888 translation of Boethius's *Consolation of Philosophy,* the transitive verb meant "to lose remembrance of," implying the act of remembering before losing hold of the thought.

In a millennium, a word can develop different senses, each with a distinct meaning. One sense of *forget* is "neglect," the intentional disregard or omission of a thought; if the forgetting had been willful, the governor may have committed a crime. That was one reason he rejected the word with such alacrity.

Poets often treated the verb as meaning the determined putting of a thought out of mind. Christina Georgina Rossetti, in 1862, wrote, "When I am dead, my dearest/ Sing no sad songs for me," leaving the choice of remembering to her dearest: ". . . And if thou wilt, remember/ And if thou wilt, forget."

Similarly, when Shakespeare's Richard II questions the willful Northumberland's failure to kneel before him, he uses *forget* in the intentional sense: ". . . how dare thy joints forget/ To pay their aweful duty to our presence?"

Another sense is "to fail to recall"; that, too, suggests some attempt to recall, and the governor was not about to admit any such thing. However, yet another sense is "to omit inadvertently," and in that meaning, *forget* would be an innocent act—as the governor said, it simply did not occur to him.

Now that we have refreshed our recollection, let us turn to a term having to do with false memory: *déjà vu.*

"Legit Déjà Vu:" headlines *Variety,* "Grosses Up, Volume Off." Anybody who is familiar with Broadway parlance has heard that before: the hits are making more than ever before, but overall attendance is down. Oh, we've been there before.

The essence of *déjà vu,* French for "already seen," is not that you have been there before, but that you have the illusion, a false impression, that you have been there before. In psychology, the term entered English usage in the early 1900s, first appearing in Frederic W. H. Myers's *Human Personality,* to describe a form of paramnesia, or false memory: the subject believes that a new experience is not really new, but has been lived through before, sometimes because it has been seen in a dream.

That nice distinction has broken down; today, *déjà vu* means "passé" and is a staple of preppy talk.

The governor, by the way, was blessed with a hung jury, and thus is a free, if forgetful, man. That's the way it so often goes: *déjà vu.*

The following quote poignantly expresses Ernest Hemingway's opinion on the lack of volition in forgetting: "A broken heart means that never can you remember and not to be able to remember is very different from forgetting."

Lisa C. Franks
Springfield, Pennsylvania

The Former Latter

I n this book you've probably tripped over a *former-latter* construction and wondered: "Why does he write that way? Getting lazy?" I've done it to make the point that we can do without formers and latters.

The *Washington Post* may have broken the habit for many of us. "The question remains," wrote the editorialist, "whether the United States is better off assuming its own strategic responsibilities in the region and, within Nicaragua proper, betting on Latin American mediation rather than on contra military action." Having posed that question, the editorialist answered: "After the raid into Honduras, as before, we would go the latter way."

We all have days like that, knocking ourselves out posing the question and not having zip left for the answer. A couple of days later, the *Post* wrote: "We mixed up a 'former' with a 'latter' in our editorial . . . it was a linguistic slip, not a political change of heart. As between Latin American mediation and contra military action in Nicaragua, we continue to favor the *former.*"

Jacob C. Fritz of Falls Church, Virginia, writes to object to former-latter pretension: "No one retains what he reads that well that he can remember what was the former and the latter without going back to read over the preceding sentence." He's right; why make the reader do the work for you, if you're too lazy to straighten it out yourself?

Belay the poor formers and mad latters. Pundits of the world, recast your sentences and re-pose your questions. "The Formers and the Latters" is a good name for a rock group.

Free Fall onto a Sandbag

"Fain would I climb," wrote Sir Walter Raleigh on a windowpane of some English palace, "yet fear I to fall."

According to Thomas Fuller, in his 1662 *History of the Worthies of England,* Queen Elizabeth wrote beneath those lines this challenging response: "If thy heart fails thee, climb not at all."

The word *fain* turned out to be fleeting, and romantic windowpane graffiti have been replaced by spray-painted slogans on subway cars, but *fall* is still with us. However, *fall*—in the sense of dropping from great heights— now requires a modifier. If the angel Lucifer were thrown out of Heaven these days, his loss of Paradise and descent into Hell would be chronicled by epic poets as *The Free Fall.*

Vice President Bush used this locution recently, and placed it in the perspective of its simile of origin: "I think it is essential that we talk about stability," he said on the eve of a trip to the land of sinking oil prices, "and that we not just have a continued *free fall* like a parachutist jumping out without a parachute."

Mr. Bush is evidently not a sky diver. For a derivation of *free fall* (I prefer two words; sky divers like one. You can use either, but stay away from hyphenation in the noun, because we need it for the compound adjective), let us consult Larry Jaffe, editor of *Parachutist* magazine, as he drifts over Alexandria, Virginia.

"*Free fall* means the time between exit from an airplane and the opening of the parachute," shouts Mr. Jaffe to an interviewer below. How long is the average *free fall?* "It can be a minimum of a second or two, or you could have an 80-second *free fall* of roughly 12,000 feet."

What does a parachutist call the period after *free fall,* when you are supported by the open parachute? "We prefer *sky diver* to *parachutist,* by the way, but to answer your question, there is no parallel word for the period after *free fall.* The technical term is *descent under canopy.*"

The neologism *driftdown* springs to mind, and the acronym for *descent under canopy* also seems apt, but on second thought, Mr. Jaffe comes up with this differentiation: "*Sky diving* refers to the portion of the jump spent in *free fall,* while *parachuting* is used more to describe the time after the parachute opens." He floated to what economists and moon shooters call a *soft landing.*

Free fall, used often by financial writers in the last decade, is a cliché adopted by experts on oil pricing, the same folks who gave us *a world awash in oil;* as a result, we are now in a *free-fall glut.* (Note the hyphenation needed for the compound adjective; aren't you glad we didn't use it for the compound noun?)

The *free* is similarly used in *free drop,* a parachute jump in which the chute is released by the jumper (which one of these things is the rip cord?), and not one in which the chute is opened by a static line attached to the aircraft. The earliest use of *free fall* was by the rocket pioneer Robert H. Goddard, who wrote in 1919: "The time of descent [of a rocket] will also be short; but *free fall* can be satisfactorily prevented by a suitable parachute."

Metaphorically, however, oil-industry sources and Calamity Janeways need a term to describe the time after *free fall. Float* is out, because it has a banking connotation; perhaps *thud.*

Any first-year physics student should be able to tell you that free fall is fall under the influence of gravity alone, without restraining forces. A body dropping in a vacuum—remember our astronauts' experiments on the moon?—descends in free fall. If a dish slips out of your hand, it crashes to the ground very nearly in free fall because air resistance is so small. But a leaf or feather floating to the ground is not in free fall because of the severe retarding effect of the air (as with a parachute).

A human being stepping out of an airplane without benefit of a 'chute encounters progressively greater air resistance as his downward speed increases. Eventually, the force of gravity pulling our unfortunate subject down is practically balanced by the opposing upward force of the air, and our man continues his descent at an almost constant *terminal* velocity—about 150 miles per hour. (The italicized word is standard physicist's usage; it has nothing to do with the victim's fate on splashdown.)

Michael Robinson
New York, New York

Free World, So-Called

A note came in from a right-wing presidential aide after I had entitled an essay about the use of color for political classification "Wave of the Fuchsia." The message was brief and pointed—"Your friends are worried"—but the notepaper caught my attention. Instead of the simple blue-on-white "The White House, Washington," there was a yellow stick-on paper with the printed heading "If This Gets into the Hands of the Russians, It's Curtains for the Free World."

The phrase *Free World* is used ironically there, to establish a bezazzy, out-of-date, "Hiya, sweetheart, get me Rewrite" tone. For nearly two decades the phrase has been in intellectual disfavor, but of late it has begun to be reasserted with pride and perhaps defiance.

Free World, capitalized, filled the vacuum created by the need for an antonym for *Communist World*. It was born in the labor movement and was organized labor's most powerful contribution to the language since the preceding century's *full dinner pail, solidarity* and *pie in the sky.*

A gathering of trade unions from Western nations that styled itself the Free World Labor Congress met from June to November 1949 in Geneva and London. The phrase first appeared in public print in the December 12, 1949, *Time* magazine: "In London's County Hall last week, 261 delegates from 53 countries, representing some 48 million members, met to launch a new international non-Communist labor organization. Provisional title: the Free World Labor Congress."

That name, however, was not chosen; instead, the group, still both free and worldly, calls itself the International Confederation of Free Trade Unions. The reason for the switch, according to Murray Seeger of the AFL–CIO, is this: "The name had to include both the words *free* and *union*, to differentiate them from the Communist-dominated organization calling itself the World Federation of Trade Unions, which still operates today from Prague." Thus, the Western labor leaders substituted *International* for the Communists' *World* and *Confederation* for *Federation* and stuck *Free* in front of *Trade Union* to cast aspersions on the unfree "unions."

Time subsequently used the rejected phrase without capitalization: "In the free world," it wrote in 1951, "there was jubilation. . . ." The Eisenhower Administration liked it: Ike wrote a memo to John Foster Dulles in 1955 about "actions best calculated to sustain the interests of ourselves and the free world."

The Russians, naturally, didn't like it. Their propagandists had already captured the words *people's, democratic* and *peaceloving*; by retaliating with the capture of *free*, the Western industrial nations implied that the Communist world was not free. Nikita S. Khrushchev reacted with a sneering modifier in 1959: "The so-called free world constitutes the kingdom of the dollar."

In the late 1960s, the phrase began appearing inside quotation marks, as the freedoms of the non-Communist world were criticized from within (or, as my right-wing friend would put it, the era of Vietnam-Watergate self-flagellation began). The phrase underwent a decline in the 1970s, as its use was recognized as "loaded" in favor of the West, although the Communists felt no such compunctions about arraying their *peaceloving peoples* against the *ruling circles* of their adversaries. In his book *How Democracies Perish*, the French conservative philosopher Jean-François Revel defined this trend within a pair of dashes: "Detractors of the United States and the 'free world'—the expression is usually employed as a term of derision, as though there were not really a free world and a slave world. . . ."

In the 1980s, *free world*—usually not capitalized—took on a new life. Midge Decter and a bipartisan group of neoconservatives organized into an unabashed Committee for the Free World in 1981. Asserts Miss Decter: "We used the term *the free world* in naming our committee four years ago. It's not *a* free world because that implies hope for achieving freedom in the future; it's *the* free world because it's here now. As a term, it denotes something rare and precious, something that involves privileges that are unfortunately not available to vast numbers of humanity."

Bill:

I recall hearing "free world" first used in World War II to refer to the non-Axis world. The phrase MAY have originated with Henry Wallace, but that's speculation. I once had a book of his speeches from the period and my recollection is that one was titled "The Price of Free World Victory." I believe the book was titled *Century of the Common Man.* You might be able to find a copy.

Anyway, a footnote on page 2 of John Lewis Gaddis's "The United States and the Origins of the Cold War" mentions a Wallace speech May 8, 1942, to the Free World Association. That definitely pins down the time period.

There was also a *Free World* magazine, which I think I first saw around 1945. Max Ascoli wrote for it, as I recall, and so did Orson Welles, who dallied in that sort of thing.

I have no firm recollection of names of any other writers. The magazine died after a few years.

> Glad [Dean Gladfelter]
> National Desk
> The New York Times
> New York, New York

You place the origins of the words "free world" in the context of growing anti-communism. In fact, the term was used at least eight years earlier in an anti-Fascist sense.

Back in 1941 a political journal, *Free World,* was founded in New York as an anti-Fascist publication. Its editorial board and staff included both liberals and leftists, plus a few card-carrying Communists.

> Dr. Jan-Christopher Horak
> Associate Curator, Film
> George Eastman House
> Rochester, New York

Was that a gathering of trade unions, or rather trade union*ists?* Unions are organizations, and to say they meet together unnecessarily anthropomorphizes them. Not that this usage is entirely improper. But wouldn't it be better, in this increasingly impersonal world, to reinforce with words the fact that these are individuals acting to assemble of their own free will?

Referring to things when we mean people, especially people in large groups, seems to be a natural tendency in the language, and I think it should be resisted. When seven heads of state gather each summer for the economic summit meeting, it is a forum not of the leading industrial nations but of their several leaders, who represent those nations. When the American Economics Association holds its convention, it is a meeting not of economics but of economists. The Socialist International is a body not of socialism but of socialists.

> Jeffrey Kutler
> Editor of Transition
> New York, New York

Full-Tilt Boogie

When the dry-cleaning man pulls his spotless truck up to my back door, I like to hand out my wrinkled pants with the order, "Give this a full-court press."

Full-court press is a basketball term, as supporters of the Bradley-Gephardt tax proposal know, meaning "a tactic in which defenders closely guard the opposing team man-to-man the full length of the court." The object is to force a mistake or steal the ball by disrupting the normal offensive game, and the phrase has been taken into the general language, meaning "all-out effort." (A *zone press*, on the other hand, is like spot cleaning.)

Forbes magazine recently wrote about tax proposals, including the one urged by Senator Bill Bradley, a New Jersey Democrat, a former basketball star, in this way: "Nobody expects anything serious to happen until next January. But then we could have a full-tilt boogie over tax reforms."

Mitch Krauss of Newark writes to ask: "Is there a *half-tilt* or *partial-tilt boogie*? Am I getting old? Is *Forbes* so with-it they've left me behind?"

Malcolm Forbes, whose letterhead reads "Chairman & Chief Executive Officer" as well as "Editor-in-Chief" (must be the boss), sends along this internal memo to him explaining the phrase: *"Full-tilt boogie* is an all-out dance to rock music, which roughly translates into an all-out effort. Apparently was a song title some years back."

I like it. We'll soon see if the cleaning man understands.

A full-court press can be either a man-to-man, a trap (where the defense may swarm to one person with the basketball, a variation of the man-to-man) or a zone (except in the NBA) where the defense players cover territory on the court rather than an individual player.

A half-court press may use the same three types of defense.

If you had your pants zone-pressed, they would still be entirely covered, unless you only asked for half a job.

In other words, the type of defense deployed is not to be confused with the area it is to cover.

Paul A. Weisenfeld
Santa Monica, California

A zone press is not a press that is applied only in certain zones of the court, but a press in which each defensive player guards a particular area of the court rather than a particular offensive player. Thus a press may be applied over the whole court (a full-court press) or only over half the court (a half-court press). Either variety may be "man-to-man" or "zone." Thus a zone press is not like spot cleaning. Sorry about that.

Kenneth Shaw
Brooklyn, New York

You define a full-court press as "a tactic in which defenders closely guard the opposing team man-to-man the full length of the court." As an erstwhile defender, I beg to differ. A full-court press means pressure defense the full length of the court, but it can be man-to-man pressure or zone pressure. The first-ranked Georgetown basketball team, for example, plays a full-court zone press, with its defenders assigned to areas of the court, and its seven-foot All-American center responsible for the area closest to the basket.

Hence, you are wrong in saying that a zone press is "like spot cleaning." The better analogy, it would seem, is that a half-court press (which again can be either man-to-man or zone) is like doing just the pants.

Paul Shechtman
New York, New York

Full Tilt Boogie, so far as I recollect, was not the name of a song. It was Janis Joplin's last back-up group. She dubbed them the Full Tilt Boogie Band early in 1970 and it was appropriate to her headlong, hedonistic style. You can hear them on her posthumous *Pearl* album (which includes my first song and generated such royalties that I left my job as a *Village Voice* music critic, moved up to the country and painted my mailbox purple).

Obviously, the phrase was in circulation when Janis chose it and someone else can probably tell you more of its origin. I believe it came out of California, as did much of the hippie culture in those days. And it meant just what it sounds like: going at it with all strength and abandon. Full tilt also makes me think of pinball machines and windmills (Quixote). The boogie part is a slightly musical underpinning but in your citation of it, I sense the usage of "Let's boogie" which means

"Let's go" or "Let's rock on out of here." Get the picture of cruising down the road at a steady, merry clip?

Johanna Hall
Saugerties, New York

"Full Tilt Boogie" was the name of the band that played with Janis Joplin on her last, and arguably her best, album "Pearl."

We early baby-boomers may have subsequently transformed into corporate tigers, flaming capitalists or astonishingly middle-class parents, but it's nice to know that our "language" is making inroads into the American business lexicon!

(Mrs.) Ellen Rand
Teaneck, New Jersey

The Gift of Words

"He who writes badly thinks badly," charged William Cobbett, the English grammarian and vituperator. That will come as a shock to all those who are certain they think brilliantly but lack the knack of putting their thoughts on paper, or concoct the excuse that they just don't have the patience to compose prose.

The corollary: By learning to write clearly, we learn to think clearly. Toward year's end, this department recommends books that make good gifts for those who want to hook their friends and relatives on writing with precision, grace, color and clarity. (And the greatest of these is clarity.)

Write to the Point, by Bill Stott (Anchor Press/Doubleday—and the publisher should use a hyphen rather than a virgule, or another formulation, like Doubleday's Anchor Press—$7.95 paperback). This is the year's best book for encouraging the beginning, or the intimidated, writer. Stott's style is punchy and breezy—"What to Do When a Sentence Stinks" is a typical subchapter—and his advice is sound. In that case: "Change it. How? Easy. Read a stinky sentence over. Figure out what it means. Now

. . . put the sentence's meaning in your own words. . . . You may have to expand the sentence into two or three sentences. That's allowed."

Edit Yourself, by Bruce Ross-Larson (Norton, $11.95), is a book to use after you have been emboldened by Stott to get started. Here can be found useful suggestions about editing: change *in order to* to *to*, *have an impact on* to *affect*, *preliminary to* to *before*. Good words to cut: *it, of course, ideally, in the final analysis, the field of, the level of, the area of, the nature of,* and *rather* as a modifier. This book came out two years ago and is still available; a paperback house would be wise to snap it up and widen its audience. (How do you get *it* out of that?)

The Origins of English Words, by Joseph Shipley (Johns Hopkins, $39.95). If you are feeling flush and know someone who digs deep etymology, Shipley's discursive dictionary is your meat. This is a scholarly tome with a willingness to discurse—to wander around a bit, chewing things over with the reader. Under the Indo-European *leubh*, root of the Latin *libet* (meaning "desires, love"), which led to *libido* and *libertine*, Shipley veers off into the lines of the Irish playwright Isaac Bickerstaffe, writing around 1800: "Perhaps it was wise to dissemble your love/But—why did you kick me downstairs?"

If you know a speechwriter who needs a lift, try Robert Orben's *2400 Jokes to Brighten Your Speeches* (Doubleday, $14.95).

For a wordlover's gift that keeps on yakking, try a year's subscription to *Verbatim*, Laurence Urdang's lively and informative language quarterly (four issues, $10; Box 668, Essex, Connecticut 06426). This periodical is getting stronger every year, so there is hope for the language.

The granddaddy of linguistic quarterlies, *American Speech*, is carrying on in the grand tradition under Ronald Butters's editorship. (A note at the end of the current issue asks if any readers have heard of *tony nut* as a synonym for *filbert*.) This sprightliest of learned journals costs $15 for four issues (University of Alabama Press, P.O. Box 2877, University, Alabama 35486).

If your interest is more narrowly lexicographical and directed to neologisms, add on *The Barnhart Dictionary Companion*, which slips behind a few months occasionally but is still ahead of the dictionaries on new words (four issues, $50; Lexik House, P.O. Box 247, 75 Main Street, Cold Spring, New York 10516). Another periodical, called *English Today*, is being launched in Britain. (A free preview issue is available from Cambridge University Press, 32 East Fifty-seventh Street, New York, New York 10022.)

As a Cobbett nut, I am giving friends the paperback reprint of his 1819 *Grammar of the English Language . . . Intended for the Use of Schools and of Young Persons in General; but more especially for the Use of Soldiers, Sailors,*

Apprentices, and Ploughboys. To Which are Added Six Lessons, intended to pre-
vent Statesmen from using false grammar, and from writing in an awkward man-
ner.

They're not titling grammars like that anymore. The man about whom
the phrase "fourth estate" was coined is no fuddy-duddy on usage: "What
a whole people adopts and universally practices, must, in such cases, be
deemed correct."

This reprint has an introduction by Robert Burchfield, editor of the
Oxford English Dictionary, and is a bargain at $4.95 in United States
bookstores and through Oxford University Press at 200 Madison Avenue,
New York, New York 10016. If this turns you on to William Cobbett, get
"Great Cobbett: The Noblest Agitator," by Daniel Green ($24.95; distrib-
uted in the United States by David & Charles, P.O. Box 57, North Pomfret, Vermont 05053).

> "By learning to write clearly, we learn to think clearly" is certainly
> *not* a corollary of "He who writes badly thinks badly." The correct
> consequence is the converse of Safire's "corollary": "He who thinks
> well writes well" (technically, this is called the contrapositive). Safire's
> conclusion isn't too arguable, however; it's a consequence of the emi-
> nently reasonable "He who thinks badly writes badly."
>
> *Jeffrey S. Simonoff*
> *Assistant Professor of Statistics*
> *New York University Graduate School*
> *of Business Administration*
> *New York, New York*

For years sportswriters and announcers have been congenitally unable to refer to the Rose Bowl football game in any way but "the
granddaddy of all bowl games." To my horror they now refer to the
Wimbledon Tennis Tournament as "the granddaddy of all tennis tour-
naments." Indeed just about any event that predates others in its class
suffers from this lamentable locution.

But never, *never* did I expect my favorite word-watcher to sink to
such depths. That you are alluding to the venerable quarterly *Ameri-*
can Speech makes the phrase especially unpalatable. What's wrong with
"the oldest" or "the original" or "the earliest"?

Mr. Safire, please give me your assurance that you will never use
this not only trite but "cutesy" expression again.

Van Cunningham
Alfred, New York

You credit William Cobbett with the quip: "He who writes badly thinks badly." Cobbett was not the first to say that; it was Pericles. He wrote: "The man who can think and does not know how to express what he thinks is at the level of him who cannot think." Those who want to learn to write with precision, grace, color and clarity should read *aloud* Plato, Montaigne, Voltaire and Proust.

                                                      Paul Mocsanyi
                                                      New York, New York

Gifts of Gab

'T is the season to shower worldly goods on wordlovers. (*'Tis* is an itsypooism for *It is*; never use a construction that began in poetry and song and has been overworked by off-key, holly-draped copywriters. Never start a sentence with "It is," either; that sort of lollygagging up to a subject puts the reader to sleep. That sentence should read, "Wordly goods should, in this season, be showered on wordlovers." OK, now—back to the Christmas spirit, tra-la-la, with our annual holiday visit to Deserved Plugsville, to guide shoppers to gifts for literate loved ones.)

Dare to give the first volume of the projected five-volume DARE—the Dictionary of American Regional English, which the with-it merchandisers at Harvard's Belknap Press say is $49.95 until year's end, and after that the bookseller will throw you out of the store for asking for it. (I don't like that "buy-now-or-you'll-pay-through-the-nose" sales gimmick, but I do like Dr. Fred Cassidy's monumental achievement in DARE's dialectology.) You cannot tell a chipmunk from a ground squirrel without this book.

If you need mnemonics to help you remember anything—and I wish I could figure out a way to remember *mnemonic*, or why a syllable beginning with an *m* is pronounced *knee*, or even why *knee* starts with a *k* and not a *g*, as in *gnu*—try Michele Slung's *The Absent-Minded Professor's Memory Book* (Ballantine, paperback $5.95). I now walk around saying "Nights Grow Darker After August," which draws curious glances from colleagues, but which is supposed to remind me of the declensions of Latin (nominative, genitive, dative, ablative, accusative). On how to pronounce *quay:* "When by the quay, think of the sea." Only problem for musicians: "Every Good Boy Does Fine" is sexist. Miss Slung (that's her real name, not the past tense of anything) is also the author of "Momilies," a good blending of *mom* and *homilies*, such as "If you swallow the stone, a cherry tree grows in your stomach."

Lengthen your life by shortening your sentences: if you do not have *Simple and Direct*, by Jacques Barzun, in your library, you're doing without a classic (Harper & Row, paperback $6.95). This year, the Modern Language Association has brought out *Line by Line: How to Edit Your Own Writing*, by Claire Kehrwald Cook (Houghton Mifflin, $14.95). This is more helpful than hortatory, with solid sections on putting modifiers in their places (avoid the lonely *only*) and how to come to grips with a comma. In an appendix of usage, Mrs. Cook has the most lucid approach to *comprise*, as opposed to *compose* or *constitute*, that I've seen: "If you are not sure that you have used *comprise* correctly, try substituting the corresponding form of *include*. If it fits, you have the right word. If it doesn't, try *compose*."

I Always Look Up the Word "Egregious" is the title of Maxwell Nurnberg's little classic, published a few years ago by Prentice-Hall at $5.95, and still around and selling (you hear that, Belknap?). In his prolegomenon, a word for "preface" dealt with recently in this space, Mr. Nurnberg explains his title by telling of a friend who used *eclectic* because "I just happened to come across it in the dictionary." He was on his way to looking up *egregious* and the other word caught his eye. Asked how he happened to be looking up *egregious*, the man replied "I always look up the word *egregious!*"

The best pronunciation guide to names since the more extensive NBC Handbook is *Klee as in Clay*, by Wilfred J. McConkey (University Press of America, paperback $3.95). It straightens out architects (Marcel BROY-ur, le core-boozy-AY, mees-van-dare-ROE-uh), reminds you that a couple writers have the first names Ayn and Anaïs—Ayn, which rhymes with nine (Rand) and uh-NIGH-is (Nin)—and even reaches out that finger to touch the Sistine ceiling painter, Mick (not Mike) el-AN-jullo.

If wordwise magazine subscriptions are your thing, try *American Speech, A Quarterly of Linguistic Usage*, $15 from the University of Alabama Press, University, Alabama 35486-2877, and the growing language quarterly *Verbatim*, $10, Box 668, Essex, Connecticut 06426.

Philip Howard of *The Times* of London has turned out an original and thoughtful book. He usually beats me to the punch on zingy titles for column collections (*Words Fail Me, A Word in Your Ear*), but this year he has written a book from scratch (and, one hopes, for much scratch) titled *The State of the Language* (Oxford University Press, $14.95). In a delectably punctuated paragraph decrying the misuse of the dash, he practices what he preaches, which writers on language like to do to reinforce their message:

"All we can do is hang on to our colons: punctuation is bound to change, like the rest of language; punctuation is made for man, not man for punctuation; a good sentence should be intelligible without the help of punctuation in most cases; and, if you get in a muddle with your dots and dashes, you may need to simplify your thoughts, and shorten your sentence."

He's right—the slapdash use of dashes is egregious—meaning "outstandingly undesirable"—which I know because I looked it up.

I suggest you try muttering "Nights Grow Darker August After" or else give up Latin. Any number of classicists will by now have advised you that the order of declension is "Nominative, Genitive, Dative, Accusative, Ablative." Or perhaps you were lacking for incoming correspondence.

As for your difficulty remembering the pronunciation of "mnemonic," try thinking of it as similar to another Greek initial double-consonant, such as "chthonic."

Paul Ambos
New Brunswick, New Jersey

Re: your interdiction on beginning a sentence with "It is," I quote the opening of *Pride and Prejudice:*

It is a truth universally acknowledged, that a single man in possession of a good fortune, must be in want of a wife."

It is good enough for me.

Sylvia Alberts
New York, New York

You say, "Never start a sentence with 'it is' . . . that sort of lollygagging up to a subject puts the reader to sleep."

Mostly, you're right. But of course there are times when you want to sidle up to an assertion; when you want to frame what you have to say with phraseology that suggests you are thinking it out as you speak; or when you want to use a narrative tone of voice.

It is also true, I think (note how I cozy up to you) that "it" is sometimes a referent-less pronoun and sometimes a tight, relative pronoun. What you wrote is not only too sweeping. It is verbally insensitive.

David Jenness
Washington, D.C.

Go with the Flow

I n a piece about the moving-around and shaking-out that took place at
the start of Mr. Reagan's second term, I recalled the time that Richard
M. Nixon demanded the resignations of everyone in order to avoid having
the country run by "exhausted volcanoes." I thought he was quoting Disraeli about Gladstone.

The Gotcha! Gang promptly struck in the person of Senator Daniel P.
Moynihan, Democrat of New York, the Nixon aide in 1972 who slipped a
biography of Disraeli into the President's night reading.

"I can't find the remark," he writes, "but I am dead certain it was not
about Gladstone but rather of the Whig (or Tory) front bench. . . ."

The Senator's recollection is only partially accurate: Disraeli's metaphor-
ical use of volcanoes was directed at Gladstone's ministers, if not the Prime
Minister himself, in a speech at Manchester on April 3, 1872. According to
Britain's Dictionary of National Biography, it was to extinct volcanoes that
Disraeli "likened the heads of departments in Mr. Gladstone's Govern-
ment, as he sat opposite to them in the House of Commons."

In *The Speeches of the Earl of Beaconsfield,* Vol. II, this passage from Disraeli erupts: "As I sat opposite the Treasury Bench the ministers reminded
me of one of those marine landscapes not very unusual on the coast of
South America. You behold a range of exhausted volcanoes. Not a flame
flickers on a single pallid crest. But the situation is still dangerous."

Good Night, Irenic

T he Harvard Divinity School is searching for a scholar to fill an endowed chair for the study of Judaism. The likeliest choice for the post
was Dr. Jacob Neusner, a Brown University professor and co-director of its
renowned Program in Judaic Studies.

That was before Professor Neusner saw that one of the qualifications specified for the position was "an irenic personality." *Irenic* means "peaceful," with additional connotations of "calm, serene, undisturbed"; Irene was the Greek goddess of peace, parallel to the Roman Pax.

That adjective, as all who know him will attest, does not describe the iconoclastic Jack Neusner. In a letter asking that his name be removed from further consideration, he wrote: "My hero has always been Jeremiah and, alas, he too never turned out to be . . . irenic." The prolific Talmudic scholar must also have been aware of the theological sense of *irenics,* "the doctrine of promoting peace among contentious Christian churches."

In an era of arms-control talk, with *peace-loving* a word the Communists have made their own, you might think we would see more of *irenic.* Careful how you use it, though—as they have learned at Harvard Divinity School, it can trigger a jeremiad (which the dictionaries still define as "a long tale of woe," but has gained the sense of "an irate blast of complaint").

The Gotcha! Gang Strikes

The Gotcha! Gang is that shock troop of Lexicographic Irregulars who specialize in correcting other language mavens. Their delight is catching grammarians with their syntax down; their symbol is the hoist petard, and their patron saint goes by the name of U. Ofallpeople.

Gotcha! gangsters in the federal government call themselves "wordsleblowers," an awkward play on *whistleblowers.* Like the latter, the "wordsleblowers" point to hidden corruption in government, specializing in exposés of linguistic or grammatical wrongdoing.

The United States Commerce Department, sometimes derogated as "the Fourteenth Street Rope-Sellers' Association" by hard-liners who deplore technology transfer to the Soviet Union, has its resident "wordsleblower." Munching on a sub rosa, this hoagy hero seeks to torpedo Secretary of Commerce Malcolm Baldrige, a political poor boy who has made much of his campaign to rid his department of the grinders of bureaucratese.

Early in the first Reagan term, Secretary Baldrige circulated a memorandum titled "The Secretary's Writing Style," admonishing those who wrote to him or for him against the turgid prose of federal officialdom. The memo began, "Clarity and brevity are key factors when preparing a letter for the Secretary." (*Key Factor* is a very small island off the tip of Florida, leeward of *Key Aide* and windward of *Key Role*. That sentence might better have read, "When preparing a letter for the Secretary, be clear and be brief.")

The Secretary was rightly hailed for setting forth such rules as these: "Use the active rather than the passive voice. Avoid wordiness. Keep sentences lean and short. Do not use nouns or adjectives as verbs, such as *to impact, to interface, it obsoletes.*" Purists were delighted by these demands: "Use the precise word or phrase: *datum* (singular), *data* (plural); *think* is mental, *feel* is physical or emotional (think thoughts; feel feelings)."

The Squad Squad saluted him for banishing such redundancies as *enclosed herewith, end result, future plans, subject matter, important essentials, new initiatives, personally reviewed* and *serious crisis.* The Bromide Brigade considered him a hero for putting a halt to the overuse of pretentious verbs like *effectuate, enhance, facilitate, orient, target,* nouns like *input, output, overview, thrust,* and the timeworn phrases that appear in so many letters from lazy government officials: *I share your concern; I regret I cannot be more responsive, as you are aware.*

Instead of *prior to,* urged the Secretary, use *before;* instead of the cravenly conditional *I would hope,* use *I hope;* instead of *more importantly,* use *more important;* instead of *at the present time,* use *at this time* (and never *in this time frame* or *at this point in time*).

These were not idle suggestions or the frenetic bleats of a Miss Thistlebottom, unable to stem the tide of solecism or wave of fuzziness. In the age of the programmable typewriter, English maven Baldrige was able to make some of his suggestions stick: when a Commerce Department typist types the bureaucratic favorite, *maximize,* into her machine, the machine's memory stops the typewriter from clicking out the word; instead, a series of *x*'s appears. That's getting tough; would that the rope-sellers of Fourteenth Street were as tough on the Russians.

Then the Secretary, afflicted with grammatical hubris, went a step further: he put out amendments to his style memo. One was to stop the *-ize* from smiling: no more *finalize, optimize, prioritize* or *utilize* (use *use*). The other was to stamp out sexism in language by using *mail carrier* instead of *postman, police officer* rather than *policeman*—both good ideas, as more workers in these categories are women, and extending to the more controversial *committeeperson* and *chairperson.*

The "wordsleblowers" of the Gotcha! Gang rose up and got their copying machines going at night. The Secretary's covering memo—if it is not a forgery—was reproduced as evidence that the preacher was not practicing: "Attached is an updated Writing Style Memorandum," Mr. Baldrige had written. Then came this garble: "It has been as amended to discourage use of elimination of gender specific language as well as all 'ize' words."

One of the moles sent it along to Lex-Irreg headquarters with a list of corrections: "Note that the second sentence has not been proofread. He should have eliminated *as* and *elimination of.* He should have hyphenated *gender-specific* because it is a compound adjective modifying *language,* and his *ize* should be written *-ize* to show it deals with suffixes." Another mole added: "*Update* is clearly one of the words that the Secretary would not like. Why not use the word *current?* And why is he using the passive voice?"

I put in a call to the house on Fourteenth Street, refusing, as is my wont, to give his assistant the subject (not subject matter) of my call. Secretary Baldrige came on the line, probably with an explanation on the tip of his tongue about why he was approving the shipment of the latest compact-disk technology to Colonel Muammar el-Qaddafi, when I blindsided him with the writing-style memo.

"Did I write that?" he asked. That was his signature on the copy, I assured him. There was that awkward pause that comes when a man finds it impossible to point out that he wished he never had succumbed to the use of an autopen, which permits others to sign what seems to be his name. "I never use *update,* always *bring up to date.* And I don't like that *person* stuff." He sighed the sigh of a man corrected for trying to aid the cause of correctness. "If it came out of my shop, I'm responsible. Sock it to me."

As one who was recently castigated for misunderstanding the phrase "Good fences make good neighbors," and having often been told by the relentless Gotcha! gangsters of the Nitpickers' League to pull up my socks, I have therefore pulled my punch. (One pulls punches; one pulls *up* socks.) Stick to your guns, Malcolm Baldrige; I am willing to approve the shipment of your jargon-zapping typewriters to the Russians.

I find it highly unlikely that the symbol of the "Gotcha! Gang" would be the "hoist petard." It is not the petard that is hoisted; it is what it is attached to, if only momentarily, that is.

A petard is an explosive device, I am sure your many readers have informed you by now, used for breaching walls; also, it was a firework used to simulate the sound of musketry. The object to which the petard was fixed was "hoist" or hoisted, rather than the petard itself.

The word petard, in the phrase "hoist by his own petard," which appears to be what you had in mind, refers specifically to intestinal gas. In that sense, in plain English, a petard is a fart, and it is he who breaks wind in a small enclosed place who is "hoist by his own pe-tard," that is, victimized by his own effluvia.

A. I. Schutzer
Tenafly, New Jersey

"As you are aware" is a marvelous multidimensional weapon in the arsenal of knowing mid-level bureaucrats. Approximately eighty percent of the time it is used, the phrase carries an important hidden meaning: "As you should be aware, but are obviously not or you wouldn't have made such a numskull proposal (or complaint)." It is perfect for use with the average Assemblyman or Deputy Commissioner. You can insult under the guise of a servile attempt at a weak compliment or a lapse of tight style and still keep your job.

Five percent of the time, the phrase is used in a conspiritorial sense meaning: "You and I are aware, but you can bet on it that very few of the defective dolts we have to deal with have the slightest idea what we are talking about."

Another five percent of the time, this noble phrase acts as an ego assuager for politically connected nabobs. Its overt and covert message intertwine something like: "OK, Congressman, so you do know something about the spawning habits of smelt. Do you want me to genuflect before or after I yawn?"

Only in the remaining ten percent of the cases is the use of this phrase a result of linguistic laziness. And, as you are aware, we need this ten percent to cover us in our other uses.

Karl E. Felsen
Albany, New York

Gypping the Pharisaic Tribe

People are becoming more sensitive to racial, religious or cultural slurs. Some take umbrage, others take offense, and a few take pen in hand to demand that whoever is in charge of the language take action to change meanings or put a stop to common usage.

One example: *tribe.*

Mangosuthu G. Buthelezi is chief minister of the KwaZulu homeland and chairman of the South African Black Alliance. He takes umbrage at anybody who calls the Zulus a "tribe." In a letter to the *Washington Post,* Mr. Buthelezi writes: "We Zulus regard it as a gross insult to be described . . . as 'a tribe.' The Zulu people were a sovereign nation with a king until July 4, 1879, when they were crushed in a defeat by the might of the British Army. . . . The fact that as a nation we were conquered does not make us 'a tribe.' " He compares the seven million Zulus with the half-million Swazis, whose Swaziland is a nation represented in the United Nations, and calls on commentators to stop insulting his people by describing them as a mere tribe.

The root of *tribe* is probably the Latin *tri-*, "three"; a *tribus* was one of three groups into which Romans originally were divided. For a time, the word meant "clan, community under a leader or chief, from common ancestors," but in time has come to connote a preliterate society. (*Preliterate* is a euphemism for *illiterate*, suggesting that literacy is surely on the way.) American Indians, who look askance at the Washington Redskins and prefer to be called "Native Americans," find no slur in the word *tribe*, though their leaders often prefer *nation*, as in *the Cherokee nation*, when referring to a group of tribes.

A couple of decades ago, denizens of a New York restaurant run by Toots Shor called themselves "the Tribe" (Shor called us "crumbums") and, for a time, American Jews used *M.O.T.*—"member of the tribe"—as a self-mocking identification. Groups as diverse as travel agents and literary lights are sometimes referred to as *tribes*, with a faint derogation.

So is *tribe* a slur or not? The word's meaning today is most often "a primitive society," secondarily "a clannish or ethnocentric group"; *tribe* can cause offense, whether or not intended, and I would not direct it at a member of the Zulu nation.

Just because some people take offense at a word, however, does not automatically banish the word from the English language. For example, the colloquial verb *to gyp*—"to cheat, shortchange, swindle"—comes from a slur at Gypsies, wandering tribes of dark-skinned people who were targets of Hitler's master-race murderers. If I were a Gypsy politician campaigning on an honesty-in-fortunetelling platform, I might take offense, but the word is deeply ingrained in the language and only one syllable of the group's name is used; therefore, it is hypersensitive to take it as a slur. Egyptians, from whose name the word *gypsy* erroneously originated, are usually unaware of the etymology and are not offended. (*Gypsy cab*, which uses both syllables, stresses the "wandering" meaning of *gypsy*, which is descriptive and not derogatory.)

That one-syllable distinction is legitimate, I think: if the common usage were *I wuz gypsied*, I would stigmatize the verb as a slur and cast it forth. I have already done that with *to welsh*, a slang term meaning "to refuse to pay a debt," especially a gambling debt; people from Wales are no more inclined to refuse to pay off than Scots or Gypsies or Zulus, and Welshmen are right to complain when the very name of their language is used as an insult.

Another example: *pharisee.* In a political piece about the fads and fashions of our society, I condemned "the fiercely fawning fickleness of foreign-policy pharisees," following up with a blast at their fecklessness by asking "What caused the pharisaic flip-flop?" (There may be a philological term for "excessive use of alliteration," but I don't want to know it.)

"Must you use the word *Pharisaic,*" writes Herbert H. Paper of the Hebrew Union College in Cincinnati, "in its traditional Christian anti-Semitic sense?"

Now hold on: "Woe unto you, scribes and Pharisees, hypocrites!" is a denunciation repeated eight times in the New Testament Gospels; *Pharisees* were members of a sect in Judaism who were portrayed as sticklers for religious observance without a true spirit of religion, and their name became synonymous with hypocrisy, self-righteousness and pitiless piety.

(Frankly, ever since adopting a career in writing, I have felt that the *scribes* were unfairly castigated. The corresponding Hebrew word for *scribe* is *sofaer,* root of my own name as well as that of the State Department's legal adviser, and there are those who believe that the biblical blast at scribes, associating us with those stand-on-ceremony Pharisees, was an early example of media-bashing. Not so; *scribes,* rooted in the Latin for "write," were interpreters of the law, adept at counting and numbering, which is why they were lumped in with the *Pharisees.*)

According to several readers who feel about Pharisees the way I feel about scribes, I have uncritically accepted the early Christian derogation of a group that resisted the teachings of Jesus. Although the Apostle Paul, after his conversion to Christianity, said, "I am a Pharisee, the son of a Pharisee," the sect, and later the uncapitalized word, took on the meaning of the charges of hypocrisy leveled at them by St. Matthew and St. Luke.

As it happens, I know the world's leading expert on the subject. Jacob Neusner, professor of Judaic studies at Brown University, is the author of the classic three-volume study of the rabbis before A.D. 70 (or 70 A.D., as some scribes prefer) and of *From Politics to Piety: The Emergence of Pharisaic Judaism.*

Back off, Professor Neusner tells me, my correspondents have a good point: "The Pharisees were a group of lay people who aspired to live in their homes as if they were priests in the holy temple in Jerusalem. They were holy women and men living in the midst of secular society."

Let us assume, purely for the purpose of linguistic argument, that Professor Neusner is right and the Pharisees got a raw deal from the Gospels, Josephus and subsequent historians. (If you disagree with his historical interpretation, write to him at Brown, in Providence, Rhode Island, not to me.) Does that mean that the long-understood meaning of the word changes? Put another way: If it turns out that Machiavelli was a nice guy, or if modern research shows that Byzantium was a place of plain dealing, do we change the meaning of the words *Machiavellian* and *Byzantine?*

No; at least, not overnight. All we do is put a little red flag next to the word in our minds, reminding us: this word is in dispute. Some people think it's a slanted word, subtle propaganda to get us to knock somebody or some idea; watch it.

In this case, the red flag has a double meaning: for some reason, *pharisaic* has become one of the favorite terms in Soviet propaganda. A check by Nexis, the supermorgue, shows Pravda slamming a human-rights meeting in 1978 with Pope Paul VI as part of a Washington effort "for fanning up its pharisaical campaign"; *Izvestia* in 1980 inveighed against West German support for Poland's workers as "dark hints, Pharisaical warnings and provocative inventions"; a Soviet United Nations representative in 1984 called the United States' interest in Andrei D. Sakharov "pharisaical preaching," and Tass described American statements before the Geneva summit in 1985 as "the ultimate in Pharisaism."

They do like that word. Evidently the Soviet propagandists like to tinge their anti-American charges with a little subtle anti-Semitism. "The word *Pharisaism,"* wrote *Pravda* after our invasion of Grenada, "has synonyms— sanctimony and hypocrisy." The word also has overtones that we would do well to understand.

I appreciate your supporting the historical meaning of the expression "M.O.T." but I do not nor did I ever consider it "self-mocking" but self-defense and/or protectivism.

I remember using the term at the tail end of World War II (I was about the last draftee from East New York Brooklyn) when I approached a mountain man or a Southerner whom I suspected of being a Jew. Asking this possible Jew or possible anti-Semite whether he was a Jew could be devastating if he was not. Asking him if he was an "M.O.T." had protection. If he knew what an "M.O.T." was, odds on he was one. If he did not know, one could safely change subjects.

Self-mocking identification? No way!

Myron Cohen
Bethpage, New York

Your statement that the Pharisees "were portrayed as sticklers for religious observance without a true spirit of religion" perpetuates an entomological interpretation rather than an etymological one.

Apparently, Dr. Neusner tried to set you straight that the Sadducees were, in fact, the sticklers and the Pharisees the liberal Jews of their day.

I recommend George Foote Moore's *Judaism in the Intertestamentary Period* and several books by R. Travis Herford on Pharisaism to further enlighten your readers.

M. *Sigmund Shapiro*
Baltimore, Maryland

You have apparently come to the conclusion that the use of the term Pharisee in the New Testament context is an anti-Semitic rebuke of Jews.

I am sure you will be surprised to learn that the derogation of the word Pharisee is still being propagated by present-day organizations. One such group is the American Bible Society, a 25-million-dollar non-profit organization with headquarters in New York City.

One of their publications, *The Good News Bible*, includes the following definitions:

Pharisees—A Jewish religious party during the time of Jesus. They were strict in obeying the Law of Moses and other regulations which had been added to it through the centuries.

Sadducees—A small Jewish religious party in New Testament times, composed largely of priests. They based their beliefs primarily on the first five books of the Old Testament and differed in several matters of belief and practice from the larger party of Pharisees.

Some passages from the same American Bible Society publications:

"Then the Pharisees left and made plans to kill Jesus."

"When the Pharisees heard all this, they made fun of Jesus, because they loved money."

"Some Pharisees and Sadducees who came to Jesus wanted to trap him."

"The teachers of the Law and the Pharisees are the authorized interpreters of Moses' Law. So you must obey and follow everything they tell you to do; do not, however, imitate their actions, because they don't practice what they preach."

"Watch out for the teachers of the Law, who like to walk around in their long robes and be greeted with respect in the marketplace, who choose the reserved seats in the synagogues and the best places at feasts. They take advantage of widows and rob them of their homes, and then make a show of saying long prayers."

The Good News Bible, which is described in a National Council of the Churches of Christ brochure as reaching for a mass audience by using simple grammar and vocabulary, also characterizes Jews as

"DOGS," "DEMONS," "JEALOUS PLOTTERS," "RABBLE ROUSERS," "LEG BREAKERS," "SNAKES," "SONS of SNAKES," and "LIARS" . . . even "TO THIS VERY DAY."

I agree that we cannot change the meaning of words overnight. However, we can act to change the context in which they are used and the negative images they are used to portray. Especially when those "hate-mongering" images are used for garnering profit or position.

Ernest Moss
Whitestone, New York

I am surprised to learn that Josephus gave the Pharisees "a raw deal." The Gospels, okay; but Josephus, no. On the contrary, he tells us (*The Life* 10–12) that he explored the different sects composing Judaism in order to "select the best." He chose the Pharisees. At several points in his works, he casts them and their "philosophy" in a very positive light.

More to the point, the question of changing long-understood meanings of words, when the word is *Pharisee* becomes more complex than, to take your example, when the word is *Byzantine*. The original borrowing of any word to describe its chief characteristic is, of course, an interpretive process and *de gustibus non est disputandum*. In Christian documents of the first two centuries *Pharisee* carried a negative connotation while Jewish documents of the same period view the Pharisees positively.

Now, while each interpretation was born in its own matrix of social, theological, and political forces, the Christian matrix is that which gave birth to the religion. The interpretation is *pari passu* with the religion's theological foundations.

No amount of modern research will change the view of the Pharisees given them by early Christian writers. Indeed, to change the meaning of this word is to deny the validity of the Gospels' understanding of the world they sought to change. What scholarship can do is to open our eyes to that world, showing it in much greater depth, breadth, and clarity, so that we can say that the Gospels' view is not complete.

Once we begin to see things differently, we assign new meanings to words and that, presumably, will happen with *Pharisee* too. But it will happen more slowly because it involves the realignment of theological foundations (ah, the power of scholarship). Now when it comes to use of the word today, the case of *Pharisee* is not merely more complex than the case of *Byzantine*, it is fundamentally different—and this is where I differ with you. The example you gave, "to gypsy" would be a better parallel, for the Jews today consider themselves as heirs to the

Pharisees. So no matter what impact scholarship may have on our understanding of the Pharisees, the adjective *Pharisaic* with its negative connotation should not be used in a religiously pluralistic and sensitive society.

David M. Goldenberg
President, Dropsie College
Merion, Pennsylvania

Pharisees I don't know much about. I always thought that had something to do with a calm ocean.

However, as an ex boy from the Bronx I know a lot about gypsy cabs. Where I came from "gypsy cab" was rather derogatory. It meant a taxi that was not licensed by the City of New York or anybody else. This derogation extended to the driver of this cab. Therefore, I beg to differ and wish to point out that, if I could help it, I never ever took a gypsy cab.

On the other hand gypsy violinists play a lot better than Pharisees.

Arthur L. Finn
Beverly Hills, California

Where do you get off deciding for us whether *gyp* is offensive or not? Be assured that it is. It hurts me when I hear it, and it hurts my children. It's right up there with *jew down*—your insensitivity surprises me.

Not only do we find the word *gyp* defamatory, but a good many of us don't care for the word *Gypsy* either. One of our periodicals has a policy of never using the word at all. Your own prejudices are apparent in your association of "gypsy" cabs with wandering, and in the inclusion of that unnecessary cartoon. The term refers to unlicensed cabs, of course. All cabs "wander," though Gypsies only do in your stereotype. Why not find out a little about our people before speaking with such authority about us and our feelings? Did you consult any Gypsies before writing your piece? We're out here, if you need us.

Yanko le Redžosko
General Secretary
World Romani Union (USA)
Buda, Texas

How would you like to go to a store and get 'mericaned?

Ian F. Hancock
Professor of English
The University of Texas
Austin, Texas

Nobody, of course, wants their "tribe," their language, or anything else pertaining to them to be used as an insult. But the term "to welsh" does not really pertain to the good people of Wales, after all. It is an adaptation of the German noun *Welsche,* and which has another specific meaning in Switzerland, namely (for the German Swiss) for those who are Francophones.

Thus, while "welshing" still means "gypping," it does not specifically refer to the Welsh and not even to Gypsies.

Gerardo Joffe
San Francisco, California

Welsh means strange or foreign.

When the Angles and Saxons came upon the Cymry, a Celtic people living in the West of what is now England, they named them the Welsh.

One story has it that these people called out Welsh! Welsh! to warn the others of intruders and were then named with their Cymric word for outsiders.

But the word *welsch* is Old German, surviving in some compounds such as *Rotwelsch*—the language of thieves or gypsies, perceived as gibberish, according to Cassell's. Partridge suggests that that word was also responsible for the naming of Wallachians and Walloons.

The verb to welsh or welch, meaning not to pay off or to walk away from a deal, does not signify a habit of any specific people. It describes the manner in which, historically, many persons have treated strangers, foreigners, intruders, conquerors, etc., who are not part of their community and do not participate in their justice system.

William J. McBurney, Jr.
New York, New York

Whatever Mr. Buthelezi contends, it is evident that the British regarded the Zulus as a tribe, or at least they did on the eve of World War II. *Zulu* was the name of one of the famous British "Tribal" Class of destroyers, very effective ships indeed. Others included, if memory serves, *Eskimo, Nubian, Ashanti* and *Sikh.*

Taliaferro Boatwright
Stonington, Connecticut

You state your preference for "Zulu nation" as opposed to "Zulu tribe," based in part on Mangosuthu Gatsha Buthelezi's protestations.

I would argue with the use of either and suggest the simpler and less ideologically charged "Zulu people."

Jane Sovern
New York, New York

On the question of *tribe*, Mr. Buthelezi is entirely correct in objecting to the use of this term for the Zulus. The point is not umbrage but accuracy. The term *tribe* is used by anthropologists for a wide range of societies in which people share a sense of common identity and are linked together through ritual or political mechanisms that give them a loose unity. The term is not, however, appropriate for societies with state organization—that is, a centralized government complete with administrative apparatus and means of enforcing legal sanctions. The Zulu clearly fit the latter category. The distinction is not a matter of anthropological nitpicking; it carries major implications for understanding societal differences. Don't blame Mr. Buthelezi for hypersensitivity or make apologies for "common usage." The problem is our society's abysmal ignorance of the diversity of the non-Western world, which leads to the assumption that one "primitive" is like any other.

Sydel Silverman
Graduate Center
City University of New York
New York, New York

I was somewhat taken aback by your use of the word "denizens" to describe those who used to frequent Toots Shor's restaurant. I have always been under the impression that the word described one who actually lived in a certain place. For example, the cliché "denizens of the deep" is generally used to denote octopii, but not scuba divers, even habitual ones. I think a better word would have been habitués.

Myra Fribourg
Stony Brook, New York

You state that the term *preliterate* is a euphemism for *illiterate*. While I understand your point, I hope you will consider my objections to it. In our literate (or post-literate, if you wish to acknowledge television's primacy) society, the word *illiterate* connotes uneducated, in addition to the lack of reading and writing skills. It is one thing to give the label *illiterate* to an individual who does not know his ABC's while all those around him do. However, it is clearly ethnocentric to refer to an entire society as illiterate, and thus uneducated. Members of a preliterate society become educated by memorizing an oral tradition. (This is an oversimplification, but in lieu of a more copious explanation I would refer you to Walter Ong's *Orality and Literacy*, London: Methuen, 1982, as well as the work of Milman Parry, Albert Lord, and Eric Havelock, assuming you are not already familiar with this material.) Much of the oral tradition consisted of songs, often sung with instrumental accompaniment (as Homer sang the wrath of Achilles). Sans literacy, the song is the only game in town, hence the equivalence between unsung and unknown (today we might say untelevised). Since education in the oral tradition was characteristic of ancient Greek culture up to the time of Plato and Aristotle, it is not surprising that the Greeks used *musical* and *unmusical* as metaphors for educated and uneducated. When Plato barred the poets from his school, he was trying to change the basis of Greek education from orality to literacy.

While I do not believe that *preliterate* is a mere euphemism for illiterate, I am not above criticizing the term. As you mention in your column, *preliterate* suggests that "literacy is surely on the way." Writing should not be viewed as an inevitable development, because the invention of writing was a unique achievement, and few things are inevitable in history. Nor should literacy be considered a natural development; spoken language is part of our genetic heritage, but literacy is man-made, and fragile. An alternative to *preliterate* is *nonliterate*, which does not make any promises about the subsequent appearance of literacy. I have some reservations about describing a society as nonliterate, however, because it only tells us what is absent, not what is present. As I mentioned above, the preliterate or nonliterate society does have an oral tradition, and a system of education based on memorization. It is for this reason that many scholars have been using the term *oral* instead of *preliterate* or *nonliterate*. *Oral* has the additional advantage of brevity, and therefore I consider it the favorite. The problem with *oral* is that all societies are oral; the post-oral culture only exists in science fiction stories where higher evolution leads to silent telepathy. Combined terms such as *oral-preliterate* or *nonliterate-oral* are awfully unmusical. Walter Ong suggests using *primary oral*, but this does not make the meaning much clearer, and may be confused with certain political speeches. In my doctoral dissertation (now you know why I have given the subject so much thought; my topic is the differences in conceptions of the hero in oral, literate, and electronic cultures, in case you are curious) I will suggest *oral-mnemonic*, which calls attention to the reliance on memory to preserve information, and the use of mnemonic techniques to insure fidelity in such a society. I think it is worth a shot, but it is a long one and all the smart money is on *oral.*

Lance Strate
Kew Gardens, New York

Although I do not suggest changing the meaning of *Machiavellian,* it turns out that Niccolò Machiavelli was, in fact, a nice guy.

Machiavelli was not an especially prominent or important politician in late fifteenth-century and early sixteenth-century Florence. If what he wrote in *The Prince* was meant to be taken literally—and significant evidence suggests this political bible was written as a warning and even as satire—Machiavelli did not follow his own advice. My reading indicates that he never indulged in any significant crimes or vices, that he was a kind, affectionate, considerate and probably faithful husband and father, and that he was a man of his word and a respected citizen —in short, a nice guy.

Perhaps, then, a little ambiguity in one's writing or a contrast between what one says and does may help one be remembered. (Being different things to different men has certainly done wonders for the reputation of Karl Marx.)

Robert Blackey
Professor and Chair
Department of History
California State University
San Bernardino, California

A related problem, which I would like to see you address in a future column, is the word "dialect." It, too, is used disparagingly to refer to the languages of non-Westernized, non-white peoples ("tribal languages"?). In fact, this usage appears with disturbing frequency in the pages of *The New York Times,* in such locutions as "he speaks five languages and three African dialects." As if Ibo, Yoruba, etc., were not real languages, but just some tribal gabble. And so, again, subtle and perhaps unconscious prejudice rears its head.

John S. Major
Director, The China Council
New York, New York

You write: ". . . the corresponding Hebrew word for scribe is *sofaer,* root of my own name . . ."

You err thrice.

First: the correct pronunciation would be not "Sofaer" but

"Sofér," with an open, Spanish-type "é," or, if you are a stickler for mid-European Hebrew pronunciation, perhaps "Sofeyr," since the "e" vowel sound (denoted by two horizontal dots underneath the Hebrew letter "f") is a *Tzeyré*, a sort of an open "e" terminating with a soft, floating "y."

Second: The scribe mentioned in your column (in the matter of Pharisees et al.) is not a *Sofér*, but a *Sofér Stamm*—that is, a special writer who inscribes holy parchments only, where *Stamm* is the Hebrew acronym for *Sifrey Torah* (Torah books), *T'fillim* (philacteries), and *M'zzuzot* (those doorpost ornaments containing a few words of scriptures). The plain word *Sofér* would more properly translate as Author.

Third and most important: the root of your own name, Safire, has nothing to do with writing—scribing or authoring. In Hebrew your name would be pronounced Safír (or perhaps Sapír, with the "f" receiving a daghesh, a hardening accent, because of the open "ā" vowel preceding it). Again, the stress would be on the last syllable, and the "í" would be a hard one, as in Spanish.

As you may suspect, the Hebrew word *Safír* (or *Sapír*) means sapphire, that translucent blue crystal of alumina that, by the order of the Supreme Scribe, Moses had had set (among eleven other precious stones, one for each of the tribes of Israel) in the priestly Ephod (a sort of breastplate) of his brother Aharon. (In case you are interested, the stones were: a sardius, a topaz, a carbuncle, an emerald, a sapphire, a diamond, a ligure, an agate, an amethyst, a beryl, an onyx and a jasper.) That sparkling breastplate constituted the Urim and Thummim, a highly magical contraption used for divinations (so claim latter-day annotators) and, no doubt, *pour épater le peuple commun.*

So whence your confusion? I think it is due to the several possible permutations of the Hebrew verb-root s.f.r. (Most Hebrew verbs have roots of three letters, which, upon conjugation, yield a treasure of meanings). Here the verb-root s.f.r. may be conjugated both as *LeSappér* (to tell, or to recount), as well as *LiSpór* (to count).

In the first case the verb-root yields *Sofér*—a writer of *Sfarim* (—books; singular: *Séfer*, or *Seyfer*, for those insisting on their *Tzeyré*), from whence: *Sifrút* (—Literature), and *Sifriyá* (—Library), as well as (with a daghesh in the "f") *Messappér*—a teller of stories (—*Sippurím*; singular: *Sippúr*).

In the second case, however, the very same root will yield *Mispár*—number, as well as *Sifrá*—numeral. And to add to the confusion, here the word *Sofér* would come to mean not a writer of books, but a counter of numbers.

A natural question arises: How, in an ancient language predating digital computers, can both counters (of numbers) and recounters (of tales) cohabit the same verb?

The answer, I think, has to do with the Cabbala. Cabbalist texts mention nine layers *(Klippot)* of grace, also called *Sfeyrot*, i.e.: Spheres (a wholly Greek word). But in other texts the double-dotted *Tzeyré* under the "f" metamorphoses into a *Chirik* (—a single dot denoting a hard "ī" sound), making the word come out as *Sfirot*—that is, Countings. I suspect that this numerical flavor of ever ascending bookish grace came to the Cabbalists from their cousins the Platonists, for whom all was number. This guess is further strengthened by the Cabbalists' favorite hobby—letter counting, also called *Guimatria* (a Greek word). The Cabbalists amused themselves (and still do) by counting letters in the Hebrew scriptures, summing up their numerical values (each Hebrew letter has a number associated with it), to divine the precise date of the End of Days.

So: the only faint connection between your name and Hebrew scribing is through divination, practiced both by the Grand Priest via his Ephod (containing your namesake gem), and by Cabbalist scribes. Other than that, I am afraid the name Safire has little to do with writing, at least in Hebrew. But I think we have taken your triple error far enough, and trust the above shall be of value to you.

Avner Mandelman
Toronto, Ontario

Haberdasher

Quick: What did Harry S. Truman do before he went into politics? He was a *haberdasher*, of course, and rarely does an account of his career omit the fact and the word. But why don't we hear the word applied to today's merchants of men's apparel and furnishings?

Just off Eastern Parkway in Brooklyn, there used to be a large neon sign over the establishment of "Joe Sass, Haberdasher." It's gone now. Few hardy hatters, it seems, hold themselves out proudly as *haberdashers*.

"The word *haberdasher* just faded from the scene," says Robert Bryan, fashion editor of Fairchild Publications. "Now people would just say 'hatter' or something. Last store I remember using it was Raleighs Haberdashers in Washington."

"We have not used *haberdasher* in our advertising in years," retorts David Nellis, a vice president of Raleighs. "*Haberdasher* does have a connotation of men's wear, but the word is obsolete. We're a full-service specialty store." Certainly no mere *haberdasher* would presume to call himself a full-service specialist.

The great old word was first spotted in English in Chaucer's *The Canterbury Tales:* listed among the pilgrims was "an Haberdasshere." The word may have come from *hapertas,* an Anglo-French word of unknown origin, which Eric Partridge broke down to *happe,* a hook or scythe, and *tas,* a "heap," to come up with an unhelpful heap of hooks.

In Britain, the word came to mean "a dealer in small articles dealing with dress, such as tape, ribbons, thread, buttons." That was not the meaning that developed in the United States; here, the haberdasher dealt in shirts, socks, gloves, mufflers, ties, belts and especially hats, but not suits or jackets —suits were down the street in the big store, specialty or otherwise.

Perhaps the *dash* in *haberdasher* made the old word too jazzy-sounding for the dignified purveyors of what we now call "men's furnishings," as if a man were a walking house. In the general gentrification of neighborhoods, however, we can hope that the resonant *haberdasher* makes a comeback. One glimmer of good news: the word is now the name of a race horse, a three-year-old chestnut colt that has competed in some of the top-money races. If this Tresvant Stable entry, trained by Sue Sedlaeck and sired by Gummo out of Lady Has a Bonnet, wins the Derby or something, the great old Chaucerian word will charge back into popularity.

Count me—hatless, tie-stained, one-gloved and unmuffled—among its ardent rooters: *C'mon, Haberdasher!*

Long, long ago, at the time when transportation was dependent on horses, the owners of the stations where the coachmen stopped to feed, take care of or change horses had to provide for their needs. Among other things they sold *oat bags,* or in German *Hafer Taschen.* Because of the different dialects or in Dutch, it became *Haber Daschen.*

The station owners soon found out that the coachmen (and the travelers) might need a clean shirt, socks, gloves, kerchiefs, hats, etc.

So they stocked and sold those articles and became known as *haberdashers.*

Harry A. Kugeman
Wurtsboro, New York

I am a researcher for World Book Encyclopedia and feel it is my duty to relate the following information regarding the etymology of *haberdasher.*

The excerpt reproduced below is from *Essays, by Francis Bacon.* New York: Hurst and Company (no date of publication, but an introduction by Henry Morley is dated November 1883).

In Chapter XXII, "Of Cunning" (p. 106 of this edition), Bacon writes, ". . . these cunning men are like haberdashers of small wares . . ."

In a footnote, an editor (maybe Morley—it is not clear) informs the reader:

> This word is used here in its primitive sense of "retail dealers." It is said to have been derived from a custom of the Flemings, who first settled in this country in the fourteenth century, stopping the passengers as they passed their shops, and saying to them, *"Haber da, herr?"* "Will you take this, sir?" The word is now generally used as synonymous with linen-draper.

I hope that this story interests you as much as it did me.

David R. Shannon
La Grange, Illinois

Your article brought back fond memories of the Brooklyn that used to be. I thought that my brother and I were the only ones who remembered "Joe Sass Haberdasher." It was located on Eastern Parkway at the corner of Kingston Avenue.

I too mourn the disappearance of "haberdasher" from our modern vocabulary. It seems to me that the word "crockery" has suffered a similar fate.

David Helfant
New York, New York

Robert Bryan's quoted remark that "people would just say 'hatter' or something," seems vague and, I suspect, not very accurate. Least of the sales made by a dealer in men's incidental apparel must be head-gear. How many males these days, even when it snows, seem concerned about protecting their noggins? Only Lewis Carroll's renowned character would be apt to embark on a business venture with such small possibilities of yielding a profit. "Haberdasher" may be "old hat" but it does cover the territory acceptably.

At the risk of appearing hopelessly out of date, I maintain there's much to be said on behalf of the old rather than the new. Why is "record player" deemed superior to "phonograph," or "hair stylist" to "barber"—a profession youngsters might well assume exists only in Seville? Do "janitors" still exist or have they all succumbed to the lure of lengthier titles? Why is "two times" so frequently employed when "twice" comes off the tongue with much less effort? Why have the three syllables of "I'm buying!" superseded "My treat!" among pub-crawlers?

Are we becoming more verbose?

Thomas G. Morgansen
Jackson Heights, New York

Shouldn't the opening be:

QUICK: What did Harry S. Truman do before he went into politics?

He *haberdashed* . . .

I know there's no such word, but my point is that your question required responding with a verb form. What he *did* was the thrust of the question, not what he *was.*

Of course you might reply that your answer implied "(What he did was) he was a haberdasher . . ." but I think you're on surer ground by giving the direct answer, which is the clearest. Gotta dash off now.

Roy E. Nemerson
New York, New York

Why, oh why do you insist on putting punctuation after the "S" in Harry S Truman? As you well know, the "S" does not stand for anything; it is Harry's middle name. I am willing to believe that this is *New York Times* policy, as I have seen this error elsewhere in the good gray pages. Nevertheless, it ain't right. Truman did not think so, and even got a ruling from Secretary of State Dean Acheson (in his capacity as keeper of the Seal of the United States) as to how his name should appear on documents.

Mark M. Lowenthal
Reston, Virginia

Hacking It

Toward the end of a political campaign, Lyn Nofziger, the longtime Reagan political associate who is now a private consultant, was observed aboard Air Force One. He was asked if he should be described as a *key aide* (one who unlocks doors for a candidate staggering home late at night) or an *adviser*, and he shunned those pretentious bogus titles. His preference reflected an inner serenity: "Just call me a *hanger-on.*"

Hey, Nonny-non

A new word has been rampaging through our language and has never been properly lexed. The word is *non* or, if you wish to call attention to its origin as a prefix, *non-*.

You've heard it a thousand times, at ticket counters or in front of what used to be velvet ropes in restaurants:

"Smoking or *non?*"

"*Non*, if you have it."

"You'll have to wait for *non.*"

In three generations, we have come from Waiting for Lefty, to Waiting for Godot, to Waiting for *Non.*

The rise of *non* is an example of identification by exclusion. The comedian Fred Allen, in the heyday of radio, had a character in "Allen's Alley" afflicted with amnesia who was trying to remember who he was by the process of elimination. "I'm not carrying an umbrella," he would say, "so I'm not Neville Chamberlain."

In the same exclusionary way, we categorize the yellow, red and black races as *nonwhite*. A decade ago, when America's attention was directed to the demands of minority groups, Ben Wattenberg and Richard Scammon once identified the real majority of Americans as "un-young, un-poor and un-black." That was an original and striking use of the elimination process;

so was *nonbook*, a condemnation of books that were published without having been written. Most often, however, *non* is linguistic evasion, sheer laziness on the part of the categorizer.

What, for instance, is the category for the article you are now reading? "We have only a negative word for *nonfiction*," writes Morton Yarmon of New York; "that is, we identify nonfiction only in terms of what it is not. Some people use 'fact articles' to identify nonfiction, but that doesn't seem satisfactory. Worth thinking about?"

Yes, especially because fiction is often fact disguised only to escape the libel suitor. Bestsellers should be listed under *fiction* for novels and *fact* for the rest of the stuff. Or perhaps *rest of the stuff* for what is now called *nonfiction*, calling attention to the need for a new word, or a new application for an old word.

Get on this, book reviewers, lest *yin* and *yang* become *yin* and *nonyin*. An escapist novel about a neologician's search for a replacement for *non* would, of course, be considered *nonfiction*.

You mentioned the increased usage of the additive "non," as in nonfiction. I immediately recalled my favorite employment of that term in the phrase "nonbank bank," which, if not puzzling to the financial wizards of the world, then certainly must confound the non-professional (i.e. amateur?).

This nonbank is an institution that either takes in deposits *or* makes loans, but certainly not both. Seems to me it should be termed a "half bank" to be distinguished from a "full bank." In football this is easily understood. A fullback's running partner is a halfback, not a nonback back!

Nonetheless, if money mongers and lawmakers persist in calling an institution the 1st National Nonbank Bank of Somewheresville, then I anxiously await the opportunity to tackle the next nonfiction fiction book I see!

William M. Roth
Chicago, Illinois

High on the Hog

One of my informants in the Pentagon, a merry person (never give away the sex of your source) who listens for leaks in E-ring elevators, called to predict that United States arms negotiators would soon cave in to the Russians at Geneva. The basis of his or her suspicion: he or she had overheard an arms-controlnik complaining of accepting a *pig in a poke*.

After an extensive stakeout at the drop site, the informant revealed (as you can tell, I expect a visit from Big Polly and am learning interrogese) that the overheard phrase was *a pig in a sack*; further probing induced the subject to refresh his (whoops! or her) recollection, and the whispered phrase became *a sack pig*.

With this accurate report in hand, Agent Lex turned to a source in DOD's telemetry encryption. (For the uninitiated: "DOD" is a Jamaican way of saying "father.") What, I demanded, was a *sack pig*, and did it mean that our boys in Geneva were buying a cat in a bag from the Russkies?

It was explained (note the passive voice, a must in interrogese) that the most common acronym in the Pentagon is *IG*. Anyone, down to the meanest subaltern, can be on an *IG*, or "Interdepartmental Group." Whenever you run into anybody across the river at State, you "have an *IG*," and can charge off a cheap lunch.

Senior officials ("senior," I think, means over twenty-eight years old, nearing pension benefits), when serving on an *IG*, turn them into a *SIG*, or "Senior Interdepartmental Group," which rates a car to transport you to the meeting. But *SIG*'s became too commonplace about a year ago, and the acronym atrophied, at least among the Star Wars superstars.

A SACPG, pronounced *sack pig*, is a Senior Arms Control Planning Group. It has no relationship to *earth pig*, current campus slang for a date that one is less than proud of, or to *pig in a poke*, a phrase that originated in Chaucer's *The Canterbury Tales*, in which the Reeve speaks of "two pigges in a poke." Buying a pig in a poke, or a bag, is the mistake of paying for something without first inspecting it: a dishonest seller might substitute a different animal, such as a dog or a cat, for the pig. As early as 1380, John Wyclif wrote of "doggis in a poke" and also translated into English the

French trope *acheter chat en sac,* "to buy a cat in a sac," which produced the later expression "to let the cat out of the bag."

However, the familiarity with IG's has an effect on all Planning Groups, which are now called PG's but pronounced *pigs.* When top brass get finished with a SACPG meeting, they hope to be invited to a *nisspig,* which is the National Security Planning Group. That can include the President, and is more frequently held than National Security Council meetings because attendance is not statutory and announcement of the meeting is not expected: anybody can be invited to a *nisspig* in the President's name.

I hope that lays the rumor of secret sellout to rest. But it raises another issue of the esthetics of bureaucratic terminology: somehow, it seems inappropriate, or even wrong, or worse yet, ugly, for a conference of our most distinguished leaders on subjects of immense significance to the fate of the nation—indeed, to the survival of humankind, formerly mankind—to be called a *nisspig.*

Subject recalls a similar problem at the beginning of the Carter Administration. In the Nixon-Ford era, major studies ordered by the President were called National Security Study Memorandums, or *nissims;* NSSM-1, for example, was the analysis of the possibility of an opening to China. When Henry A. Kissinger and his Nixonian followers cleared out desks for the Carter men to take over, it was felt that a change in the terminology was needed to signify a fundamental change in philosophy. Zbigniew Brzezinski decreed that his strategic studies would be called Presidential Study Memorandums, until somebody told him what the acronym would sound like, at which point he hurriedly amended his decree.

In like manner, let the nomenclature nomenklatura in the Pentagon and National Security Council come up with a less porcine name for great deliberations. Off the *sacpigs* and the *nisspigs!*

DEPARTMENT OF STATE
Washington, D.C. 20520
NEED TO KNOW

MEMORANDUM FOR ASSISTANT SECRETARIES AND OFFICE HEADS
Subject: Expanded Interdepartmental Group
(IG) Subgroups

With the warm reception given the Department's recent revival of the Interdepartmental Group (IG) and the Senior Interdepartmental Group (SIG), Department principals have decided that it is essential to move promptly to expand the concept to the subgroup levels. Specifically, bureaus are expected to convene appropriate subgroups as follows:

1 *Military Interdepartmental Group (MIG)*—MIGs should be numbered for easy identification. Example: MIG 15, MIG 21, etc.

2 *Junior Interdepartmental Group (JIG)*—JIGs should be identified by the country concerned, example—the Irish JIG.

3 *Senior Advisory Group (SAG)*—SAGs should be instituted in close liaison with SIGs (see above). Example: Military Fitness SAG.

4 *Zairian Interdepartmental Group (ZIG)* and *Zairian Advisory Group (ZAG)*—The ZIG and the ZAG will focus on this key African country. An active ZIG/ZAG will demonstrate to key allies greater consistency in U.S. foreign policy.

5 *Financial Analysis Group (FAG)* and *Group on Analytical Yields (GAY)* will consider special preferences. Security clearances for all FAG/GAY participants will be reviewed.

6 *Deputies' Review Action Group (DRAG)*—DRAG will review dress codes for the Department.

7 *Budget Interdepartmental Group (BIG)*—BIG will deal with large budget issues. Two subgroups will consider smaller matters:

  A Working Interdepartmental Group (WIG)—BIG/WIG will focus on appropriate issues.

  B Zero Based Interagency Group (Z'BIG) will focus on bureaucratic problems left by the previous administration.

8 *Policy Interdepartmental Group (PIG)*—PIGs will focus on meatier issues, particularly for the high level analytical meetings (HAM). Subgroups include:

  A *Haitian Output Group (HOG)*

  B *Syrian Output Working Group (SOW)*

  C *Policy Economic Network (PIG/PEN)*

  D *Budgetary Analysis and Coordinating Output Network (BACON)*

9 *Joint Budget and Policy Interdepartmental Group (BIG/PIG)*—BIG/PIG will root around in all issues.

10 *Financial Interdepartmental Group (FIG)*—FIG will work to reduce long-term spending plans with a view toward turning over a new leaf in government.

11 *Foreign Operations Group (FOG)*—FOG will coordinate cover for clandestine operations. Deep cover will be handled in a thick FOG.

12 *Bilateral Operations Group (BOG)*—BOG will generate procedures to handle paper flow.

13 *Congressional Operations Group (COG)*—COG will confine its efforts to turning around the big wheels on Capitol Hill.

The Secretary looks to each of you to make maximum use of these important organizations. Participation in any IG, SIG, JIG, SAG, ZIG, ZAG, FAG, GAY, BIG, WIG, Z'BIG, PIG, HOG, SOW, BIG/PIG, PIG/PEN, FIG, FOG, BOG or COG should be on a strict need to know basis.

You refer to a French phrase "to buy a cat in a sac," which produced the later expression "to let the cat out of the bag." The intent of these phrases is to show the mistake of paying for something without first inspecting it. The origin is more sinister.

In the Royal Navy during the eighteenth and nineteenth centuries the cat-o'-nine-tails was kept in a red baize bag tied to the mainmast. It was only removed for a flogging. The phrase "the cat is out of the bag" means it is too late to turn back, events will take their inexorable course. It is possible that the two expressions developed independently. All things are possible but I consider this unlikely. If there is any evidence to support this thesis I will ungraciously withdraw my gotcha.

The lore of sailing ships has produced a number of expressions which are in common use today by persons unaware of their nautical origin. Two of these are "touch and go," meaning to ground briefly and move on, and to be "taken aback" or "taken all aback," referring to a square-rigged ship pointing directly into the wind and causing it to lose its forward speed. This usually occurred when a square-rigger was sailing as close to the wind as possible only to be betrayed by a sudden shift in wind. "Gone by the boards" is another one referring to something washed overboard.

James R. Hillas, Jr.
Morristown, New Jersey

Dear Bill:

Your Pentagon "PIGS" have a civilian side, Public Interest Groups. These are representatives of state and local governments seeking to maximize federal intergovernmental assistance, aka "feeding at the federal trough." The National Governors' Association, the National Association of County Officers, the League of Cities, the Conference of Mayors, the National Association of State Legislators and the National Association of Housing Development Officials were once referred to as the "Six PIGS."

Bill Green
15th District, New York
House of Representatives
Washington, D.C.

Nissims means miracles in Hebrew. Maybe that is what we need instead of Nisspigs.

Heskel M. Haddad, M.D.
New York, New York

Hit the Ball, Schlep Morris

"**M**y monumental *schlep*" is what the entertainer Bette Midler called a concert tour a few years ago, using the Yiddishism as a noun. The novelist Erica Jong used the verb form as she recently derided "affluent Americans, who *schlep* from the Cipriani pool to Harry's Bar and back again, buying gold jewelry en route at inflated prices." And Jeane J. Kirkpatrick, former United States delegate to the United Nations, asked if she would run for the Presidency in 1988, replied with the use of the word as part of a gerund phrase: "I can imagine myself doing the job. I can't imagine myself running for it. I don't mind the campaigning or *the schlepping around*. For me, the difficulty of running is the asking—and the risking."

Schlep has dragged itself into the English language and is apparently here to stay. The lexicographer Sol Steinmetz, in his thoughtful *Yiddish and English: A Century of Yiddish in America* just published by the University of Alabama Press, defines the verb and noun as "drag," and a *shleper* as "a bum"; he spells the words without the *c*, and does not double the *p* (as I do, to avoid the confusion with *sleeper*).

Extended usages exist. A *schlep* is a "loafer" to some, but is gaining the meaning of "one who drags himself around"; its meaning is slopping over into *schlepper*, "one who carries," a caddy or a *gofer* (one who will "go fer coffee"); a mechanical *schlepper* is the device intended to help you roll baggage on wheels but makes a surgical strike at the traveler with clawing bungies.

The Kirkpatrick usage is current and correct: *schlepping around* is "wearily dragging oneself from place to place." A presidential race, in Miss Midler's usage, would indeed be a "monumental schlep."

Dear Bill,
Many thanks for citing my book. It was thoughtful (= considerate) of you to characterize my book as thoughtful (= carefully reasoned).

Incidentally, on page 54 I point out that the idiom *shlep around* is a partial loan translation of Yiddish *arumshlepn.*

> Sol [Steinmetz]
> Clarence L. Barnhart, Inc.
> Bronxville, New York

Schleppen, meaning to drag or tug, is an eminently respectable German word, and its entry into English may owe as much to our large German ancestry as to Yiddish.

Two wars against Germany have left some reluctance to credit Germany as the source of anything that might be considered military or fascist, but *schleppen* belongs to the opposite or gemütlich side of the German nature, and its German origin would therefore be quite acceptable, along with beer and oompah bands.

> Arthur J. Morgan
> New York, New York

Your *schlep* story roused memories.

As no doubt you are aware, the word *schleppen* is a perfectly legitimate German verb. Even in Holland, where the word is *slepen,* we always referred to the "Volga Boatsman" song as: "Der Wolgaschlepper."

Many, many years ago as a fledgling designer in The Hague, I was given the assignment to create a stage gown for the soubrette of a Viennese Operetta Company then resident in The Hague. The leading lady would get her wardrobe from a local fashion house: Maison de Paris. When I arrived at the theater to supervise the fitting of my gown, unbeknownst to me the Maison de Paris creation was being tried on as well. Waiting outside the dressing-room door for the lady to get attired, I suddenly heard the anguished cry: "Die Schleppe ist zu kurtz!!!" ("The train is too short!!!") Luckily, it was not the train of *my* gown that was thus deficient.

As you have correctly surmised, the female noun *Die Schleppe* is the train of a garment (in Dutch: *"de sleep"*).

> Leo Van Witsen
> New York, New York

I'll bet that your research would never turn up possibly the first use (1837) of *schlepp* in its modern meaning. In his tempo instruction to musicians, Felix Mendelssohn admonished:

"Andante: Dieses Stück darf durchaus nicht schleppend gespielt werden"
(String Quartet Opus 44 No. 2, third movement).

Arthur J. Mitteldorf
Pebble Beach, California

Hot to Redact

You don't get a call from the assistant attorney general in charge of the Criminal Division of the Department of Justice unless you are in heavy water or deep trouble. When this division's chief is on the phone, the person on the other end usually trembles. For that reason, every couple of years I like to call whoever is in the job to give him a hard time.

Stephen Trott is the man who strikes terror into criminal hearts these days, so he was the recipient of my query: why had he not cooperated with the House Judiciary Subcommittee investigating the E. F. Hutton affair? With a smooth asperity, he replied, "We've been redacting thousands of pages of documents for a month."

Redacting? I remembered, years ago, receiving mail from Daniel Morgaine, a journalist in Paris, with the letterhead title "Rédacteur en chef," which I assumed meant "editor in chief." Although its written use dates to the fifteenth century, this was the first I had heard the word *redact* as an English verb.

"It means to purge it of 6-e stuff," explained Mr. Trott. Translated from prosecutorialese, that means he was removing the material that Rule 6 (e) of Title 18 of the United States Code requires be kept secret, as part of grand-jury proceedings.

Redact is a good verb that deserves wider use. It means "make suitable for presentation," from the Latin word for "reduce." *Redact* is more precise in its legal connotation of removing that which is unsuitable than *edit*, more purposeful than *shorten* or *compress*, more formal than *boil down*. Also, if you are snipping something embarrassing out of a document, it is a fine euphemism for *censoring*. Try it, next time you have to pass along some information: one man's *redact* is another man's *sanitize*.

Dear Bill:
A word on *redact*. The verb in French is *rédiger* and although *re + agere* etymologically mean push back, reduce (as you said), in

modern use it means compose, frame, set down, put (thoughts, words) in order—hence rédacteur-en-chef.

But *he* doesn't *rédige* anything; his reporters *"rédigent leurs articles"* and his other writers *rédigent* the editorials *(topos)* and the columns *(chroniques)*. So it's a question whether we should adopt *redact* as you suggest, with a meaning no longer attached to the French, especially when we have reduce, boil down, pare down, edit to do the job.

> Jacques [Barzun]
> Charles Scribner's Sons, Publishers
> New York, New York

You quite naturally find the word in legal reference, in light of OED's first reference (1430): "The great Pompeius was the firste whiche willede to haue redacte the lawes in to bokes."

But the word has wider use now than you seem to realize. In biblical studies it refers to the use of earlier sources (oral or written) for literature in the Bible as it has come to us. More necessary in the Old Testament, the Synoptic Gospels (Matthew, Mark, Luke) in the New Testament most appropriately and profitably yield to this type of critical study.

Biblical scholars commonly ask what use of earlier accounts of the life of Jesus Christ did the Gospel writers make? Each redacted those accounts, or indeed each other, to shape his account to fit the specific purpose for which he wrote. They were all redactors.

The term seems to have been brought into this discipline by Willi Marxsen about 1954. Many seminaries teach a course on Redaction Criticism, and many books use the term in their titles, e.g., D. A. Carson, *Redaction Criticism: The Nature of an Interpretive Tool* (Christianity Today Institute, 1985).

If you correct the language errors of this letter, you edit it. If you use some of the information and apply it to redaction of legal documents, you redact it—especially if you do so in order to publish.

> Wallace Alcorn
> Austin, Minnesota

You write that "redact" comes from the Latin word for reduce. The Latin word for reduce you probably refer to is *reducere*, which in fact seems to have nothing to do with "redact" since it means "to lead back."

Redact is actually based on the past participle of the Latin verb *redigere (redactum)*, which, to go a little further back into etymology, is made up of the prefix "re" (repetition) and the verb *agere* (to act), between which a "d" has been inserted to avoid the hiatus (double vowel) e-a, or e-i.

José de Vinck
Allendale, New Jersey

I first met *redaction* while studying theology as part of my Jesuit training. In scripture scholarship, the word has gained such currency that it risks the danger of overuse.

I have consulted a standard reference—*The Jerome Biblical Commentary*—for a definition of redaction as employed in New Testament criticism. Its use among English-speaking scripture scholars derives from the German word *Redaktionsgeschichte,* or "the study of redaction." A school of German exegetes adopted the term while pressing their view that those who produced the gospels of Mark, Matthew and Luke did more than simply compile preexisting materials. That is, they became creative theologians in their own right. For instance, the author of Luke grappled with the fact that the period between the resurrection and the second coming would not be brief. Scholars maintain, thus, that his *redaction* deliberately and radically diverged from the conventional treatment of available materials. It did this in order to accommodate an elongation of the expected interval between the resurrection and the end of time.

Colin Campbell, S.J.
Georgetown University
Washington, D.C.

You described one with severe difficulties as being "in heavy water or deep trouble." At the risk of being banished to the "Gotcha! Gang," I hasten to point out that problems of such severity usually get one into "hot water" (shades of cannibalism) or "deep (. . . ah, shall we say . . .) mire."

As a chemical engineer who worked on several Canadian heavy water projects in the late 1960s, I know something of this *aqua densa* of which you (perhaps inadvertently) write.

Technically, heavy water, or deuterium oxide (D_2O), is the combustion product of a natural, heavier isotope of hydrogen called deuterium. It occurs throughout nature mixed with "regular" or "light" water to the extent of about one part in 7,000. Heavy water is difficult to concentrate because, although the pure product *is* (just) slightly more dense than good old H_2O, it is physically, chemically and physiologically very similar. In fact, you could very easily be up to your aspirate vowels in heavy water and never notice the difference.

Heavy water is used for its nuclear properties in both power reactors (allegedly peaceful) and H-bombs (decidedly not) and, as a result, may have become politically undesirable. However, I do not believe that man's (mis)use of this innately inoffensive isotope should forever damn it to the negative aspects of our language in the way your usage has. Please, let's keep troubled waters "hot" and not make them "heavy."

On the other hand (he indicated ambidextrously), you have very nearly touched upon a public service in that "heavy" is how our recent wave of Russian immigrants initially translates "difficult" ("Heavy day today. No?"). You should come close to being applauded for almost pointing this out to your readers.

Daniel Snyder
Brooklyn, New York

"Inartful" Dodger

Political life, as we shall see, follows art.

Governor Cuomo, the New Yorker whose name is often bruited about as a potential Democratic candidate for President, was asked what he thought about some of the vitriolic letters that came to him from opponents of a bill to require wearing seat belts in automobiles.

Apparently the Governor had been quite worked up over such intemperate and embittered correspondence, and he lashed back at his epistolary tormentors by comparing them to "hunters who drink beer, don't vote, and lie to their wives about where they were all weekend."

You can with impunity zap a group of hunters for being a bunch of drunks and adulterers, but to call them nonvoters is to invite a counterblast. When the president of the National Rifle Association, an organization of three million Americans, many of whom vote, wrote to demand an explanation, Governor Cuomo put on his seat belt and shifted into reverse.

"My response was *inartful*," he readily admitted, "and could leave a false impression of disrespect for the National Rifle Association and its many members. I regret that. I would not like to be perceived as disparaging any large group." He went on to point out that he had recently signed a bill lowering the minimum age permitted for possession of rifles or shotguns by young New York State licensed hunters.

That did not mollify the association. "One speech triggered your meteoric rise to fame," wrote Alonzo H. Garcelon, the organization's president —who uses verbs like *triggered* whenever possible—"and one sentence may shoot down your national political aspirations." (The gun lobby's chief also favors *shoot down*; he blazes away with a limited but consistent metaphor.)

In his column in the rifle association's official journal, Garcelon continued his sniping at the apologetic Governor: "He uses the word *inartful*," he fired back. "In other words, he meant what he said, only wishes he had said it differently. Look up *inartful* in the dictionary. If you find it, let me know. I couldn't."

Inartful is in no dictionary because it is not a word. The aim of this piece is to consider the two meanings of *artful,* not to empty both barrels at the retreating form of the Governor, who writes more of his own material than most politicians.

An early meaning of *artful* was "performed with skill, dexterous." In a 1728 translation of *The Satyrs of Persius,* Thomas Sheridan used this sense: "Horace was more artful, and in a merry Way touched upon his Friends' Faults without putting them out of Humour." That meaning of the word has atrophied, however, its function taken over by *skillful.* When we want to say "filled with art" or "artist-like," we use the adjective *artistic.*

What happened to *artful?* It came to mean "adroit," then gained a more pejorative connotation, almost "crafty, wily." Charles Dickens applied the word to a pickpocket who befriends Oliver Twist: "Among his intimate friends he was better known by the sobriquet of 'the artful Dodger.'" I once wrote a speech for Richard M. Nixon and asked Clark Clifford, who had written speeches for Harry S. Truman, what he thought of it. "Artful," he replied, which I took to mean "Machiavellian" and considered a left-handed compliment.

If *artful* now means "crafty, wily, slippery," what would *inartful* mean? Take *disingenuous* as an analogy: *ingenuous* means "innocent, naïve," and *disingenuous* means "falsely frank, calculating." Thus, with *artful* meaning "wily," *inartful* would mean "not wily" and would be a compliment.

That's why Governor Cuomo's "My response was *inartful,*" meaning "I goofed," makes no sense. Depending on his specific intent, he could have chosen *insensitive, cruel, thoughtless* or even *impolitic.* His apologists will have to sharpen their apologies if they expect the gun lobby to join the Cuomo boom.

State of the Inartful

I may have been unduly harsh on the Governor who bids fair to become the next Democratic candidate for President of the United States. Mario M. Cuomo was castigated for his use of the undictionaried locution *inartful.*

Because *artful* means "crafty, wily" more often than "skillful," I held that *inartful* seemed to mean "not crafty," which was not what the Governor of New York meant in apologizing for a bumbling statement about hunters. Moreover, I asserted with fine disdain that because it was in no dictionary, *inartful* was "not a word."

However, in the legal field it is a term of inart. "Many specialized terms elude dictionaries," writes Fred R. Shapiro, head of reference services at the New York Law School (I think he's chief librarian). *"Inartful* is a widely used word in the specialized vocabulary of law." He punched up the word on Lexis, the computerized compilation of judicial opinions, and found the word used hundreds of times, most often to describe poorly drafted documents.

Carl L. Distefano of New York City, who found 1,286 uses on the system in both adjectival and adverbial form, uses a couple of nice hunting metaphors to instruct me further: "I suspect it was *inartful,* the law word, that Governor Cuomo intended when he took back his potshot at the hunting set. If my suspicion is correct, then Alonzo H. Garcelon, the National Rifle Association president, missed the mark when he ungraciously turned down the Governor's retraction."

OK, Guv, you win—*inartful* is not, as I put it, "not a word." However, it is not a precise word, no matter how hoary its precedents in the law. Here's a contribution to your next campaign, in which you will not want to appear legalistic: try *artless.*

This brings up a more profound subject: when a word's meaning is changing, when does it stop meaning what it used to mean?

Some semanticists say we should not go with the flow of meaning shift, but retain all meanings: "To deny multiplicity of meanings for a word would hog-tie our language," writes Robert A. Herrig of Stamford, Connecticut. "For instance, one could no longer use the word *green* to mean 'youthful, vigorous,' because a more recent connotation, 'inexperienced,' has been associated with the word. The fact that *nice* is now used primarily as a synonym for 'pleasant' would preclude its being employed to mean 'punctilious.' In such cases, context dictates meaning, as it does in the Cuomo case."

Those of us in the language dodge are not so powerful: we can neither banish nor preserve different senses of the same word. However, we have some influence (I cannot get my daughter to stop referring to one young man as a *geek*, but I can get the Governor of New York to think twice about *inartful*). That influence should not be in the direction of relying ever more on context for meaning; when a word change reaches a critical mass, I turn to the new meaning and reject all others, lest I wind up with a critical mess.

For example, in saying "Nice guys finish last," a phrase attributed to Leo Durocher, I do not want any confusion about the old and new meanings of *nice*. Context makes it clear, but all too often context can be ambiguous, and words with single, predominant meanings help the cause of clarity in communication. Let *artful*'s secondary meaning of "skillful" continue to atrophy; when we use it, let the image of craftiness loom up unencumbered by nice-guy distinctions.

> You'll hear from a lot of lawyers on "inartful." Around the courthouse—the New York County courthouse, which I cover for the New York *Post*—it's mainly used adverbially: "The complaint, while inartfully drafted, does indeed state a cause of action." I.e.: "The plaintiff's lawyer, *qua* writer, would find a paper bag an insurmountable opponent, but we can discern, however barely, how he thinks the other guy done him wrong. Motion to dismiss denied. Go to it."
>
> It usually suggests the plaintiff is a chump. I don't think Cuomo was going that far in self-description.
>
> *Hal Davis*
> *White Plains, New York*

> I disagree with your suggestion that Governor Cuomo replace "inartful" with "artless." I feel "artless" is inappropriate as a substitute for "inartful."
>
> There are both explicit and connotative differences in describing one's actions or thoughts using the suffix "-ful" and using "-less."
>
> The suffix "-less" means "without, free from." Use of "-less" is powerful, negative, self-demeaning. For example, "It was artless of me." "It was tactless of me." This tells the other person, one had *no* art, tact.
>
> However, the suffix "-ful" refers to "abounding in," as in "Gee, I

wasn't so abounding in tact." This is a milder correction of the self than saying "I had no tact at all."

So, "-ful" and "-less" are not interchangeable. Inartful may not be correct according to the dictionary. ("I was not artful" might be a better expression of the thought.) Yet, I wouldn't want my governor groveling with words by announcing to the public that he's "artless."

Regina Berenback
Larchmont, New York

Contrary to what Robert Herrig wrote and you published, "green" is not a valid example of a word whose meaning is changing. It has meant "inexperienced" since the time of Shakespeare. In *Hamlet*, I, iii, 101, Polonius says to Ophelia, "You speak like a green girl/ Unsifted in such perilous circumstance." Want another example? In *Antony and Cleopatra*, I, v, 73, Cleopatra speaks of "My salad days,/ When I was green in judgment."

"Brush up your Shakespeare."

Irving Genn
Flushing, New York

In Re Pot

"Has high court's spelling gone to pot?" asked a headline in *The National Law Journal*. The subhead in this usually sobersided publication read: "You Say 'huana, I Say 'juana."

The facts are not in dispute. As the article by Tony Mauro of *USA Today* made clear, the problem about the spelling of *marijuana* (probably the Spanish word for the drug's nickname, "Maria Juana," in English "Mary Jane") arose in March when Justice Byron R. White wrote the Court's opinion in *Malley v. Briggs*.

The police may be sued for making some unconstitutional arrests, whizzed White, no matter if they have arrest warrants. The Justice used terms of dope-smoking art in describing the arrest—*toking* and *doing her thing*—and defined them for his less hip colleagues as "smoking marihuana" for the former and "rolling a marihuana cigarette," in the instant case, for the latter.

Not everybody blows *marihuana* with an *h*. That's Castilian Spanish;

American or Mexican Spanish generally spells it with a *j* (although sometimes with an *h* or even a *g*), and that more local spelling is preferred in most United States dictionaries. In the report issued recently by the President's Commission on Organized Crime, headed by the up-to-date Judge Irving R. Kaufman of the United States Court of Appeals for the Second Circuit, a zinging *[sic]* was placed after the *h* spelling in quoting a previous report. In 1984, the Government Printing Office Style Manual switched from *h* to *j*, after a meeting in what one may assume was not a smoke-filled room.

In an accompanying opinion in *Malley v. Briggs*, which is becoming known in legal circles as "Marihuana v. Marijuana," Justice Lewis F. Powell, Jr., used both spellings in a footnote's single sentence: "At trial, Mrs. Briggs denied seeing any marihuana at that party or receiving a marijuana cigarette."

Justice Powell is a careful fellow, and one of the Court's most courtly; friends say he did that because his opinion was a partial concurrence and a partial dissent. If so, that is one of the subtlest and most effective digs at a fellow jurist in modern legal history.

Queried about this through a Court spokesman, Reporter of Decisions Henry C. Lind says only that on review of the controversy, the Justices decided to change the Court stylebook to conform with the modern *j* spelling. No reasons given; the Supreme Court sometimes acts that way, and we'll never know the judicial tugging and hauling that went into it. "Henry Lind says that's it," reports the spokesman, adding, "He expected your call and wants to know how you spell Qaddafi."

You make no reference to the whim of the United States Congress. Throughout the statutes banning drug abuse marihuana is the employed spelling. See, *e.g.*, 21 U.S.C. §812(c)(10).

While I had been an aficionado of spelling the controlled substance with a j, my opinions have bowed to the Congressional usage. In spite of Judge Kaufman's distaste for the "h" and the GPO Style Manual, I undoubtedly will, as a non-activist jurist, continue to hew to the statute.

John T. Elfvin
Judge, United States District Court
Buffalo, New York

Invasion of the Verbs

"The fact is I think I am a verb," wrote the dying Ulysses S. Grant to his doctor, "instead of a personal pronoun. A verb is anything that signifies to be; to do; or to suffer. I signify all three."

The fact is I think he would have left us a punchier quotation without the first five words, but no editor stepped in to make it read "I am a verb. . . ." Even so, Grant's self-identification with a verb showed he understood the essence of that part of speech: action. No verb, no plot. You just sit and plan, like General George B. McClellan.

After a short period of decline, while wishy-washy writers in passive voices lolled around in dull, bureaucratic constructions ("the program was implemented"), the verb is back with a vengeance. Sixty-second managers shift to the active voice to snap, "Implement this," and their bosses, two-second managers, bark a gutsier action word: "Do that!" The superboss, or split-second manager, says, "Dotted-line the responsibility to him, and straight-line the reporting to the other guy."

Huh? A *dotted-line* denotes a non-hierarchical relationship, as between two executives in the same echelon or on different levels exchanging information rather than direction, but a vogue verb in executive suites is "to dotted-line it," which is a verb meaning "tell him, but it's not an order."

New verbs are being coined every day. Like body snatchers, the alien verbs are investing and seizing the souls of every interesting new noun. "We're looking *to fast-track* that," Maine's Department of Transportation planning director Gedeon G. Picher told the Brunswick, Maine, *Times Record.* Only yesterday, the *fast track* was one of the hottest nouns in chic-speak, until it was shunted aside and passed by the *fast lane.* Now it's up out of the cinders and back in the trendy running as a verb, *to fast-track,* and will soon be overtaken, if history repeats, by *to fast-lane.* (I detect a shading of difference: you *fast-track* a program, but *fast-lane* a person. Welcome to life in the fast language.)

"The last two cars of this train will not *platform* at Talmadge Hill," announces the conductor. Fred McClafferty of N. W. Ayer in New York sends that in, urging resistance, and adds that he will fight two other new verbs, *to parent* and *to network.* (That advertising agency is trying to style itself "N W Ayer" on its stationery, eschewing periods. The N. W. stands for Nathan Wallin, and the founder's name demands periods, but the graphic designers at the agency evidently do not platform at periods.)

Other Lexicographic Irregulars wince at such back-formations as *to surveille* and *to liaise,* activities that the French might consider voyeurism, and some high-tech types shudder at *to satellite* or even *to videotape.* Julian Bercovici of Hollywood sends me a statement he received from Group W Cable announcing "Service charges will be *statemented* the 22 of each month." A spokesman for the gas-station owners of New York was quoted as saying, "There seems to be a tremendous movement *to exodus* the area." Here is one of Manhattan District Attorney Robert M. Morgenthau's comments on the subway vigilante's case: "We *post-mortemed* this thing to death," which is surely a case for the Squad Squad.

The verb invaders have *accessorized* the fashion industry, *concertized* around the world, *funeralized* their casualties, *mainstreamed* their thinking, *leafleted* their neighborhood and *credentialed* their coverage. (I know this because I've *sourced* it.) The new verbs threaten to *angst-out* their critics, as the new functional shift confuses the dee-fense.

What cooks with this rampant verbification of nouns—or, as the vogue-verb set would put it, what *rotisses* here? My colleagues in columny are also shuddering at the nominal body snatching: "I think it's worth wondering about role models," wrote Ellen Goodman in the *Boston Globe.* "Or about *role modeling* if you belong to the *interfacing, accessing, networking* school of verbing." Harold C. Schonberg of *The New York Times* takes issue with an Atlanta editor who said fresh news "mooted the story." Says Harold: "I hoot at the moot." And Phil Gailey of *The Times* noted how governors like to *sunset* legislation and compliment each other for *profounding* the issues. Am I *demagoging* or *cheap-shotting* to suggest the vogueverbers are *excessing?*

Let us chew this over with William A. Kretzschmar, Jr., of the University of Wisconsin-Whitewater, who edits *The Journal of English Linguistics.* He applies two tests to the functional shiftiness—one of newness, the other of logic and aesthetics. "Of *commentate,* for instance, I ask whether the form offers any new shade of meaning. I think it does, since the action of a commentator is specialized; we noncommentators can *comment,* but you commentators can *commentate* because of your special position and authority."

In the same way, he likes *administrate* because he detects a shade of meaning different from *administer*. But he rejects *orientate* on aesthetic grounds: "It seems to me an ugly duplication of *to orient*." He'll buy a locution like "lunches are *satellited* from the regional high school" but does not countenance *to dialogue* because "I find it impossible to see how any subject person or group could unilaterally impose a dialogue on or with somebody else." Linguist Kretzschmar adds: "I shouldn't make such judgments, and should just believe in the doctrine of usage, but I can't help it— I won't abdicate my own right to decide what I am willing to say or write."

Nobody can deny a nonce verb its moment in the sun, and sometimes they come to stay, though some people still grump about *finalize*. (*Grump*? From the noun *grump*, probably out of the verbs *to grunt* and *to grumble*. So why not use the old *grumble*? Because *grumble* kind of rumbles, and *grump* jumps and bumps.)

David B. Guralnik at Webster's New World Dictionary is laid back about functional shift, which has roots deep in the language. The form it takes is largely accidental: *civilize* could as easily have been *civilate*, and *pacify* could have been *paxilate*. I asked him, if he had to decide what ending to use for "to make a verb out of a noun"—*verbize*, *verbate*, or *verbify*—which he would choose and why. The lexicographer, who has no trouble verbalizing, said: "-*ify*, from the Latin *facere*, 'to make,' is specific; -*ize*, from the Greek suffix -*izein*, means 'to become' as well as 'to make'; -*ate*, from the Latin -*atus*, is not as specific as -*ify*. So I would choose *verbify*. Or just *verb*."

Others, come to think of it, would also choose *verb*, with no suffix at all: "Don't verb nouns" is an obvious fumblerule. But where does that leave us? Should we hoot at the mooters, and despise-*prioritize*?

My advice is to take it a case at a time.

Uniqueness counts. Does the new verb do a job that no other word does? I cannot think of an exact synonym for *to cheap-shot*. *To exodus* sounds silly, but it does not mean merely *to exit*, rather "to leave in droves" —I might use it, if I had not used a vogueverb in a previous page of copy, and if I had just used "leave in droves."

Aesthetics counts. *Prioritize* strikes me as ugly, and *priorify* would horrify, probably because the word is used huffily by prissy people. Anybody who says, "Nutshell this," ought to be boiled down, because such finger-snapping locutions have the ring of jargon. And overuse of the shift puts too many of your men in motion: you cannot *party*, *host* and *R.S.V.P.* in the same sentence without *hangovering*.

Tradition counts. If two words like *make clear* do the semantic trick, use them, or use a standby like *specify* or *illuminate* if that is precisely what you mean—but do not strain for *disambiguate* just to be in academic vogue. And before you reach for *disincentivize,* ask yourself—will *discourage* do? At the same time, if a new verb has lasted a few years, don't take it upon yourself to give it the functional shaft. *To intuit, to babysit, to curate, to position* all have made it out of noncehood, so start accessing them.

I don't like "to curate," falsely derived from curator, one who (from the Latin) takes care of an art collection. He also organizes temporary exhibitions. The other meaning is to cure as in preserving ham, fish, etc., and the English curate who is entrusted with the cure of souls.

Readers will surely understand better what happens when you organize an exhibition rather than curate it. To curate is merely chichi, but to baby-sit is very clear and acceptable as you note.

As a retired curator I may be prejudiced, but time may cure me of my prejudice.

> *Gustave von Groschwitz*
> *New York, New York*

Let me offer an item for your collection of verbified nouns:—"cul-de-sacked." I heard it for the first time recently when one of my colleagues advised in a briefing that we should not let ourselves "get cul-de-sacked" (as in painting ourselves into a corner) by being too hasty in choosing a particular piece of computer equipment.

I like "cul-de-sacked." It has unmistakable verve and cascades delightfully off the tongue. I hope you like it too.

> *J. R. Champion*
> *Englewood, Colorado*

I've collected a host of "needless variants" (Fowler's term) over the years:

> improvisate
> variate
> summarization
> vandalist
> analysization
> determinated
> manifestate
> conferencing
> conservationalist
> unusuality

signaturize
destruct (for "destroy")
observating
scrutinization
sensationalistic
eventuate
combinate
experimentate
delimitate

My favorite is "coronate" (for "crown"), a word which appeared in the *Times Magazine* itself a few years ago.

Arthur L. Block
New York, New York

When a fielder doesn't chase a fly hard enough, Phil Rizzuto likes to say that he "nonchalanted" the ball.

Stephen B. Labunski
New York, New York

N. W. Ayer was *not* the founder of the advertising agency that bears his name (the oldest such firm in the U.S.).

The founder was *Francis Wayland Ayer*, and he was twenty-one years old. It was a one-man firm, so he made it look more substantial by calling it "N. W. Ayer & Son." His father, N. W. Ayer, was never in the firm.

John Maass
Philadelphia, Pennsylvania

Is a Problem

"I am being driven slightly crazy," writes the moderately distracted Ann Shanahan of Smith College, in Northampton, Massachusetts, "by the rampant misuse of the word *problematic*. Would you care to deliver yourself of some instructions on the matter?"

Horseradish. That is not an expletive, but the subject of the clipping she attached, an article by Steven Greenhouse of *The New York Times*: "Wil-

liam J. Keller, a ruddy, muscular man who grows 50 acres of horseradish
. . . asks himself why he continues to grow this problematic root."

In another part of the paper, an editorialist wonders: "What of deposi-
tors in the small number of banks that lack Federal coverage and rely
instead on problematical state insurance?"

Also in my *problematic* dossier, which is horseradish-redolent because I
have been working on this piece over a dish of Eastertime gefilte fish, is this
letter about my advocacy of the Star Wars defense doctrine from Michael
Huelshoff, a lecturer in political science at the University of Pennsylvania,
castigating me for "relying upon defensive systems whose feasibility is at
best problematic."

First, which is correct—*problematic* or *problematical?* The answer is un-
equivocal: both are correct, with the shorter form preferred in most dictionaries. Do not search for consistency here: *grammatic* is wrong and *grammatical* is right, though *erratic* is right and *erratical* is wrong. Don't look for
rules; be practic.

More important, what does the word mean? In one sense, considering
the horseradish "a *problematic* root," the word means "giving problems."
Farmers find the horseradish an ornery crop to grow, digging it out of 16
inches of dirt while trying to keep their eyes from watering.

A closely related sense is "giving or having problems," as in this use by
the language writer Steele Commager in *Forbes* magazine: " 'Stock' is a
more problematic word," with sixty-five meanings listed in the Oxford
English Dictionary.

That leads to another sense: "puzzling, hard to solve or decide." John
Donne wrote in 1624: "His happinesse is but disputable and problemati-
call." Questionable.

Now we're getting away from a word lying on a couch, often a predicate
adjective ("It's problematic") having all those problems, to a plain adjective
casting doubt on a noun. The more common meaning of *problematic* has
been "dubious, uncertain," as expressed by our editorialist derogating state
bank insurance and my correspondent knocking the feasibility of a serious
zap-you're-dead defense system.

I suspect that the most common meaning of the word is changing from
"dubious, doubtful, not to be relied upon" to "problem-filled." Perhaps it
fills a need (not a "felt" need, a real need) to describe a time in which many
of us are getting anxious about too much angst. In this transitional phase,
the word is soft at the edges, slopping over both senses. Linguistic stalwarts
at Smith College who like its "dubious" meaning are a tad mad about
those who use it in a "having problems" sense.

In this stage, if clarity is your object, stay away from the word. If you're puzzled, say so; if you have problems, try horseradish and have a good cry.

A side issue: note Mrs. Shanahan's use of "deliver yourself of some instructions," which I have dutifully done. In that phrase, the words *yourself of* are not necessary, but they serve a rhetorical purpose. They make the verb *deliver* reflexive.

A reflexive verb's subject and object refer to the same thing. Why do I mesmerize myself with such pedagogic declarations? Because the grammatical reflection—as in "I deliver myself of these views"—is a device that makes a phrase round and renders prose mellifluous. Severe editors take note: readers tire of spare prose. Loosen up a little. The style is the person himself and all that. This is the fourth punchy sentence in a row, and already this piece reads like "The Killers."

We are taught tautness and told that our sentences must be as lean as the best corned beef, but sometimes a little reflexive horseradish helps the medicine go down. The stylish stylist usually observes the strictures about no unnecessary words, but crosses 'em up now and then.

In *The Garden of Eloquence*, Henry Peacham in 1577 gave this example: "When for *rhetoric*, we say *the art of speaking well*; for *logic*, *the art of reasoning*; for *tyrant*, *an oppressor of the laws and liberties of the commonweal*; for *man*, *a wight endowed with reason*."

Or for *give*, the more mouthfilling *deliver yourself of*. Reflex, ye slimmers, before it is too late.

Surely, surely there is more than a grammatical and stylistic difference between *deliver* and *deliver yourself*. Used reflexively, it assumes a different meaning: you'd never say "deliver yourself" when it is a matter of delivering a package or a message. "Deliver yourself" has an association with "bring forth," "give birth," and is more descriptive than the straightforward transitive form of the verb.

You are known to consider matters of style and grammar carefully, and to express your conclusions and recommendations forcefully; you are now assumed to have given the matter of *problematical/problematic* some thought; now, please, let us share in your views after the preceding period of gestation: "deliver yourself . . ."

I think this form would also be used to encourage an interlocutor to come out with it, stop shilly-shallying and pussyfooting when the point has obviously not yet been made: "Come on, deliver yourself!"

(Mrs.) Lu Fenton
New York, New York

You state that your *problematic* dossier was horseradish-redolent because you worked on it over a dish of "Eastertime gefilte fish." Where do you get Eastertime gefilte fish? From the Passover Bunny?

Harvey Margolin
Yorktown Heights, New York

Kotcha!

E dward Koch, a bestselling author who moonlights as a city official, referred to a compatriot under investigation by hordes of leaky law-enforcement officials as a "close friend—*in the abstract.*"

This is a new category of political friendship. One meaning of *in the abstract* is "apart from material objects"; its synonym is "theoretical," its antonym "concrete." An *abstract friendship*, then, is a tie that binds in theory but that does not suggest participation in the sharing of material objects, such as cash and other valuables that could be construed as graft.

Mayor Koch has used other words recently that bear investigation. In his defense of a policy of permitting his department heads to hire their aides without prior approval from him, the Mayor explained: "I don't want commissioners to ever be able to say to me, 'I could not perform because you decided to give me *palookas.*' "

"My recollection of Joe Palooka," writes a *New York Times* colleague, "was that he was dumb but honest. If that's so, Mayor Koch might be better off with *palookas* rather than what he's had."

The American slang term *palooka* was adopted by, but did not originate with, the cartoon character of an amiable prizefighter drawn by Hammond Edward (Ham) Fisher. According to *Webster's New World Dictionary*, the word was coined by Jack Conway, a baseball player and, later, a sportswriter, and is considered "Old Slang" (that label doesn't refer to Old English, says the lexicographer David Guralnik, but to "aging slang words mostly used now by older people like me"). The *Dictionary of American Slang* by Wentworth and Flexner says that the coinage was ascribed to Conway (without a citation) by Abel Green, editor of *Variety*, for which Conway wrote until his death in 1928. The following year William Henry Nugent wrote in *The American Mercury* that "*Palooka*, now signifying a fifth-rate pugilist, derives from a pure Gaelic word." The *Oxford English Dictionary*'s supplement dismisses all this and says, "Origin unknown," extending its meaning from pugilist to "any stupid or mediocre person; a lout." Its first use in print is cited in 1925; two years later, Dashiell Hammett, in *Black Mask* magazine, was writing about "a paluka who leads with his right." Despite the uplift given the word's meaning by the cartoon character, a *palooka* is still generally considered a punch-drunk or inept fighter, and Mayor Koch used the word correctly.

When savaged by a right-wing civil libertarian for publicly calling a suspect in the case a *crook* (a colloquial term in use since 1879 to mean "swindler, thief"), the Mayor explained that his prejudicial comment was no more than "a primordial scream of rage and anger" because he felt betrayed.

He meant *primal scream*. *Primal, primeval* and *primordial* are all synonyms for "earliest, original, primitive, first in time," from the Latin *primus*, "first." The phrase *the primal scream* is from a 1970 book of that title by Arthur Janov, a psychologist who espoused treating mental disorders with *primal therapy*, in which patients are encouraged to reenact infancy or express strong emotions by means of shouts and screams. Apparently this is the therapy that Mr. Koch believes he engaged in by calling his friend-in-the-abstract a *crook*.

Finally—not to pick on the beleaguered Mayor (*beleaguered* is more defensive than *embattled*), but this cleans out my Kotcha! file—the Mayor sought to make a dramatic statement, complete with dramatic pause, but ruined it with bureaucratese. He told reporters of the time he discussed with Governor Cuomo the potential removal or resignation of his abstracted friend and, according to *The New York Times*: "The Mayor then paused and said, 'The time factor has arrived.'"

This made me want to emit a primordial groan. Some of us remember when the dramatic phrase was "The time has come," but you have to factor in an extra word when you are dealing with palookas in the abstract.

Whatever the etymology of "Palooka," Ham Fisher surely meant his readers to think of "Polack," which amiable blond Joe assuredly was.

Hugh Kenner
Baltimore, Maryland

I think I may be a palooka. Ham Fisher may have been one too.

Back in Wilkes-Barre in the late '20s or early '30s when he was a subject of some discussion as a local boy who was making good, my mother explained the origin of the Joe Palooka name.

Her family and Fisher's, she said, emigrated to this country from the Ukrainian shtetl of Priluki, about a day's journey (50 miles?) from Kiev. Prilukers, on the lower East Side at the turn of the century, were considered amiable unsophisticated country bumpkins, and they came to be called Palookas. That's what I've always believed was the origin of the term. You could look it up?

Incidentally, before he went national, Ham Fisher was the cartoonist and caricaturist for the *Wilkes-Barre Times Leader*. Mostly I remember he did caricatures of people in attendance at functions like Rotary meetings or volunteer firemen's clambakes. My father was neither, but I remember being impressed that he was once a subject. Also, for what the information may be worth in a game of Trivial Pursuits, Knobby Walsh, Joe Palooka's manager, was a caricature of Joe Walsh, city editor of the rival, now defunct, *Wilkes-Barre Record*.

Marvin Williams
Philadelphia, Pennsylvania

It is not often that one has an opportunity to emend the O.E.D.'s supplement, but the origin of "palooka" seems to provide such an occasion. An available source* predates Jack Conway and Dashiell Hammett (whose proper spelling of the word lacks only a circumflex) by some sixty years.

Pâluka is an "Eskimo" word, meaning "my gloves, mittens".** The Americanized connotation of boxers and their mitts, especially in an era before large padded gloves were worn in the ring, is clear. A

---

* Eskimo-English dictionary, compiled from Friedrich Erdmann's 1864 Eskimo-German edition (Church of the Ascension Thank-Offering Mission Fund, Hamilton, Ontario, 1925). NYPL call #: HBQ (Eskimo) 84-205
** entry 255, B 14

person holding up both mittened hands in front of the chest would appear to be in a pugilistic posture, even though innocently declaring *pâluka!*

Beyond the fact that the "u" is pronounced as "oo," one of the suffixes denoting who is the possessor of the noun is "-look"—*pâlo, pâluk, pâlut (pâlook, pâlooet):* gloves, mittens.***

"Eskimo" languages are among those which offer great charm in discovering the thought process which transcends mere translation. The following examples illustrate this point:

ahamarik: yes, it is indeed so; literally, a full-grown yes.

naegligijaksak: something to love; something which one should love, but does not as yet.

kapoktalik: there is froth, foam; said of a man who speaks many and beautiful words, and one is convinced that they are empty, idle, unmeaning words.

Russell Eliot Reif
New York, New York

Some (but not all) dictionaries give as one meaning for "abstract"— "theoretical, not practical or applied" or "theoretical rather than practical." But this is not the major or the main meaning given. By proposing "theoretical" as *the* synonym for "abstract," you suggest that this is the best or preferred word to use in its place.

Unfortunately, equating "theory" with "abstraction" caricatures the former. There is a perfectly good and concrete (though seldom used) synonym for "theoretical" and that is "explanatory." A theory is, to put it quite simply, an explanation, and if something is not "explanatory," there is no reason to regard it as "theoretical."

Many things that are "abstract" get passed off these days as "theory," to the discredit of the latter. Nothing should receive this honored designation unless it actually *explains* some phenomenon or relationship. To identify a proposition or an argument as "theoretical" simply because it is "abstract" is to derogate the meaning and pursuit of "theory."

Abstraction may be an important part of the process of developing theories. But observation, speculation, conceptualization, measurement and testing are each at least as essential to establish tenable explanations of phenomena or relationships. The quest for theory will become more concrete, and probably more productive, if the goal is seen as explanation rather than as abstraction.

Norman Uphoff
Ithaca, New York

*** entry 255, B 13

Lavish It On

"From the glow of the tapers on the 4-foot candelabra," reads the lush advertising copy for New York's Helmsley Palace hotel, "to the 100-year-old pastel panels of a royal court in amorous play, Leona Helmsley ensures the grandeur. . . . What better way to lavish her royal family."

Soon after that ad appeared, a *New Yorker* cartoon by Lee Lorenz showed a wealthy-looking couple coming out of a fancy entrance to a French restaurant, with the man saying, "I'd say we were served adequately but not lavished."

Lavish is best known as an adjective, from the Latin *lavare*, "to wash," root of *lavatory* and *lather*. A torrent of rain washing over the land was considered by the French to be *lavasse*, "abundant," even "excessive"; hence, *lavish* in English means "extravagant" or "profuse."

But what about *lavish* as a verb? Parsimonious lexicographers have always known of the intransitive use of *lavish*, meaning "to be lavish," and can cite examples from the Oxford English Dictionary showing a transitive use as well. Nicholas Udall's 1542 translation of the apothegms of Erasmus was first: "Those persones, who of a ryottousnesse did prodigally *lavesse* out and waste their substaunce. . . ."

The transitive verb has also been used with an immaterial object: "But I have lavished out too many wordes," wrote Sir Philip Sidney in 1581. More recently, we have been awash in the usage *to lavish (something) on:* "He attracts the attention a nation lavishes on its heroes," wrote Murrey Marder in the *Washington Post* about Henry Kissinger. *The Economist* wrote in 1976, "The government is also proposing to lavish on itself executive reserve powers. . . ."

Therefore, Mrs. Helmsley has every right to reach back and give new currency to the transitive verb form in seeking to "lavish her royal family. You. Her guests." (Avoid sentence fragments. Including those.) Lavish it on, Leona, or to put it intransitively, lavish away, Leona! They may poke at you at *The New Yorker,* but nobody can knock the etymology of your ad copy.

In a closely related linguistic development, the word *slather* has been coming on strong. This from the current *Mademoiselle* magazine: (You like that crisp introduction? I stole it from television-telegraphese: "Now this word.") "Sit with ankle resting on the opposite thigh. Slather lotion or oil onto hands. Stroke calf muscle with your thumb and fingers, squeezing. . . ." Or this, on foot care, from the same publication: "Mix 2 mashed avocados with several drops of lemon juice and 2 Tbs. honey. . . . Slather on feet. Place each foot in a plastic bag and elevate legs for 10 mins."

In 1978, the *Washington Post*'s Carol Krucoff described the way office workers grabbed a few moments of sun: "They slither into swimsuits, *slather* on the Deep Tan, slip on their sunglasses . . ." In 1980, Florence Fabricant wrote in *The New York Times:* "Frequently the barbecue chef *slathers* on a basic red sauce right from the bottle," and in 1984, the *Washington Post*'s David Remnick criticized a sportscaster who "*slathers* on the schmaltz with a broad knife."

Slather was first cited in 1876 as a noun, meaning "a great quantity," and is still used that way: people who lounge around stroking and squeezing their calf muscles usually have *slathers* of money. Merriam-Webster has its first verb citation of *slather* in 1881 and has as its primary meaning "to spread thickly or lavishly," with an extended meaning of "to use or spend in a wasteful or lavish manner."

Where does *slather* come from? An 1818 glossary of Cheshire words defines it as a verb meaning "to slip or slide." This was the sense Rudyard Kipling had in mind when he wrote in 1909: "I hate slathering through fluff." There could be a link, as yet missing, between the slippery glop of

Cheshire and the oily substance that the sun-worshiping office workers smear on their pale bodies.

The easy part of all this has been to readily accept a revived use of an older English verb and to welcome the wider use of a colorful bit of slang. And now to the hard part—the synonymy of pouring it on. As transitive verbs, how do *lavish* and *slather* differ?

Lavish means "treat with extravagance, pamper, fuss over, heap goodies upon." By lavishing praise, we do a positive thing to some admitted excess; the verb has a connotation of pleasure. *Slather* means "to besmear, to lay on almost obscene quantities." By *slathering* on the butter, we approach gluttony; the verb is almost always used pejoratively.

Lavish us, Leona, but *slather* us not. And send up a bellhop in a hurry: I can't get my pickled feet out of these plastic bags.

Lavish it on. OK. But can you lavish him or her? Among your citations I find none to justify the use of *lavish* as a transitive verb with a person as the object. So where do you derive your definition: *Lavish* means "treat with extravagance, pamper, fuss over, heap goodies upon."

It is possible to imagine some old-time Eastern potentate lavishing concubines upon a friendly prince, but in such case these ladies would be being treated as non-persons—scarcely the sense in which Leona Helmsley wishes to "lavish her royal family."

To defend her etymology seems to me ridiculous, so I can't help thinking your real purpose is to test how many Nitpickers will scurry out of the woodwork.

> Harriet V. Reinhard
> San Francisco, California

I think your column on *lavish* misses the point: using *lavish* to mean "treat with extravagance, pamper, fuss over, heap goodies upon" is a novelty, and a superfluous one. As a transitive verb, its standard meaning is to "give, spend, or pour forth generously or liberally"; this is the sense in your examples from the *Washington Post* and *The Economist* and in the older ones from the OED. When she lavishes attention *on* her guests, Leona Helmsley properly gives new currency to this old form, with the imprimatur of Sir Philip Sidney. But when she insists on lavishing her guests directly, she commits a solecism or coins a neologism (depending on your point of view). I think it's a solecism;

she may pamper (or *indulge* or *coddle*) her guests, but with all those choices on the menu she doesn't need to lavish them.

Alan Wachtel
Mountain View, California

Let a Simile Be Your Umbrella

The umbrella, that symbol of appeasement of two generations ago, has been jerked out of its stand and metaphorically applied to a different diplomatic maneuver.

"We need to extend the arms-control process," President Reagan told the United Nations, "to build a bigger umbrella under which it can operate; a road map, if you will, showing where during the next twenty years or so these individual efforts can lead."

The *road map* metaphor never got unfolded, but the *umbrella* did. After the election, a White House aide listed six areas, from weapons in space to conventional weapons in Europe, that could be discussed under what he termed *umbrella talks.*

The Soviet Union, in the person of Ambassador Anatoly Dobrynin in Washington, replied cautiously, joking about the strange term: "You introduced something new in the history of Soviet-American relations, the umbrella. What is it?" he asked at a reception. "A *mackintosh* we can understand, but this must be studied."

Many Americans would not catch the meaning of *mackintosh,* a Briticism for a raincoat made of a lightweight waterproof fabric, originally of rubberized cotton, named after Charles Macintosh, a Scottish chemist and inventor who died in 1843. The word was first used in 1836 and may have gotten its *k* through a confusion with *mackinaw.* That short coat of heavy wool, often plaid, was named for Mackinaw City, Mich., once an Indian trading post. *Macintosh,* however, has no meaning in diplomacy and was just used by my friend Anatoly to throw us off, so forget this paragraph unless you are interested in rainwear or disinformation.

Umbrella, taken from the Latin *umbra,* "shade," was snapped up into English in the seventeenth century as a noun for "the thing that turns inside out in the wind and leaves you soaking on a rainy day," to use the technical definition. It has been called a *brelly, brolly, roundtop, shower stick, blub-blub* and *bumbershoot.*

In this century, the word has been used to evoke "protection" in many ways: during World War II, the commando raid on Dieppe was covered by an air armada called an *umbrella*. In 1950, when the New York Giants under coach Steve Owen introduced a pass defense of a six-man line with one linebacker and four defensive backs fanned out behind the line, this was dubbed the *umbrella defense*. More recently, the word has added a meaning of "embracing a broad range of factors," and Merriam-Webster's Ninth New Collegiate quotes Diane Ravitch's phrase "building new colleges under a federation umbrella."

That brings us to Mr. Reagan's usage in what his State Department speech drafters thought would become known as his "famous *road map* speech." The previous description of items combined into a comprehensive proposal was *package*: Defense Secretary Charles (Engine Charlie) Wilson startled an Eisenhower Cabinet meeting by putting Korean negotiations together with recognition of Red China and asking, "Is there any possibility of a package deal?"

Fearlessly, President Reagan took up the symbol that British Prime Minister Neville Chamberlain made famous in his return from the Munich Conference in 1938 announcing after dismembering Czechoslovakia that he had brought "peace for our time." (Not "peace *in* our time," as often misquoted; the second phrase comes from the Anglican Morning Prayer.)

Curious, that Mr. Reagan should use the old umbrella symbol in his own search for peace for this time; it has the wrong associations. Democrat Al Smith wrote in Depression-racked 1931: "The American people never carry an umbrella. They prepare to walk in eternal sunshine."

I work as a lighting director for film and video, and umbrellas (either white or metallic finish) are used to "bounce" light off of, in order to create a broad soft source of light, yielding a natural look. Under *our* umbrellas there is no shadow, no *umbra*—in fact, just the opposite. *Lighting umbrellas* is an anomaly that might take a fair amount of explanation, some generations from now. Reflective parasols? No better.

Jerome E. Noonan
West Newton, Massachusetts

I beg to differ with the suggestion that the term "umbrella" has no other meaning in diplomacy than that given it by Mr. Chamberlain in 1938. I would not want to suggest that your memory of the Nixon administration is short. But it would appear that Ambassador

Dobrynin, after more than twenty years, is infected with the ingrown-toenail spirit of our nation's capital.

From March 1970 through August 1971 the ambassadors of the United States, Great Britain and France in Bonn, and the Soviet Ambassador to the German Democratic Republic negotiated an umbrella agreement—the Quadripartite Agreement of 3 September 1971. Under the terms of the legal umbrella provided by the Four Powers, agreements and arrangements "implementing and supplementing" it were negotiated by the "competent German authorities"—East and West.

This international legal sense of the term, as then used by the Berlin Allies, probably derived from the German term *Schirm*, used alone in speech to mean umbrella—properly *Regenschirm*—but found in many compounds connoting protection of one sort or another. These include *Abschirmdienst*, counterintelligence service, and *Schirmherr*, patron, *inter alia*, as of a club.

The *idea* of a four-power umbrella, under which the Germans themselves were allowed to make certain "inner-German" trade arrangements, modest easements in the rigors of the *de facto* division of the country, may be found in the Communiqué of the Council of Foreign Ministers of 20 June 1949. As I recall, the English text of this document does not use the word umbrella. Rather, this sense evolved from translating it, from translating the will of the Four Powers into German. Implicit in it is a legal complication now rarely if ever mentioned in public: residual responsibilities of the victorious World War II allies for "all Germany and Greater Berlin."

> *K. Martin Johnson*
> *Former Army Historian*
> *New York, New York*

Your talent for taking a word literally often leads you down a blind turn. I believe Mr. Dobrynin used the word "mackintosh" as an allusion to the cloak-and-dagger state of relations that has prevailed between the Soviet Union and the U.S. He obviously was not making a simplistic association between the waterproof properties of the mackintosh and Mr. Reagan's "umbrella," a point you argue tediously.

No, the mackintosh is synonymous with spies. It is the uniform of the secret agent. Mackintosh thus does have "meaning in diplomacy" insofar as it is a subtle reference to the intrigues of cold war politics. It appears then that Mr. Dobrynin was not being disinformative as you clumsily suggest, but rather, quite ironic. I just hope the ambassador's candid wit was not as easily lost on our diplomats as it was on you.

Richard Linnett
New York, New York

I wonder whether you intentionally laid a trap in referring to a mackinaw as "of heavy wool, often plaid." "Plaid" (properly pronounced plade) is "the shawl-like outer garment of the Highlander's national dress" (Fowler, second edition). While the Americans and English will not notice, perhaps you may hear from a Scot if the exchange rate is not too high for the postage.

Paul W. Lunkenheimer
Philadelphia, Pennsylvania

The Linear Camel

Nora Ephron, the novelist, underlines a couple of curious usages in a story by Jane Gross of *The New York Times* about Fred Lebow, the marathon runner and promoter.

Mr. Lebow comes up with marketing ideas that no high-powered committee could be expected to produce, according to Kathrine Switzer, a former runner. "People who think linearly get frustrated by that," says Miss Switzer. "They're afraid of change. They camel an idea to death."

First, *linear*. This word is claimed by many disciplines: to an artist, it is a graphic design where lines and forms are emphasized over color; to a mathematician, it involves terms of the first degree or an equation whose graph is a straight line; to a botanist, it is a description of narrow, uniform leaves or grasses; to a physicist, *linearity* is the extent to which an effect is exactly proportional to its cause; to an educator, *linear learning* is that step-by-step process requiring correct responses before proceeding in programmed learning.

Linear made the front page of *The New York Times* in a story by James Gleick about Dr. Narendra Karmarkar's discovery of a problem-solving algorithm, which "set off a deluge of inquiries from brokerage houses, oil companies and airlines, industries with millions of dollars at stake in problems known as linear programming."

Linear programming is the way that mathematicians examine the variables in a system to figure out the most efficient route to the goal. (That fairly straightforward definition will elicit letters with holes on the edges from terrible-tempered technocrats; those who wish to send their billions of variable definitions to me electronically should be on notice that I check my electronic mailbox for messages every two years.)

To the rest of us, *linear* used to mean "extended in a straight line" or "strung out in a line." Today, to those of us who ain't got algorithm, it has another meaning: *linear thinking* is formal logic, a brand of thinking that moves steadily from cause to effect to the next cause and so on.

The question: Is calling someone a *linear thinker* a compliment or an insult?

The phrase is sometimes intended to have a pejorative cast, as a type of thinking devoid of emotion or unseen by insights. Linear thinkers, muses the inspirationalist, rarely shout "Eureka!" Miss Switzer jogs past them and sneers. Bunch of clods and plodders.

For example, Tom Zito of the *Washington Post* wrote in 1983 that a psychology professor "suggested that games also teach children a large number of cognitive skills, multilevel (rather than linear) thinking. . . ." That puts down *linear*. Timothy Leary, the 1960s enthusiast of LSD, recently said proudly, "I've totally toasted all those circuits in my brain that lead to linear thinking."

On the other hand, there are those who use *linear* to describe thinking that is rational and produces results. Writing about mysticism and science in *The New York Times* in 1982, William Stevens reported that some analysts said Hindu convictions are "contrary to the linear-thinking spirit of discovery and the ever-evolving, ever-changing picture of reality that science paints." Thus, disciplined linear thinking is more likely to lead to "Eureka!" than are meditative methods.

On the third hand, the phrase has been used because it has a nice scientific sound. Political pollster Pat Caddell said in 1979 that by the use of "focus groups," panels of typical people who go into the tank in depth, "you get insights that go beyond your numbers. You get a linear thinking process that explores all sorts of unexpected dimensions to the campaign." In that use, *linear* seems to mean "intuitive" rather than "rational," but pollsters can be Humpty-Dumptian in their usage.

Now to the verb that might puzzle linguistic historians of the future if its origin is not explained here immediately. "They *camel* an idea to death," derides Miss Switzer. That verb is based on the anti-bureaucratic definition of a camel: a horse designed by a committee. *To camel* is evidently "to act ploddingly and uninspirationally, as in a linear-thinking committee."

As one who pioneered the field known as "Linear Programming," I believe you missed the point. All your examples, although dressed in different clothes, defined linear as a step-by-step process like beads on a chain with the possible exception of Pat Caddel's use which defies classification.

In mathematics, linear means a straight line in two dimensions. In three dimensions, it is a plane. In higher dimensions, it is a "hyperplane," sometimes called a "flat." In linear programming, we deal with systems that have many constraints (like don't spend more than you are budgeted). Each constraint is expressed in the form of linear *inequalities*, meaning lying on one side of a hyperplane.

The point is that linear programming is the antithesis of a step-by-step process like beads on a chain. The relations express the fact that all parts of the system (e.g., the economy) are interacting simultaneously on all the other parts over time.

George B. Dantzig
Department of Operations Research
Stanford University
Stanford, California

As part of your disquisition on "linear" thinking, it would have been most appropriate to mention "lateral thinking," an approach of which I am a great exponent. The classic bit of lateral thinking was, of course: "Don't raise the bridge, lower the river." But see Edward DiBono's book *Lateral Thinking* for more details.

Guy Henle
Scarsdale, New York

You use the word "technocrat" to describe what I think is a technologist. A technocrat, I think, is an adherent of, or member of, government by technicians (technocracy), while a technologist is a specialist in technology (such as Linear Programming).

Erik Wiik
Engineer and, I think, Technologist
South Charleston, West Virginia

Madame Esquire

A barrister in Britain was once called a *green-bag*, from the color of the briefcase he carried; in American slang, a legal eagle also became known as a *green-bag*. Then the British bag color changed, and a barrister was called a *blue-bag*. (Thus, it became possible for hardworking blue-bags to brown-bag at the Temple Bar, while lubricious green-bags brown-bag it in American restaurants.) In almost every case, however, the lawyers address one another in writing with *Esquire* after the name.

Comes now Charlton Heston, the actor, engaged in filming a series for ABC in which the character he plays has a daughter who is a lawyer.

"The script refers to a nameplate on her desk," writes Mr. Heston, "inscribed *Monica Colby, Esq.* 'Come on, guys,' I said. 'You've got this lady calling herself *Monica Colby, Gentleman.*'

" 'No, no!' they said." (Mr. Heston likes dialogue.) " '*Esquire* means "lawyer" now.' To me, it means, or meant in the Middle Ages, a squire serving a knight. This definition declined in the nineteenth century to 'gentleman' and eroded in the twentieth to a dusty honorific. . . . The Oxford English Dictionary extends it to include 'barrister.' "

"I concede a shaky justification," concludes this voice from the bulrushes, "for including lawyers among the professional gentlemen who can add *Esq.* after their signatures, if they choose. But to make it a genderless label for the legal profession seems to challenge the prime meaning of the word. What's your ruling?"

Cut! No camera rolls until this is resolved. The word *esquire* originally meant "shield-bearer," conjuring the image of Sancho Panza, the squire, schlepping Don Quixote's gear. Later, the term was applied to men of gentle (that is, noble) birth who were not quite knights but were considered more than mere gentlemen. Barristers, who could plead at the bar, were entitled to *Esq.*; solicitors had to beg for what dignity was left over.

Lawyers, looking for a way to give themselves the honorific clout that doctors had with *Dr.* and *M.D.*, adopted *Esq.* It was and is purely an affectation. Many women who are lawyers like it, because it shares the pomposity equally. "Now *esquire* has general acceptance," says Irene Redstone, president-elect of the National Association of Women Lawyers. (I would say "female lawyers," but prefer to avoid litigation.) "The idea is to represent the individual as an attorney regardless of gender. The sooner we all accept *Esq.* as a term without gender, the better." (I would say "sex," rather than gender, because I don't mind dirty words.)

The root is sexless: anybody can go around bearing a shield, or a bag of golf clubs (a *caddie* can be male or female, though a *cad* is still exclusively male—he should have at least offered to marry the girl). It was a job, or role in life, assumed in olden times by men, but when that all changed and women picked up the shields and clubs and started bearing them, they became entitled to be called *Esq.* as well. The sex of *esquire* is incidental to, and not central to, the etymon. The magazine *Esquire*, originally called "the magazine for men," can now accept perfume advertising. (Come to think of it, men's perfume has been a big advertiser for years.)

My ruling: if a female lawyer wants to be a pretentious oaf, she can call herself *Esq.* with impunity, same as the status-hungry male lawyers who affect the term. The word is being stripped of its male sexual connotation, and can be defined as "an appendage to a name seeking to assert importance or status; when accompanying a signature, an affectation, and when added to the name of an addressee, a form of flattery bordering on the obsequious."

Okay, Chuck, roll 'em.

I read with interest, not to say delight, William Safire's item entitled "Madame Esquire." How fascinating to find this arcane corner of English snobbery alive and well in these United States. The usage of the term esquire is peculiarly English and restricted to service officers of the rank of major and above, Church of England clergymen, the holders of some decorations, sons of knights and, as Mr. Safire says, barristers.

However, if the lawyers really wish to rake up their English inheritance, then they should remember that one of the key rules of snobbery is that you never give yourself a title. His Grace the Duke of Newcastle will simply sign and introduce himself as Newcastle. So, if female lawyers are the snobs they would like to be, they should wait for someone else to give them a title. Sadly, this was only possible prior to 1776.

> *Peter N. Jones*
> *Budd Lake, New Jersey*

Your discussion of usages of "esquire" as "Esq." is incomplete to the point of ineptness in failing to mention the usage by tens of millions for tens of decades among the British as their equivalent of "Mr." in addressing mail to untitled males. The point in time when the usage dropped below the 50 percent level is probably within the last ten years.

> *E. H. Leoni*
> *New York, New York*

In medieval Germany the *nebige,* just like the English *esquire,* was a farmer not bound to the land. He got that name as follows. Like everybody else a free farmer had his obligations within the framework of feudal society. His was to remain next—*nebig* in medieval German —to a knight and carry his arms.

As a free man the nebige as well as the esquire occupied a social position of some distinction. Thus, esquire became an honorific term. But in war such a person's lot—keeping up with a horse while carrying a heavy load—was anything but enviable. Thus, the nebige turned into the nebbish, a term of petty and derision in Yiddish and German slang.

It is my understanding that this explanation of the word nebbish is not universally accepted. I have been told some linguists believe it derives from the Hebrew for "one to be laughed at" (*nebboach*).

> *Michael Zuntz*
> *Arlington, Virginia*

You are correct that, among lawyers, "Esq." means "attorney at law" or "lawyer," rather than a rank of gentry. However, few lawyers refer to *themselves* as "Esq.," or sign their names with the "Esq." appended. Among lawyers, "Esq." has long been a customary term of courtesy and respect between brothers (and—if you want to genuflect to the reigning feminist *Zeitgeist*—sisters) at the bar and, as such, is used when addressing or referring to *another* lawyer. Thus, a lawyer who used the "Esq." after his own name would likely be regarded as something of a jerk by other lawyers. In writing to or about another lawyer, however, professional courtesy dictates use of the honorific.

Those lawyers who truly want to be status-hungry, pretentious oafs, as you so charitably put it, do not use "Esq." to get their point across. Instead, they sign their names using their law degrees, *viz.*, J.D., LL.B., or LL.M. (I hope you didn't mean to suggest that lawyers have cornered the market on status-hunger, pretention, and oafishness; I'd estimate that journalists and pundits are neck-and-neck with us in those regards, as they are in most measures of conduct.)

You may be interested to know that "Esq." is not used by lawyers in all parts of the country. In some states, lawyers refer to each other as "Attorney," as in "Attorney William Safire," or "The Honorable," as in "The Honorable William Safire." In New York, the latter mode of address is reserved for judges and other magistrates.

Thomas M. Bower
New York, New York

Situations do arise when it is important to designate the "players," e.g. lawyers and/or clients. Even after almost ten years in practice, I find that, without a designation, women attorneys can be and often are ignored or slighted. (I remember once sitting at the counsel table with my male client. The judge, who happened to be female, smiled at my client, giving him permission to begin *his* opening argument. The judge thought that *I* was the social worker, not the attorney.)

Since I do not want to be known as a "pretentious oaf," I'll gladly consider another term that describes me as a lawyer. One female senior partner in a major Los Angeles firm uses "Esquire" for the men, "Atty" for the women.

You disparage the use of "Esquire," but you've provided no creative alternatives. Any suggestions?

Jill Switzer
Los Angeles, California

NOTE from W. S.: Drop it for everybody.

Marginal Tax Day

On income tax day, the *marginal tax rate* is on everyone's lips. *Marginal* has become a vogue word, like *problematical,* but its different senses are tearing the word's meaning apart.

In business, *marginal* usually has a positive meaning: many companies base their increase of output on the marginal cost—that is, the cost of each extra unit produced. The last widget produced costs less than the first, and if you can sell the last one, it produces a greater *profit margin* than the first.

In our progressive income tax, the *marginal tax rate* is what we pay for additional income. "Let's say you make $30,000," explains George Carlson, director of the Treasury Department's Office of Tax Analysis. (I couldn't call the Internal Revenue Service on this—its phones are plugged into its crashed computers.) "When you check that amount in the table in your I.R.S. booklet, you find in the left column that your income falls into, say, the $28,000–$34,000 range. Within that bracket, everyone pays an average tax rate—in this case, say $5,000. In addition, the next column gives your *marginal* tax rate—that's the percentage of extra tax you pay on the extra income in your bracket. If the minimum in your bracket is $28,000, and you make $30,000, the marginal tax rate is the percentage you must pay on that extra $2,000."

Thus (good word, "thus"—means "Wake up! Here comes the part you need to know"), the more you make, the greater the percentage you pay on the last dollar you earn, a bite into profit that can remove incentive. "Economic and political decisions are made at the margins," says Mr. Carlson, as we contemplate the onrush of the tax-rate flatteners, "—whether the extra income earned will be worth the higher percentage of taxes."

Not everyone is in love with the action at the margin. *Marginal* was defined in 1658 as "belonging to the margin or margent . . . the brink or brim of any thing." That "close-to-the-edge" meaning, which carried danger in it, competed with a newer "on-the-side" meaning, which connoted unimportance. That clash of meanings is what makes *marginal* confusing today.

In politics, a *marginal district* is one in which either party can "edge out" the other; in psychology, *marginal consciousness* is at the mind's edge, far from the sharp *focal* consciousness; in finance, *marginal trading*—buying "on margin"—extends the buyer's purchasing power beyond the edge of his own money; in zoology, the *marginals* are the feathers on the tips of a bird's wings.

In vogue usage, however, the warning inherent in living in the margin now appears to be taking over from the "inconsequential" sense. The National Conference of Catholic Bishops, in last year's letter on economic justice, wrote of the poor's "being marginalized," presumably forgotten on the fringe of society.

When you begin verbifying the adjective, the original noun takes a beating. Back to taproots: Shakespeare, describing the face of young Paris in *Romeo and Juliet*, uses the metaphor of a book in an unfamiliar but breathtaking passage: "Examine every married lineament/ And see how one another lends content/ And what obscur'd in this fair volume lies/ Find written in the margent of his eyes."

Whatever usage may appeal to the Internal Revenue Service, the word that applies to the situation you described is "incremental," not marginal. That is, a different, invariably higher, tax rate attaches to the incremental income—that over the upper end of the range of income taxed at any given rate.

When one deals with the word "marginal" in an economic context, the usual idea is that the firm is justified, in a perfect market, in manufacturing one more unit of production so long as the marginal revenue which flows from its sale exceeds the marginal cost of making it. Under this concept, the (marginal) profit on this final product unit may approach zero, while all other profit is thought of as, or measured against, some optimum, and will probably be less than that on the first unit.

These are subtle distinctions, and of no particular import, since our world is anything but perfect. In fact, the only sure thing I learned in Economics at the University of Chicago is "some is better than none, and more is better than some."

David W. Nicholas
New York, New York

I question the suggestion that "marginal trading" is the same as "buying 'on margin.' " If you don't want to use "buy on margin," then I think you should say "margin purchase" to refer to the case where you buy securities through a combination of cash plus a loan from the broker. In fact, if one were to use the term "marginal trading," I would infer, unless the context clearly indicated otherwise, that he was referring to a small amount of trading.

Charles L. Merwin
Washington, D.C.

Medium-Rare Book Lingo

O what is so rare as an afternoon spent browsing through an antiquarian bookstore, tenderly examining used books that have made themselves scarce?

The O that begins this piece is the poetic, sighing-for-attention O, always capitalized, as in the odes of the great poets. When the same sound is spelled *oh*, the exclamation signifies wonderment, surprise or pain; when followed by a question mark and accompanied by a lifted eyebrow, it means "I didn't know that about her; tell me more." When changed to *ah*, the exclamation means "There, that's the spot; rub some more" or "I thought I had my tonsils out when I was a kid, Doc"; when stretched and flattened in pronunciation to *aah*, it means "To hell with it." This exploration of the subtleties of a single sound is to show speakers of Chinese that theirs is not the only language that shifts meanings totally with minor changes of pronunciation or a curl on a brush stroke. Those readers who discover a meaning of warning in a combined form of the sound will exclaim, "Oho, *uh-oh!*" and those irritated by these parenthetical peripatetics will say, "Aah, O.")

In my lead sentence, if anybody can remember back that far, the words *rare, used* and *scarce* are laid out for comparison. For the person who tosses out catalogues selling electronic marvels and flimsy nighties but snatches up the latest listings from the steeped-in-tradition Maggs in London or the tiny Appelfeld Gallery in New York, those are the words that confuse.

Used is a beat-up, kicked-around word that nobody uses unless he must. Pedants and bureaucrats, sharpening their implements, change the past tense of the verb *use* to *utilized*; used-car dealers change the adjective to the chichi *previously owned*. About the only people who use *used* with pride are sellers of secondhand books, who think they are getting away with a euphemism for *secondhand*. But even booksellers seek to put a spin on *used*: "If you open a store dealing in just 'used books,'" confesses John King, owner of the great used-book store in Detroit, "the customers won't come as they would to a store of 'used and rare books.' " *(Used bookstore* says "a book-store that was previously owned"; *used-book store* is accurate but looks bookish; to solve the problem, use *store of used and rare books.)*

Used, at least, has a clear meaning of "not new." But what is the differ-ence between *scarce* and *rare?*

Some booksellers use *scarce* loosely, to mean "I haven't seen this around much lately." Others, like Dan Siegel of M & S Rare Books in Weston, Massachusetts, limit it to twenty-five copies known to be extant (compared to only five, which he thinks of as *rare):* "Books like James Joyce's *Ulysses* (1922), published in various editions totaling 1,000 copies, and Newton's *Principia* (1687), of which Owen Gingerich's census has located about 270 copies, are not really very scarce. There are both large numbers in institu-tions and sufficient numbers (at a price) to satisfy one wanting a copy and willing to wait a few months and to pay $5,000 or so for the Joyce or $20,000 for the Newton." If the books were scarcer—really rare, with a handful of copies in the world—the price would be much higher, consider-ing their importance.

In the general language, *scarce* means "inadequate supply" and *rare* is of such short supply as to be highly valued; in "booksellerese," *scarce* means "hard to find, unless you grab this one or hire somebody to conduct a search," and *rare* means "very few around in private hands and available for purchase, which is why it costs so much." I like the honest advertise-ment for Wayward Books of Washington, D.C.: "out-of-print, used and medium-rare books."

And now to the bookbuyer's main concern, the condition of the book: "This ranges from *fine* to *good* to *fair* and then to *poor,* which might mean the copy is falling apart," explains Allen Ahearn of the Quill & Brush in Bethesda, Maryland.

Unfortunately, the meanings of these terms of condition are all too subjective. A *poor* copy is sometimes euphemized as a *reading copy,* which the Modoc Press's *Collector's Guide to Antiquarian Bookstores* describes as having "no intrinsic value other than the fact that it is in a condition that it can be read." (This guide is a good new book, published by Macmillan. It tells you all you need to know about the nation's dealers in used and rare books. My thumbed and marked copy is already just a *reading copy.)*

"What may be *fine* to you may be only *very good* to me," says John T. Zubal, whose huge store is in Cleveland. "*Fine* means 'virtually as new,' just as a book was when taken off the press. You might come across dealers who use *mint* for books in the best condition, but that's a term from numismat-ics and stamp collecting. If the book really is 'as new,' why not say *as new?*

Out of every two thousand used books, maybe as many as ten would be *as new."*

Beware of *foxing,* a process that leaves a book *foxed* or *dampstained.* These are the brown or reddish-brown marks on the pages of old books, and the etymology is obscure: some suggest it has to do with the use of foxtails in dusting books; others can see the prints of a fox's feet or the color of a fox in the marks. Herbert Weitz, a bookseller and bookbinder in New York City, defines the term with exactitude: *"Foxing* means the brown discoloration that occurs on paper as a result of oxidation. When there is iron in the paper—in a book with steel engravings, for example—and the book becomes damp or lacks ventilation, the result is iron oxide. Actually, it's a very light accumulation of rust." (Because Mr. Weitz binds books in leather, I asked about the word *dentelle,* which I have always assumed meant toothmarks along the edges. No, "it's a French word for a pattern of lace and is the border on the inside of the cover that can be seen even when the book is closed.")

Now to the back of the catalogue, where you find the *exotica* or *erotica*— we all know what that is and can do better in the videotape catalogues— and *ephemera.*

Ephemera is a hot word these days in the antiquarian trade, from the Greek *ephemeros,* meaning "lasting only a day." *Ephemera* in the general language means "matter of no lasting significance," but the book trade has given it a specialized meaning: collectibles originally with little, or ephemeral, value, but which now cost an arm and a leg. "It can mean any printed item other than a book," says Craig Anderson, the head of the rare-book collection at the Strand Book Store in New York. (Of the big used and rares, my favorites are the Strand in New York, Zubal's in Cleveland, John King in Detroit, Goodspeed's in Boston, Second Story Books and Estate Book Sales in Washington and Francis Edwards in London.) Anderson adds: *"Ephemera* includes pamphlets, clippings, posters and broadsides— those are single sheets printed on one side and suitable for posting or framing. Some small presses have done broadsides of a single poem by an author, and it can be framed to hang."

Oh. (*Oh* now has an *h* when the *O* sound is followed immediately by punctuation. "O Mistress Mine" has no punctuation after the O; "Oh, I stubbed my toe" does. Another important use of the naked *O* is in what the Greeks called *apostrophe,* not the high-riding possessive comma but the rhetorical technique of addressing someone who is not physically present: it is the difference between "O Lord" and "Oh, waiter!")

May I suggest a very plausible etymology of "foxing": The Latin-based term for rust, *ferrus oxide*, is easily shortened by taking the first letter of *ferrus* and the first two letters of *oxide*.

Joel B. Miller
New York, New York

Foxing, depending upon which dictionary you consult, can mean a variety of things. To the conservator of paper and books it is a disfiguring, little understood biodeterioration process involving microorganisms known as fungi. This was known and bemoaned some 122 years ago, with later research beginning again in the early 1930s.

Foxing does not leave a book dampstained; these are two independent offenders of paper. Damp stains are birthed of prolonged moist environments and not consequences of foxing.

Mr. Weitz's definition of foxing is marginal at best. Not all brown discoloration of paper is foxing. Oxidation of paper can result in pigmentation, but it doesn't have to. Iron oxide is not always the result of iron content paper "being damp or lacking ventilation." Iron is readily attacked by oxygen in the presence of moisture to form rust. This can produce iron oxide and, further, as concerns paper, can lead to iron-induced degradation. But this is *not* foxing. The distinction is clear.

The etymologist should recognize the uncertain identity of the term foxing and would do well to review the existing literature. The challenge, as I perceive it, is to determine when and why foxing took on a negative sense, and when did it become associated with fungal attack? When wine and beer went "off" it was said to be foxed. A foxed person was a lunatic, etc. Perhaps the most intriguing of all is the biblical use—"Take us the foxes, the little foxes that spoil the vines."

Elizabeth Morse
New York, New York

I have always felt a little peculiar in describing my vocation as that of "rare book dealer," preferring to introduce myself as a dealer in rare books. Does the distinction seem significant to you? It seems to me that the use of "rare" as an adjective for book dealer is ambiguous.

Ralph B. Sipper
Joseph the Provider
Santa Barbara, California

Noting warily the fact that a number of the establishments named contain the word "store" in their titles, I submit that the correct name for a retail premises selling one general class of goods is *shop*.

> *Louis P. Dolbeare*
> *Washington, D.C.*

The ubiquitous bibliographic irregulars have reported your quotation from Dan Siegel misdescribing my research as a census of Newton's *Principia*.

For over a decade I have been trying to locate every possible copy of Copernicus's *De revolutionibus* (Nuremberg 1543), no mean task, especially when you consider that such a census has been attempted for only three other major books: the Gutenberg Bible, the Shakespeare first folio, and the Audubon elephant folio. Because I depend on a certain amount of publicity in order to ferret out copies in private collections or unexpected institutional libraries, I was naturally disappointed that the opportunity was botched. Anyway, I have located 258 copies of this first edition and have personally inspected 253 of these. At $60,000 a copy, Dan Siegel would say that the book is expensive but not rare—it is so common that even he owns a copy—but such strictness flies in the face of the ordinary usage in the book trade.

Incidentally, I also collect locations on the *second* edition of Copernicus' book (Basel 1566) and so far have 292 on the census. It is worth much less, although I did testify in Federal Court last summer that a copy was typically worth over $5,000. The thief was convicted.

> *Owen Gingerich*
> *Astrophysicist, Smithsonian*
> *Professor of Astronomy and the*
> *History of Science, Harvard*
> *Cambridge, Massachusetts*

I thought that I learned many years ago in high school that *and* was only used inside of sentences to list parallel items. More and more I notice in the press that writers are starting sentences with *and*. Then I found some writers starting paragraphs with *and*.

And now I find the High Priest of English Usage starting a paragraph with *and*.

And now would you please explain what is going on, so that my old

English teacher, Miss Roaring Lucille Smith, will stop turning in her grave.

> Henry E. Hirschland
> Rochester, New York

If the book is like new, why not say like new? As new sounds as hell, and is ambiguous.

> William M. Farrell
> Huntington, New York

Moon of My Delight

In the language of the heavens, myth has become reality. You cannot look into the night sky without knowing your gods and goddesses, and cannot speak of space without an ear for current pronunciation.

Triumph and tragedy, to use Churchill's alliteration, have been felt by Americans watching the skies in recent weeks. A few queries came in about language used in connection with the space shuttle Challenger, and it is not to trivialize the nation's sense of loss to deal here with matters of grammar associated with the event.

Why is there no comma before the proper noun *Challenger?*

The absence of the comma is easily explained. If written as *the space shuttle, Challenger,* the phrase before the comma would specifically describe the noun, meaning "Challenger is the name of the space shuttle," as if there is no other space shuttle. But there exist three others, which is why the correct phrase is *the space shuttle Challenger.*

Let us turn now to the happier story on the same subject: the space probe Voyager 2 (again no comma, because there is more than one space probe) passed by the seventh planet from the sun and caused great consternation among those who would pronounce the name of the planet correctly.

"I was raised in New York," writes Joyce S. Cohen of Morganville, New Jersey, "where the name of the planet Uranus was pronounced *u-RAY-nus,* not *YURR-in-us,* as the newscasters of late and the dictionary clearly say. I have polled everyone I know in New Jersey, where I now live, and they also say it incorrectly. It sounds like an affectation to say it 'correctly.' Should I continue my mispronunciation because 'everyone else does it'? Things like this drive me crazy."

The everybody-did-it defense never helped a former boss of mine, but common usage counts in pronunciation; frankly, I have always pronounced *Uranus* much the same way I pronounce *uranium*, and at first I suspected the announcers were coming up with a pronuncieuphemism. I called a couple of astronomers:

"The seventh planet's name comes from the Greek *Ouranos*, or 'heavens,'" replies the best-known name in stargazing, Carl Sagan, "and in Greek myth that figure is two generations before Zeus—Zeus's grandfather, I suppose you'd say. Because the Greek word means 'heavens,' it seems logical that the astronomers of William Herschel's day should name the outermost planet then known 'Uranus.'"

The pronunciation? "That involves a continuing debate," says Mr. Sagan, whose name is pronounced *SAY-gun*, not to be confused with the French author of the same name, tristesseful Françoise Sagan, who pronounces it *sa-GANH*. "The debate is not unlike that of the pronunciation of Io, the innermost major moon of Jupiter. Should that moon be pronounced *EE-o*, as the people of the Mediterranean first said the name, or should it be pronounced *EYE-o*, as the Oxford unabridged dictionary indicates?"

My problem is not with Old MacDonald's moon, I explained, but with this planet now in the news.

"Predominantly the planet is pronounced *YUR-in-us*. Why it's often heard as *yur-A-nus*, I don't know. I say *YUR-in-us*. And I pronounce Jupiter's moon *EE-o*, because I think the original pronunciation deserves to be used."

Always get a second source, they tell us in investigative lexicography; I turned to the world-renowned astrophysicist Owen Gingerich, Smithsonian Professor of Astronomy and the History of Science at the Harvard Center for Astrophysics, known to bibliophiles as the census-taker of every possible copy of the first edition of Copernicus's *De revolutionibus*. (I give him this big plug here because in a piece on rare-book lingo, his research was misdescribed as a census of Sir Isaac Newton's *Principia*. Ever since, he has been plagued by queries for his expert opinion on the wrong book, and gets a little testy about it. Please stop calling Professor Gingerich about Newton; as far as I know, he flunked Newton, but if you want a man who has personally inspected 253 of the 258 known copies of the Copernicus book published in Nuremberg in 1543, Gingerich is your man.)

"The correct pronunciation of the seventh planet is *YUR-in-us*," says this modern Copernicus, who is unfailingly cooperative but who would dearly like to drop a hard apple on my head. "The confusion of *yur-A-nus* began when some high school teachers were afraid that students would titter at the correct pronunciation." These teachers wanted to avoid the sound of the first two syllables, and caused a pronunciation in which the last two syllables were stressed. A generation later, the second combination of syllables made up a word that was more to be avoided than the first, and the prior pronunciation returned. That answers Joyce Cohen's question.

Professor Gingerich explains that William Herschel wanted to name the planet he discovered after his patron, King George III, but the French resisted and vindictively called it Herschel; when both French and English astronomers spotted an eighth planet, a deal was made: Neptune, with its associations with Britannia, was to be its name, and Herschel (the planet) was to be called Uranus.

We are now into mythology. Earth (*Gaea* to the Greeks, *Tellus* to the Romans) married *Uranus* (in Greek, *Ouranos*), the heavens, and their descendants included many gods and goddesses for whom planets were named: using the Roman names, *Mercury*, the swiftest god, for the planet that completes its circle of the sun fastest; *Venus*, goddess of beauty, for the most brilliant; *Mars*, god of war, for the red planet, and *Jupiter*, supreme god, for the largest planet. Farther out, *Saturn* was Jupiter's father, and *Uranus* was Saturn's father. *Neptune* was Jupiter's brother, as was *Pluto*, the god of the underworld, fitting for the darkest and coldest planet.

Moons are given wonderful names, often derived from the stories of their planets. The first four moons discovered around Jupiter were named after some of that god's seductions: *Io* (we know all about her), *Europa*, *Ganymede* and *Callisto*. The two moons of Mars are named, according to one version of the myth, for the children of *Mars* (the Greek *Ares*): *Deimos* (Terror) and *Phobos* (Fear).

Uranus, however, has four of its moons named after characters in Shakespeare: *Oberon* and *Titania* are king and queen of the fairies in *A Midsummer Night's Dream* and *Ariel* and *Miranda* (great photographs of Miranda sent back by Voyager 2) are from *The Tempest*. The *Miranda* decision of the astronomer Gerard P. Kuiper was especially apt: she is the daughter of the magician Prospero, kept from other men, who falls in love with Prince Ferdinand, virtually the first man she has met, and later exclaims, "How beauteous mankind is! O brave new world/ That has such people in't!"

Voyager 2 (why no Roman numerals?) has discovered ten new moons of Uranus. If the International Astronomical Union does not see fit to name one of them *Ferdinand*, I for one will forever call its planet *Herschel*.

Fortunately, I already know how the name *Sagan* (Françoise, not Carl) is pronounced, so I don't need to decipher your statement that she "pronounces it *sa-GANH.*" The only orthographies that I know of in which the combination *nh* is used are Portuguese and Vietnamese, where it stands for a palatalized *n,* but that's not the sound that you're trying to represent here. Have you adopted the policy of writing *h* to indicate an unspecified deviation from the sound normally represented by the preceding letter? Your instructions on how to pronounce the name are not completely uninformative (you at least specify correctly what syllable is stressed), but are almost so.

Three inches down the same column, I am not sure whether Carl Sagan's statement that "the original pronunciation deserves to be used" is supposed to apply to "*YUR-in-us*" (Uranus) in the preceding sentence. The pronunciation in this case is of course not the original one but an adaptation of the original pronunciation to the phonology of modern English. Note in particular the *Y,* which English puts before *U* in an open syllable, even in words (such as *Cuba*) that are borrowed from a language that doesn't have a *Y* there.

James D. McCawley
Department of Linguistics
University of Chicago
Chicago, Illinois

I read with interest about Uranus, Ouranos, etc. One thing I missed was your referring to the adjective form of Uranus—Uranian, a term that appeared several times in newspaper accounts of the finding by our spacecraft of "Uranian" moons. You may or may not recall that Uranian had a few years ago another meaning: it was a term used around the turn of the century by some rather hifalutin English literary lights (lights of not much brilliance, alas) to refer to what we now call "gay" or "paederast" amours. The word appears, oddly in quotation marks, in the title of a book not found on everyone's bedside table: Timothy d'Arch Smith, *Love in Earnest: Some Notes on the Lives and Writings of English 'Uranian' Poets from 1889 to 1930,* Routledge & Kegan Paul, London, 1970.

The word, in this context, doesn't pop up in daily conversation; but I've friends who enjoy chatting about questionable matters in public places and code words are often helpful. In a restaurant one can nod towards a curious-seeming duo at the next table and murmur to one's companions, "a Uranian attachment, evidently!"

(Name withheld)

I think you were not fair to Jupiter in saying that Ganymede was one of his "seductions." Io, yes; Europa, certainly; and Callisto, by all means. But, as I learned the myth, Ganymede was simply snatched up by Jupiter to take Hebe's place as cupbearer to the gods. While admittedly he was a very beautiful young boy, there does not seem to have been any suggestion of hanky-panky. And in fact Homer (says Bulfinch) wrote that Ganymede was carried off by the gods, collectively, not specifically by Jupiter, and there are later stories which attribute the carrying to an eagle, not to Jupiter in the form of an eagle. There is no report that Juno, who was notoriously jealous and vigilant in respect of her husband's escapades, ever did anything about Ganymede, although she was certainly hard on Io and Callisto, and that is some evidence in itself. (On the other hand, she apparently did not punish Europa either.)

The case against Jupiter is, in my view, not proved.

Shirley Boskey
Bethesda, Maryland

Murder Most Foul

A member of the Squad Squad, on guard against repeated redundancies, has alerted me and called my attention to a mistake I made in a political column.

My subject was terrorism, and I wrote of "the vicious bombing-murder" of an Arab-American. John Moran of Manhattan College's philosophy department asks: "What sort of distinction do you have in mind? Are there perhaps bombing-murders that are not 'vicious'? That usage sounds like 'traumatic shock' and 'wet water' to me."

That thought nagged at me as I wrote the phrase, but it was in a piece about Arab terrorism and I wanted it to be clear that this murder should be condemned with equal fervor. I figured the redundancy would get by. Nothing gets by.

Same thing with *brutal murder*. I suppose there is some difference between a killing done with a blunt instrument and another accomplished with a stiletto, but a powerful noun loses force when it is modified by anything. All bombings are vicious, even when justified in war; all murders are brutal. Even the phrase *mercy killing* carefully avoids the word *murder*, because *murder* contains a condemnation of the neutral *killing*. Any adjective straining to strengthen a killer of a word like *murder* is a weakener.

Shakespeare faced the same problem. "Murther most foul," he had the Ghost tell Hamlet, adding, as if expecting immediate retribution from the Squad Squad of his day, "as in the best it is." He knew nothing gets by.

William Safire is quite correct in concluding that "vicious murder" is a redundancy. But in more than a dozen states, men still live or die on a jury's ability to conclude that some murders are more vicious than others.

In Georgia, to pick one quite typical example, an "aggravating circumstance" that triggers the death penalty is that the murder was "outrageously or wantonly vile, horrible or inhuman in that it involved . . . depravity of mind, or an aggravated battery of the victim." Numerous other states apply a similar "vileness" test to select the few murderers who will die from the many who will be allowed to live.

> *Peter Huber*
> *Washington, D.C.*

You quoted a letter which criticized your use of "vicious bombing-murder." The writer stated, "That usage sounds like 'traumatic shock' and 'wet water' to me." While I can agree that the initial phrase might be redundant, the other two are appropriate terms.

"Shock" is defined as a failure of the circulatory system and can be caused by external trauma (e.g. vehicle accident or gunshot wound) or by internal problems, such as cardiac failure, an injury to the nervous system, or even a bee sting. Thus, "traumatic" is an appropriate modifier for "shock" and is necessary to ensure appropriate treatment for the condition (which might, of course, result from a vicious attack).

"Wet water" is a chemical additive used in fire suppression. It is a detergent which, by breaking down the surface tension of the water, allows it to soak in more quickly and thus makes it a more effective fire suppression agent.

> *Richard A. Narad*
> *Santa Rosa, California*

Professor John Moran perhaps does not know that traumatic shock is one of many kinds of shock; other kinds are cardiogenic, systemic, anaphylactic, etc. Also, the Rand Corporation tried wet water with the New York City Fire Department in the late '60s or early '70s. The firefighters' union resisted!

Redundancy may be in the eye of the beholder of language when it is a necessary tool for the practitioner, in which case it isn't redundancy.

Edward Pearce
Boston, Massachusetts

"All bombings are vicious, even when justified in war; all murders are brutal."

Upon reflection, not so. To the extent an act is "justifiable" it cannot be "vicious" in that word's broadest sense: full of vice. The two terms are contradictory.

Again, to the extent one takes a life reverently and with regret, murder can be both humane (*e.g.*, the attempted assassination of Hitler; the shooting of a pilot trapped in a burning plane) and other than "brutal": "characteristic of a brute: cruel."

Sweeping generalizations can be dangerous. In any event, they are often wrong, as here.

Winthrop Drake Thies
Maplewood, New Jersey

Wrong! All murder is not brutal. After all, "brutal" suggests an action which is both savage and cruel. There is nothing savage or cruel about a wife who takes special pains to murder her husband with a quick-acting poison so as to avoid all suffering. A procedure of this type must be termed, shall we say, a very "civilized" (as opposed to brutal) way of dispatching a person whose demise is considered necessary and appropriate.

In any event, as you well know, the judicious application of adjectives is one of the most important aspects of good composition. Let us suppose you are writing about an individual who was hacked to death and left dismembered in a pool of blood. I cannot believe that you would be content to merely remark that "Mr. Brown was murdered." How unimaginative can you be? To drive home the horror of the crime it would be imperative to use some phraseology like "the hapless Mr. Brown was murdered in a most brutal fashion." Doesn't that convey a better impression of the nature of what must have transpired? And isn't accurate communication the purpose of language?

Zounds! I am appalled. For without the liberal interspersion of descriptive adjectives and adverbs, the English language would be dead —murdered, if you will (although not "brutally").

Frank K. Haszard
Santurce, Puerto Rico

Muscle-bound Dollars

A pejorative adjective slights, belittles, disparages and depreciates the noun it modifies. For example, *weak* is pejorative (from the Old English *wac* for "yielding" or "feeble"); nobody likes a weak President or weak coffee.

The opposite of *pejorative* is *aggrandizing, extolling* or *laudatory*. For example, *strong* is a laudatory word; we all admire strong leaders and think well of Jane Fonda for doing sit-ups to strengthen her tummy.

What, then, do we do when *strong* becomes pejorative and *weak* is not all that bad? Consider the dollar.

Senator Daniel Patrick Moynihan, Democrat of New York, was explaining the difficulties of a New York-based company, Kodak: "What it can't do," wrote the senator in his newsletter to constiutents, "is overcome the effect of the overpriced dollar." He then shifted into a discussion of semantics: "Here there is a real problem with the words we use. We say *strong dollar*. Strong dollar, strong America, right? Wrong. But there you are. Overpriced is a better way to put it. If the dollar is overpriced, American exports are overpriced; imports are underpriced."

The trouble with the Moynihan solution is that *overpriced* and *underpriced* are as value-laden as *strong* and *weak*; needed are words of comparison, neutral or at least fair-seeming, that describe the status of the dollar in relation to other currencies.

Try *high* and *low*: "The dollar was high today against the franc," or "The value of the dollar lowered today, while rupees and zladniks soared." Unlike *strong*, the word *high* is not always unassailably good, and though *low* is not a good word for most moods, it is a happy description of tensions and temperatures. At least it would not make us feel as unpatriotic as rooting for a weaker dollar.

Name That Dog

Canine nomenclature is taking a turn toward the human. More and more, we are giving dogs the names we used to reserve for people.

In olden times, we often named dogs for their disposition. *Rover* was chosen for dogs who liked to wander off, or *Fido*, from the Latin for "faithful," for those who preferred to hang around. *Friskie* was considered appropriate if the animal was not unduly lackadaisical, and sometimes a touch of sarcasm was added by calling a lazy mutt *Lightnin'*. In those days we named dogs for their appearance: *Spot* was popular, and *Rags* for the disheveled; no neighborhood was complete without a Labrador retriever named *Blackie*.

Regal qualities were a source of names: *King, Prince, Duke* and *Baron* were popular, along with *Queenie, Princess* and *Duchess*. Ever title-conscious, and slightly behind the times, President and Mrs. Reagan have just chosen the name *Rex* for their new Cavalier King Charles spaniel; *Rex* is the title of a reigning king, and a questionable choice made by a leader of a democracy

(Gerald R. Ford's dog was the suitable *Liberty*), but Mrs. Reagan explained that the dog was named after a member of the White House staff.

Disposition and appearance are still sources of dog names, but lately we tend to give our dogs the names we had left over for children we never had, or we name them after favorite uncles or cartoon characters or rock stars. Instead of turning verbs and adjectives into proper nouns (for example, by calling a puppy that likes to nip your finger *Nipper*), we are using proper nouns directly, calling the little nipper *George, Daisy* or *Charley.*

I used to have a German shepherd named Henry, after Henry A. Kissinger, because at one time I was irritated with my Nixon Administration colleague and wanted to be able to say "Down, Henry!" after a hard day at the West Wing. Years later, after wiretap passions had cooled and we resumed our friendship, Henry the strategist came to the house for dinner and Henry the dog came over to say hello. When Henry the K asked the dog's name, I did not want to revive old tensions, so I lied: "We call him *Zbigniew.*" Mr. Kissinger patted his head and said, "Nice, Zbig," and a new era of confrontation was avoided.

My evidence of the growing humanization of dog-naming is more than anecdotal, however. Four-hundred-and-ten Lexicographic Irregulars read a query on the subject barked in this space a few months ago, and responded with about 12,000 names for dogs. It may be the most extensive such survey recently undertaken, and I have the correspondence piled up in little categorized mounds around the office; the place looks like my backyard.

The biggest pile is "Names of People," and the names that appear most frequently in it are *Max, Belle, Ginger, Walter* and *Sam. (Sam* is a dog; *Samantha* is a cat.) One correspondent reports a dog called *Dot*, derived not from Dorothy but from *Sadat*; another dog in that family is *Knock*, presumably from *Menachem.*

The names of cartoon characters appear often: *Snoopy* and his beagle brother *Spike* are obvious sources that also embody characteristics, but *Poindexter* is a pure "name" taken from a smarty-pants human character in *Felix the Cat*, and will surely be adopted by national security staff members in naming their pets.

Some common human names are rare in dogs: you don't find *Bill, Bob* (although David Letterman talks on television about his dog *Bob), Barbara* or *Jane* as often as *Winston* (big in bulldogs) or *Sheba.* We're beginning to see more of *Fred* in both humans and dogs, and there has been a recent run on *Vanessa* and *Rebecca.* My own golden retriever is *Rufus,* the name of Churchill's dog, and my Bernese mountain dog is named *James.* The snapping, neurotic cur in Anne Tyler's novel *The Accidental Tourist* is named

Edward. In these cases, the trend is toward the full name, not the diminutive. Lane Kirkland, head of the A.F.L.-C.I.O., has a dachshund named *Stanley*, who, when told to "assume the State Department position," lies on his back and howls.

One tradition that continues is the linking of breeds identified with specific countries to names of people from those countries. "Sled dogs—malamutes, Siberian huskies—often have the Russian ending *-asha* in their names," reports Elizabeth Watson, a breeder and trainer of Brackenbriar Kennels in Middleway, West Virginia. "Awful lot of *Sasha, Tasha* and *Masha.*" Similarly, too many Irish setters are named *Kelly,* German shepherds *Fritz,* and huskies *Nanook.* Several correspondents say they call their French poodles *Phydeau,* which shows some originality; it beats *Fifi.* Be careful about calling out *Max* at a Doberman show.

Not all dog owners are bestowing human names on animals, however. Disposition is still a source, but the names are symbolic: *Pepper* is an example of disposition once removed, rivaling *Bandit* and *Misty* in popularity. Some watchers of beer commercials call their animals *Gusto,* and hound owners like *Sad Sack.* Although *Rover* is now rare, similar qualities are recalled in *Solo, Gypsy, Scooter, Streaker, Rascal* and *Scamp.* This carries on the grand tradition cited in Shakespeare's *The Two Gentlemen of Verona,* in which the clownish Launce has a dog named *Crab:* "I think Crab my dog be the sourest-natured dog that lives . . . a stone, a very pebble stone, and has no more pity in him than a dog."

Certain syllables recur: *-ie* and *-y* are the favorite endings, perhaps because large animals seem less frightening if named with a diminutive like *Binky.* (Conversely, owners of tyke-like breeds like to call their tiny friends *Killer, Monster* or *Godzilla.*) *Uf* is a hot sound: "Dozens of pets at the Anderson Animal Center, in South Elgin, Ill.," reports Leslie Mann Smith, "are named *Buffy, Duffy, Fluffy, Muffy* and *Puffy.*" (That sounds preppy; sure enough, citations include *Preppie, Binky, Muffie, Yuppie, Worthington, Percival, Cambridge* and *Andrea.*)

Boozehounds name their dogs after their favorite drinks. *Brandy* is one of the most popular canine names, perhaps because it is also the name of a color, but *Whiskey* (for Scotties, it is spelled *Whisky*) is cited frequently, as are *Boozer* and *Tonic, Soda* and *Chaser.*

Foods are also used, because people like to name animals after things that provide enjoyment. *Cookie, Candy, Taffy, Peaches, Oatmeal, Gingersnap, Noodles* and *Cinnamon* abound, with more with-it types adding *Yogurt, Tofu* and *Mayo.* (Hold the *Mayo!*)

Color? *Blackie* still prowls the neighborhood, but is likely to be shadowed by *Ebony, Charcoal, Sooty* and *Midnight.* (I once claimed to have a pet named

Peeve and was hailed by a man with a *bête* he called *Noire.*) "Dogs used to be called *Old Yeller*," reports Sean Blackmore of Ventura, California, "but now they're called *Amber.*" Old *Rusty* is still with us, but runs with *Snow-flake, Topaz, Raspberry, Nugget* and multicolored dogs like *Patches* and *Plaid* (perhaps after "Plaid: A Dog," which Albert Payson Terhune never wrote).

The nicknames of the jobs of owners are often applied to pets: lawyers like *Shyster* and *Escrow*; doctors prefer *Bones*; tennis stars try *Topspin*. A veterinarian, Dr. Ira H. Silver of Chevy Chase, Maryland, reports that the baseball pitcher Tom Seaver had one dog named *Casey*, probably after Casey Stengel, and another named *Slider.* Technocrats have named their dogs *Glitch* and *Ergo* (probably rooted in "ergonomics," if the dog is owner-friendly). One stereo engineer came up with a superb choice: *Woofer.*

Another veterinarian I know, Dr. Steven H. Steinberg of Gaithersburg, Maryland, spots a trend: "Dogs now come in better dressed than we are. You should see them—jeweled collars, fancy vests, some even dressed in ear-warmers. To reflect that look, they need the names they are given—like *Madonna.*"

So farewell, old *Sport*; nobody names you that anymore, or *Ace* or from Jack London's *The Call of the Wild, Buck.* A pundit I know calls his Rhodesian Ridgeback *Zim*, after Zimbabwe, the new name for Rhodesia; we're getting sophisticated. The most appropriately named dog I ever knew was a German shepherd owned by Herman Wouk, the novelist: *Barkis* was his name, after the character in Dickens's novel *David Copperfield* who liked to say, "Barkis is willin'." That was a good name for a dog.

It must now be more than thirty years ago that I vowed that if I ever owned a dog (which, alas, I do not), I would name him Willis, so that whenever he gave tongue I could lift a finger and exclaim, "Ah, hark! Willis is barkin'."

Frank W. Lindsay
Schenectady, New York

William Safire's article on the gentrification of dogs' names reminded me of a Shakespearean scholar I knew at a university where I once taught. He was a cat person, but grudgingly consented to tolerate a mongrel his children dragged home one day. Predictably, they named the dog Spot, though the professor would have preferred something along more classical lines, like Malvolio or Caliban. Inevitably, the children soon lost interest and the burden of looking after the dog's needs fell on the cat-loving professor. But he had his donnish revenge. When the dog scratched at the back door wanting to be let out, he would throw it open and shout, "Out, damned Spot! Out, I say!"

> *Ernest Paolino*
> *New Brunswick, New Jersey*

I have always been told that a dog should have a one-syllable name so he would respond to a command, probably saving his life, if he started across First Avenue against the traffic lights. However, I think dogs have a right, if they are dignified members of the family, not to be called Spot or Fido.

Salukis have a regal dignity. One could never call one of them Buck, Prince or Rufus. Mine is named James Fenimore Cooper, but I call him Fenn. He has a brother, a champion Saluki, whose name is Henry David Thoreau, but, in heavy traffic in the city, is called Thor.

> *Maurine P. Rothschild*
> *New York, New York*

I recently had the opportunity to spend some time with members of the family of Barbara Tuchman, an opportunity that included encounters with the family dog, Coucy. Directly Coucy was introduced to me by name, I marveled, once again, at Mrs. Tuchman's vast erudition and subtlety. How clever was she to name the dog "Coucy" (or Cusi or Cuthi), after members of the obscure tribe, identified in the Talmud, of reluctant converts to Judaism. According to Jewish tradition, the Cusim (or Cuthim) were considered to be in some respects Jews, in other respects Gentiles. The name, it seemed to me, beautifully reflected a world of conflict and ambivalence, of identity and universalism, all devolved upon this poor dog. Hound, you are one of us, but are you really?

"What are you talking about, Jerome?" queried Alma, Mrs. Tuchman's daughter. "What on earth is a 'Cusi?' This dog's name is 'Coucy,' after the hero of Mother's book [*A Distant Mirror*], Enguerrand de Coucy. Please come back to earth, Jerome." Oh.

> *Jerome A. Chanes*
> *New York, New York*

I wrote, and sold, my first article to *The New York Times*, back, I think, in 1920 or 1921. Subject: names that people give their dogs.

In your current list I missed only Bulova, obviously a watchdog.

> *Herbert R. Mayes*
> *New York, New York*

Many years ago I saw a film which starred Janet Gaynor and Douglas Fairbanks, Jr., called *The Young in Heart* and featured Roland Young and Billie Burke. There were two Great Danes and one was called Get off the Rug and the other was called You, Too.

Milton Goldman
New York, New York

We named our Beagle "Bagel," with the intention of breeding him, and his firstborn son would be called "Lox, Son of Bagel."

Benis M. Frank
Washington, D.C.

You never mentioned the name "Checkers."

Jan R. Harrington
New York, New York

Name Your Poison

A rose by any other name would smell as sweet, Shakespeare posited, founding a school of linguistics later led by Alfred H. S. Korzybski and popularized by Stuart Chase. Their point: the name is not the thing. A word is only a word, a label, a symbol, and we should not endow that symbol with the reverence we would pay the object, or referent, itself.

People who get paid to name perfumes sniff at that semantic notion. To them, the name is part of the package, along with the bottle and the logo, and all the symbolism has a measurable effect on the way the customer thinks the perfume smells. In that ambiance-chasing world, the name fuses with the thing and takes on a reality of its own.

Time was, the names of perfumes were often descriptive of the odor, usually innocently floral: *Lily of the Valley, Hyacinth* or *Jasmine.* Then came the names that described feelings, like *Joy, Hope* and *Moment Supreme.* Femininity was emphasized in *Femme* and *Jolie Madame* and, later, *Miss Dior.*

But, back in 1937, along came *Shocking,* then *My Sin,* and hoo-boy! (*Hoo-boy!* has never been the name of a perfume, because it would not be understood by non-English-speaking perfume buyers.) Sex had entered the field, and the scent would never be the same. *Tabu*—the original Tongan spelling was used—meant "forbidden, proscribed by tradition," and to this day, whenever I write of a word that cannot be used in a family newspaper because it is taboo, I see myself with a violin in one fist and my face buried in the neck of some poor woman who only wanted to play the piano.

Although the obsession with sex continues (there are fragrances called *Obsession* and *Sex Appeal)*, the operative word has more often been *love*, from *Amour, Amour* to *Aphrodisia* (from *Aphrodite*, Greek goddess of love). It is only a matter of time before the new euphemism for sex, *gender*, finds its way to a bottle, and *syndrome*, with its psychological connotation of moral turpitude in an astrodome, seems a natural.

Among men's perfumes, *musk*—from the Sanskrit word for "testicle"— is popular, and *Brut* was inspired because it can be found on some bottles of very dry champagne, but many buyers read it as "brute," from the French word for "rough," connoting domineering, if not deliciously caddish, behavior. *(Macho* sells well, but *Cad* never made it.)

Proper names, usually masculine ones adopted by women, enjoyed a recent boom: *Charlie* (from Charles Revson), *Maxi, Babe* and *Smitty* sounded like a bunch of guys snapping towels in the locker room, but appealed to women. Seizing an old idea from Coco Chanel, who put her name on a perfume with *Chanel No. 5,* designers have attached the name to the bottle directly, with no "by" to interrupt the cognomenclature: *Lauren, Giorgio, Y* (for Yves), *Halston, Norell* and now *Coco*, which the company evidently felt would sell better than *Chanel No. 99. (Coco* is described in the patois of the trade as "an amber chord with wood nuances and a leather accent.")

A late development in the mass marketing of fragrance is the use of television names in perfumes: from the television show "Dynasty" comes *Forever Krystle*, but it is too late for a men's after-shave called *Bunker*.

Andy Warhol, the artist-celebrity-partygoer, was seen at a party for *Manhattan, inc.* magazine (an outfit that makes great use of puns in headlines) with an atomizer of a new perfume named *Beautiful*, spraying it about, saying in his heavy leather accent: "It's all in the name, you know. People can say you smell *Beautiful."* Then he was quoted as adding this wooden nuance: "I was thinking it might be fun to start my own perfume line and call it *Stink."*

He was kidding, but the artist has a nice sense of semantics. A trend is now discernible that gives a spiked-hair, punk-rock, razor-blades-around-the-neck sense to perfumes. *Metal* hints at it tastefully (recalling Robert Frost's "as a metal keeps its fragrance"), and *Decadence* proclaims it proudly. A few years ago Yves Saint Laurent sought to give a good name to narcotics with *Opium*, which was highly successful, and now one awaits such entries as *Heroin, Angel Dust* and *Needle Park* to win the Order of the Odor.

"The names reflect our society, what's happening now," says Annette Green, executive director of the Fragrance Foundation (look, they weren't going to call it the Smell Society), "and are an outgrowth of our video/rock culture."

What's happening now is what has Paris all atwitter: Christian Dior's latest, to be introduced in the United States a year from now, *Poison.* Presumably, it will be sold at counters flying the Jolly Roger, a skull and crossbones on each bottle.

Halston, who thinks the name *Opium* was "kind of an odd social statement," finds the naming of *Poison* to be an example of "the true decadence of the fashion business. I think it's just being done to create controversy. You can't tell people to go in and ask for a bottle of *Poison.*"

For all I know, it may smell like *Lily of the Valley,* but its appellation gives the product a sinister odor. The Olfactory Workers Union has succeeded in infusing the nice thing with the nasty name, which must be spinning Korzybski in his grave.

There's nothing wrong with what you said about *semantics.* What is wrong is to infer, however innocently, that Alfred Korzybski was concerned primarily with *semantics* as the term is commonly understood. Korzybski's work did touch on semantics, as well as syntactics, pragmatics, and a lot of other tics, but he called his work *general semantics,* a very important distinction that you will find ignored in almost every encyclopedia and biographical dictionary in which the name Korzybski, Alfred, appears. General semantics is not the study of words or the study of meaning but a theory of relationships between (or assumptions about) language (symbol) systems and human behavior.

If I had to say in ten words or less what, exactly, Korzybski did set out to accomplish, it would be this: Korzybski attempted to formulate a theory of sanity. He felt that the more closely the *structure* of the language matched the way we (ought to) evaluate the *structure* of the world, the healthier would be our nervous systems. The key here is the *structure* of the language, not the words themselves.

In short, Korzybski wasn't a word man. And he certainly didn't mean to found a school of linguistics. Unfortunately, the semanticist and linguist labels became almost impossible to remove from Korzybski's name after some of his students, notably Stuart Chase, whom you mentioned in your column, and S. I. Hayakawa skillfully extracted

and oversimplified some of Korzybski's more accessible linguistic notions—words and what they do to you, for example.

Some of Korzybski's friends considered this treasonous at the time,
but you should know that Korzybski's own magnum opus, *Science and
Sanity: An Introduction to Non-Aristotelian Systems and General Semantics,*
is almost impossible for the average intelligent layperson to understand. (Rumor has it that Albert Einstein, one of many non-Aristotelian thinkers to whom Korzybski dedicated *Science and Sanity,* tried to
read his free copy and gave up.) Those relatively few who persevered,
however, consider Korzybski's *Science and Sanity* one of the great writ-
ten-but-unread monuments in Western thought. I am indebted to *general semantics* in my own work as a writer and historian, but I have to
admit that even though I have lived with a copy of *Science and Sanity*
since infancy, I cannot claim to have read it all the way through.

> *Molly Nelson Haber*
> *New York, New York*

Juliet did not say, as you put it, "A rose by any other name . . ."
She did say, "That which we call a rose/ By any other name would
smell as sweet."

The four words that you leave out have significance. They show, as
do the lines that follow, the playwright's awareness of what Alfred
Korzybski, whom you cite, named the science of general semantics. It
teaches, among other things, the distinction between concrete objects
and the abstract labels that human language attaches to them.

To me, the omission ranks with the almost universal misapplication
of Hamlet's remark about "a custom/ More honour'd in the breach
than the observance." He meant, as I know you realize, that it was
more honorable to disregard an evil practice (in this case courtly ca-
rousing) than to follow it. He did not mean, as most people seem to
think, that the custom was more often ignored than observed.

> *Walter Barthold*
> *Douglaston, New York*

You spelled the word "ambience" (English) in its French version of
"ambiance", but without italicizing it—which might (mis)lead an un-
generous soul into suspecting you of being an indifferent speller.

> *Joseph Rothschild*
> *Class of 1919*
> *Professor of Political Science*
> *Columbia University*
> *New York, New York*

I believe the connection between Yves Saint Laurent's *Opium* and Christian Dior's latest, *Poison,* is even more demented than you merely hint at in jest.

While you await "such entries as Heroin, Angel Dust and Needle Park," you should know that on Manhattan's Lower East Side, where the heroin trade is prolific, the most enduring product over the past five or six years is called (whattayaknow) *Poison.* The glassine envelope of each dime (ten-dollar) bag displays an ink stamp of a skull and crossbones, with a Jolly Roger flying behind it. The word "POISON" is printed in block lettering below that. (These artful designs are helpful to customers seeking authenticity in a highly unregulated marketplace.)

The perfume merchants have gone beyond "giving a good name to narcotics." They've proven their capacity for manipulation to be as sublime and slimy as the lowlifes selling dope in the streets. Or is it the other way around?

John Decker
New York, New York

The Odd Decouple

Allaying allied concerns about American space-defense plans, Secretary of Defense Caspar W. Weinberger said, "There's not the slightest possibility that America would be decoupled from Europe by the pursuit of this vital initiative."

A year before, Vice President Bush used the verb in a similar alliance context, though somewhat more awkwardly. "The Soviet Union," he warned, "having already deployed sufficient missiles to intimidate Western Europe, is now trying to decouple our security from each other."

A few years ago, if you gave a free-association test to a diplomat, when you said *alliance* he would respond *disarray*; now, the intimately linked word is *decouple*. The word is not brand-new—*Science News* was writing in 1970 that "the northeastern Pacific and the South Pacific were decoupled sometime during that period [the last sixty-five million years]"—but it broke out in a rash of usages at the end of the 1970's. Astronomers liked it and spoke of radiation and matter decoupling just before the formation of supergalaxies; economists picked it up, writing of the decoupling of energy and economic growth; and in 1979, in a piece by Fred Kaplan in *The New York Times Magazine,* the word made its military-lingo debut, in the context of suspicion that "America was 'decoupling' its own defense from that of NATO."

The verb *decouple* means "to separate, disjoin, unlink"; if you want an informal synonym, try *split up* or *part company;* for a surgical feel, use *sever* or, if you want an offbeat word, *sunder. Divide* will even do the trick, if you are not hooked on the mechanical-linkage metaphor; if you are and like to use plain words, there's no need to pull the plug on *disconnect.*

Why, then, the sudden popularity of *decouple?* Why, if *coupling* is so popular to alliance diplomats, was the much more familiar word *uncouple* overlooked? The last time anybody used *decouple* in English was in 1602, taken from the French verb *découpler;* for centuries, it was *un-*couple in English, *découpler* in French. What undid the *un-?*

The answer is the rise of *de-. De-* is to prefixes what *-nik* was to suffixes (*sputnik, beatnik, nogoodnik, freezenik*) and has surpassed the use of the suffix word *-wise,* coinagewise. The prefix *de-* is now one of the hottest neologism-producers in the language. Its rival, *un-*—which only recently produced such locutions as *unpoor* and *unblack*—is on the decline, losing out to *non-* (as in *nonbook*) and *de-.* For wordniks, here's the nonstory, *dewise:*

Remember when Lady Macbeth ordered spirits to "unsex me here"? Change that to *desex,* or *degender,* in modern use. Lawyers *decriminalize,* lion tamers *defang,* naval architects *demothball,* labor leaders *decertify,* spooks *debrief* and somebody at the Department of Defense is supposed to *declassify* —but don't hold your breath. One of the new words in Merriam-Webster's 9,000 Words is *demister,* which raised my eyebrows, but it turned out to be a noun, not a verb, and has nothing to do with unsexing; it is the British word for what we call a *defroster.*

De- is a prefix that helps timid speakers out of a fix: it often offers a fix to those addicted to shyly averting their eyes from hard, abrasive words. Museum directors, fearful of provoking criticism from donors by doing something as straightforward as "selling," prefer to *de-accession.* When this obvious euphemism drew hoots, some curious curators launched *de-acquisition,* the backflipping language sweetener of the decade. The noun *acquisition* had long ago been formed from the verb *acquire;* the marble-hall gang then proceeded to royally prefix the noun, creating *de-acquisition,* first a noun and more recently a verb meaning "to sell, trade, or give the damn thing away, I won't have it hanging on my wall."

Naturally, when a method of euphemism becomes available, Washington soon snaps it up. Budget-cutters, who shy from gutty verbs like *gut,* now croon unctuously about *defunding* programs. (Envision a crowd of budget-cutters at a football game, yelling "DEE-fund!") This sounds less harsh than *cutting off the money* or *drying up the resources*. However, *defund* has at least the merit of brevity, which is not the case in that other new bureaucratic favorite, *dejustify*.

"If you want to spend less, you have to dejustify and then get rid of programs," said Donald Moran, deputy to the blow-dried Grim Reaper at the Office of Management and Budget. The logic: to *fund* a program, you must *justify* it; to *defund* that program, you must first *dejustify* it. Verbs not considered in the budgetorium include *criticize, condemn, denounce, reprehend, attack*; phrases that did not make it include the coolheaded *argue against*, the laborious *demonstrate its unworkability* or the heated *show the whole thing to be a boondoggle*. If *dejustify* gets ridiculed out of existence, however, it will probably be replaced by *devindicate*; there's no stopping the prefix fixation, especially the rise of *de-*.

Which brings us to the meaning of demeaning, or the definition of the prefix *de-*. In one sense, it means "off," as in *derail*; in another, it means "down," as in *depress*; in a third, rare sense, it can mean "completely," as in *defunct* (*funct*, of course, means "not functioning" and deserves wider usage); and finally, *de-* means "reverse the action of" or "do the opposite of," as in *decontaminate, de-escalate*.

In this last sense, *de-* and *un-* go head-to-head, and *de-* is clobbering *un-*, which clings to its particular meaning of "not." *Un-* is losing its active sense—*unearth* is safe only because *de-earth* is awkward—and is slipping down toward a state of being, like *unblessed, unsung, unfastened, unborn*. More clergymen are being *defrocked* than *unfrocked*; the *de-* is where the action is.

The unsuspecting reader has been drawn into a quick prefix, a discussion of the device we use to turn an old word into another, new, one, ordinarily a stupendously uninteresting subject. It was aimed at those inclined to be more disinterested than uninterested and who would rather appear unpressed than depressed.

In your list of the newest "de" words, you missed one of the best sources—the A.T.&T. *divestiture* case.

My first encounter was with "deaveraging" appearing in FCC docket #78-72, "In the Matter of MTS and WATS Market Structure." Apparently averaging is an important way of presenting telephone rates to the FCC and state public utilities commissions (PUC's). (An aside here is that it is impossible to read telephone material without a full glossary of acronyms.) Now, with competition, the regulated companies would like to have competitive rates for competitive situations as concentrated business lines and therefore want to use "deaveraging." Since averaging is the norm, apparently one can't just use the individual number without first averaging and then *de*averaging.

With Second Computer Inquiry (C.I. II) FCC Docket #20-828, "detariffing" appeared with the major issue being the detariffing of CPE (customer premises equipment). I believe this is the *de*coupling of the rental or acquisition of your actual phone from the cost of telephone service.

> *Phyllis Kahn*
> *State Representative*
> *St. Paul, Minnesota*

Surely, Bill, "decouple" is a long-established word from the railroad jargon? I can't remember a time when I shouldn't have said, for example, "the excursion cars were *decoupled* and left on a siding near the picnic place."

Unless I'm mistaken, you will find the word in Kipling—perhaps *Captains Courageous.*

> *Joseph W. Alsop*
> *Washington, D.C.*

Note from W.S.: Joe Alsop, who died in 1989, was a frequent correspondent on the subject of language; as in his foreign policy views, he was an unreconstructed anti-accommodationist.

The "sudden popularity of *decouple*" may be due to the transfer of this word, which has been widely used for decades in scientific circles, to general use. In nuclear magnetic resonance (NMR) experiments, the nuclei being tested are often found to *couple* to one another: the resonance of a particular nucleus is altered by *coupling* to another nucleus. The NMR experiment can be done in a way that removes this coupling. In the parlance of science, it is thus possible to *decouple* an NMR experiment. Furthermore, *decoupling* during NMR experiments is so common that the absence of decoupling is known as *undecoupling* or *nondecoupling*.

NMR has been widely used for a few decades in chemistry and physics. More recently, NMR has been applied to biology, and most recently NMR has been used in medicine. The increased public awareness of NMR as a result of the medical work with NMR may have something to do with the apparent surge in popularity of *decouple*.

The ubiquity of technical ways in our culture leads to a technical source of new words.

Mark Rubino
Department of Chemistry
Northwestern University
Evanston, Illinois

I have to question your statement that "lawyers decriminalize." It seems to me that it is legislators who decriminalize, such as the members of the New York State Legislature which decriminalized public intoxication in the 1970s. Although many legislators are also lawyers, they do their decriminalizing in their capacities as legislators.

Martin M. Heit
Rochester, New York

You stated, "The logic: to fund a program, you must justify it; to defund that program, you must first dejustify it." The part of the quote after the semicolon is the obverse of the first part of the statement. What any student of deductive reasoning would tell you is that if a statement is true, its contrapositive is true. A statement does not prove or disprove the truth of its obverse. Permit me to illustrate: If Socrates is a man, then Socrates is mortal. The obverse of that statement is: If Socrates is not a man, then Socrates is not mortal. Assume for the moment that Socrates is now a turtle. Socrates would thus not be a man and still be mortal. Thus a statement may be true, while its obverse may be false.

The contrapositive of a statement, however, will always be true if the statement is true. The contrapositive of my original statement is: If Socrates is not mortal, then Socrates is not a man. If we assume that your statement, "to fund a program, you must justify it," is true (a highly unrealistic assumption given governmental inefficiency) then we can rightfully conclude that if we can dejustify a program, then we can defund it and save us all tax dollars.

Douglas J. Workman
Los Angeles, California

Well, you've done it again: *funct* "of course" does *not* mean "not functioning."

Functus is the perfect participle of the Latin verb *fungor* which means "to perform an assigned duty," "to discharge a public office." With the addition of the intensifying prefix *de-*, the word means "to discharge completely and have done with."

The poet Vergil applied the word to "life" (viewing life, in good Stoic fashion, as an unpleasant duty to be manfully borne) and so minted a new coinage. Later authors picked it up and eventually *defunctus* by itself came to mean "dead."

A propos the growing popularity of de-; I recall that as early as 1964, when I was a Peace Corps Volunteer, to wash out of training and be sent home was known tactfully as "deselection."

> Bruce Macbain
> Brookline, Massachusetts

My Second edition of Merriam-Webster omits *funct* although *functus officio* is listed. Could you offer more support for your assertion concerning *funct* meaning "not working?"

> David E. Knoop, M.D.
> Mendham, New Jersey

Re "funct":

Hey, c'mon, Bill! You know as well as I do that there's no such word, and never has been. I've checked the O.E.D. and four other dictionaries. Anyway, if there were to be such a word, it would mean "working, discharging its duty" etc. Then the "de-" would not be an intensifier, but a negating prefix. "Defunct" would mean "no longer funct," or "not working," which is what it actually does mean.

I like the word, tho. It's the nearest we get in English to the expressive German word *kaput*. I like that word even better. Now as to your idea that we should use "funct" (even if we meant "functional" rather than the reverse), I think your idea would be better off kaput.

> Doug McGarrett
> Jamaica, New York

Of Special Interest

The special interests were the bête noire of Harry S. Truman. Others have attacked lobbyists for particular industries or organizations who indulge in what critics call *pressure tactics* and what the lobbyists call exercising their constitutional right to petition their government for redress of grievances.

As a phrase, *special interests* is getting tired, and I have been on the lookout for any term that bids fair to challenge it. In a recent conversation with Senator Gary Hart of New York, I asked what it would take for President Reagan to get his tax-simplification plan through the Congress. He replied, "He'd have to show he was willing to take on the newsletter set."

This was not a speechwriter-coined phrase, because it was not spoken in quotation marks or as if capitalized. Senator Hart just said it in passing, as if everyone knows what the *newsletter set* is—organizations that have their own newsletters, which can marshal support against proposed legislation that might affect their special interest. A newsletter is inherently special-interest, targeted through the mail to a select audience.

Let us keep an eye on that phrase. One day I will do a piece on the language of newsletters (which will **probably** look like *this*, with every word underlined that is not already boldfaced or italicized). That'll stir up the newsletter set.

You refer to Harry S. Truman. It so happens that I knew Captain Harry Truman when I also was a member of the 42nd or Rainbow Division, and at that time he had no middle name or letter. It was during one of his first political campaigns when someone suggested that he get a middle name or initial that Capt. Harry approved putting the letter S in his name and at that time, and later on, he asked the press never to place a period after it, as it was merely a matter of euphony.

And, it might also amuse you to know, that I have just finished reading proofsheets of my next book (which I will not name as I am not seeking publicity, please believe me) and the name of the 33rd President appears as Harry S. Truman, followed by a footnote saying there is no period after S!

> *George Seldes*
> *Windsor, Vermont*

Dear Bill:

Okay—we know to which period Harry S. Truman belongs, but what period belongs to Harry S Truman?

You used a period after the "S"—some would have left it out, and according to "strict grammarians," whoever they may be, this would have been correct.

A check with John Laurence Kelland, reference librarian at the University of Rhode Island, reveals this:

Truman's parents gave him no middle name, but to spare him the anguish of being a plebeian with no middle initial, they provided him with that "S," which, strictly speaking, stands for nothing.

But there was a reason for the choice of letter: Truman's grandfathers were Anderson Shippe Truman and Solomon Young—so each was able to believe the "S" honored him.

Truman himself, unless Harry was in a hurry, used the period in signing his name, as you did, so you are in the clear on this one.

But Kelland and others like to argue that you don't use a period after an initial that stands for nothing.

Our own editors disagree, apparently (or some have never even heard of this teapot tempest) and I have seen it both ways in the *Journal.*

Anyway, I believe HST wouldn't have given a damn what we did with it.

> *Gerry [Goldstein]*
> *Chief, South County Bureau*
> The Providence Journal-Bulletin
> *Providence, Rhode Island*

If the "special interests" were plural, wouldn't they have been the "bêtes noires" of Harry Truman?

> *Clifford H. Ramsdell*
> *South Orange, New Jersey*

The last time I wrote you that you had made a mistake ("beyond the pail") I got impaled. But I do think that Senator Gary Hart is from Colorado. Unless there is a State Senator from New York, which, considering my luck of late, there probably is.

> *Peter K. Oppenheim*
> *San Francisco, California*

Of "The" I Sing

As the code-breaker in Edgar Allan Poe's "The Gold Bug" taught us, the most common word in the English language is *the*. Because familiarity bred Aesopian contempt, we tended to take *the* for granted. Not anymore.

Consider the coverage of the tragedy that befell the astronauts in one of our spacecraft. The careful reader will have noted the repeated use of the phrase *the space shuttle Challenger*, always with a *the*, never with a comma. Why the use of the article *the* in front of *space shuttle?*

The first reason is that we seek to avoid "bogus titling." For example, Ralph Nader is usually anointed a *consumer advocate:* nobody elected him to that nonofficial post, however, and careful editors—even those who accept the stilted phrase—fashion him *the consumer advocate Ralph Nader.* The useful article *the* is usually dropped in newsmagazines from all occupational descriptions—they prefer the clipped *writer Norman Mailer* and *astronomer Carl Sagan*—but editors who want to preserve the distinction between a description and a title insist on the *the.*

That's why most of us referred to *the space shuttle Challenger;* if *space shuttle* were a title rather than a description, we would drop the *the* and capitalize the title, like this: *Space Shuttle Challenger.* But that would be fuzzy because three other space shuttles exist, and give us another good reason for using our definite article: the use of *the* makes our designation specific without ignoring the fact that there are others.

A fine point: when the description is placed in front of the proper noun, the reader is informed but not insulted. We already know not to write *Challenger, the space shuttle,* because that would say it was the only one; but we also do not write *Challenger, a space shuttle,* because our readers are not idiots.

In the same way, we do not often write *Norman Mailer, the writer,* because that implies that we are not referring to the other Norman Mailer, the milkman; worse, it seems to say, "I am describing what Norman Mailer does, which any fool should know, but you may not." By placing the description ahead of the name, we are less likely to offend people who know all they want to know about Norman Mailer. Changing the article from *the* to *a*—*a writer, Norman Mailer*—suggests that he is a journeyman scribbler and will get you vilified in his next novel.

This brings us to the real value of *the:* it particularizes and specifies. In this all-too-intangible and ethereal world, *the* is the *definite* article.

A bomb can be any bomb, but *the* bomb is the symbol of the nuclear threat. When we write of *a* president, we do not even capitalize, unless we mean a specific job as head of state; but when we change that to *the* President, it's you-know-who. When Alice Walker titled her novel *The Color Purple,* I think she meant to emphasize a fascination with that specific color, which includes a variety of shades; but the title of Michael Bennett's musical *A Chorus Line* made the point that the story being told was not unique, but universal—that every musical had a chorus line.

Now we come to vogue uses of *the. Superman: The Movie* has been followed by *Santa Claus: The Movie.* I am tempted to call this "On Language: The Column," but that would be wrong (who used to say that?), because the use of *the* by moviemakers in those instances is correct. They legitimately employ the restrictive function of *the:* it's not "Superman" the radio program or comic book (actually, that was originally *Action Comics,* but you know what I mean) and not the Santa Claus that no politician ever shot.

Now try this use of *the,* noted by Paul Trapido of New York City: "A phrasing that seems to me self-consciously upscale is *ten dollars the serving.* Am I seeing yuppies under every tablecloth? . . . Why does *ten dollars the serving* sound more pretentious than *ten dollars each* or just *ten dollars?*"

It sounds pretentious because it is. The menu writer asks the maître d' what these cost, and the answer is "ten bucks a throw"; he then takes a general statement about the price of every such item in a category and erroneously particularizes. If you are tempted to do this, think of Ruth Etting standing on stage in a 1930 Rodgers and Hart musical, her dress torn, shoes scuffed, makeup askew, changing the title of her song to "Ten Cents *the* Dance."

I never thought of you as naïve; however, the description of "vogue uses of the" may qualify you for the club. *Superman The Movie* was so titled in order that LCA (The Licensing Corporation of America, a subsidiary of Warner Communications) could charge an additional royalty to its pre-movie licensees for the use of their Superman character and logo. If a licensee was unwilling to pay the extra percentage, *Superman The Movie* was licensed to a competitor who got to use *the* movie promotion, *the* paraphernalia and *the* logo. This policy brought some hard language, legal action or a backing down by LCA. I know, because Chinook Equities among its earlier (Indian, Salmon or North

Wind) incarnation(s) was named Rob Roy Company Inc., which was a
Superman licensee. I was the company's president.

All linguists may have to become lawyers.

Allen L. Boorstein
New York, New York

Michael Bennett was not prompted by his respect for the niceties of
semantics when he decided to call his show "A Chorus Line." He
made his choice on the supposition, since proven, that it would guarantee the show being listed first in *The New York Times* ABC theater
listings.

Lee Leonard
New York, New York

Of Yobbos and Gits

Britain's Parliament, like the American Congress, has a list of proscribed words that members must not call one another. Decorum
must be maintained, which suppresses most of the colorful slang terms that
political people use in private debate.

On occasion, a word pops up that has not been ruled upon. One such is
yobbo, a term now sweeping Britain that has not yet made an impact across
the Atlantic. In the House of Commons, when Norman Tebbit, the Conservative Party chairman, derided a group called the Militant Tendency
within the Labor Party, Neil Kinnock, the opposition leader, led his supporters in what was described in the *Daily Telegraph* as "uncontrolled gig-
gling" and "tie-slicking." This demonstration caused the Conservative to
label his tormentors, who would not let him speak, "a bunch of *yobbos.*"

A *yobbo* is a ruffian. On a recent visit to London, I asked Mr. Tebbit for
his definition of the slang word, and he promptly replied, "A low-grade,
street-corner thug." (A Labor front-bencher called Mr. Tebbit "a street-
corner lout," which is synonymous, though *lout* is standard English.) The
noun *yobbo* has lent itself to adaptation in the adjective *yobbish* and a
second noun, *yobbism*, which is presumably a belief in the values of hanging
out on street corners and being a *yob*.

We have now reached the original word, *yob*. A call to Robert Burchfield,
the editor of the Oxford English Dictionary Supplement—the etymology

of the term will appear in the forthcoming last volume of the supplement— elicits this:

"*Yob* is backslang for *boy.* The first citation is in Hotten's dictionary of slang in 1859," says lexicographer Burchfield, "and the word came into general slang use after World War I."

Backslang is the technique in cant of spelling or pronouncing words backward. According to Derek Seymour, a driver in *The New York Times* London bureau, who has had some training in the butcher's trade, useful to slang etymologists, "butchers' backslang" was used as a code to conceal from customers the nefarious messages between meat-cutters. "Give her the *dee-low team*" meant "give her the old meat" (*dlo team* is similar to "old meat" backwards). Similarly, *kay-rop* meant "pork" and *bee-mal* "lamb."

A *yob* was a butcher's boy, an assistant or a delivery boy, and as the extension *boy-o* was used, so was its backslang *yob-o.* Indeed, after the Tory leader had denounced the "rugby club tactics" of the opposition, which was followed by an if-you-were-my-age challenge from Mr. Kinnock, Mr. Tebbit was reported to have said, "I wish I were your age, boyo." This accentuated the boyo-yobbo connection.

(I will not be sidetracked into the history of the insulting -*o* formation. Americans use *kiddo* and *wino,* and Britons broaden the usage to *aggro* for "aggravation" and have used *commo* for communist. Australians add *garbo* for garbage. There should be an interesting hyphenated expression for "aggravation stimulated by a drunken, garbage-throwing teen-age communist" or, as Americans would call the blighter, *pinko.*)

"A *hooligan* has recently been taken to mean 'rowdy at a soccer match,' " observes Mr. Burchfield, "and that meaning of that word tends to be restricted to violent young men. A *yobbo,* however, operates in other spheres as well, and is applied to anyone of whose behavior you disapprove." According to Harrap's Slang Dictionary, the French translation of *yobbo* is *petit loulou,* a young lowlife who usually wears a *blouson noir.*

This episode of the purportedly tie-slicking yobbo was not the only evidence of the growing use of slang in the Commons. The same week, Labor M.P. Brian Sedgemore called a Conservative a *deadbeat.* Although this word has a nautical history as an adjective describing a type of compass, the slang noun is an Americanism that originally meant "a man beaten down into worthlessness" but has come to mean "a cheater," more specifically, "one who fails to pay his debts."

Nigel Lawson, the Chancellor of the Exchequer, provided a riposte to the *deadbeat* charge by saying of Mr. Sedgemore that "to describe him as a pest would be unfair to pests." This caused Mr. Sedgemore, whom most Conservatives would call a quintessential parliamentary yobbo, to refer to the man responsible for financial policy in the Mother of Parliaments as a "sniveling little git!" The Speaker of the House of Commons professed not to hear the remark, probably because it would have required a ruling on the suitability of the slang term.

A *git* is British slang for "worthless person," circa World War II, rooted in the verb *beget,* which begat the noun *get,* which has meant "offspring" since the fourteenth century. It carries a slightly sharper or fiercer connotation than *deadbeat.* In 1960, the playwright Harold Pinter had a character in *The Caretaker* say, "Who was this *git* to come up and give me orders?" *Git* is a variant form of *get,* which was used by the Beatles in 1968; lyrics in the song "I'm So Tired," from the *White Album,* derogated Sir Walter Raleigh as "such a stupid *get.*"

Sniveling is a great derogation, standard English for "running at the nose," hence any sniffling, whining, teary-eyed action. Words that begin with *sn* are often lip-curlingly pejorative, including *snide, snarling, snickering, sneaky, sniping, snoopy, snookered, snippy* and *snuffling.*

"A slanging match" is what *The Times* of London called this contretemps, which it said marred the debate. Derogatory slang has its honored place in language, but that place is not a formal setting, such as a legislative body. That is where we expect speakers to use standard language to express themselves, which in no way limits the depth of discernible disdain.

For example, when asked his opinion of the Militant Tendency, that Trotskyite party-within-a-party tugging Labor to the left, the Tory chairman, Tebbit, told me, "I recently heard it described as 'just the tip of the dung hill.' I rather like that. I think I shall pinch it."

The British press, which tut-tuts at the slanging matches but reports them in delicious detail, is adept at the opposite of derogatory slang: newspapers in London seem to have an informal agreement about the use of euphemism, more to save court costs than sensibilities. One newspaper described Mr. Kinnock's appearance on the night in question—catch the Agatha Christie quality of "the night in question"—as *unabashedly cheerful.* I am told that this is sometimes intended to suggest a mild degree of inebriation—a stimulated merriness that Americans like to call "tipsy." (In a similar way, when British newsmen want to say that a suspect was grabbed and is undergoing intense interrogation in a local slammer, they write with infinite restraint, "A man has been detained and is cooperating with the authorities.")

Margaret Thatcher, the Prime Minister, does not indulge in slanging matches. Although the shadow Home Secretary accused her of having a hard heart at Christmas time, and her premiership as being one of "Scrooge and swindle," she refused to descend into linguistic yobboism.

Lest I leave the lady's language uncriticized, however, I should point out her words in a Disney-produced message televised worldwide in the holiday season: "Perhaps I may borrow a phrase from one of my fellow country-men, Charles Dickens, who at the end of his famous book *A Christmas Carol* said: 'God bless us every one.' "

As each and every member of the Squad Squad knows and realizes, *fellow countrymen* is redundant. You may address your fellow citizens, fellow human beings, fellow members of the family of man, but your countrymen are already your fellows. *Fellow countrymen* is a solecism, no matter who says it.

What, then, of *God bless us every one?* Doesn't *us* cover *every one* of us? Yes, but *every one* in this case is used for emphasis—a perfectly proper intensifier, not a redundancy. Anybody who knocks Tiny Tim for that is a *sniveling deadbeat yobbo git,* and a pedant to boot.

You suggest "yobbish" as the adjective corresponding to "yobbo," but you cite no examples. (A prissy formation, isn't it, for a ruffian?) Indeed, in the final sentence of the article you seem to use "yobbo" itself as an adjective.

Similarly, in Tom Stoppard's play for television *Professional Foul* (New York, Grove Press, 1978), a drunken professor of philosophy holds forth on what he calls "the yob ethics of professional football-ers" (Scene 10).

The same character also refers to "yob violence." Perhaps this for-mation was suggested to Stoppard by the rhyme with "mob violence."

Incidentally, in the same scene parallels are drawn between foot-ball/yob ethics and cricket/working class ethics. Does this mean that "yob" implies, not only a ruffian, but an unemployed ruffian?

John T. Durkin
Boston, Massachusetts

The British comedy troupe Monty Python once performed, as seen on the telly, a short parlor sketch that dealt with surnames. It involves a formal cocktail party in which the host introduces to one of his guests his neighbor, an obnoxious, seemingly constipated fellow named Snivelling Little Rat-Faced Git. He is accompanied by his wife, a large, gross, flirtatious woman, Dreary Fat Boring Old Git. Although the sketch rapidly deteriorates into a disgusting, but nevertheless funny bit, I recommend it as a pictorial footnote to your examination of the word "git."

John H. Hall III
Oxford, New Jersey

Concerning "dead-beat," although you are correct in stating that it describes a type of mariner's compass, that is a fairly late designation. The word originated in the mechanical world long before such compasses were developed, and identified a mechanical device that made a strike or "blow" without recoil, such as an escapement making successive movements with intervals of rest but no backward impulse. A galvanometer is an early electrical instrument in the same category.

Robert G. Herbert, Jr.
East Northport, New York

Office Pool

Linguistic office pool:

1. Cliché most likely to drop from exhaustion in the coming year is (a) academic use of *modalities*; (b) punditular use of *disarray*; (c) adolescent use of *I mean, y'know*; (d) catalogue copywriters' use of *wicks away perspiration*; (e) *sprightly* as used by newsmagazine writers to describe all newsletters.

2. Coinage credit will be resolved on the minting of (a) *privilegentsia* to describe the Soviet *nomenklatura*; (b) *one on one*, in dispute among football, basketball and Star Wars fans (the latest entry, submitted by Adam Clymer, my *New York Times* colleague: Garland F. Pinholster, basketball coach at Oglethorpe University, lists "one-on-one" drills in the 1958 Encyclopedia of Basketball Drills); (c) *scanty*, now attributed to Shakespeare, if a recently found poem supposedly written by him is authenticated; (d) *yuppie*.

3. The phrase the President will eschew in the coming year will be (a) *standing tall*; (b) *make my day*; (c) *truly needy*; (d) *evil empire*.

4. The gap in the language most likely to be filled is (a) the lack of a feminine form for *avuncular* (auntlike?); (b) the lack of a masculine form for *uxorious* (husband-loving?); (c) a suitable retronym for publications from publishers who also produce "in-house" publications; (d) a name for the missile defense system to help a truly needy President make his day in standing tall against the evil empire.

5. The word most likely to be replaced by another is (a) *reduce*, shoved aside for *draw down*; (b) *continuing*, supplanted by *ongoing*; (c) *excellent*, to be replaced in teenagers' cant by *choice*.

My selections? No, thanks; I'll not blow my expertise here, too.

Dear Bill:

There is indeed a masculine form for *uxorious*. It is *maritorious*, meaning, according to Webster's Second, "excessively fond of one's husband." To be sure, the word is labeled obsolete; but then to be excessively fond of one's husband may be obsolete too.

Willard R. Espy
New York, New York

You call for a feminine equivalent of *avuncular* and a masculine counterpart of *uxorious*.

The words in question are, of course, from Latin: *avunculus* is the uncle who was the mother's brother (*patruus*, "father's brother," is overlooked in the English derivations). For "aunt," Latin had *amita*, "father's sister," and *matertera*, "mother's sister." These might produce, if I may be so bold, the following coinages: *amitable, amititious* or *materterous, materteral*.

To match "uxorious" with a masculine opposite brings us to the two Latin words for "husband": *vir* and *maritus*. These might produce, if you will permit me, the following: *virable* (it would be fun to have *virsatile*, but that would be too bold) or maybe *marititious* (another good one would be *maritorious*, maybe).

Herbert H. Paper
Cincinnati, Ohio

You note the lack of opposite numbers for the words *uxorious* and *avuncular*, and you suggest, respectively, *auntlike* and *husband-loving*. But in my view, to be truly satisfying, the required words should parallel their mates in coming from the same source: in these instances, the Latin.

What one must do, to fulfill this ideal, is to find the best Latin word (closest in meaning to what one wants) which is at the same time easily adapted to English. In the case of *uxorious*, which comes from the Latin *uxor*, "wife," we must look for words for "husband." *Vir* won't do, since it also means simply "man" (i.e., the male of the species); *coniunx* won't do, because it means "spouse," i.e., either husband and wife, depending on context. *Marítus* is the only possibility left.

Avuncular comes from *avunculus*, "mother's brother." "Father's brother" is *patruus*, which would yield the English adjective *patrual*. The word we are looking for, then, I take it, is *matértera*, which means "mother's sister." The English adjective would be *materteral* or *materterine*, both of which were used in the nineteenth century. The OED labels the usage "humorously pedantic," but that needn't stop us, since *avuncular* is invariably used in the same way. A more serious consideration is that the words are rather unwieldy. Better, perhaps, would be *amital*, from *amita*, "father's sister," from which *aunt* comes.

I have long felt the need for an opposite term to *phallic*; for though I don't believe in phallic symbols myself, it seems to me that the people who talk about such things are being rather unfair and sexist in never referring to the female equivalent. I finally hit upon the word *colpic*, from the Greek *kolpus* ("bay," "womb," "vagina"), from which we get the words *colpitis, colpalgia, colposcope*, and so on.

Henry Ansgar Kelly
Department of English
University of California
Los Angeles, California

On Surgical Strike

M odern war needs modern lingo. In today's attackerese, the United States did not merely *conduct a raid*, *mount an attack* or *deliver a blow* to the Qaddafi forces in Libya. What took place was a *strike*, which is sometimes described as having been conducted by a *strike force*.

The only suitable modifiers for *strike* are *preemptive*, which became famous during the 1967 Arab-Israeli war, and *surgical*.

Preemptive is still used by briefers who want to stress the deterrent effect of attacks on terrorist bases. The word is rooted in the Latin *praeemere*, "to buy beforehand," a trick used by ancient Roman real estate sharpies to check the bid of another buyer; the verb *preempt*, back-formed from *preemption*, extends the meaning to stopping another's action in any field by acting first. All *surprise attacks* are now called *preemptive strikes*; the former sounds sneaky and dastardly, the latter cunning and upright, because *preemptive* is an explanation of motive: the attacker is attacking only to deter attack.

The big new modifier for *strike* refers to tactics, and gives a humane coloration to a military exercise: *surgical* means "precise, quick, clean, incisive."

During the weekend before the bombing, news reports were filled with *surgical*. The *Financial Times* wrote, "Officials said they believed that both Congress and the American public would generally support . . . a "surgical" strike with few American casualties." As always, after the strike, reports of civilian deaths cast aspersions on the surgical nature of the attack.

The first use of the phrase recorded in The Second Barnhart Dictionary of New English is from an article in *Harper's* magazine of November 1971. "Even [in] the language of the bureaucracy," wrote Richard Barnet, ". . . the 'surgical strike' for chasing and mowing down peasants from the air by spraying them with 8,000 bullets a minute—takes the mystery, awe, and pain out of violence." The internal quotation is usually the sign that the writer is not coining a phrase, but is referring to a previous use.

A 1981 article by Murrey Marder in the *Washington Post* contains a clue: "Following a conversation with President Kennedy, the late Stewart Alsop wrote in *The Saturday Evening Post* that 'a surgical strike' against China's gaseous diffusion plant at Lop Nor was under serious consideration." Strenuous thumbing-through of old *Saturday Evening Posts* turns up no such phrase; the term Alsop reported was "the nuclear sterilization of Chicoms." But there is a good possibility of the origin of *surgical strike* in the early 1960s; a decade later a Nixon aide, H. R. Haldeman, repopularized the term by writing that Henry A. Kissinger had talked the Soviet Union out of conducting an attack of that nature against the Chinese nuclear plants.

Relatedly, Pentagon officials told reporters that *gravity bombs* had also been used. This is to differentiate them from ballistic missiles, cruise missiles and laser-guided munitions called since 1972 *smart bombs*, which have homing (not honing) devices to direct them to the target.

A *gravity bomb* is an old-fashioned bomb pulled to the earth by gravity, but nobody in the military likes to say any equipment is old-fashioned, hence the retronym. For a brief period, bombs that were not smartened with homing devices were called *dumb bombs*, which is not as pejorative as "old-fashioned" to the military mind, but *dumb*, meaning "stupid," is a slur of a handicap meaning "unable to speak," and was accordingly dropped from the nomenclature. Asked if any category exists between smart and dumb bombs, Major Richard Ziegler, an Air Force spokesman, replies: "I know of no medium-intelligence weapons."

Secretary of Defense Caspar W. Weinberger, at a breakfast for serious columnists (we are thinking of calling ourselves *gravity writers*), explained that civilian casualties may have been caused by a *hung bomb*. We all went back to our offices and dug out John Quick's 1973 Dictionary of Weapons and Military Terms for the definition: *"hung bomb:* a bomb which accidentally remains hanging to the bomb rack after the releasing action has been taken."

Finally, this note on pronunciation. On occasion, a difficult or relatively unfamiliar word is used by a President and is parroted by his spokesmen as if no synonym existed; this has the effect of educating the public on the meaning or pronunciation of the Word of the Week.

The hot adjective used in connection with the provocation of the raid on Libya was *irrefutable*. The preferred pronunciation is "ir-REF-utable," though a switch of emphasis to "irre-FUTE-able" is not incorrect. A generation ago, you could tell a highbrow from a lowbrow by the way he pronounced words like *despicable, lamentable, hospitable*—the dictionary preference put the emphasis on the first syllable, but most people liked to hit the second syllable hardest. Mr. Reagan chose the elitist pronunciation of his *irrefutable* evidence, and many of us silently applauded; the value of such an example is incontrovertible.

Surgical strike definitely was in use in the early 1960s, along with *preemptive strike*. Entries on both topics are included in my Dictionary of Euphemisms & Other Doubletalk (Crown, 1981), illustrated in each case with quotations from Theodore C. Sorensen's *Kennedy* (1965). Sorensen used quote marks around *surgical* but not *preemptive*. In both cases, he was discussing the Cuban missile crisis of 1962. Here is the *surgical strike* cite: "The idea of American planes suddenly and swiftly eliminating the missile complex with conventional bombs in a matter of minutes—a so-called 'surgical' strike—had appeal to almost everyone first considering the matter, including President Kennedy . . ." This entry in Euphemisms & Doubletalk also includes an example of the use of *surgical strike* in an extended sense, with a quote from a State Department spokesman who said the Soviet government was conducting "a surgical strike against dissidents" after it arrested two of them.

I haven't tried to check it out, but imagine that Sorensen and other members of the Kennedy White House picked up *surgical strike, preemptive strike, escalate, option, scenario*, and other war-gaming words from the Pentagon, or from debates by academics over John Foster Dulles' policy of massive retaliation, and that all date in their military senses to the late 1950s.

Hugh Rawson
Roxbury, Connecticut

I have always assumed that "surgical strike" is an elegant update to the older "tactical" strike, with the word "strike" itself being a euphemism for "bombing." (In fact I cannot recall hearing of an infantry, artillery, or naval "strike.")

In World War II, under an apparent "different strikes for different folks" policy, the distinction was between "strategic" and "tactical" bombing. "Strategic" bombing was defined by one of Mussolini's generals, Giulio Douhet, with the goal of terrorizing an enemy population, so that that population would force its government to sue for peace. The main assumption was that strategic bombing would end the war quickly, hopefully before the bombing nation needed to mobilize its army and navy.

During the War, it was tried for the first time, unsuccessfully, by the Russians against the Finns (the Russians finally had to resort to numerical superiority), and by the Germans against London. Even the apparent American strategic successes against Hiroshima and Nagasaki achieved their political goals because of Hirohito's will, not because of an outraged populace. The Allied bombing of Dresden is another example of the failure of strategic bombing, which if anything, succeeds only in strengthening the will of the civilians being bombed to continue the fight.

The implied meaning of a "surgical" strike, on the other hand, is that the bombing nation has more limited goals (specific targets rather than general terror), and is presumably more professional than the strategic bomber, in the same way that a surgeon is presumably more professional than a knife-wielding assailant. There is the unspoken analogy that, just as a surgeon must kill healthy cells to remove the tumor or medical problem, so too must a surgical striker, in the course of his efforts, take innocent lives.

Steven Shore
Columbia, Maryland

One Flu Over

My eyes water as I write this: I am afflicted with *coryza.*

That's a fancy but time-honored name, pronounced "kuh-RYE-zhah," for what some doctors call *the common cold.* They never use the words *common cold* in front of patients, nor do the sniffling sufferers call what they suffer from a *common cold,* because *common* trivializes the ailment. Think about it. Did you ever say, "I have a common cold"?

You might more likely say, "I have a *cold.*" That name for a disease causing inflammation of the nasal mucous membrane was called a *cold* because it was associated with chills, a frequent concomitant of fever. But what do you call a cold when it is unaccompanied by a chill?

"What happened to *the grippe?*" wonders Alistair Cooke. My friend Cooke is a student of the language who coined the word *extro* to denote the televised afterword at the end of a dramatic presentation, contrasting with the *intro* at the beginning. (A *foreword* has an *afterword*; a *prologue*, an *epilogue*; an *intro*, an *extro*.) "In England," he adds, "we had a *cold*, or *the flu*, or *catarrh*."

Aha! *Catarrh* is rooted in the Greek for "to flow down," and has nothing to do with chills and fever; it is a more accurate description of a runny nose (also a *running* nose, but *runny* is more specifically descriptive). *The flu* is short for *influenza*, a more serious and sometimes killing respiratory disease, which some people—who wouldn't be caught dead with anything as common as a *cold*—like to call their *sniffles*. Because of this use to cover mere *colds*, *the flu* no longer carries the danger implicit in the whole word, *influenza*.

What happened to *the grippe*, from the French word for "seizure," synonymous with *flu?* It sort of died. Nobody catches *the grippe* anymore. (We don't even grip *grips* anymore; we carry on *carry-ons*.)

I don't have *the grippe*, or *the flu*, and I've already forgotten how to pronounce *coryza*. I got a code id da node and ub gonna bed.

The grippe has not disappeared. I had it just last month. It is the affliction known in my family, familiarly, as "the whoopsies & the runsies" or "the green-apple quickstep." And it comes upon one either as the twenty-four-hour grippe, or just the grippe. Mine was the twenty-four-hour type and after just that amount of time one is perfectly well.

I believe "grippe" is an accurate description of the gripping pains and cramps accompanying and distinguishing the malady.

Cindy Foster
Branford, Connecticut

I was surprised you didn't mention a word that pops up at least once a month in the *Times* crossword puzzle, usually with the clue "flu." I'm talking, of course, about "ague." A great word, what with all its malarial connotations and all.

Dan Woog
Westport, Connecticut

While "extro" seems to be perfectly suited for the job, radio and television stalwarts have long used the term "outro" to indicate the opposite of "intro."

Eric Boardman
Los Angeles, California

Passages

How do you sound when your nose is stuffed up?

In a recent piece about *coryza, catarrh, sniffles, grippe* and *flu* (Jacques Barzun, who thinks *Coryza* would be a lovely name for a girl, adds *sinusitis* to the list of words we use to avoid *common cold*), I concluded with this muffled message: "I got a code id da node and ub gonna bed."

That spelling—that series of represented sounds, to be precise—was in error. "As any speech teacher could tell you," writes Robert N. Williams of New York, "the problem with speaking when you have a cold in the head is usually that the nasal passages are stopped up. This congestion prevents the normal pronunciation only of the three English consonants that are made through the nose: the nasals *m* as in 'some,' *n* as in 'sun' and *ng* as in 'sung' or 'rang.'"

"These three sounds," he sniffs, "will most often change, when the nasal passages are blocked, into those voiced plosives made with the same articulatory adjustments. Thus *m* will become *b*, *n* will become *d* and *ng* will become *g*. You can easily check this by holding your nostrils closed as you say the sentence."

I am conducting that experiment even as I write this, and my correspondent is correct. (My colleagues at the newspaper, passing by as I do this, offer words of encouragement because they think I am too critical of my own work.)

"The other sounds of English speech," instructs Mr. Williams, "though their resonance may be dulled and dampened in some cases, will not usually change in nearly such marked degree as the nasal consonants. Possibly the discomforts of a cold could leave one unable to make the effort needed to speak as clearly as usual, and could result in your 'code' for 'cold,' or in the lethargic substitution of *d* for the voiced *th* that you have indicated for 'the.' But such pronunciations as these are as likely to result from careless slurring as from the physical effect of a head cold."

What, then, would be the proper way to write the words "I got a cold in the nose and I'm going to bed" if you want to accurately record the sounds of a runny-nosed, watery-eyed, chill-suffering speaker?

The prescription's description: *I got a cold id the doze add I'b gudda bed.* The Lexicographic Irregular, who does not make house calls, adds an alternative to *gudda*, namely *go-ig*. Let's hold noses and try that—yes, *go-ig* is a far more graphic depiction of the sound. (Yes, I often sit here writing this way; and no, I have no problems with self-esteem.)

One-on-One Dukeout

There sat Ronald Reagan and Mikhail Gorbachev in front of the fireplace, alone except for interpreters. "The summit's greatest surprise," wrote a *Sunday Observer* team, "was the five hours the two leaders spent tête-à-tête (or, as the Americans insist on calling it, 'one on one')."

We insist on calling it that because *one on one* is a slam-bang new phrase denoting competitive intimacy. *Tête-à-tête*, or *head-to-head*, in its English translation, connotes closeness without tension; you have a little *tête-à-tête* talk at some secluded rendezvous when you want to conspire to defect. In the same way, the Geneva phrase *unter vier Augen*, "under four eyes" (that's two persons' eyes, not one guy with glasses), implies conspiracy or at least complicity. *One on one*, however, means "matched for competition," closer to one *against* another than one *with* another. The preposition *on* in this case conveys the meaning of "to cover," as one player "covers" the moves of an opposing player, which is more accurate than *one to one*, or *one facing one*; in addition, *one on one* has the internal wordplay of inserting a word minus one letter between words carrying the extra letter. (You see, my dear *Observer*, but you do not observe.)

I hyphenate the phrase when using it as an adjective, as in *one-on-one meeting*, but resist hyphenation when using it adverbially, as in *they met one on one*.

You think it's from football, don't you, as the opposite of *zone defense?* ("Wrong!" cry basketball fans, who were using it years before.) Hah! Both are mistaken: the first use cited in the Oxford English Dictionary Supplement is from the February 20, 1967, issue of *Technology Week*, describing, of all things, defenses against missiles long before *Star Wars* was written: "In the one-on-one, relatively 'simple' intercepts run during the 1962–63 test series, the 'old' Nike-Zeus scored on 10 of 14 attempted live ICBM intercepts." That usage persists in technocratese; *Aviation Week & Space Tech-*

nology in 1975 wrote that communications satellites had to be "invulnerable to anything but one-on-one direct attack."

Score one for the space age: not until the early 1970s did *one on one* become sports lingo. (This certitude would be shattered if some researcher, going one-on-one with the world of lexicography, came up with an earlier printed or recorded usage in a sports context.)

"The long 'one on one' talks," wrote Richard Beeston in *The Telegraph*, another British newspaper that revels in discovering Americanisms, ". . . must have been agonizing for such Pentagon hawks as Mr. Weinberger's deputy, Richard Perle, whose nightmare is that Mr. Reagan, if left on his own, might 'give away the store.' "

To give away the store was indeed the cliché most used by hard-liners at Geneva, a summit at which I was present to record the coinage or overusage of memorable phrases. *Giveaway* is a conservative's attack word, sometimes applied to welfare payments (called *entitlements* by liberals) but more often to the work of painless irredentists, as in "the *giveaway* of the Panama Canal."

I recall Richard M. Nixon's using the phrase "to give *up* the store" frequently during his administration. The earliest use I can find on my computer's Nexis databank is this quotation of a TRW official in *Business Week*, May 31, 1976, in a corporate, but not exclusively retailing, context: "We want controlled expansion only—we won't *give away the store* to build volume." I suspect a much earlier retailing use based on the overuse of "loss leaders." The phrase appears in this metaphoric form as Representative Samuel S. Stratton of New York, a hawk, rose on the floor of the House on February 2, 1977 to wonder if Paul C. Warnke, the Carter administration's arms negotiator, "would be likely to *give away the store* in a mistaken mood of guilt and goodwill." Hard-liners adopted the retailing phrase as their own.

At the Geneva meeting of the superpower leaders, Robert C. McFarlane, the National Security Adviser—who used *fora* as the plural of *forum*, which is not incorrect, but is not preferred even by those of us who use the classical plural of *memorandum* and *referendum*—suddenly shifted linguistic course to colorful slang in describing a struggle, using the expression "they'll just have to duke it out."

To duke it out is, I think, a modern marriage of *put up your dukes* with *fight it out*. One version of the origin of *duke* meaning "hand," or specifically "fist," is in Cockney rhyming slang: fingers were referred to as "forks," and the slang rhyme to conceal the word was *Duke of Yorks*; hence, the hands became *dukes*.

Thus, as the British press was picking up on the Americanisms *one on one* and *give away the store*, the President's adviser (known when seeking not to upstage the Secretary of State as merely a "senior official") was piercing the summit air with the latest twist on Cockney rhyming slang. That trade went unnoticed, but was more give-and-take than took place one on one.

After reading your article, I consulted one of my favorite boyhood books, *Cincinnati Power Basketball*, by Ed Jucker (Prentice-Hall Inc., Englewood, N. J., 1962). Ed Jucker coached the University of Cincinnati Bearcats to NCAA championships in 1961 and 1962. His innovations in team pattern offenses set the standards for college basketball in the 1960s. (The current head basketball coach for University of Cincinnati, Tony Yates, played on both championship teams. Much of Jucker's system was designed for Yates, whom Jucker called the "best defensive player in college basketball.")

In his book Jucker outlines game strategies, but also practice drills. In Chapter 10, "Specific Drills," he discusses "five-on-five rebounding," two-on-two guard series," "*one-on-one* with pivot offense drill," and "*one-on-one* with offensive trailer drill." The "one-on-one" citations are on pages 106 and 111. You can look it up.

I side with sports fans who claim "one-on-one" as a basketball term. The citation from *Technology Week* concerning defenses against missile power may have been derived from *Cincinnati Power Basketball*.

Robert A. Clark, M.D.
Professor of Radiology
University of Cincinnati
School of Medicine
Cincinnati, Ohio

The phrase "one on one" definitely was sports lingo before the early 1970s.

Clair Bee, who for many years was the basketball coach at Long Island University, used the term in his book, *Basketball for Everyone*, which was copyrighted in 1962.

On page 38 of the Ace Star Book's paperback, Mr. Bee states, "The one-on-one is probably the most important play in basketball. . . ."

Burt Soloman
Bedford Hills, New York

You state, "I hyphenate the phrase when using it as an adjective, as in *one-on-one meeting*, but resist hyphenation when using it adverbially, as in *they met one on one.*"

You did not resist very long. One paragraph later you wrote, "(This certitude would be shattered if some researcher, going one-on-one with the world of lexicography, came up with an earlier printed or recorded usage in a sports context.)"

I believe that the latter *one on one* is as adverbial as it gets.

Robert L. Robertson
Granville, Ohio

Your zing on hyphenating *one on one* hit the mark except for subject complements after the verb.

Inconsistency! "This certitude would be shattered if some researcher, going *one-on-one* with the world . . ." That's a subject complement after an intransitive verb, or linking verb.

Note that you wrote it right: "That trade went unnoticed, but was more give-and-take than took place one on one" only at the end. You hyphenated the subject complement (a predicate adjective in other lingo), though both come after the verb. *Went, was,* and *took place* are all the same sort of parallel construction.

Says *The Chicago Manual of Style*: "If the compound adjective occurs after the noun, the relationships are usually perfectly clear, and the hyphen is not needed: The sculpture on the terrace was free form." (1982: 164)

It's the same use of the adjective whether one *went* Democratic or Republican, if one *is* attentive to heads who meet tête-à-tête or one on one, with or without give-and-take, the much-needed noun in diplomacy today.

Le Moyne A. Farrell
Ithaca, New York

"Tête-à-Tête" may perhaps be used to conspire a defection, but it also has a far more common meaning of a romantic get-together. When two lovers meet, they are unlikely to have a "one-on-one" (the connotation is too competitive, as you correctly noted) but quite probably a "tête-à-tête" at a "secluded rendezvous".

Alexander Shatton
Washington, D.C.

"*Giveaway* is a conservative's attack word, sometimes applied to welfare payments (called *entitlements* by liberals) . . ."

Not quite. The best liberal term for welfare payments is probably *transfer payments*, because the justification for the subsidy in liberal thought involves its redistributive effects. *Entitlement* is a legal term, used because the law mandates that the payments be made in certain amounts. Thus the recipient is *entitled* to the money and, as a matter of constitutional law, cannot be denied it without *due process of law*—another bizarre and misused phrase, and one that will, I hope, provide grist for one of your future columns.

> *Stephen L. Carter*
> *Professor of Law*
> *Yale Law School*
> *New Haven, Connecticut*

The Duke of Wellington had a big nose and that a device used to break a big nose—i.e. a clenched fist—became known as a duke buster. Fists were then known as duke busters. Over time, the final word disappeared and the term "put up your dukes" arose as an invitation to a fight.

I suggest that "dukes" is only used as a term for hands when the hands demonstrate a clenched fist, never when they demonstrate a fork (consider the children's game of scissors cut paper, paper wraps stone, stone smashes scissors—only the stone is in duke format). One might note that a clenched fist is not much use in football or basketball, but perfect at hitting a missile-firing button.

> *Jan R. Harrington*
> *New York, New York*

Only Foolin'

The President of the United States, discussing pre-summit maneuvering, told a group of wire-service reporters that the time had come to "stop this *futzing* around."

No White House spokesman rushed in to say that Mr. Reagan had "misspoken himself." No eyebrows were raised by the reporters. The headline writer for *USA Today*, a respectable family publication, put "Stop This Futzing Around" across five columns.

The Yiddishism *futz* is listed in Merriam-Webster's Ninth New Collegiate as an intransitive verb meaning "to fool," customarily used with *around*. Webster's New World defines it as a slang term for "to trifle or meddle." The Oxford English Dictionary Supplement cites its earliest use in print in

James T. Farrell's *Studs Lonigan* novel in 1932: "Studs kept futzing around until Helen Shire came out with her soccer ball."

In 1943, Julius G. Rothenberg wrote in *American Speech* magazine that *"futz* has undergone an internal change to make it less obviously vulgar. Creators and users of such slang delight in skating over the rubber-ice of the conventions." He pointed out, as do our dictionaries, that the etymon is the Yiddish *arumfartzen,* and adds that in its changed form, *futz* is "seemingly innocuous."

The presidentially schlepped Yiddishism (apparently directed to those *schmegegges* and *schlemozzles,* not to say *momzers,* in the Kremlin) is a good example of a word that has been cleaned up and now is suitable for use as a euphemism. The most common word to follow *futz* is *around,* and the *around* construction, so central to our growing vocabulary of annoying relationships, deserves pop-scholarly examination.

Horsing around, kidding around, messing around are synonyms denoting playfulness, while *fiddling around* has more of a potentially serendipitous connotation, as in "I was fiddling around with this laser beam and, gee, it became this nuclear shield."

Playing around suggests adultery; *noodling it around* suggests useful rumination; *futzing around* can be synonymous with *kidding around,* even when used as a euphemism for obscene or scatological terms of similar sound. In one of those quirks of slanguage, reversing previous usage, an obscene *around* term has been used so much as to have gained an innocent connotation, while the previously harmless-meaning *fooling around* suggests the promiscuity formerly represented by the obscene term. (You think it's easy to cover my arcane beat, explicating the etymology of the expressions of our nation's leaders? Those of us who try to tread the path between scholarship and salaciousness are not just futzing around.)

You maintain, on the authority of a certain Julius G. Rothenberg, that the word *futz* is an anglicized derivative from the Yiddish etymon *arumfartzen.*

After searching through several Yiddish dictionaries, as well as Nahum Stutchkoff's renowned thesaurus, I must report that there "ain't" no such word as *arumfartzen* in the Yiddish language.

I have no doubt that Mr. Rothenberg encountered this contrived street-word somewhere in his peregrinations, but the Yiddish language has long been victimized by similar distortions of its vocabulary.

From the point of view of etymological credibility, it is more likely that the expression "futzing around" was derived from an old and somewhat earthy Yiddish colloquialism: "a-rum-drey-en zikh vi a *fortz* in ro-sl," which literally means: "to bounce around like a f_____t in the broth (or brine)," but which connotes aimless and ridiculous motion.

Mordecai Povzea
Valley Stream, New York

A spade is only a spade, but a *futz* (Anglo-Yiddish) is a *Furz* (German) or a "fart" (English). Is that one of the unprintable quadriliterals, for the editors of the *Times?* The American Heritage Dictionary admits it as a vulgarism and my old Concise Oxford Dictionary calls it indecent, but it is the only accurate translation, nevertheless.

Leonard Burkat
Danbury, Connecticut

The Yiddish "futzing around" shared usage with "fah-tootsing around" in my early Bronx days.

Lester Zimmerman
Jackson Heights, New York

While you may be right that "futzing around" has now been cleansed of its scatological meaning, the word "futzer" and more particularly "old futzer" was as recently as 1962 the source of a major politico-linguistic controversy at the University of Colorado.

The words were applied as a sobriquet in connection with Dwight Eisenhower in a newspaper article written by a graduate philosophy student. The term was seized upon by Republican legislators who then attacked the president of the university for allowing this obvious moral looseness into a student newspaper. After a maniacal freedom of speech debate, the president resigned—he was the former Democratic mayor of Denver—and subsequently many deans who were apparently tired of all the political futzing also decamped.

My question is, has futzer lost its punch? And if so, can putz be far behind?

Stephen Strauss
Toronto, Ontario

Anent *momzers:* (1) cognoscenti (note the Latinate plural) would probably spell it *momzerim* (note the Hebraic plural). The word, as you know, comes to English from Yiddish, which in turn swiped it from Hebrew. (2) On second thought, cognoscenti would probably not spell it at all, especially in a family newspaper such as the *Times.* The only meaning I know for the word indicates that the known number of

parents that a child had at his (note gender) birth was exactly one—
i.e., the exact meaning of *momzer* is *bastard*. Only in rare situations
would the *Times* permit the latter word be used in describing people.
Why then is the former permitted?

> Myron R. Myerson
> Staten Island, New York

You were on the verge of indicating the well-known differences between a shlemiel and a shlemazel. The former is one who if he waits
on the table, spills the soup. The shlemazel is the one he spills it on.

> Rabbi Samuel M. Silver
> Delray Beach, Florida

Open Mike

American presidential speechwriters, on their way to the celebration
of détente in Moscow in 1972, were sternly warned by State Department cultural-affairs officers never to use the phrase "Russian people," but
to say and write "Soviet peoples," plural.

That's because the Soviet Union contains millions of non-Russians in
ethnic groups from Ukrainians to Uzbeks to Georgians. It would be a
diplomatic booboo, we were told, for a United States official to betray an
ignorance of this essence of the Union of Soviet Socialist Republics.

Comes now Mikhail S. Gorbachev, the Soviet leader, as he is called (not
"the Russian leader," although he is a Russian), speaking to residents of
Kiev in June, in an appearance that was broadcast on local Ukrainian
television, monitored by Bohdan Nahaylo of Radio Liberty. Here is the
verbatim English translation of his mistake, his realization of that mistake
and his revealing reaction to cover it up:

"For all people who are striving for good, Russia—I mean the Soviet
Union—I mean, that is what we call it now, and what it is in fact—for
them it is a bulwark."

So the Soviet Union is Russia? Or did he mean that Russia is the Soviet
Union? Whichever he meant, he tried to correct his mistake by pretending
it was no mistake and, in trying to pull his foot out of his mouth, he put his
other foot in.

In America, if the President were caught in such a political-cultural gaffe, the White House spokesman would be out ten minutes later to explain that the President "misspoke himself." In Russia (or in the Soviet Union, take your pick), when the top man makes a mistake, his locution is no longer a mistake.

Your choice to comment on Mr. Gorbachev's Freudian slip and his attempt to vindicate himself was perceptive. I would like to present for your consideration a further elaboration of the topic. More specifically, I would propose exploring the implications of Mr. Gorbachev's faux pas within the context of the Soviet Union.

The process of Sovietization of society in the U.S.S.R. is in a constant conflict with the diverse and numerous nationalities, languages, cultures and religions which cumulatively represent the Soviet Union. Soviet society has been officially perceived by its leaders to function at the optimum level when universal conformity within the Soviet Union is achieved. Individuality has been traditionally viewed as anti-Soviet and verges on the unlawful. In this context, it is important to comprehend the fine distinction between tolerance of limited individuality resulting from the diversity within the U.S.S.R. and the official process of implementing conformity by the bureaucracy.

The Russian language as well as selected segments of Russian culture have evolved as important means to augment the process of creating a perfect Soviet society. In doing so, a paradox has been created. The non-Russian citizens, who soon will account for over 50 percent of the population, must first be molded into pseudo-Russians before the process of Sovietization is complete. Soviet leaders from Lenin to Gorbachev, notwithstanding the faux pas, have always been very careful to de-emphasize any blatant manifestation of this Russification process. Therefore, Mr. Gorbachev's slip of the tongue is a significant event within the Soviet Union.

It soon may become clear that the words *Russia* and *Russian* have transcended their meanings to represent a wider range of official Soviet use. Ironically, this phenomenon has also evolved in our own permitted use. It is common practice to refer to the Soviet Union as "Russia" and the various nationalities as "Russians." Few political entities offer such a variety of reference because the Soviet Union can be referred to as the Union of Soviet Socialist Republics, U.S.S.R. or the Soviet Union. Yet the need to further augment these terms with the use of "Russia" is beyond my comprehension. I can understand the political connotations and advantages of such usage within the Soviet Union but not the unquestioning acceptance of this substitute in our news media and educational systems. Such a practice helps to reinforce the process of uniformity within the Soviet Union. In this context, a word can be mightier than the sword or government force.

Roman Zabihach
Morris Plains, New Jersey

Oral Hygiene

I n my diatribalist capacity, I wrote that Getty Oil's deal with Texaco broke a *verbal agreement* with Pennzoil. Michael Murray, professor of management at DePaul University in Chicago, writes that "All contracts are *verbal,* unless you can think of an agreement by smoke signal or other nonverbal sign." *Verbal* means "dealing in words," and what I should have written was *oral.*

John Simon, the prince of prescriptivists, caught me on that six years ago, and I corrected myself. On sober second thought, I have decided my correction was in error: after enough time, words come to mean what most people think they mean, not what we say they ought to mean.

To most people, a *verbal agreement* is an oral agreement, and anybody who tries to make the meaning carry over to *written agreement* is out of touch with the language as it is. The distinction is now between *written* and *verbal,* not between *oral* and *written.* Jacques Barzun will be disappointed in me, but that's my call and I'm climbing down off that rampart; the lingo, she is a-changin'. As Sam Goldwyn's press agent said, intending a malapropism: "A verbal agreement isn't worth the paper it's written on."

Dear Bill:

Got your message. I am with you in wanting to follow the changes in the language, especially when they add or amplify meanings. But one must look ahead; what will you think when you hear:

"Johnny couldn't get into the college of his choice because he did poorly on the verbal part of the test."

Again, will you tolerate: I want you to report as soon as possible—in any form, oral and/or verbal (The and/or is bound to crop up here)?

Is there, besides, a loss of a general term in lowering the general one to a narrower meaning?

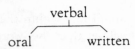

The opposite being *inarticulate* in either mode. "She's full of ideas but can't verbalize—you should listen to her talk or read her letters."

I hope you read mine, and repent.

> Yours,
> *Jacques [Barzun]*
> *Charles Scribner's Sons, Publishers*
> *New York, New York*

I was disappointed to read that you have surrendered. The barbarians have been invited into your midst. Now who is to be the guardian against slovenly speech and writing? The distinction between verbal and oral is no small one. I have personally denied tenure, salary increases, and permission to apply for research grants to any faculty member I catch confusing these two words.

> *Robert E. Doherty*
> *Dean*
> *New York State School of Industrial*
>   *and Labor Relations*
> *Cornell University*
> *Ithaca, New York*

Fowler says "the supersession of *oral* is not yet so complete that those whose care for the niceties of language leads them to prefer it need fear a charge of pedantry."

I couldn't have said it better myself.

You were the one who turned me on to "oral" and "verbal"; writing and teaching real estate I have used the distinction often, and have raised the consciousness of more than one lawyer on the matter. Now you've abandoned me.

If we can't count on you, what is there left? Next thing, I suppose, you'll endorse those purveyors of lite foods who boast of less calories.

> *Edith Lank*
> *Rochester, New York*

If "the distinction is now between 'written' and 'verbal,' not between 'oral' and 'written,' " does this mean that the future is one of verbal declarations, verbal proclamations and verbal sex?

> *Stanley Budner*
> *New York, New York*

You are definitely right about the meaning of "verbal" vs "written" (let's not forget, after Saussure, that in a language, the lexemes function by opposition to one another) and the first meaning for *logos* or *verbum* was "speech," as opposed to writing.

Lazare Paupert
Northampton, Massachusetts

You approve the phrase "verbal agreement" with the comment, "after enough time, words come to mean what most people think they mean." I should hope so! This sense of the word "verbal" has been used since at least 1591, according to the Oxford English Dictionary, which cites usages by Pepys, Swift and Scott, among others, as literary illustrations. Searches on the LEXIS computerized legal research system pull up 2,812 American judicial opinions employing the term *verbal agreement*, and 1,308 opinions employing *verbal contract*, demonstrating that this meaning is well established in legal discourse.

Fred R. Shapiro
New York, New York

Your choice of the remark by Sam Goldwyn's press agent ("A verbal agreement isn't worth the paper it's written on") as exemplifying an intended malapropism raises further complications. What is amusing in that remark, even if intended as humor, is not the misuse of any word in it; no replacement of any single word in it by another word could set things wholly right. Indeed, this remark illustrates (in my view) neither a malapropism nor any of its first cousins. The humor arises here from the relations of the meanings of the elements of the sentence; they are literally inconsistent with one another. The remark you quote is an exemplar (even an archetype, but certainly not a prototype) of that wonderful class of self-contradictions known as "Irish Bulls."

The Irish Bull, like the malapropism, is ordinarily—perhaps essentially—unintended; the failure of the speaker to recognize the enormity of the blunder in his utterance can prove hilarious. Writes the schoolboy: "The climate in the center of Australia is so terrible that the inhabitants have to live elsewhere." Bertrand Russell once reported that he had received a letter from a distinguished logician who told him "that she was a solipsist and was surprised that there were so few others." A number of remarks attributed to Yogi Berra (e.g. "That restaurant is so crowded nobody goes there anymore.") amuse because they are Irish Bulls. And the foreman of a jury who announced: "We find the man who stole the horse not guilty!" has the knack of it. I am a longtime collector of Irish Bulls—and I will be grateful for any you can contribute. Warm thanks.

Carl Cohen
Professor of Philosophy
The University of Michigan
Ann Arbor, Michigan

Our Pluralistic World

"Superpower relations are like octopi making love," I wrote in a summitary thumbsucker about the need to link issues and interests, "and all the tentacles must intertwine."

That was trope-a-dope at its best, I thought, filing the copy with some glee; political pundits enjoy taking an abstract subject like linkage and expressing a thought about it in a deliciously entangling metaphor.

Imagine my horror when the sentence appeared in *The New York Times* reading "like *octopuses* making love." An Op-Ed page copy editor who has saved me from countless embarrassments had gone too far, I thought. Ordinarily, she will call to ask: "Are you sure you want to say 'compared *to*' in showing dissimilarity? Shouldn't that be 'compared *with*'? Or do you disagree with the usage books, and especially our stylebook, which uses *to* to show similarity, and want to do it your way?" That's my kind of copy editor, guarding me against unintended errors, but prepared to tolerate my stylistic statements. But in this case, the correction was made as if I were wrong and had no basis for argument.

Octopi, in my mind, has always been the plural of *octopus*. I also drive through Arizona being prickly to the *cacti*, friendly to the *alumni*, and yawn back at the *hippopotami* in the San Diego Zoo. Yes, there are those who say *octopuses*, but these are not among the cognoscentuses; to buttress my case, I followed the advice of Doc (a friend of Squawks McGrew, the Thurber baseball manager) who used to say, "You could look it up."

Octopi is listed as the second choice in both *Webster's New World* and *Merriam-Webster's Ninth New Collegiate*, which prefer *octopuses*. That did not bother me; both dictionaries prefer the pronunciation "LAMentable," when present usage has become "laMENTable," and I'm with it and they're not, so let them rend their garments and wail. But a flat statement in Fowler's Modern English Usage stopped me: "Pl. *-uses; -pi* is wrong and *-podes* pedantic."

Uh-oh. *Octopus* comes from *okto,* "eight," and *pous,* "foot." The Greek plural of *pous* is *podes,* pronounced "pode-eez," as in *antipodes,* "with the feet opposite," which is why the islands Down Under, on the other side of the earth, are called the Antipodes. Ain't no way to make *pi* the Greek plural of *pous;* it's wrong, wrong, wrong.

The only reason *octopi* is in dictionaries as a second use is that a group of priggishly mistaken people keep using it, mistaking it for correct Greek. So I am no longer sore at the copy editor. If you want to be a pedant, say *octipodes,* which establishes your bona fides in the classical world, but if you want to call over more than one octopus in normal society, the thing to yell out is "Here, octopuses!"

This does not mean we cave in to the *-uses* crowd in the plural of *cactus, alumnus, hippopotamus* or even *magus,* each of which ends in *-i.*

This is not pedantic at all; it saves space and is easier to say. The use of the Latinate ending is also helpful in identifying sex: "Those are *alumni,*" say the kids about the old-timers at a boys' school, and "Those are *alum-nae,*" snicker the kids about the health-food fanatics who return to Welles-ley. I would use *alumni* to cover both male and female fogies at reunions, but feminists prefer the egalitarian concealment of *alumnuses* or *alums.*

Do not carry this too far; no *-i* ending is in use for *sinus* or *hiatus,* and anyone who pluralized *apparatus* as *apparati* would be considered an ignora-mus. On occasion, the difference in endings helps us with a difference in meaning: *geniuses* can be grand masters at chess, while I prefer *genii* for spirits that can be called up from the vasty deep. Often, if the word is associated with science or medicine, the Latinate ending is preferred in common use, too: there are *fungi* growing in the *radii* of my circles.

Which brings us to *um.* Scientists like the Latinate ending of the plural of *bacterium,* and most laymen lay out great sums for antibiotics to kill *bacteria,* not *bacteriums.* Academics prefer *curricula,* sociologists like *strata,* ethicists choose *criteria,* and a big fight goes on between grinds and jocks over the plural of *stadium*—those erudite no-pass, no-play Texans say *sta-dia,* while the flunked-out linebackers say *stadiums.*

You have to make a decision about *memorandum, medium* and *datum.* The Associated Press stylebook says *memorandums, referendums, stadiums;* I dis-agree on all, saving space and avoiding the mumbling of "ums." The A.P. accepts the Latinate ending for the plural of *addendum* and *curriculum;* come on all the way, fellas, and be consistent. Again, on occasion, the ending helps with meaning: *media* are those dreaded opinion-manipulators, while *mediums* urge us to join hands and feel the table move and listen to the thumping.

On *datum*, nobody argues that the plural is not *data* (*datums* is a baby-talk word for one's boyfriend), but the question is: do you ever construe *data* as singular? Answer: say *Data show* when you are talking to your fellow mathematicians about the ignorant hordes who are corrupting the meaning of your parameters, and say *Data shows* when you are speaking to those who dig the parameters of your concern. Specifically, if you mean "bits of information," *data* is plural, and if you mean information in a lump, it is a collective noun and should be treated as singular. When Ted Bernstein wrote that "the preference in good usage is to keep it plural," Laurence Urdang wrote in *Verbatim*: "Since *datum*, the singular, is confined chiefly to surveying, *data* used as a plural strikes me as a pedanticism."

However, never, never construe *media* as singular—always say "the media are," not the conglomerating "the media is"—because the press is sensitive (not "the press are" anything) and will come and get you.

Readers with eight arms will recall that what got me off on this was the plural of *octopus*. This tirade was triggered by a letter from Daniel Silver of Mobile, Alabama, holding that "your analysis of octopus courtship, while very romantic, demonstrates less than consummate knowledge of animal behavior." He cites this passage in The Encyclopedia of the Animal Kingdom, by Maurice and Robert Burton:

"In mating, which may take several hours, male and female sit apart. There is almost no courtship display, although the male may expose certain particularly large suckers near the base of the second pair of arms, as if 'making a pass' at the female. The only contact he has with her is through a single arm which he extends to caress her."

That turns out to be a curiously apt metaphor for superpower summit negotiation. Sweeping figures of speech about diplomacy should be handled the way porcupines make love, the old gag on which my metaphor was bottomed: "very carefully."

Frankly, what I had in mind was the giant squid, the plural of which is "giant squids." When terrified, they squirt ink.

I can hardly believe my disappointment. Here I sat week after week extolling your many virtues to my fellow editors here at Bell Communications Research. Here I sat supporting your every letter, but it's all over now. You have made the final faux pas. No, it wasn't a misused word or phrase. In fact, it wasn't a slip of the pen at all. It was much worse, a slip of the logic.

How can you possibly defend the use of *data* as singular by saying "if you mean information as a lump, it is a collective noun and should be treated as singular?" Collective nouns have plural counterparts. For example, family has families and flock has flocks. Why, groups of pheasant groups even have nides. *Data,* however, has no datas. (That last sentence, the careful reader will observe, is one of the rare cases where *has* and *data* will appear so close together.)

Data has datum and that is final.

Wayne R. Cavanaugh
Red Bank, New Jersey

Dear Bill,

Surely, there is a typo in "If you want to be a pedant, say *octipodes* . . . ,*" for which read *octopodes.*

One of the more common problems (probably because it is so often used in business) is "prospectus," the plural of which is not prospecti but prospectuses. Only second-declension nouns and adjectives in Latin, ending in -us, have -i as a plural; those ending in -um have -a as a plural. But that is Latin, not English, and the degree to which those words have been assimilated into English, being a matter of opinion, affects individual editors' opinions about the plurals of words like "memorandum."

Of course, not all words ending in -us in English come from Latin—"octopus" is a typical example. And not all words in Latin ending in -us form plurals by changing to -i: the plural (in Latin) of "prospectus" is, properly, "prospectūs" (with a long -oo- sound; that of "onus" is "onera," of "opus," "opera," of "corpus," "corpora," and so on.

Most English dictionaries (which traditionally show the plurals only of nouns that may cause trouble and, similarly, the inflections of other words) also show the plurals of nouns ending in -a, -i, -o, and -y. That takes care of words like alumna/alumnae, shoji/shoji, tomato/tomatoes, and candy/candies.

One particularly nasty example is "jinn," which is a plural to begin with in Arabic, the singular being "jinni." Anyone trying to sort out the various spelling forms in English together with their attendant plurals may acquire, before he's through, a lot of hair on his djinni, jin, djin. (And I am of the opinion that the English borrowing of Latin *genii* "spirit," as a plural of *genius,* represents a possible confusion between the forms and languages.)

All the best,
Larry [Laurence Urdang]
Editor of Verbatim
Essex, Connecticut

You state that "no -i ending is in use for *sinus* or *hiatus*" and that "anyone who pluralized *apparatus* as *apparati* would be considered an ignoramus." I am surprised that you did not point out to your readers that even a Roman who used *apparati* would have been branded an ignoramus. All of the above nouns belong to the fourth, not the second declension in Latin and have nominative endings in -us, not -i. What is surprising is that the OED gives *apparatus* as a proper but rare plural of the English noun *apparatus*. Indeed, the editors provide the following example of its use: "Which of the two apparatus would your Graces recommend?" (Bentham, *Church of England,* introduction, 50, 1818). With all due respect to Mr. Bentham I believe that the use of *apparatus* today would be inappropriate and confusing and would advise, as you do, the use of *apparatuses.*

George W. Shea
New York, New York

I was somewhat surprised that you concluded, from Fowler's remarks, that *octopi*, as a plural of *octopus*, was incorrect. After all, you did find a dictionary which sanctioned the psuedo-Latinate *octopi*. And I am sure that you could find a dictionary which sanctions the pronunciation of *antipodes* with the accent on the penultimate syllable, the only construction I can think of which will justify the syllabification which produces your *"pode-eez."* I have never in my life heard it pronounced except with the accent on the second syllable.

I suppose, like most old duffers, I tend to resist the evolution of pronunciation which I think is converting so much of oral English to Pablum. LAMentable seems to me to be more euphonius; the argument for laMENTable escapes me. Maybe the latter is easier to say, as may be, I guess, peJORative, which joined my vocabulary as PEJorative. It isn't even EXquisite any more, but the phony (to my ear) exQUISite. Maybe the answer is that any pronunciation should be permissible, any spelling which does not obscure the meaning, acceptable. On that basis, let's embrace *octopi.* It sounds so learned. And isn't it easier to say?

Robert L. Mattingly
Morristown, New Jersey

You have the following double-error sentence: "I also drive through Arizona being prickly to the *cacti,* friendly to the *alumni,* and yawn back at the *hippopotami* in the San Diego Zoo."

For shame! How am I to teach my editors about parallel structure if "even Safire" does it wrong? Your sentence reads, literally and grammatically:

"I also drive through Arizona being prickly to the cacti; I drive through Arizona being friendly to the alumni; I drive through Arizona being yawn back at the hippopotami."

All it would have taken would have been an *and* instead of the first comma and perhaps an additional *I* before *yawn* for felicity. As it is, of course, the alumni bit is a phrase and the *drive* is its verb, but the *yawn* bit already has a verb. Or you could have added a whole new verb for the alums—"reune being friendly to" comes to mind, since that's what alumni seem to do best, if you happen to accept reune as a verb, which I do not. . . .

Renée Cafiero
Brooklyn, New York

I approve your preferring the *-i* plurals over the *-uses* ones, as *alumni* and *cacti*.

And, like you, I thought *octopi* was a proper plural—as a Graecist I should have known better—but *octopi* is in one of my dictionaries, and *octopods* in another.

HOWEVER, I cannot, simply cannot, go along with *cognoscentuses* as a variant of *cognoscenti*. The singular is not *cognoscentus*; it is not *from* the Italian, it *is* the Italian *cognoscente*. And the plural *is cognoscenti*. If there were a variant it would be *cognoscentes*, but there ain't.

Paul R. Betz
Professor of English
Saint Joseph's University
Philadelphia, Pennsylvania

My Merriam-Webster's New Collegiate gives this beast a plural of *-uses* or *-i*. Ah me. *Hippopotamus* comes from two Greek words: *hippos,* "horse," and *potamos,* "river." The plural for each of these nouns is, coincidentally, *-oi,* as in "hoi polloi." Now, one never says "huses polluses" or "hi polli," so what I would like to know is why the hoi polloi say "hippopotami."

Lucinda Dwight
Cambridge, Massachusetts

Oxy Gored

An *oxymoron* is the jarring juxtaposition of opposites, usually an adjective headed one way *(cruel)* modifying a noun headed the other *(kindness)*.

David A. Stockman, who spent most of his time in the Reagan Office of Management and Budget and some in the Reagan woodshed, was on the receiving end of a half-oxy for years: we called him *the blow-dried Grim Reaper*. He has returned with a new book containing a phrase that popularizes a superb oxymoron: President Reagan, he says, is afflicted with *terminal optimism*. This variation on "terminal dandruff," a macabre play on "terminal illness," was probably coined by the *Washington Post* writer Ward Sinclair in a 1979 piece about Ivan Hill, head of an organization that cheerfully promotes capitalism and ethics.

Piggyback Slam-Dunking

When political operatives of the putative presidential candidate George Bush asked a poll taker for the Republican National Committee to frame a few questions their way, the metaphorical roof fell in: not only did Senator Bob Dole of Kansas demand to know if the supposedly neutral national committee had suddenly become "Bush headquarters," but a spokesman for former Senator Howard H. Baker, Jr., stormed that any over-$5,000 expenditure by the Bush committee for polling would be a *slam-dunk violation* of federal election laws.

Supporters of the former senator, who is not the tallest of candidates, might be expected to eschew basketball terms in their quest. ("Never speak of rope," said Franklin Delano Roosevelt about the Republican use of *Depression*, "in the house of a man who has been hanged.") According to Tim Considine's *The Language of Sport*, published by Facts on File, *slam-dunk* was coined by Chick Hearn, a Los Angeles broadcaster, and was first applied to the vigorous way the seven-footer Wilt Chamberlain leaped and stuffed a basketball down through the rim. That compound noun is now being used in general speech as a compound adjective whose meaning slops over "egregious" to "especially forceful" to "brutal."

The Bush people were only *piggybacking,* said defenders of the Vice President, who may be presumed to be wholly innocent in this affair. In pollster parlance, *piggy-backing* meant that the Bush forces were paying to add a few questions onto a poll about to go into the field, a frequent practice in today's politics.

The poll taker absolved the Bushmen of all blame, but John Buckley, a spokesman for Jack F. Kemp, a candidate who knows something about pigskin, got his foot into the ball with "If this is piggybacking, it's a case of a dump truck piggybacking on a bicycle."

OK: the first word for the observers of the 1988 presidential campaign to know was *piggybacking.* It has already become the greasy pole's greasy poll.

The word is perfectly kosher: pigs have nothing to do with it. Although *to be on the pig's back* is listed in the Dictionary of Newfoundland English as "to be prosperous," similar to our "high on the hog," the origin of *piggyback* is clearly nonporcine: *pick-a-pack* or *pick-a-back* is the root, from the action of picking up a pack and pitching it on the back to be carried. *Pickbacke* dates to 1565; not until 1888 did the corruption to *piggyback* appear in print, and ever since, children have been asking, "Can I have a piggyback ride?" on the aching backs of parents.

Lately, the figure of speech has lent itself to descriptions of any supplementary load, now called an *add-on* rather than an addition. In 1959, *The Wall Street Journal* described the way railroads could use rail cars designed for *piggybacking;* nine years later, the same publication was the first to extend the metaphor dramatically: "To the degree heroin does *piggyback* on marijuana, it seems more due to the law than to the pushers."

Banks now seek *piggyback financing* to get around regulations holding down the percentage that may be lent on a mortgage, and transportation companies have spawned *fishyback* and hatched *birdyback* additions, or add-ons. (Soon to come: *subtract-offs.*) And when political managers who cannot afford a complete poll ask the age-old plaintive question—"Carry me?"— poll takers can be expected to answer by providing *piggyback questions.*

I object to your use of the word "putative" as in "putative presidential candidate."

The actual meaning of "putative" is not only "believed to be," but "believed to be, while it actually ain't so."

The classical example of this usage: St. Joseph was the putative father of Jesus.

José de Vinck
Allendale, New Jersey

I was fascinated by your language column on the use of the word "slam-dunk." For those of us who don't play anymore, this shot, combining ballet and athletics, is obviously very difficult and demanding. However, in the investment banking world, with which I am now associated, I heard the word used in a different context, so that it means, in effect, "a piece of cake."

For example, on a recent trip I made with Lou Gerstner, the president of American Express, he used the term when we came out of a meeting in which he thought that a deal could be made relatively easily. "That's a slam-dunk," he would say.

Similarly, yesterday I heard one partner say to another, "You may think this deal is a slam-dunk, but it is going to take us at least six months and it won't be easy." I guess what this adds up to is that one man's slam-dunk is another's "easy layup." Come to think of it, a slam-dunk *is* an easy layup to Dr. J.

Richard Holbrooke
New York, New York

Plain Vanilla

E ric Dickerson, the great Los Angeles Rams running back, explained to the sports columnist Scott Ostler why his team almost lost that day: "I think we were just too *vanilla.*"

How hath the mighty fallen. *Vanilla* is a word that has been blitzed, reddogged and run out of the ballpark. First, its pronunciation has been mangled: I think the vast majority of American ice-cream lovers says *vin-EL-la,* and a minority becoming minuscule says *vuh-NIL-uh,* with that dwindling band of correctniks also saying *min-US-cule* rather than *min-ISS-cule.*

Originally, the word carried with it the very essence of zest and flavor: "Ah, you flavor everything," wrote Sydney Smith in 1845, using the French word for it, "you are the *vanille* of society." That metaphor was bottomed on the *vanilla bean,* which produced an aromatic substance much desired by confectioners to flavor ices and custards. The word had a real tang. Its etymology is interesting: from the Latin *vagina*, which means "sheath, pod, encasement," and we will now quickly turn from etymology.

For a time, even its slang use carried a connotation of delectability. Every former soda jerk (now beverage dispenser, or squirtperson) knew that the call of "Vanilla!" was code for "Come out of the kitchen—there's a chick just walked in that'll knock your eye out!"

Then the word's meaning was tackled: in slang terms, *vanilla* came to mean "exaggeration." In recent years, it has suffered a late hit: instead of "flavored with vanilla extract," the most frequent slang meaning changed to "unflavored." *Vanilla* was not as vividly colored as other ice creams, and it was a standard flavor; that led to "plain vanilla," with its pejorative connotation of "tasteless."

Now we have *Business Week* writing, "Learjet now builds a standard 'vanilla' airplane—free of paint, upholstery, or any optional avionics or conveniences." *Time* writes of "what the trade calls a 'plain vanilla' radio—*i.e.*, one without options." (Time likes *i.e.*, from the Latin *id est*, "that is," clarifying the meaning of the preceding clause; *e.g.*, abbreviating *exempli gratia*, "for example, such as, "gives a free example. Do not confuse the two. If you prefer clarity to saving space or showing off your Latin, use *that is* or *such as*. Where was I?) Neologistic *Newsweek* drops the quotation marks around the metaphoric use of *vanilla*, writing of a dull movie: "after it's over you feel a vanilla chill settling over history itself."

Here, then, is a word coming to mean in slang the opposite of its standard meaning. Farewell, tasty vanilla. When my favorite football team plays lackluster ball, and the front four fall asleep on their three-point stance, I turn to a synonym for *vanilla, e.g., flat—i.e.*, not all nice and fizzy as when you first drop the tablet in.

> The great jazz saxophonist Lester Young was admonishing his sidemen back in the '30s, '40s, and '50s to keep their musical accompaniment free of cluttered embellishments by telling them to "just play vanilla."
>
> *Paul H. Falon*
> *Washington, D.C.*

. . . But before we call the whole thing off, a couple of thoughts which might serve as addenda:

1) About the time Ira Gershwin penned the lyrics for *Shall We Dance?* (1937), the expression "I'll take vanilla" was popular, at

least with writers of movie dialogue. It was usually delivered out of the side of the mouth by tough customers like Ward Bond or Veda Ann Borg, and the locale was more apt to be a dime-a-dance joint than a soda fountain. The phrase connoted a skeptical rejection of whatever had just been suggested; that people didn't riposte "I'll take chocolate!" or "I'll take strawberry!" seems to show that vanilla was held in higher esteem in Depression-era America than it is now.

2) Something a little tangier, now; better file this item under the same "not for a family newspaper" heading as the etymology of vanilla: Among gay men who practice sadomasochistic, or "leather" sex, more conventional (and presumably less painful) gay sexual relations are known deprecatingly as "vanilla sex." That this term isn't more widely known probably shows that most gay men favor hanky-panky over hanky-spanky.

Bruce Medville
New York, New York

Your disquisition on vanilla reminded me of a conversation I overheard on a bus recently. A passenger (black) and the driver (likewise) were quietly discussing various bus routes they had driven.

"I don't enjoy driving the X-11 line," said the passenger. "All vanilla."

I assumed he was describing the passengers on that line, and so I thought to myself, "Chocolate is beautiful." Which is true, but so is vanilla!

Arthur J. Morgan
New York, New York

Player-Manager

Henry Kissinger was once asked why he took time from his lucrative private practice of diplomacy to serve as chairman of a bipartisan commission on Latin America. "It's important to be a *player* occasionally," he replied. Cryptic? Not to the students of powerspeak. A *player* is a participant, one who sits at the table and engages in the game, in contrast to the observer, the commentator, the kibitzer and the hanger-on.

"Now we have *players* everywhere," writes David R. Jones, *The New York Times*'s national news editor. "People who bid for companies are *players*; people involved in Washington political stories are *players*. Might there be a story in what is going on here?"

In a piece on specialized discount stores, business reporter Isadore Barmash wrote, "Three leading *players* closed their doors last year . . ." C-Span, the television service that covers Congress, was described as having "become an important *player* both on the Washington scene and in state government." Observing the way President Reagan was trying to avoid involvement in the deficit-reducing process, Senator Bob Dole said, "The President's got to be a *player* . . ."

We have here a spinoff of a dying cliché. The predecessor phrase was *a role to play*, based on the metaphor of a stage play mirroring reality, first popularized by William Shakespeare in *Hamlet*. For a time, everything and everybody had "a role to play"; the vogue construction began to peter out as a real actor bestrode the national stage in 1980.

Supporting the *player* metaphor is the business adoption of a sports metaphor, *in play*. A corporation at which a run has been made by investors or predators is said to be *in play* even if it fights off the attack; hence, those who are in the takeover game are *players*.

OK, you players, the manager says: off the field. Once a vogue word has been overdone, it becomes a walking shadow, "a poor player/That struts and frets his hour upon the stage/And then is heard no more . . ."

Playing in Pretoria

Speaker Thomas P. O'Neill, Jr., did not like the way President Reagan took away the House's thunder at the Government of South Africa. Congress was readying a bill to apply sanctions; the President, to head off Congressional seizure of the setting of foreign policy, announced his intention to put forth a series of sanctions by executive order.

"It will be seen for what it is," grumbled the Speaker, "by the people suffering under the yoke of that government." His point was that the slightly less onerous restrictions would be taken lightly by apostles of apartheid. The Speaker let loose his scorn in a searing phrase: "This package will play in Pretoria."

That was a deft shot. The phrase *play in Pretoria* is a play on *play in Peoria,* substituting the capital of South Africa for the city with a similar name in Illinois. I had not heard that Nixonian phrase for many years, and can cite chapter and verse on its coinage.

John D. Ehrlichman, who in 1968 was the chief of Nixon advance men, used the phrase to mean "go over well in a non-elitist environment" in a "school" he ran for the organizers of parades, hoopla and local welcome in cities to be visited by the candidate. *"Play in Peoria* appeared in a *Wall Street Journal* story after I'd run the school in New York and used the expression there," recalled Ehrlichman years later. Why Peoria? "Onomatopoeia was the only reason, I suppose. And it personified—exemplified—a place, removed from the media centers on the coasts, where the national verdict is cast, according to Nixon doctrine." (I think John meant *alliteration,* the repetition of an initial sound; *onomatopoeia* means "imitative, echoic," like *tinkle* for the sound of glass touching glass. I run this school for advance phrase-coiners, of which Mr. Ehrlichman is a star student: he also contributed *twisting slowly, slowly in the wind.)*

The word most frequently applied by Mr. Reagan to apartheid is *repugnant;* whenever asked about that racial policy, the President almost always uses that adjective, although usually in a subordinate clause. That word is rooted in the Latin for "to fight back," and its most frequent meaning is "objectionable, distasteful." Other synonyms available are *offensive, loathsome, repulsive.*

Sanction is a word that appears to go in opposite directions. As a verb, *to sanction* means "to permit, ratify, approve, validate," but as a noun, a *sanction* is a penalty or method of coercion. What gives? The word comes from the Latin *sanctus,* past participle of "to make holy," and it is the root of such words as *sanctuary* and *sanctimonious.* It began as an ecclesiastical decree, and the meaning split early: the verb implied approval, but the noun came to be associated with the threat contained if the church's order was not followed. In law and ethics, sanctions could be positive as well as negative—"inducements" as well as "coercions"—but in international relations, the word came to mean only the penalties threatened or carried out to force a course of action. That's the context of most usages of the noun now: a *sanction* implies a good type of pressure, but *pressure, threats, coercion* and *penalties* connote imperialist bullying.

While we're at it, *Pretoria* is a city named after Andries W. J. Pretorius, the Boer leader who defeated the Zulus at the Battle of Blood River in 1838. His name was probably rooted in *praetor,* an ancient Roman magistrate, a rank below a consul, leading to the phrase *Praetorian guard,* the soldiers protecting a Roman emperor. *(Peoria,* north of Springfield in central Illinois, comes from *Piwarea,* an Algonquian Indian word that perhaps means "he comes bearing a pack on his back.")

I have always found it curious that my Nixon colleagues chose Peoria as the epitome of squareness, because I heard Everett M. Dirksen, who in 1969 was the Senate minority leader, use the name in a wholly different sense. "I was born in Pekin, Illinois," he recalled, "a lovely town, kind of on the quiet side. But for those young rakes who wanted excitement—not too far away were the bright lights of Peoria."

As I read "Playing in Pretoria," it became apparent that John D. Ehrlichman has been up to his old tricks again, and has misled William Safire by taking credit for coining the phrase "play in Peoria," while he was a member of the Nixon inner circle.

In reality, the phrase originated many years ago, during the vaudeville era.

As a boy, growing up in Peoria during the late 1930s and '40s, I recall having heard the phrase "Will it play in Peoria?" on the Jack Benny and Fibber McGee and Molly radio programs, among others.

When I asked about the origin of this expression, my grandmother explained that Peoria was known on the vaudeville circuit as one of the toughest towns in which to get a laugh, and consequently, if a new act or comic skit were likely to "play in Peoria" it would play, or be successful, anywhere.

David H. Bremer
Newport Beach, California

John Ehrlichman may think "playing in Peoria" was generated only by onomatopoeia and he may be dutifully corrected by William Safire to ascribe it to alliteration, but from what I am told by my friends in Peoria there is likely another origin that lurked in Mr. Ehrlichman's subconscious.

Peoria is a test town for marketing new products. It has been considered a typical American city with a diverse population.

Thus, how well a product "plays in Peoria" is used as a measure of how well it is likely to sell nationwide.

Paul M. Copeland
Salem, Massachusetts

I hope that you receive 5,267 letters of objection from old-timers who care as much about the origin of our wonderful language and its phrases as you do—which is why we read your essays at all; that is, if there are 5,267 people left who remember "play in Peoria" as a marvelous bit of American show biz.

Yvonne Gallagher
Los Angeles, California

The origin of "to play in Peoria" was definitely prior to 1968 and Richard Nixon (and John Ehrlichman). When I was a child (circa 1945) growing up near Peoria, I asked my father what that phrase meant. He claimed that it was a vaudeville saying meaning that if Peoria audiences liked the show, it would be a hit anywhere. I always felt it had something to do with the selectiveness of Peoria taste, but I can't vouch for that.

Margaret Real
Maplewood, New Jersey

Since you were more or less present at the birth, it would be cheeky to challenge your account of John Ehrlichman's "playing in Peoria" line, but I would like to suggest a possible source, albeit from a somewhat different context. It comes from the old "Fibber McGee and Molly" radio program from the 1940s and was one of those catchwords listeners used to anticipate and then laugh at—well, chuckle—when it finally came, somewhat like the famous front-hall closet. In one of his rambling nonconversations with almost anyone, but usually Molly, McGee (Jim Jordan) would reminisce "I remember when I and Fred Nitney (Knitney?) played vaudeville back in Peoria . . ." or some such locution.

I assume that Ehrlichman, like most of us, misspent enough of his youth listening to this kind of pre-trivial pursuit to have encountered this little line and that it was lurking somewhere in the inner reaches of his memory bank awaiting the opportune moment. In any event, as I remember when I was growing up in the Middle West, Peoria, as a referent, was roughly interchangeable with "Podunk," to include the pejorative overtone—precisely, I think, what Ehrlichman had in mind.

Bruce Radde
Fairfield, Connecticut

I would imagine, however, that Mr. Ehrlichman, being "a star student" in your "school for advance phrase-coiners," had *onomatopeoria* in mind.

Mary Susannah Robbins
Cambridge, Massachusetts

As every young student in an introductory sociology course soon discovers, sociologists use the term "sanction" to mean the enforcement of a rule. The enforcement can be through either formal or informal means and it can be done in either a positive or a negative way. In common terms, either the police or your next-door neighbor can impose a sanction and the sanction can be either a carrot or a stick. If I save the neighbor's cat from a tree, they are likely to give me an apple pie along with many thanks. This is an informal, positive sanction. On the other hand, if I run over their cat with my car while I am drunk, the police are likely to lock me up. This would be a negative formal sanction.

G. Duncan Mitchell, in his Dictionary of Sociology, traces the sociological use of the word to W. G. Sumner in his 1906 book *Folkways.* In addition, Mitchell notes the article on sanctions written by the anthropologist A. R. Radcliff-Brown in the 1934 edition of the Encyclopedia of the Social Sciences. Radcliff-Brown developed the distinction between diffused and organized sanctions. The former refers to the informal, non-codified sanctions discussed above, where organized sanctions are "those incorporated in legal enactments."

Thus, while sociology is often noted for its turgid prose, usually by those poor students in introductory sociology, it has, at times, added a bit of precision to the language.

Richard Ling
New York, New York

Port Manteau

Coiners get a break in this space. When I hailed *Time* magazine's editors for the happy blending of *television* and *evangelist* in a piece on Pat Robertson to make the portmanteau word *televangelist,* I overlooked a flock of previous usages.

Professor Irving Katz of Indiana University's history department directs me to a *New York Times* book review in 1981, which in turn reveals an earlier use: Jeffrey K. Hadden and Charles E. Swann wrote a book that was published early in 1981 about electronic ministries titled *Prime Time Preachers*, and the subtitle was *The Rising Power of Televangelism*.

If an earlier citation is found, we'll run it up the portmanteautempole and see if it salutes.

The Post-Holiday Strip

I n Paris, they're *au régime*; in Berlin, they're *diätleben*; in London, they're *slimming*; here at home, after stuffing ourselves for the holidays, we're *dieting*.

Perhaps I used that term too quickly. According to Joanna Green of Weight Watchers, the current euphemism for dieting is *being careful.* Only a generation ago, that phrase was a euphemism for contraception, which shows how our worries change.

If you've been *fressing* or *noshing* (Yiddishisms based on the German *fressen*, "to devour," and *naschen*, "to eat surreptitiously") or *snacking* between meals or *grazing* all day, then you, like most of us, have been *overeating*, or *stuffing yourself*. As they say at Weight Watchers (parodied by National Lampoon as Weighty Waddlers), you were *being bad.*

But who could pass up the celestial potato latkes, silver-dollar-sized, at Daniel and Li Schorr's annual Hanukkah bash? What Scrooge-like calorie-counter would turn down the toad-in-the-hole (English sausages in a Yorkshire pudding batter) and bubble and squeak (fried potatoes and cabbage) at the Boxing Day post-Christmas festivities at Liz Drew and David Webster's? What Sisyphean spoilsport would keep pushing his regimen in the presence of the crispy egg rolls stuffed with shrimp at Marge and Mel Elfin's, where every New Year's Eve rings in 1942? (This paragraph brightens a language column with celebrated names, enlivens an abstract discussion of terminology with vivid examples of temptation and saves three thank-you notes.)

OK, everybody, the good times are over; now we're into *fiber*. That's the hot new word in the language of diet. It means "the part of food that is indigestible cellular matter"; in the bygone days when waitresses giggled to hear you order bran flakes with a side of prunes, *fiber* used to be called *bulk* or *roughage.*

Empty calories is another phrase you come across while nibbling your way through diet books. The calories themselves are not "empty," but they come from food with little or no nutritional content. (What jargon am I accepting with *nutritional content?* The simple English word is *nourishment.*) This pseudoscientific term has replaced the familiar *junk food. Junk,* by the way, permeates the language; I'm speculating, but I think its modern use is a back-formation from *junkie,* a heroin addict, which led to *junk food, junk mail, junk jewelry.*

Reliance on high-energy foods spawned the current phrase *carbohydrate-loading,* popular among runners of marathons who stuff themselves with whole-grain pasta before trotting off to the day's race. Most dieters, who do not exercise enough as it is, frown on loading themselves with carbohydrates.

In that regard, every health-food nut knows what *gorp* is: a mix of cereal grains, peanuts, raisins, dates, little bits of chocolate or sugar candy. Some hikers and campers go for *gorp,* or *trail mix,* on the theory that its high energy content gives them a lightweight kick. Some folk etymologists contend that *gorp* is an acronym for *granola, oats, raisins, peanuts,* but that smacks of the *port out, starboard home* malarkey about the origin of *posh.* To me, the word seems formed like Lewis Carroll's creation of *chortle* by combining *chuckle* with *snort: gorp* is a wedded *snort* and *gulp.*

Because those of us who shovel food in our faces ravenously are addicts, the vocabulary of addiction has been adapted to dieting. You can O.D. on the mocha buttercream Ilona tortes in George Lang's new *Café des Artistes Cookbook;* O.D. comes from *overdose* in drug usage and not from the Southern *pure O.D.,* an often-forgotten reference to ox dung. The suffix *-aholic* or *-holic* is now being applied to lovers of darkly delicious sweets, as in the word *chocoholic.*

The words used by dieters to revile nondieters include *pig out* and *binge,* taken from the noun that described the lost weekends of alcoholism. *Wolfing* is what fast eaters do, and this term has been bastardized to *woofing,* adding a canine dimension.

The biggest verb in this fast-food-for-thought category is *scarf,* "to wolf down"; this verb originated in the black English term for food in the 1930s, *scoff,* which Wentworth and Flexner's Dictionary of American Slang suggests has an African origin. Farmer and Henley's Slang and Its Analogues traces the word *scoff* to 1893 hobo use. Clarence Major's Dictionary of Afro-American Slang defines *scoff/scarf* as meaning "to eat," synonymous with "grease (one's) chops."

In the lexicon of lip-smacking, an *epicure* is fastidious in his choice and enjoyment of food, just a soupçon more expert than a *gastronome;* a *gourmet* is a connoisseur of the exotic, taste buds attuned to the calibrations of deliciousness, who savors the masterly techniques of great chefs; a *gour-mand* is a hearty bon vivant who enjoys food without truffles and flourishes; a *glutton* overindulges greedily, the word rooted in the Latin for "one who devours." After eating, an *epicure* gives a thin smile of satisfaction; a *gastro-nome*, burping into his napkin, praises the food in a magazine; a *gourmet*, repressing his burp, criticizes the food in the same magazine; a *gourmand* belches happily and tells everybody where he ate; a *glutton* embraces the white porcelain altar, or, more plainly, he barfs.

What do you call a person who has become corpulent, portly, or—let's face it—fat? You call him, or call yourself, *blubber-guts, fat stuff, five-by-five, porky, tubby, bucket o' lard, solid suet, beef trust,* or *hippo.* (For many of these terms, I am indebted to the Dictionary of American Regional English.)

What would I like you to call me if I can get these fifteen pounds off and then go into a maintenance mode? One name fits all: *Slim.*

Not meaning to scoff, but what your column says about *scarf,* to "wolf down" food, is something I can't swallow. You rightly connect it with *scoff* as a variant form—the *r* is the way an *r*-dropper would spell it. But it has been in the language much longer than the sources you refer to (Wentworth-Flexner, Farmer-Henley, Major) are aware. The Old Scots form *skaff* was the earliest (fifteenth century), taken into English as *scaff* "to eat voraciously" (1797) and as a noun *scaff* "food, provisions" (1768), which developed into *scoff,* both verb and noun, in the nineteenth century. The ultimate source (uncertain) is probably Dutch or German.

In American use it easily became an underworld word, used by hoboes and others who would scrounge and gobble any food, drink, or other provisions they could get their hands on. Jack London wrote that the hoboes called Reno "a hard town for scoffings" (*My Life,* 1892). It's still an active slang word, used by Blacks among others, and spread into the world of drugs and street crime. But there is no evi-dence of African origin—its ancestry is European and antedates the European explorations of Africa.

My chief sources are the Scottish National Dictionary and, of course, the big old Oxford English Dictionary, which is what one should always consult first. There's a bit of etymology for your readers to scarf!

Frederic G. Cassidy
Chief Editor, Dictionary of American
Regional English
Madison, Wisconsin

Dear Bill:

I am that Scrooge-like figure (no calorie counter, ever, but simply Scrooge with a discriminating taste in food) who would discover a pressing, forgotten, appointment if ever I was offered the Websters' ordure. As a Lancastrian; I suspect and decline anything manufactured in Yorkshire—their celebrated "pudding" is a slab of wet lead. (In New England and the South, on the contrary, I have had excellent pudding which at once shames and glorifies the dreadful county of the White Rose.) I could certainly be enticed to Marge and Mel Elfin's, but not to the racist Schorr's. Potato latkes, indeed! You are more of a meat-and-potatoes man than the—culinarily speaking—benighted Jack Kennedy. But, please, no more reminders in your column of the dank evenings at Jesus College, Cambridge, with its Windsor soup, bubble and squeak, grey lamb (and black falcon on special occasions) —winding up with toad-in-the-hole or devil-on-horseback as a savoury.

Once that's out of the way, let me say that this is really about slimming. "Banting" was the invariable word in Britain in the 1920s, and I do believe that John Hawkesworth, who could be marvelously accurate in these things, used it in an episode of either "Upstairs, Downstairs" or "The Duchess of Duke Street." The word came, of course, from association with the recently famous Sir F. Banting—of insulin fame. That's what I was told, but Sykes now tells me that it derives from a famous popular work of one W. Banting "an English undertaker and dietitian, d. 1878." Certainly, Sykes is right to put "arch." I never heard the word in America.

That's all, brother. Come to New York, or London, some time and I'll introduce you to edible food.

> *Yours,*
> *Alistair [Cooke]*
> *K.B.E., C.G. (Crispy Gourmet)*
> *New York, New York*

When I first encountered the term *gorp* over thirty years ago, it was explained (by an uncle who implied he had coined the word) to derive from an unbalanced conflation of gourmand/gormandize and pig. *This* folk etymology has the advantage over the two you suggest of allowing gorp to function equally well as noun or verb (a gorp is a person who gorps his food).

> *David Rife*
> *Williamsport, Pennsylvania*

About *gorp:* where do you get *snort* and *gulp?* Much more likely as the elements of the portmanteau are *gorge* and *gulp.*

Throat and swallowing words often contain the throat-produced "g" and "r" sounds, i.e.: Gorge, gulp, gobble, guzzle, gargle, gormand-ize, regurgitate. Even the slang word for food—"grub"—and the un-happy result of gobbling and guzzling too greedily, "gripe."

Note the derivations for some of these elemental eating and swal-lowing actions (mostly Middle English).

gulpen—drink greedily
gurga—(M.E. from L.L.) throat
gobet—mouthful
gobbe—large piece of food
gripen—to grip, grasp
grubben—to dig (for food?)
gurgle and gargle—both probably imitative; M.E., *gargoullier*
gurgitare—L.L., to engulf
gargantuan—from the Rabelaisian giant king with a great capacity
    for food and drink

Just saying the word "gulp" requires a sort of—well, *gulp.* And so with burp and slurp. (Not in my dictionary, but a well-known euphe-mism for "vomit" is "urp.")

Janice M. Jensen
Syracuse, New York

Please tell your chums Liz Drew and David Webster that it is BRUS-SELS SPROUTS, not just cabbage in bubble and squeak!

Obviously you don't have a dear English mum who served it up all lovely and proper, dearie!

M. J. Barrell
Hershey, Pennsylvania

In your translation of the German verb *fressen:* you are correct in saying that it means "to devour," but only in a particular usage. The word's first and most common application is as the ordinary verb for "to eat" for animals. (German, you may know, has a separate vocabu-lary for animals.) Only when it is applied to humans does it take on the meaning of "to devour," or "to eat like an animal," and it has connotations of grossness and vulgarity. (The Yiddish derivation is much more lighthearted and humorous; the German usage is a rank insult.)

My second quibble is with your speculation about the origin of "junk" as in "junk food." I, too, am only speculating, but it seems to me that the noun "junk" predated the usage and an adjective, or the noun "junkie." It's first meaning in this sense is surely "useless trash" such as what is collected by "junk dealers" and sold from a "junk yard." I imagine this meaning was adopted for the "useless trash" addicts shot into their arms, and that their use of "junk" gave them the name "junkie," not vice versa. The terms "junk food," "junk mail" and "junk jewelry" seem more related to the meaning "useless trash," and probably evolved from that original connotation rather than the habit-forming-drug sense. "Junk food," after all, isn't really addictive—it just doesn't provide any real nourishment. The sense is clearly closer to "trash food" than to the other synonymous adjective for "junk," which would make it "dope food." The fact that this phrase doesn't make much sense seems to bear out my contention.

Richard E. Kramer
New York, New York

Your column contained a usage error that stems in part from the social confusion caused by unmarried adults living together. I refer to your reference to a party "at Liz Drew [sic] and David Webster's."

Unless "Liz Drew" describes "Webster," it must take the possessive form, "Liz Drew's." I gather that your intent was for the phrase to indicate that the two people are a couple, as in "Bob and Mary Anderson's," but it doesn't work in the form you used. If you meant to indicate that David Webster is the major investment partner (*i.e.,* his house), it might be fitting to give him the single possessive, but Liz Drew might think that was a put-down overriding your public sharing of your invitation list.

John P. Richardson
Washington, D.C.

My favorite portmanteau word, *bletch,* was coined by my sister Margaret when she was a child.

A combination of "blotch" and "blemish," *bletch* describes any unsightly, but unidentifiable, mark on skin or clothing. Examples: "I have a bletch on my nose—I hope I'm not getting a pimple." "Ugh! There's a bletch on your hat."

Try it—it's very useful!

Kathryn Lance
New York, New York

The last time I heard the word "scarf" was in the Army during WW II. The meaning then was "to steal" and I always heard it accompanied by scooping action of the right hand.

Lawrence Goldstein
Syracuse, New York

Prexy Isn't Sexy Anymore

I read in the *Hollywood Reporter* that a "restructuring"—we used to call it a shake-up—of a division of Paramount Pictures has taken place, "with Barry London and Buffy Shutt being promoted to president of distribution and marketing and president of marketing respectively."

This is an outbreak of the Olive-Size Phenomenon, in which "mammoth" is medium, "giant" is larger, and the big ones start at "colossal." The olive-naming blight has seized moviedom and is appearing elsewhere in the world of business.

Ever since Nelson A. Rockefeller derogated the Vice Presidency with "I never wanted to be the *vice* president of anything!" vice presidents have been brooding about their titles. No longer did the root word *vice* bring forth the meaning of "one who stands in the place of," from the Latin ablative of *vicis*, meaning "a change." (That meaning of "stepping into the place of" is expressed by the word *vicar*, and is probably why George Bush got sore when Al Haig described himself as the President's foreign-policy *vicar*. Only one *vice* at a time.) The *vice* of "Miami Vice," on the other hand, derives from the Latin *vitium*, meaning "fault," and there's plenty of *vitium* in video.

For a while, vice presidents tried to put pep and authority in their titles by adding modifiers. The title of *executive* vice president, however, suggests that the other veeps are not such executives, much as a Distinguished Professor in a university leaves the other profs undistinguished and a little shabby. A *senior* vice president, everyone knows, is the Old Guy who was passed over for the top slot, and an *administrative* vice president keeps track of paper clips, disapproves expense accounts and stays out of the way of the moneymakers.

When the modifiers didn't work, vice presidents—Barry, Buffy and their ilk—began to seek a new approach to define their status. What do you do when a title doesn't do the job? The advice of the vices: call a vice president a president.

This triggers the riddle: "If you call a tail a leg, how many legs has a dog?" The answer is four, because "calling a tail a leg does not make it a leg." Calling a vice president a "president of a division" robs a chief executive of a good title, which does not enrich the division head and leaves the boss poor indeed.

Although *President* remains a strong word in politics, its authority is waning in the business world. *President*, "one who presides over," is rooted in the Latin for "to sit before," much as a president sits at the head of the table, in the place of authority. However, the *chairman* of the board of directors, more often than not, sits at the head of the table, which diminishes the president.

The fight between the words *chairman* and *president* is over who sits in the key seat. The *president*, etymologically, must sit in the place of authority, but the *chairman* is the man in the most important chair. King Arthur, to solve this problem, invented the Round Table, which in corporate life is the office of the president.

The word *president* is further undermined by the change in meaning of its root verb, *preside*. John Hancock *presided* over the Continental Congress of 1775, and the verb then connoted great authority and decisiveness; now, authority has been sapped from the word, and *to preside over* connotes standing (or sitting) idly by while others debate. An activist President, we say, does not merely *preside* over the Cabinet, he *takes charge* of the Administration. The zip has gone out of *preside*, and has been assumed by *execute*. Whoever heard of a hands-on presider?

So, while vice presidents seek to drop their quick *vices*, and lust after the title of president ("Fleagleman, formerly vice president, international, of the Widget Corporation, has been promoted to president of Widget International, a not-yet-disowned subsidiary"), the real presidents look for ways to shore up their own titles.

Stand by for a hot management insight: *Nobody calls himself only "president" anymore unless he is only president.* Whoever really runs the place is "president and chief executive officer," or "president and chairman," or, if top dog but desperately insecure, "chairman, president and chief executive officer." Only if the executive is the No. 2 (the recently renamed executive vice president) does he or she hand out cards with "president" on them. Some No. 2's, trying to hype their mere-president titles, call themselves "president and chief operating officer"; this is a suitable title for a surgeon also running a hospital, but strikes me as straining for effect when used by business executives all too conscious of what they are not yet.

A truly honest No. 2 would have on his card "president but not chief executive officer," which business lingo would quickly abbreviate to P.B.N.C.E.O. But sometimes full disclosure asks too much.

The hard fact is that the title the vice presidents are seeking is the title that the bosses are shucking off. The cost of living may have been brought under control, but title inflation is rampant.

Dear Bill:

If you had ever been a Member of the Cabinet, you would know that the President does not sit "at the head of the table in the place of authority." We who have *been* Members of the Cabinet know that the ultimate seat of authority in our system of government is located at the *middle* of the table where the President sits. This, of course, is the British style and is maintained meticulously in the Cabinet Room. However, when the President leaves the Cabinet Room for the Roosevelt Room, he sits at the head of the table in the manner you suggest, but then that is because he is emulating bureaucratic practice as against presidential prerogative.

Sometime I would like to take you around the White House and show you some of these interesting aspects of American life.

Daniel P. Moynihan
United States Senate
Washington, D.C.

Public Diplomacy

F irst came plain old *diplomacy*, from the Greek word for a letter that has been folded over so that its contents cannot be readily seen.

Then came the march of modifiers, usually casting aspersions on the noun. *Dollar diplomacy* was first, in a 1910 blast by *Harper's Weekly* at the way President William Howard Taft's Secretary of State, Philander C. Knox, was buying up politicians in Honduras. (Nobody names a baby Philander anymore, but that has not reduced adultery.) Two years later, President Taft praised the idea of "substituting dollars for bullets" in what came to be known as his "Dollar Diplomacy" speech.

Gunboat diplomacy was next coined in 1927 to describe big-power domination of China early in the century, and popularized in the 1937 "Panay incident," in which a Japanese bomber sank a United States gunboat on the Yangtze River. Ironically, in the case that made the phrase a household word for foreign-policy fans, the gunboat was on the receiving end of the force.

Not until 1973 did the word *diplomacy* find a new mate, and the matchmaker was Henry A. Kissinger, who, *Time* magazine in 1974 reported, went to the Middle East "for another round of 'shuttle diplomacy.' . . ." The presence of quotation marks around the reference suggests an earlier use, but I have not been able to find it. (The National Aeronautics and Space Administration's "space shuttle" plan was then in the news, the phrase based on Eastern Airlines' intercity back-and-forth flights.)

That made *diplomacy* a big coinage device again, like *-arama* and *-nik* in their day. *Ping-Pong diplomacy* described the initial attempts to bring about the opening to China, and *media diplomacy* was applied to satellite telecasts that brought together opposing statesmen.

Amid all the noise, Secretary Kissinger let it be known he preferred *quiet diplomacy*, a formulation that diplomats liked because it seemed to describe action and promised results from behind-the-scenes maneuvering.

In January 1976, with Ronald W. Reagan trying to snatch the Republican nomination from President Gerald R. Ford, the puissant-but-neutral party leader Bryce Harlow asked Richard Allen, the foreign-policy analyst, to write the national-security section of that year's party platform. Mr. Allen agreed, on the proviso that it not be cleared with Henry Kissinger.

"A strong and effective program of global public diplomacy is a vital component of U.S. foreign policy," read the document, and this *public diplomacy* was taken, as intended, to be an emphasis different from the *quiet diplomacy* that led to the détente that held sway during the era of Henry the K.

"It meant a strong and effective United States Information Agency," recalls Mr. Allen today, "taking the offensive in the war of ideas against the Soviet Union." The phrase was considered more acceptable than *propaganda*, a term that has a long and honorable history concerning the propagation of the Christian faith but gained a pejorative connotation under Joseph Goebbels.

Although Mr. Reagan lost the nomination fight to President Ford, who lost the election to Jimmy Carter, the phrase *public diplomacy* remained in moderate use during the Carter years. It found a sponsor in the reporting of the *Washington Post*'s Don Oberdorfer, who wrote in 1977 of "Carter's unorthodox style of public diplomacy" and how "Carter and his team are now beginning to experience the severe problems of public diplomacy— inflexible positions, international bad blood, open confrontations flowing from open declarations." (Woodrow Wilson had an equally hard time living with criticism of his "open covenants, openly arrived at.")

In the Reagan era, the term *public diplomacy* has prospered, although President Reagan likes to use the phrase *quiet diplomacy* from time to time. Gilbert A. Robinson, Mr. Reagan's first deputy director of the United States Information Agency, moved to the State Department in 1983 to become special adviser to the Secretary of State for public diplomacy, and started the Office of Public Diplomacy that is now a part of Foggy Bottom. Not surprisingly, when he left office a month ago to return to his own consulting business in Washington and New York, Mr. Robinson named one of his companies Public Diplomacy Associates.

How does he define the phrase? "Governments are learning," says my former colleague, "that while bilateral diplomacy has its place, a television special on a given policy can often have more impact on a foreign government's actions than a host of traditional diplomatic exchanges."

What's next for the tried-and-true combining form of *diplomacy*? The obvious step is *private diplomacy*, but that seems too close to *quiet diplomacy*. The phrase is waiting to be made. Watch this space.

I was intrigued by your recent column on public diplomacy. After reading it, I went back to Harold Nicolson's *Peacemaking* (1919) to test my recollection that he had employed the expression "democratic diplomacy." Indeed, he does use this expression but I can't determine whether or not he first used the expression at the time of the Versailles Peace Conference or later. In either event, it belongs somewhere in your chain of "diplomacy" terminology. Here it is: Democratic diplomacy possesses many advantages: yet it possesses one supreme disadvantage: its representatives are obliged to reduce the standards of their own thoughts to the level of other people's feelings: were it not for the time-lag which affects democratic wisdom, this necessity might prove a safeguard rather than a danger: but in circumstances requiring great rapidity and breadth of decision democratic diplomacy does in fact constitute a danger more insidious, and far less manageable, than the most unscrupulous intellectualism of the older system.

Also, I always associate the expression "gunboat diplomacy" with the appearance of the German gunboat *Panther* off the coast of Agadir during the Moroccan crisis of 1911.

Robert Bookman
Executive Vice President
Columbia Pictures
Burbank, California

"On the proviso"? As a lawyer, I always said *"with* the proviso." Incidentally, "provided that" means "but only if." Many too many lawyers use "provided that" when they mean "except" and sometimes to mean "oh, and here's another idea."

George D. Braden
Scarborough, Maine

I have read with great interest and usual enlightenment your piece on public diplomacy.

Let me simply add a footnote that this expression was in circulation somewhile before it surfaced in the 1976 GOP platform. For example it is used by Dr. Frank Stanton in our 1975 CSIS study on "International Information, Education, and Cultural Relations: Recommendations for the Future" which as you recall blueprinted the reorganization of USIA. It is used with considerable precision in our 1976 Washington Paper #40 on "Culture and Information: Two Foreign Policy Functions." Specifically it is discussed on page 56 of that report, a copy of which is enclosed. Whether this paper came out in January of 1976 or not I don't recall exactly. My only point is that the expression enjoyed substantial currency among professionals prior to January '76.

M. Jon Vondracek
Director of Communications
Center for Strategic & International Studies
Washington, D.C.

Come, come . . . the NYC shuttle has run for many years from Times Square to Grand Central . . . and probably this was so called from the *shuttlecock* of the old English game of badminton, whereby the "cock" was sent back and forth over the same route.

Jerome J. Katzman
Watertown, New York

Resume Speed

First, there was the *curriculum vitae*, from the Latin for "course of life"; this is still the preferred name in academia for a quick rundown of a life story on one page (references on request). That is frequently shortened to *vitae*, as in "Send me your vitae," from school administrators who like to receive lives. Professors like the Latin touch; that's why they speak for honoraria, not fees.

Then there came the *résumé*, the French language's contribution to American business. Some purists still give it the French pronunciation, with the pursed-lips *u*, and spell it with acute accents on both *e's*, but most now put a schwa in the middle and say *rezuhmay*. It is also jocularly pronounced *rezoom*.

Now, from Tom Reid of the *Washington Post*, this news: "I was covering a story today and ran into a fellow who gave me his résumé. Only he didn't call it a résumé, or a curriculum vitae, or just a 'vitae.' He called it a *biodata summary*. I laughed when I saw this, but the more I think about it, the more I like it. *Biodata summary*. Has a nice high-tech ring to it."

I am a low-tech man and like a *thumbnail sketch*.

Dear Bill:

You will hear a thousand academic voices telling you that the short form is *vita* (nominative) and not *vitae* (genitive needed to "course *of* life").

But it hardly matters, for I think the term is dropping out of use in favor of résumé (pronounced in ways ranging from *rezmay* to *rayzeem*).

Jacques [Barzun]
Charles Scribner's Sons, Publishers
New York, New York

As a certifiable academic, I have often heard *vita* as a synonym for *curriculum vitae*. *Vita*, as you know, means "[one's] life." I have never heard *vitae* used except as a plural noun, e.g., "The candidates' *vitae* are available for inspection by the search committee." That Latin term is surely easier for those who were not Latin students in their salad days than the fuller but equally correct *"curricula vitarum"* to describe several résumés.

Gratuitously, I'll add a plea to use "academe" rather than "academia" to refer to higher education collectively. I believe the phrase "the groves of academe" occurs in Milton, but I can't recall an exact citation. "Academia" conjures up for me a malfunction of the higher cortical functions (therefore, often not an inexact term). I think it is in the same order of pseudo-Latinism as *vitae* is in your usage.

William J. McKeough
Greenvale, New York

Professors prefer honoraria to fees not so much because of their predilection for the sesquipedalian tergiversation of Latinate constructions as for their growing sophistication (shrinking naïveté?) in the ways of the IRS. In short, honoraria generally qualify as non-taxable income; fees do not.

David Rife
Department of English
Lycoming College
Williamsport, Pennsylvania

Sack Pig's Aperiodic Non-Life-Style

Cavalrymen from Parthia, an ancient land southeast of the Caspian Sea, gained fame by shooting over their shoulders while running away; the technique became known as the *Parthian shot,* and is now often corrupted to *parting shot.* In this tradition of defiant retreat, President Reagan's recently departed National Security Adviser, Robert C. McFarlane, has left his imprint on military bureaucratese.

National Security Decision Directive 196 established the policy of using polygraphs, misnamed "lie detectors," ostensibly to protect our secrets from pilferage; in practice, it would inhibit all government officials with access to secrets from talking to reporters.

This NSDD (pronounced *nizz-did*), drafted under McFarlane's supervision and recommended to the President at a meeting at which McFarlane was chairman, reads: "The National Security Planning Group also recommends that the U.S. Government adopt, in principle, the use of *aperiodic, non-life-style, CI-type* polygraph examinations for all individuals with access to USG sensitive compartment information, communications security information, and other special access program classified information."

In the words I have italicized, the CI in *CI-type* stands for "counterintelligence," and the *-type* is a military-jargon suffix for "brand, style." ("Dogfood, dehydrated, kibble-type.") That's easy, and the acronym for National Security Planning Group will be a subject for closer study below. But *aperiodic* requires an immediate trip to Merriam-Webster's unabridged Third New International Dictionary (permissive-type): *aperiodic* means "of irregular occurrence: not periodic," and is used all the time by cryptographers who want a certain herky-jerkiness in their codes to avoid telltale rhythms and make the encryption tougher to break. (Cryptographers write the codes that cryptologists study, just as lexicographers write dictionaries using the words that lexicologists study.)

In regular, periodic testing, you could say, "It's Thursday, I have to take my Valium so I can beat the lie detector." However, in an *aperiodic* scheme, Cap the Truthful could skip the test on Thursday and hit you with his blood-pressure armband and little box the following Tuesday.

Non-life-style, to my knowledge, is an authentic neologism, and will be remembered as the McFarlane Contribution, much as *nuanced* and *caveated* will forever bear the situation-room brand of Alexander M. Haig, Jr. Its root, *life style*, was coined by the psychiatrist Alfred Adler in 1929 to denote a person's basic character, formed early in life, which governs that person's behavior later. In the revolution in sexual and living habits of the 1960s, when hippieness was next to godliness, the term was revived and changed to mean "way of life, style of living," and was derogated in a Spiro T. Agnew speech as a deadening conformity—"a life style that has neither life nor style."

According to a Reagan Administration official who demands anonymity, *non-life-style* means "nonintrusive"—that is, not intended to go into your love life, drinking habits or kinky avocations. This is intended to reassure the suspicious that the polygraph examination will be strictly businesslike: when you give an affirmative response to "Do you know Mata Hari?" the operator of the sweat-measuring paraphernalia will presumably refrain from asking how well you know her.

The predecessor to the compound adjective *non-life-style* was not *impersonal*, which means "not referring to any particular person"; rather, it was the more bureaucratic but accurate *nonpersonal*, "not dealing with matters a person considers private or intimate." If the directive were to be reduced to English, it might include a sentence like "From time to time, the Government may ask employees questions related to official duties but not dealing with their private lives." But officials who have great faith in the divining nature of machines do not talk that way.

"Cryptographers write the codes that cryptologists study . . ." Let me broadly define that cryptology is the science that embraces cryptography and cryptanalysis. Cryptography does not conceal the presence of a secret message, but renders it unintelligible to outsiders by various transformations of the plain text (encoding or enciphering). Cryptanalysis is the re-rendering of cryptographic texts (encoded or enciphered) into the original plain text by decoding or deciphering. Thus, you are right that cryptographers may write the codes/ciphers; however, it is the cryptanalyst rather than the cryptologist who does the study. In short, cryptology embraces both the cryptographer and the cryptanalyst.

Walter L. Pforzheimer
Washington, D.C.

Say *"Uncle"*—And Make My Day

"I have only one thing to say to the tax increasers," said President Reagan, delighting in a mock-tough line submitted by one of his writers. "Go ahead and make my day."

Mary McGrory, the liberal columnist, responded: "At last a slogan for the second term of Ronald Reagan. It's short, provocative . . . a shade more genteel than 'Drop dead,' which is what it really means."

Not quite. In current usage, it means "Give me the long-sought opportunity to respond devastatingly," and its route to the current meaning shows the movement of meaning at its quirkiest.

One of the many meanings of the verb *make* is "to secure the success of," which can be found in John Lyly's 1579 observation: "It is the eye of the master that fatteth the horse, and the love of the woeman, that maketh the man." Shakespeare used it: "This is the night," said Iago in *Othello*, "that either makes me or fordoes me quite." The dictum of Polonius in *Hamlet*, "The apparel oft proclaims the man," was shortened in common use to "clothes make the man"; that sense is transmuted now to "dress for success," but the big achievers still use the colloquial phrase *making it*, which is far more fun than *having it all*.

Then, in her 1909 novel *The Rosary,* Florence Barclay wrote, "I knew I wanted her; I knew her presence made my day and her absence meant chill night; and every day was radiant, for she was there." That made the day for "made my day." P. G. Wodehouse followed that up in 1935 with "That . . . will be great. That will just make my day." The Briticism crossed the Atlantic and appeared in the soft rock of Carole King's song "Brighter," published in 1971. Author William Styron told *Newsweek* in 1979 of his satisfaction in writing: "If it's only one paragraph, but it's felicitous, that makes my day."

The sunniness of this image began to be clouded in the 1970s. "Go on, dare him," said a shady character in Hugh McLeave's mystery *Question of Negligence,* in 1970: "It'll make the evening."

The sinister side of day-making approached its zenith in 1983 in *Sudden Impact,* one of the Clint Eastwood Dirty Harry movies, script by Joseph Stinson, its central character a cop who gives short shrift to the civil liberties of the accused, in Mickey Spillane's grand Mike Hammer tradition.

Interrupting a stickup in a diner, Dirty Harry Callahan aims his Smith & Wesson at a thief and challenges him with a snarled "Make my day." That is to say, he invites the robber to resist arrest or make a threatening move, thereby enabling the police officer to have an excuse to kill him, which would give the officer the warm feelings of good will, cheeriness and pervasive optimism associated with a day so "made."

Mr. Eastwood capitalized on the attention given the phrase by recording the song "Make My Day" with the country singer T. G. Sheppard, which was a moderately successful exploitation.

" 'Make my day' is much used in the New York subway system," continues Miss McGrory, "where life is raw and tempers are short and even brushing a fellow passenger's sleeve can lead to unpleasantness just short of an encounter with Bernhard Goetz."

The phrase is becoming the rallying cry of vigilantism, thanks to the Dirty Harry association and the subsequent episode in the New York subway when a passenger shot four youths he says he felt were threatening him.

By using the expression jocularly regarding his reaction to those who would reduce the deficit by increasing taxes, President Reagan has deepened the phrase's roots in American colloquial speech. You can imagine what he has done for students of slang.

Secs Appeal

"**D**o you know what *secular humanism* is?" asked Norman Lear, subtly knocking the term in a letter to what he called "a number of well-known educators, artists, and public officials like yourself." Myself, I prefer *like you*, and don't know exactly which direct-mail category applies to me, but I will try to illuminate and aggravate the controversy about the phrase.

A spokesman for Mr. Lear's People for the American Way says, "Trying to define *secular humanism* is like trying to nail Jell-O to a tree." (Good metaphor, often used; would the coiner step forward?) In making the point that the phrase has different meanings to different people, the organization sought to show that the phrase has no widely accepted meaning and thus did not belong in legislation.

Definitions do vary. *Secular humanism*, to the evangelist James Kennedy, is a "godless, atheistic, evolutionary, amoral, collectivist, socialistic, communistic religion" posing a threat to schoolchildren. To Michael J. Rosenberg, editor of *Near East Report*, "*Secular humanist* has become the new label employed to indict anyone who opposes school prayer, believes in evolution, or disagrees with the religious right's views on abortion." Roy R. Torcaso, an outspoken atheist who was plaintiff in the 1961 case in which the phrase was popularized and is still one of the few people who calls himself a secular humanist, cites the definition given by Corliss Lamont in his book *The Philosophy of Humanism*: ". . . joyous service for the greater good of all humanity in this natural world and advocating the methods of reason, science, and democracy."

I would describe most secular humanists as ethical atheists who try to do good without believing in God. But that is not "the" definition, as many humanists are agnostics, and some who accept the label are churchgoers. No pop lexicographer can lay down the law on what the phrase means; I can only report what disputants say it means, and put forward a definition that encompasses its different senses.

People in the word dodge can, however, trace the history of a term, and the etymon teaches us where the attacker or defender is coming from. (Not *comes from*, which means "place of origin"; *is coming from*, which uses the present progressive *is coming* instead of the simple present *comes* to show continuing action, is colloquial English meaning "the context or experience in which the speaker has reached his conclusion," and should prove useful enough in time to become Standard English.) (The preceding is a *parenthetical remark.*) (Both preceding parenthetical remarks constitute a *tangent.*)

In 1984, Senator Orrin G. Hatch of Utah wrote a paragraph in an education bill saying that federal money for magnet schools may not be used "for courses of instruction the substance of which is *secular humanism.*" Last year, the United States Department of Education decided not to define the term, but to leave its definition up to local schools. That raised a further ruckus. Senator Hatch's spokesman explained the intent of the original phrase in the legislation was to make sure that magnet schools improve their curriculums and not get into "soft stuff" such as personal values or courses in life styles; the controversial phrase was dropped in the current legislation. The civil liberties groups, and Mr. Lear, won this round.

The phrase was probably taken from a footnote in the decision written in 1961 by Justice Hugo L. Black in *Torcaso v. Watkins,* which in turn was taken from an amicus brief in that case written by Joseph L. Blau, professor emeritus of religion at Columbia University. The footnote's point: "Among religions in this country, however, which do not teach what would generally be considered belief in the existence of God are Buddhism, Taoism, Ethical Culture, Secular Humanism and others."

Go back further, to 1952, and an essay by C. Wright Mills: "Liberals have repeatedly articulated a secular humanism, stressing the priceless value of the individual personality. . . ." The first citation in Merriam-Webster's files is from a religious work in 1933, William G. Peck's *The Social Implications of the Oxford Movement,* in which secular humanism is opposed to Catholicism: "In face of this *secular humanism,* the return of the Oxford leaders to Catholic doctrine and practice necessarily signified a criticism of the secular standpoint, and the provision of a positive alternative." If you have an earlier citation, join the fun.

How does this etymology help us understand the furor raised by the phrase?

Secular is an adjective that means "worldly, not religious or otherworldly"; *humanism* is "a concern for the human condition." The modifier *secular* emphasizes the nonreligious character of the fuzzy noun *humanism.* I think the phrase was construed by a growing number of clergymen, especially evangelicals, to be a euphemism for *atheism.*

No doubt a goodly number of secular humanists are atheists; to them, however, the phrase subsumed atheism in a much broader philosophy of ethical values stressing individualism, acting rightly unmotivated by the fear of God or promise of heaven.

That broadening made *secular humanism* an even more inviting target to preachers than atheism, because "godlessness" had been denounced so heatedly for so long. Here was a way to slam opposition to prayer in schools, to castigate sex education in schools, to blast abortion—all potent social issues—while mixing in disapproval of the drug culture, permissiveness, pornography, short skirts and live-in lovers, and tying all these in to a rejection of belief in God. The target was Heaven-sent, or heaven-sent, as you prefer.

People who disagreed with many fervent religionists on one or more of the social issues, but who firmly believed in God, resented being lumped in with atheists and all the others. They saw *secular humanism* as a linguistic bludgeon, a chance to beat over the head all who oppose "the religious right" with a club incorporating all the issues.

That's what the fight over a phrase is about. *Secular humanism* may be defined as: 1. a philosophy of ethical behavior unrelated to a concept of God; 2. a characterization of an emphasis on individual moral choices as having the common denominator of atheism; 3. an attempt to besmear political opponents by impugning their faith in God.

It's a bare-knuckles fight, and etymology, lexicography and semantics are right in the middle of it.

Dear Bill:

Harking back to *secular humanism,* I would point out that the phrase, now full of political TNT, is a description turned into a tautology. The clue is in the writer you quoted who said *"a* secular humanism." He was qualifying *humanism,* as who should say "a religious faith." Humanism by itself is secular, since it makes man and his concerns primary—man the measure, instead of God.

Of course, there are other, equally confusing uses of *humanism* (-istic), which are related to literature and the humanities. The terminology is a quicksand for those who do not read the dreary scholarship that uses all these variants as if they were clear.

Jacques [Barzun]
Charles Scribner's Sons, Publishers
New York, New York

In historical context, humanists were not always "secular," that is, without allegiance to God. Desiderius Erasmus and John Calvin were classical humanists. Hence the term "secular humanist" distinguishes the commonest class of modern humanists.

Since the Humanist Manifestos (I and II) were published, the humanists, by their own definition, seek independence from God, primarily the biblical one. Thus a "humanist," as the term implies, believes in the Renaissance doctrine that "man is the measure" of all that is true and good.

Judeo-Christians maintain that man without God is like a ship without rudder. Such a man or society has no guideline except subjective, self-defined interest for value or truth. This, say the Judeo-Christians, is a dangerous human and social condition.

William H. McDowell
Professor, Philosophy and Religion
Florida Southern College
Orlando, Florida

Nailing Jelly

"A man's speech must exceed his grasp—else what's a metaphor?" That nice jerk-around of Robert Browning was sent in by Dr. Arthur N. Huttner of Youngstown, Ohio, occasioned by my comment on "like trying to nail Jell-O to a tree," which I called "Good metaphor, often used," and asked the coiner to step forward.

But I did not use the precise word. *Metaphor* is implied comparison— "life is a river of solecism"—while another word exists for specific comparison. "So pack up your babble in your old kit bag," writes my instructor, "and simile, simile, simile!"

My half-mistake was in using the general term, *metaphor*, rather than the specific word called for, *simile*. A *metaphor* is implicit; a *simile*—a category of metaphor—is explicit, so explicit that it bangs you over the head almost always with the words *like* or *as*, proclaiming its status like a bullfighter waving a red farewell.

Metaphor comes from the Greek *metapherein*, "to transfer," a combining of the roots *pherein*, "to carry," and *meta*, "over" or "beyond." A metaphor transfers or carries over the meaning in a comparison. Henry VIII first used the word in English in a 1533 letter: "And rather then men would note a lye when they know what is meant, they will sooner by allegory or *metaphor* draw the word to the truth."

Simile, an older English word first used in 1393 in William Langland's *Piers Plowman*, comes from the same root as "similar": the Latin *similis*, "like." The use of *like* or *as* signals the reader to the comparison, as in the poetry of Robert Burns: "O, my Luve is like a red, red rose."

Notice the difference: it's definitely a *simile*, an explicit comparison, when a gardener says, "My love *is like* a rose." It may or may not be a *metaphor*, however, when the gardener says, "My love *is* a rose."

Most metaphor correction has to do with mixed metaphors: when singing the praises of similes, you have to make sure you don't get off on the wrong foot. However, an unexplored avenue of research in this trope-a-dope is the outdatedness of certain figures of speech. When Edward Bleier of New York complained recently of being *stuck on the flypaper*, who under fifty knew what he was talking about?

More to the point of the tree or wall dribbling a gelatinous substance, who was the coiner of that simile about nailing Jell-O?

Some Irregulars pointed to the 1981 book *Nailing Jelly to a Tree*, by Jerry Willis and William Danley, Jr., about the nebulous world of computer software. Another found it in a 1976 Federal court opinion by a judge having difficulty defining "public figure" in a libel action.

The earliest use—at least until an earlier one is found—was submitted by Prof. Joe E. Decker of the University of Tampa: "You could no more make an agreement with them," wrote Theodore Roosevelt in 1915, describing his troubles with the Colombian government leaders during negotiations for rights in the Panama Canal Zone, "than you could nail currant jelly to a wall—and the failure to nail currant jelly to a wall is not due to the nail; it is due to the currant jelly."

That, of course, is metaphor, by a master of metaphor in the political language, Teddy Roosevelt, coiner of "lunatic fringe." After a historian noted his expression, the former President, pleased as all of us are when anybody notices a nice figure of speech, wrote, "You are welcome to use my simile of the currant jelly."

He was in error on that last. As Ted Dow of Arlington, Virginia, points out, the original line about currant jelly has no *like* or *as*; it is metaphor, and Teddy was mistaken to call it a simile. I identify with the old trustbuster on this late hit; but, as he would say in defiance, it is not the critic who counts. . . .

Surely you should know that the quote "A man's speech must exceed his grasp—else what's a metaphor?" is not only a nice jerk-around of Robert Browning but also of Amy Lowell and her poem "Patterns." ("Christ! What are patterns for?")

If you can't flag your sources correctly, what's a semaphore?

Richard Hall
Oakland, California

Please back up and stand by T.R. Though the most unusual explicit verbal signs of a simile are not present, the explicit verbal is present in "no more . . . *than.*" There are also other verbal signs and arrangements that can make a comparison explicit. Consider the Shakespeare sonnet, "Shall I compare thee to a summer's day?/Thou art more lovely . . . etc."

Simile is an explicit comparison in which the logical form is "X *is like* Y." A *further* condition of simile is that there be adequate *difference* between the elements of the comparison. "John is like Richard" is a comparison but not a simile, not a *figure* of speech. In metaphor, the logical form is "X *is* Y," a form which is actually a violation of logic. Furthermore, the predicate may be unexpressed (see Robert Frost's "downy flake" in "Stopping by Woods . . .").

Arthur W. Hoffman
Department of English
Syracuse University
Syracuse, New York

The Self-Clasping Squeeze

D an Rather noticed it, and scooped the world by instantly reporting the gesture.

President Reagan, at the conclusion of a United Nations address, was acknowledging the applause rolling out from every delegation except those of the Soviet bloc. He nodded thanks, as almost every speaker does; then he moved his shoulders slightly in a hint of a bow, which is a graceful way of bowing without formally bowing. Finally, he clasped his hands in front of his chest and squeezed them, accompanying that characteristic hand signal with a tight half-smile.

"Nice gesture for the President, responding to the applause," said the television reporter immediately; Rather, master of the sleeveless cardigan, knew a good picture when he saw one. Sure enough, the newspaper and newsmagazine pictures accompanying the text of the address showed Mr. Reagan, hands clasped, with the tight-lipped expression.

That was not a new gesture by the President. Richard V. Allen, an early Reaganaut, recalls Reagan's using the self-clasping squeeze in the campaign of 1980, "at slightly more formal moments, when the aw-shucks handwave would not be appropriate." Its use in a world forum has now made it a Reagan trademark. He has sent an unmistakable signal to semiologists the world over: we can expect the chest-level, self-clasping squeeze to be copied, because it fills a vacuum that orators call The Acknowledgment Problem.

The Problem: The audience is going wild; waves of applause roll toward you; feet are stomping and the cottoning is high. You have left the microphone; you have nothing more to say; how do you let the audience know you hear them, you are grateful to them, you even love them?

William Jennings Bryan, it is said, held his arms straight out at his sides and extended all fingers, as if to gather in the multitude.

Winston S. Churchill, with "V for Victory" the slogan of the day, made a memorable picture every time by holding up his index and middle fingers in the V sign.

Dwight D. Eisenhower carried the V sign further, sticking his arms up in the air at that angle, seeming to make his whole body cry out "victory" in motorcades and at political conventions.

Richard M. Nixon copied the Eisenhower arms-in-the-air gesture, adding the Churchill V symbol with each hand, sometimes wiggling them for emphasis. (This has been parodied. After it was announced that Mr. Nixon would arbitrate a dispute between baseball-team owners and umpires, the cartoonist Jeff MacNelly showed Nixon behind the plate in his familiar double-V pose, with the ump saying, "He loves it when the count goes to 2 and 2.")

When the Soviet leader Nikita S. Khrushchev came to the United States, he surprised some American audiences by responding to applause in the traditional Russian way—by clapping back. That response no longer surprises; the speaker's applauding the audience that is applauding the speaker makes sense, because each is thanking the other.

In a pictorial era, the identifying gesture gains importance. Whenever you see a couple of politicians posing, look for the one who is gesticulating; that man is running that year, his listener is not. If a political or religious leader can invent or adopt a hand gesture that sets him apart, he need pose with nobody; his hand will provide the caption.

Mohandas K. Gandhi used the traditional Hindu salute, with palms and fingers pressed together as if in prayer. This has also been the gesture favored by popes; in addition, Christian leaders have available the widely recognized sign of the cross, and rabbis and others often use the hands-up, palms-down gesture of benediction.

The raised fist is the near-universal gesture of defiance; black-power advocates popularized it again in the 1960s, and its use by some United States athletes at the Mexico City Olympics in 1968 infuriated many and pleased a few.

Some evangelists use a raised index finger to both acknowledge a response and make a point: the message of the single finger often is "One Way," the path to Jesus.

Nelson A. Rockefeller understood the message of a hand signal that had been previously considered obscene, and raised a middle finger at hecklers; the wide publication of the picture lessened the impact of the gesture by others. (If it appears in a family newspaper and is used by a national figure, how obscene can it be?)

John F. Kennedy perfected the three-fingered wedge-shaped jab, which was picked up by Gary Hart in his 1984 campaign.

Even as we analyze, candidates are working on hand signals that will make them distinctive, that photographers will be looking for at the conclusion of speeches. One is working up a three-finger wedge-shape double-V prayer sign, but that unifying gesture requires seven fingers and needs editing.

Rest assured, Ronald Reagan's chest-high self-clasping squeeze will be used again and again and again, as Franklin Delano Roosevelt, waving his cigarette holder, used to say. The Reagan gesture seems taken from boxing, after the winning boxer's arm has been lifted by the referee; then the winner raises both hands above his head and clasps his hands. The current President's contribution is in lowering the clasp to chest-level, thus modifying it to seem more appreciative than triumphant.

Thank you and God bless you. Thank you. (One-hand above-the-head wave.) Thank you very much. (Two-hand deprecatory wave.) You're too kind. (V sign.) I don't deserve it, really. (Palms together with head-bob.) Thanks again, you're really a terrific mob, I love ya. (Self-clasp, chest-high with tight smile.)

The implications of Winston Churchill's "V for Victory" sign go even deeper into history.

The Welsh archers who in 1414 were responsible for the English victory at the Battle of Agincourt used the first two fingers of the right hand to draw the string of their longbows. Charles d'Albret, Constable of France, had threatened to cut the archers' fingers off after this battle, which he was so confident France would win. Instead, d'Albret was to suffer the defiant gesture of the Welsh archers as they cheered and raised their intact two fingers when he led away from the battlefield his defeated troops.

Churchill, who lived and breathed history, adopted this sign to proclaim Britain's defiance of the Germans in the face of what then seemed unsurmountable odds—no doubt bearing in mind that the French outnumbered the English by five to one at Agincourt. The meaning of this sign could not have escaped most Britons, for whom school has made Agincourt and its lore as vivid as if it had happened yesterday, not five centuries ago.

The "V for Victory" translation this sign underwent was useful in furthering its initial purpose. The "V" appeared on walls in Axis-occupied territory around the world, and translated into Morse code it echoed the opening notes of Beethoven's Fifth, thus putting the German composer to work for the Allies wherever his work was performed. But these and other mutations should not make us forget the highly civilized origins of this sign, which was much more than "the slogan of the day."

Claudio Campuzano
New York, New York

Churchill's "V for Victory" gesture with his index and middle fingers was made with the palm-side of the hand facing his audience. The same sign made with the back of the hand toward the crowd means in Great Britain much the same as Nelson Rockefeller's famous "doigt du seigneur"!

Richard Restrepo
Philadelphia, Pennsylvania

Since you love precision, I decided to try my hand at enlightening you on your reference to the Christian message of a certain gesture. "Some evangelists use a raised index finger to both acknowledge a response and make a point: the message of the single finger often is One Way, the path to Jesus." The final two words in this statement indicate a possible misunderstanding of the theology in question.

Jesus comes to a person. One may ask Him to come to oneself, or ask to be graced with a closer walk with Jesus (as in the song, "Just a Closer Walk With Thee"). Then again, Jesus is quoted as saying "Come unto me, all you who labor and are heavy laden. . . ." Yes, it would be correct to say one ought to come to Jesus, but there must be at least as many ways to come (paths) to Jesus as there are individuals created by the Father, through Jesus.

My point is that the "One Way" message is to indicate that Jesus *is* The One Way, that is, to the Father (God), to heaven (the Father's house, mansion), to eternal life. "I am the Way, the Truth, and the Life," says Jesus. To live as Jesus lived, to walk closely with Him, to draw nearer to Him and receive His Holy Spirit—these are all part of His message and the path to eternal life. He is the One Way. But the path *to* Jesus is many-faceted. Hence the technical incorrectness of " 'One Way,' the path *to* Jesus."

Therefore, a simple change in your phrasing, from "path to Jesus" to "path *of* Jesus" would make your sentence theologically correct.

Margaret A. Kelly
Bloomington, Indiana

You left out a poignant example and one very meaningful in light of the feature article on U.S.–Russian viewpoints. Namely, Dave Garroway's closing on the "Good Morning" show on NBC in the fifties, the palm facing the viewer and Garroway whispering, "Peace."

Bruce R. Blaustein
New York, New York

Shape Up or Ship Out

The picture in the ad was of a well-built young woman wearing what looked to me like a white bathing suit with lace around the top and bottom. The headline identified her garment as a *shapesuit.* What was the model wearing?

It used to be called a *girdle.* This word was born with the earliest nouns in the language, appearing about the year 1000, with the meaning of "a belt worn around the waist to secure or confine garments." Shakespeare's Puck said, "I'll put a girdle round about the earth in forty minutes," using the word to mean a kind of sash; in modern times, the "confining" meaning came to the fore and the "circling" meaning atrophied.

As the holding-in function grew, euphemists took a deep breath and laced in the language tightly: the use of the word *girdle* was squeezed out. In the *shapesuit* ad that caught my eye, the advertiser was the Olga Company of Van Nuys, California, and the garment was identified as a *shapesuit* and further as a *Secret Hug:* "It gently stretches to fit you beautifully. The lightest bit of underwire." This seemed to hint that the product might perform the restraining function of a girdle, but the noun itself was carefully avoided.

Because the slogan of the company is a proud "Behind every Olga there really is an Olga" and features a small picture of the woman who is presumably the company's founder, I called to see (a) if there really is an Olga, and (b) if there is any hope for a return to the original word.

Olga Erteszek is listed as the company's vice president of design, but she was described as "traveling and unreachable" for a week or so. Thus, I cannot confirm that there really is an Olga.* However, there really is a Gerald Cohen, vice president of advertising, who said indignantly, "Our *shapesuit* is not a *girdle*. The *girdle* historically begins at the waist; it may have a skirt bottom or, if it has legs, it's known as a *panty girdle.*"

Why the resistance to the name *girdle*, other than in the constricted, modified form as *panty girdle?* "It would imply a garment that is restrictive," explained the real adman. "We use lightweight fabrications that function as a girdle but are more comfortable and allow more freedom." One company, Playtex, goes so far as to attack the word directly in the name of its garment: "The I-Can't-Believe-It's-a-Girdle Girdle." (Montgomery Ward has advertised a ripoff called "You'd-Never-Know-It's-a-Girdle Girdle.")

Another word rarely found in advertising copy is *corset*, a form of girdle that incorporates a bodice. *Corset* comes from the Old French *cors*, "body," and originally applied to the short jackets worn in medieval times and called in England *jerkins*. These were supported by whalebone, until elastic came along, and have been called *foundations, all-in-ones* and *smoothers*; in the 1920s, undergarments that combined the function of *camisole* and *knickers* were called *camibockers*, but that has vanished, along with the irreverent *Old Ironsides*.

The "Be Slim" girdle is known as a *Bodyshaper*; evidently *shape*, as noun and verb, is in fashion. At International Playtex, the preferred words are *shapers* and *undershapers*; their girdles that run from the waist to midcalf are called *pantliners*, and their corsets go by the name of *body-briefers*.

Keep your eye on *briefs*; taken from the men's department, they are replacing the word *panty* and have recently taken on a restraining function: *body-briefers* are corsets, and *tummy-control briefs* are girdles. *Briefs* have replaced the word *drawers*, a noun formed from the verb *to draw on*, akin to the Old Norse for the word *drag*. (To be *in drag* was a term first used by male actors wearing women's petticoats on stage in the 1850s; the slang term may have come from the Norse etymology, but more likely from the unfamiliar drag of women's underclothing felt by the actors. This column follows a story wherever it leads.)

Let's be frank: we have been forthrightly using the language of *underwear*. When that word became too embarrassing for the easily shocked to

* Olga Erteszek died at seventy-three in 1989.

bear, it became *undergarment*, then *unmentionable*, with the less confining items called *scanties* (a meld of *scant* and *panty*). Before department stores became impersonal, elevator operators would shyly announce *"Intimate apparel"* when the car stopped at that floor; no man dared to get out.

However, *wear* as a combining form is now all the rage. *Bathing suit* changed to *swimsuit* and is now categorized as a minor item in the vast field of *swimwear* (also encompassing caps, goggles, waterproof watches, foot webbing and oxygen tanks). Eyeglasses are making spectacles of themselves by becoming known as *eyewear*. Nylon shells and woolly mackinaws are *outerwear*. In that inexorable linguistic fashion, the clothes that shape and mold the figure can be called *Shapewear*, and Mr. Cohen points out there really is an Olga trademark on the word.

The word *brassiere*, first used in English in 1911, has been replaced by its clipped version, *bra*, coined in 1936; in France, the item has long been called a *soutien-gorge*, meaning "something to hold up the throat."

The one adjective that you never read in girdle advertising is *tight*; it is as taboo as the word *hard* in mattress advertising. With the mattress crowd, the permissible hard word is *firm*; in the girdle world, the acceptable restraining adjective is *trim*.

What you and other landlubbers call whalebone is baleen—a horny substance akin to keratin, of which fingernails, claws and horns are composed. Baleen extends in long thin plates from the roof of the whale's mouth to its lower jaw, forming a sieve which traps plankton and other food. Whales that have baleen instead of teeth are called— appropriately enough—baleen whales, and include in their number the fin whale (*Balaenoptera*), the blue whale (*Balaenoptera musculus*) and the right whale (*Eubalaena glacialis*).

Frank Salvidio
English Department
Westfield State College
Westfield, Massachusetts

Your current column suggests a linguistic or "feel" origin for "drag" as describing a female impersonator. While I can cite no source, it was my understanding that the term was an acronym from DRessed As a Girl.

Bearing in mind that the nature of an appearance is derived from what the audience calls it, the "unfamiliar drag of the clothes"—

which could only be felt by the performer and not noticed by the audience—would seem an unlikely candidate.

Jan R. Harrington
New York, New York

You refer to the Montgomery Ward version of Playtex's I-Can't-Believe-It's-a-Girdle as a "ripoff." I believe you are referring to a "knockoff." A ripoff is generally an overcharge or a theft, while a knockoff is an unauthorized, slightly changed copy.

While it is true that knockoffs are ripoffs in the sense that they are thefts, the use of knockoff would be more precise in the instance you refer to.

Herman R. Silbiger
Tinton Falls, New Jersey

As a scuba diver, I have to fault you on your reference to "oxygen tanks" in the list of swimwear. That usage is a common error; actually, scuba tanks contain compressed air, not oxygen. But I have no idea what you meant by "foot webbing"—not swim fins, surely? Also, scuba "goggles" are properly termed "masks."

(Mrs.) Pat Withner
Bellingham, Washington

In French, *gorge* has several meanings: "breasts," "throat," and "bosom" are the most usual. *Soutien-gorge* means the maintenance or holding up of the breasts—not, as you put it, "to hold up the throat."

In any case, one *soutien-gorge* usually does double duty.

J. Vuillequez
New York, New York

I don't consider the "bra" definition a complete bust, but I do believe you missed the boat by not mentioning the very literal, very descriptive German word for that garment—*Bustenhalter!!* 'Nuff said?

George Lawrence
Sag Harbor, New York

Shut Up and Deal

"**D**o you have a word in your language called *sandbag?*" asked Secretary of State George P. Shultz in the middle of lunch with Turkish officials in Istanbul. "I have been brought here in order to have a nice luncheon and get hit behind the ear."

The Secretary was protesting the way his hosts in Turkey had surprised him with their complaints about United States quotas on the import of Turkish textiles. The free-traders at the editorial page of *The Wall Street Journal* promptly leaped into the fray.

"*Sandbag* is an unusual word," began *The Journal.* "It is one of the few Americanisms whose definition in the classic second edition of Webster's dictionary is incorrect." Presumably, the editorialist refers to Merriam-Webster's unabridged New International Dictionary; its Third Edition, selling briskly since 1961, was criticized as permissive. Some linguistic ramparts-defenders stick grimly to their beat-up Second Editions.

"The word, Webster's says, means to hit someone with a sandbag or, colloquially, to coerce with crude force.

"These definitions," states the writer (I suspect it is Robert L. Bartley, who prides himself on his poker face), "are either archaic or revisionist. The word means to entice someone into putting money into a poker pot— either by not betting yourself or by betting only a small amount—and then raising back with a large bet later."

I'll ante up on that. A few years ago, I defined the verb *sandbag* in this space as "to hit from behind," and cited the definition in the Farmer and Henley 1904 slang dictionary as rooted in the noun for "a long sausage-like bag of sand dealing a heavy blow that leaves no mark."

The Wall Street Journal editors, who probably sit around playing seven-card stud with one-eyed jacks wild, instead of playing serious poker, consider that definition archaic. To be sure (and I am not sure anybody uses *to be sure* anymore in an of-course world), the word is in fashion around the poker table, where the buck stops. "*To sandbag* in poker is to check and raise," wrote Elizabeth A. Zitrin of San Francisco when I dealt this hand last time around, "to check (pass) at the beginning of a betting round and then, after another player has opened the round by betting, to raise that bet rather than just seeing (meeting or equaling) it. To be *sandbagged* at the poker table is, as in the rest of life, to be hit from behind."

OK, everybody in? Now I'm pushing in my whole pile of chips.

To a New Zealander, *sandbag duff* is army pudding made from ground biscuit. To a United States Navy man, *sandbag*, like *Mae West*, has often been used as the name for a life preserver. To a crook, a *sandbagger* is a blackmailer, and to a golfer, it is a mug-hunter with an inflated handicap. To a hot rodder, it is a driver with a very heavy foot. Had enough? Folding already? Here is a final shot to the nape of the neck from a chess fan, David Stoughton of Venice, California: "*To sandbag* is intentionally to lose some games in a tournament in order that one's 'rating' will drop sufficiently to enable one to play in a lower section in a subsequent tournament. The idea is to encounter weaker players, win more games and take a money prize."

As I stuff the contents of the pot in my pockets (what does *The Wall Street Journal* know from slang?), I should answer the rhetorical question posed in Istanbul by Secretary Shultz. The equivalent term in Turkish is *gafil avlamak*, which means figuratively to hit someone by surprise. There's a *sandbag* shoring up duplicity in every language.

All right, I'll stick around for one more hand, but then I gotta go home.

I have been looking for some time for a source to cite regarding the use of the term "sandbag." The word needs a good, general definition; your column yesterday didn't provide one. Let me try:

> To sandbag is to conceal one's resources and abilities, or true interests, in hope of gaining an advantage at a later time.

The unabridged Webster's Third New International Dictionary contains the definition, "to trap (another poker player) by checking a strong hand and then raising if he bets." That's a good example of what a sandbagger does, but the word has evolved into much broader usage.

There are sandbaggers in auto racing, in golf, in bridge, and, apparently, in Turkey. (Personally, I like to sandbag in hands of 500 rummy). An added definition of the word is needed to capture its expanded meaning. I submit the one above for lexicographers of yet-to-be-published dictionaries.

> *Louis J. Ganim*
> *Clifton Park, New York*

Bill:

When I was at Dartmouth in the early 1960s, back before sex and demonstrations, one of the main events of the spring party weekend was a highly competitive singing tournament called "Hums." Fraternities and dormitories formed glee clubs, and the whole thing was taken remarkably seriously.

Apparently, the judges rewarded quantity as well as quality. My fraternity's glee club had four-part harmony: tenor, baritone, bass and sandbag. Sandbags like me who could not carry a tune were interspersed among the other three parts, and we mouthed the words while the rest of the guys sang.

If you'd like, I can give you my sandbag rendition someday of "Watchin' All the Girls Go By."

David [Rosenbaum]
The New York Times
Washington, D.C.

The first term that popped into my mind when reading about Mr. Shultz getting ". . . hit behind the ear" was that of being sapped—hit from behind with a leather pouch filled, not with sand, but with lead shot, New Jersey style. The only thing an upstanding, self-respecting Jersey hoodnik uses sand for is to make cement, not carry around with him in his back pocket!

From the description of what happened to Mr. Shultz at the luncheon, I believe "bushwhacked" would be more precise. Or, as my old Olympic Rifle teammate John R. "Pinky" Edwin from El Paso, Texas, would say: "Dry-gulched is what Mr. Shultz was." Suckered into a cul-de-sac and then pounced upon.

John R. Shelter
Caldwell, New Jersey

In the theater, "to sandbag" is to hang around (literally) performing some marginally useful and invariably invented activity—something which could be just as effectively accomplished with the placement of a 50- or 100-pound sandbag, such as hanging onto a piece of scenery. In this sense, the word takes on the meaning of one serving as "dead weight," or more generally, to procrastinate; while appearing to be doing something vital and useful, one is, in fact, scheming to avoid any sort of strenuous activity whatsoever.

Elizabeth Rothwell
Brooklyn, New York

Sand bag as a noun (more properly a sandbag) is a canvas bag used to hold sand and is attached to a line set or a pipe to assist in raising and lowering scenery in a hemp house (a pre-counterweight fly system in theaters).

To sandbag (a verb) means to drop said device onto an unsuspecting person. Hence most of the other definitions.

Theater terms are a treasure trove of derived and original word usages. I am surprised that terms such as dutchman, dead hung and apron haven't appeared in your fascinating column.

> W. Stuart Russell
> Nyack, New York

"Here is a final shot to the nape of the neck from a chess fan . . ."

What other kind of nape is there besides the cervical variety? (Or could it be that you are a naughty boy who plants something to lure people like me into shouting "Redundancy!" so that you can later pounce on us? If so, please pounce.)

> Gaines Kincaid
> Fort Stockton, Texas

Sleepmanship

The ad in the Amtrak office window downstairs reads: "Sleep in and still get there first. . . . Takes you downtown to downtown while you get a good night's sleep."

I've been wondering about the phrase *to sleep in* ever since my grown offspring began to use my house as a place to crash. It bothers Miriam Silverberg of Jamaica, Queens, too: "High-powered executive couples take turns on weekends caring for the children and letting the other *sleep in*," she writes, wide-awake. "Obviously, they mean *sleep late*, but why don't they say so? Or do they mean sleeping in a bed as a special treat, as opposed to the floor? Is this new?"

Since 1918, *sleep in* has been in American, and especially Canadian, use. Originally it meant to *oversleep*—that is, to sleep later than intended—but by 1931 had come to mean to sleep late intentionally, which many of us do on weekends, and some of us who shall be nameless do during the week.

Where did the *in* come from? Probably from *to stay in*, to stay at home sleeping. "The usage is still mainly dialectical," reports Sol Steinmetz of Barnhart Books, "but it is spreading southward." He cites this quotation from the *Tuscaloosa* (Alabama) *News* in 1972: "Now I get to stay up late and watch the late movies and sleep in. It's great!"

Keep an eye on intent: *to oversleep* is unintentional, *to sleep late* can be either planned or not, but is most often planned, and is used by an older generation (which really needs the sleep, believe me); and *to sleep in* is to lollygag in bed with laziness aforethought.

A quick check of the Oxford English Dictionary—always the first stop in these matters—shows a citation from R. H. Dana's *Two Years Before the Mast*, dated 1840: "The steward and the cook are allowed to sleep in at night"; and another from a less well known writer, one G. McDonald, dated 1888: "I had to be up early, and I feared I would sleep-in." This latter is I presume British.

My own best citation, which I do not find in any dictionary, is from Chaucer's *Troilus and Criseyde*, which of course carries us back very far indeed, to the fourteenth century. The wily Pandarus, taking advantage of the rainstorm to persuade Criseyde to stay overnight in his house, declares: "Lord, this is an huge rayn! This were a weder for to slepen inne. . . ." For the rest of this very amusing story, you must go to Chaucer. But it does provide us with a first-rate example of the same verb-formation, "to sleep in."

Of course, such a formation is very much in the grain of the English language. In all the Germanic group of languages (of which English is one), the verbs have a remarkable tendency to attract adverbial (or prepositional, if you will) particles to themselves. We can "sleep on," "sleep off," "sleep in," "sleep out," and so on, in a rich variety of modulations. Most of our verbs are capable of this function, and the word order is not fixed: "Will you bring in the dog?" and "Will you bring the dog in?" are equally normal usage in English. We might even say that the root verb in this case is something like "to in-bring." And that is exactly the way such verbs are formed in modern German: *abhängen* is the basic verb meaning "to depend upon." But in actual usage, the *ab* is usually separated from the *hängen*, and is most often found at the end of the sentence. Dozens of German verbs function in exactly this way (to the bewilderment of persons trying to learn that language).

All of this is by way of suggesting, then, that the formation "to sleep in" is quite characteristic of English. The only further question to be asked is this: Is there a change in meaning, depending on whether the stress (as linguists use the term) falls on the verb itself, or on the preposition/adverb? In other words, is there a distinction to be made between "sleep *in*" and "*sleep* in"? I suspect not. But in any case, the

Chaucer selection is clearly stressed on the "in"—as scansion of that line will show, according to the usual pattern of iambic pentameter.

So . . . yes, the history of the phrase "to sleep in" goes back many centuries. And this fact merely reminds us of the truism that there really are very few genuine innovations in language usage. Certain forms may become dominant, and other forms may be submerged—for generations, or even for centuries. But they remain. And then, through complex workings of social change, they may reappear. This is precisely the marvelous way in which languages are capable of constantly renewing themselves.

> *Stephen C. Bandy*
> *Associate Professor of English*
> *Pace University*
> *New York, New York*

I think Mr. Steinmetz means "dialectal," not "dialectical."

> *Robert W. Wheeler*
> *Glendale, Arizona*

Spirit Willing But . . .

No sooner had Soviet Ambassador Dobrynin expressed mock puzzlement over our mysterious "umbrella proposals" than a White House spokesman piped up with this statement: "The entire idea has not been fleshed out to the Soviets. We would like the opportunity to flesh it out."

When a figure of speech gets two mentions in a single statement, its composers are not playing trope-a-dope—they want that integumentation metaphor to be used.

The origin is in the idea of embodiment—specifically, clothing a skeleton in flesh. The first use of *flesh out* spotted by the Oxford English Dictionary cite-seers was in an 1886 novel: "A dainty bit of . . . word-painting, fleshed out and rendered thinkable." However, the O.E.D. has a use without the *out* that shows that the meaning goes back at least to 1661 and may have been popularized in this sense by sculptors: a verbal illustration in Merriam-Webster's Third New Unabridged is, "The modeler builds up his figure by fleshing a wire frame with clay."

A snag in the fleshing-out, however, came with objections from Moscow about the translation of a word in a cultural agreement. The dispute is about defectors: the Russians want us to guarantee "security"—which, to Soviet authorities, means that ballet dancers who are sent over here to dance do not dance off. We won't give any such guarantee that would undermine the right of political asylum. The only thing we will guarantee is their safety.

The Russian word for *safety* is *bezopasnost*, which, as Bernard Gwertzman of *The New York Times* pointed out, is the same as the Russian word for *security*. We will go along with *bezopasnost* as long as the English translation says *safety*; the Russians, who take the position that all defectors are seduced or kidnapped, shake their heads and execute a *grand jeté*. Presumably, the solution to this will come under the fleshed-out umbrella.

You discussed the phrase "fleshed out" and stated that the Oxford English Dictionary "has a use without the *out* that shows that the meaning goes back at least to 1661." I thought you might be interested to learn that Shakespeare used "flesh" as a verb at least seventy years earlier, in *Henry V* (first produced in 1599), Act II, Scene iv, line 54, where the French King says of Henry V:

The kindred of him hath been fleshed upon us;

The Folger Library General Reader's Shakespeare edition of *Henry V* explains "hath been fleshed upon us" as follows: "have already tasted our flesh (so that King Henry will have inherited a taste for it). The metaphor is from hunting; hounds, as well as hawks, were trained to hunt by being given a taste of the flesh of the quarry."

Frankly, I'm not sure I can see a logical progression from Shakespeare's use of "fleshed" to the modern use of "flesh out." I also can't fault the OED or anyone else for not citing the use of "fleshed" in *Henry V*; I wouldn't know of it myself if I hadn't once played the French King.

Jonathan P. Marget
Washington, D.C.

Stop, Klepto!

Former President Ferdinand E. Marcos of the Philippines has been called a great many names recently, but none more esoteric than *kleptogarch*. This was the coinage of Representative Robert K. Dornan, Republican of California, who defined his term as "a new name for thievery." It sounds like a blend of *kleptomaniac*, one with an abnormal impulse to steal, and *oligarch*, one of the rulers of a state ruled by the few. The key root is *kleptes*, Greek for "thief."

Representative Dornan stole that idea from Tom J. Farer, president of the University of New Mexico, who testified before the Kissinger Commission on Central America that the Somoza family's rule in Nicaragua was a *kleptocracy*.

My favorite derogation of a government is another word long in the language, but one that has fallen into disuse: *kakistocracy*. It means "government by the worst people." I expect it will be lifted soon by some kleptogarch.

The *g* in *oligarch* is part of Greek *oligos* "few," and the second element is from Greek *archein* "to rule." Thus, we should say *kleptarch*, not *kleptogarch*, just as we say *monarch*, not *mongarch*, and *patriarch*, not *patrigarch!!*

Louis Jay Herman
New York, New York

The word kleptocracy appears in an essay "Thieves, Ancient and Modern" by Leigh Hunt, in a discussion of the heroes of some of the Spanish picaresque novels of the seventeenth century. The essay originally appeared in his newspaper, *The Indicator*, which was published from 1819 to 1821.

Roger F. Gans
Rochester, New York

When a kakistocracy is run by a uniformed junta, does it become a khakistocracy?

David B. Sachar, M.D.
New York, New York

Summitspeak

"D efinitions are critical," an unidentified spokesman told a diplomatic reporter last week. "If we can come to some broad agreement on terms and if the Soviets are convinced that Reagan is both serious and flexible, then it might be possible for the negotiators at Geneva to work out a specific agreement after the summit." "That," concluded this skilled practitioner of summitspeak, "would be a real breakthrough."

Ever since Winston Churchill called for "a parley at the summit" in 1950, face-to-face diplomacy at the highest level has been called *summitry.* He warned that such dealing "should not be overhung by a ponderous or rigid agenda or led into mazes of technical details," and took a potshot at the conference preparers (later called *sherpas,* after those Himalayan tribesmen who help mountain climbers reach their summits), giving the back of the Churchillian hand to "hordes of experts and officials drawn up in a vast cumbrous array."

For an explanation of the terms and phrases to be brought into play at the Reagan-Gorbachev summit, I have turned to a spokesman almost legendary in his ability to leave no footprints, V. Cumbrous Array.

"You are correct," confirms Mr. Array, "in referring to this as the *Reagan-Gorbachev summit.* It is not, repeat not, the *Geneva summit,* as some press agents for the Swiss Chamber of Commerce would have you believe. The Swiss get 'the Geneva arms talks,' and that's all. I should add that my Soviet counterpart refers to this meeting as the *Gorbachev-Reagan summit.* We have agreed to disagree on the billing, but agree on the hyphenation."

Is that a *breakthrough?*

"No. It is evidence of *progress,* showing a certain mutual *flexibility,* part of the *ongoing process.* Hard bargaining lies ahead."

Is such billing a good idea?

"We do not use the word *idea* at summits, except in the denunciation, *no new ideas.* What you call an idea, privately presented, is a *walk in the woods,* and when bruited about, it is labeled a *proposal,* which when written down becomes a *formal proposal,* requiring a *counterproposal.* Two formal proposals are an *initiative.* The only adjective permitted *initiative* is *bold."*

V. Cumbrous expects a run on terms about the steps necessary to create a space defense. Four stages exist between the time an idea forms in the mind of a President and a space shield makes its appearance, blinking and peeping, in the sky.

First comes *research*—in Russian, *issledovaniye;* no problem there, as Mr. Gorbachev already indicated to *Time*'s editors in the presummit skirmishing; besides, research is not verifiable by *national technical means* (spy satellites, seismographs), so nobody will try to stop that.

Then comes *testing,* or *ispytaniye;* Mr. Reagan considers that to be part of research, but Mr. Gorbachev says that is a no-no, or *nyet-nyet.* (This latest jocularism, not yet adopted by Russians, should not be confused with the American business expression *net-net,* meaning "ultimate bottom line," which we can expect to hear in conversation between a network anchorman and his chief diplomatic correspondent: "Net-net, Marvin, is it a *breakthrough* or merely a *repackaging* of old proposals?" "Net-net, Tom, I'd have to call it *old wine in new bottles."*)

Somewhere in the late stages of *research,* probably during *testing,* comes *development*—in Russian, *razrabotka*—a wide term, which will be the battleground of limitation. If agreement is reached on a definition of the word *development,* there will be new hope for mankind, or as Mr. Reagan evenhands it, humankind.

Finally comes *deployment*—meaning "to spread out on a wider front," from the French for "unfold, display," in Russian, *razvyortyvaniye*—which Mr. Reagan has already agreed to negotiate before undertaking. Therefore, a scrap is not expected on both ends of the spectrum—*research* and *deployment*—but much hassling may be anticipated on the words *testing* and *development.*

Some confusion may be anticipated on the verb *to table.* Senator Sam Nunn said on the "The MacNeil/Lehrer Newshour" that "the good news from the Soviets is that at last they are tabling something." Sylvia Williams of Middletown, Connecticut, writes: "It took a few contextual nudges, but I finally got the good news: the Soviets are bringing specific proposals to put on the bargaining table at Geneva. Well. When did this switch take place? . . . My dictionary says *to table* means 'to postpone consideration of, to shelve.' OK, yes, it also says 'to put or place on the table,' but doesn't usage count?"

V. Cumbrous Array, with his usual disdain, replies that *to table* may mean "to shelve" in Congress, but in summitspeak it means "to place on the table" for consideration, usually neatly bound and with translations.

What are our characterizations of their proposals? *One-sided* is a favorite, usually accompanied by *taking unfair advantage*, part of the *charm offensive* unless they are part of the general *stonewalling*; but a new State Department term—*contains seeds to be nurtured*—is an optimist's view that uses a vogue verb of motherhood (State prefers *seeds*; the National Security Council likes *nuggets*; Defense calls both *propaganda*). *Seeds* and *nuggets* are considered vivid improvements over *contains positive elements*, and must always be followed by the caveat *hard bargaining lies ahead*.

Soviet characterizations of American proposals are led by the often-repeated *propaganda*, often modified as *patently absurd*, leading to *a new low point in East-West relations* and, when a hint is needed that this one really will not get off the ground, *risking nuclear war*.

East-West can be NATO vs. Warsaw Pact or Free World vs. Evil Empire, but usually is taken to mean the Soviet Union and the United States; *North-South* is the Industrial World dealing with the Third World. Strictly on background, and not for attribution even to "a senior official" as the source, V. Cumbrous Array is thinking of floating out *East-South* to mean Soviet dealings with Africa, but that would trigger the *West-North* metaphor, a concept too arcane for discussion in this century.

The most disdainful characterization of an opposite side's proposals is *not serious*. That is a heavy term in summitspeak, reflecting its etymology: *serious* is rooted in the Latin for "grave, heavy, weighty," and has come to mean "sober, solemn." In diplomacy, *a serious proposal* means "one in which we know in advance the other side will find something to accept," and *not serious* means "beneath contempt," or "lying hogwash," although I am assured that these harsh words are not used by V. Cumbrous Array personally. Continuing the metaphor of heaviness, the adjective *concrete*—the cement of Henry Kissinger mixed with the sands of time—is high approbation, and *atmospherics*, which used to mean "static interfering with radio reception" but now means "mood," is considered a mild derogation. ("Nothing *substantive* today, Dan—only *atmospherics*.")

Short of a *breakthrough*—first used as a noun in a military context by London's *Daily Express* in 1918, the closest Russian equivalent of which is *perelom*—what can a summit achieve? Here we have the product of Local 55 of the Conceptual Frameworkers International Union. Its members can turn out anything from a *framework for future discussion* to a *statement of general principles*; short of that, if the corners of the frame don't meet, a *memorandum of agreement* may be signed, or if the conference falls apart completely, a *memorandum of understanding*, which needs no signature, may be put forward as a fig leaf.

V. Cumbrous has slipped me, on a will-be-denied basis, this handy rundown of his true meaning in characterization of the talks. If Mike and Ron start throwing shoes across the room, and if the Kremlin strategic forces go on red-white-and-blue alert, the discussion will be described as *frank and serious*.

However, if they merely holler at each other, but to some good end, the spokesman's phrase will be *candid and productive*. If the talks go well, we will hear *serious and productive*. If they really go well, beyond expectations, the talks will rate the summitspeak accolade, an *important exchange*.

Now hold on to your hats. If that then escalates to *important and fruitful exchange*—beyond *serious*, beyond *productive*, with those well-nurtured seeds yielding real fruit—then we will have ourselves a regular *perelom*, a *break-through*.

If that happens, and the bells peal around the world while investors dump swords and plunge into plowshares, what will be the hosanna from V. Cumbrous Array?

"Hard bargaining lies ahead."

Taking Cides

Blurbuage—the lingo of the inside flaps of dust jackets—is usually replete with literary clichés: all prose is *taut*, all opinion *trenchant*, served up with *brio*, a zesty Italian musical term that goes well with chablis. On occasion, the flap displays a good new word.

One such is *execucide*, which wraps around a book entitled *Our Own Worst Enemy: The Unmaking of American Foreign Policy*, by I. M. Destler, Leslie H. Gelb and Anthony Lake. "The making of policy," goes the copy, "has become a kind of blood sport, or 'execucide,' in which we encourage our leaders to kill each other off."

I asked my *New York Times* colleague Mr. Gelb where the term appears in the book; unfortunately, it has been cut out, which is going to pose a problem for citators. (Is what is *on* a book considered *in* a book?) The term is useful in a wider context, as world leaders more frequently become assassination targets. *Regicide* deals with the killing of a king, but there is no term for the killing of a chief of state.

In a related macabre development, this query from Jerry Oster of New

York: "*Uxoricide* means the murder of a wife by her husband; *mariticide* means the murder of a husband by his wife. I'm unable to track down the word for the murder of someone *else's* spouse by that someone's lover, surely a popular form of the practice. Any ideas?" My correspondent, fortunately, does not seem to be in a hurry for an answer.

Dear Bill,

You quote Jerry Oster regarding *uxoricide* and *mariticide*. He's right about *uxoricide*, but (see *Webster's Third*, p. 1382, col. 2) not necessarily about *mariticide*, which is a broader term, covering the murder of either spouse by the other. True, *husband* is *mari* in French, *marito* in Italian, *marido* in Spanish—all from *maritus -a -um*, the Latin adjective —but the Romans used the masculine, *maritus*, as a substantive for *husband*, and the feminine, *marita* (logically enough) for *wife*. *Marita* was so used by both Horace and Ovid, and that may indicate that it was only a poetic term, but my Latin dictionaries do define *marita* as "wife." So, by joining the stem *marit-* via the copulative *-i-* with *-cide*, you wind up with *mariticide*, a word indifferent to the sex of either murderer or murderee.

Now, as to Mr. Oster's commendable search for a word meaning the murder of someone else's spouse by that someone's lover, all that I have been able to dream up thus far is the unsatisfactory *cuckoldicide*, not only an ugly-sounding word, but one limited in two ways: first, a cuckold is a deceived husband, and I can't find a word for a deceived wife; secondly, *cuckoldicide* would cover the case of anybody's killing the poor chap—not necessarily the naughty wife's paramour. But I'll keep trying.

Norman [Schur]
Weston, Connecticut

There is a term for killing a Chief of State; it's tyrannicide. To you the victim may have been simply and objectively a Chief of State, but obviously to the assassin, who cast such a drastic and effective a vote of no confidence, the victim was a tyrant.

Finally, and again obviously, a person who kills one's own lover's spouse is a pragmatist.

E. J. Turner
New York, New York

Terminate the Neutralize

"I t is possible to neutralize carefully selected and planned targets," wrote the author of a Central Intelligence Agency manual for insurgents in Nicaragua, "such as court judges, police and state security officials, etc."

In that context, what did *neutralize* mean? Spook-spokesmen hustled to their dictionaries to point out that the word came into the English language in 1759, meaning "to make chemically neutral" with that chemical definition extended to "to counteract the effect of, make ineffective." Viewed benignly, the manual's verb could mean merely to reduce the effectiveness of local officials, and to replace them with "friendlies."

Most readers aren't prepared to allow the manual writer such dexterity, especially with the word "targets" as the verb's object. Moreover, *neutralize* has carried for centuries another meaning: "to destroy by an opposite force." Edmund Burke, in his 1795 letter on the proposals for peace with the Regicide Directory of France, criticized the author of a pamphlet for claiming "It was the monarchy that rendered France dangerous: Regicide neutralizes all the acrimony of that power and renders it safe and social." The Regicides were the killers of King Louis XVI, and Burke's use of *neutralize* in connection with them lays a historic basis for its use in the CIA manual.

What other bureaucratic euphemisms were available for murder? In the Vietnam War, special forces were said to use *terminate with extreme prejudice.* This was a lawyer at work ("Let's terminate all the lawyers," Shakespeare almost said). When litigation ends "without prejudice," the case is settled but the plaintiff is free to bring the same case back in the future. When the case ends "with prejudice," that ends it; serve your papers elsewhere. There is no legal *extreme prejudice;* that was some assassin's creative intensifier, and it became catnip for spy novelists. The CIA never authorized the phrase in manuals or in the locker room at Langley.

Dispatch has been overlooked lately in cutting orders for cutting life short. This verb began with the meaning "to send off with speed," but by 1530 had gained the sinister connotation of "to kill with swift efficiency." The English poet Algernon Charles Swinburne, agreeing with Thomas Carlyle, wrote, "If any poet or other literary creature could really be 'killed off by one critique' or many, the sooner he was so dispatched the better. . . ."

A quick review of thesauri offers *rub out, knock off, wipe out, bump off,* the specialized *frag* and the all-purpose *zap.* The headline-writer's favorite remains *slay,* and reporters like *execute gangland-style* (not even in Chicago are victims *taken for a ride* anymore—and whatever happened to *fit him for cement shoes?*). English novelists still *do in,* but political heavies no longer *send up Salt River;* they prefer the intellectual *eliminate* or *liquidate.*

Pity Arnold Schwarzenegger. He is just coming out in a movie titled, with all ominous intent, *The Terminator,* when the hot new thing to be in the executioner's world is *The Neutralizer.*

A check with others who taught clandestine operations at the Special Warfare Center in Fort Bragg in the '60s would confirm data more accurate than the apparent guess about "lawyers" as the source for "terminate with extreme prejudice."

Spookery teaching for future Green Berets stressed a simple rule. The major rationale, and official definition, was that any connection of clandestine operations with the government could be plausibly denied *at any time.* Those last three words were taken very seriously.

An acceptable plan for any operation had to set forth in realistic detail the steps to be taken if at any time the operation was aborted. This was the plan's *termination* section. Obviously its more sensitive elements provided for ending the employment of the human sources who had been recruited for it. *Termination* referred to an infinite number of ways, whatever was appropriate under the circumstances, of severing contact with the persons concerned. "Extreme prejudice" emerged in that context, and never in a truly serious or official manner. The fact that realistically one *didn't* simply kill such people was used to impress upon students the vital need for constant readiness to deal with this problem, and the difficulties which it poses for writing sensible, realistic plans even when conditions of war are assumed.

Thus was TWEP brought to the Special Forces vocabulary. Nothing to do with lawyers. Supervision and control over such efforts involved the usual bureaucratic methods. If "termination section" of an "operation plan" seems "bureaucratic" in origin in that sense, so be it. But I'd suggest that this, like most "bureaucracy," is merely normal rationality turned into rules and routines for a large organization. In this case fairly sensible rules!

Thomas O. Schlesinger
Professor, Political Science
Plymouth State College
Plymouth, New Hampshire

Your lexicography of "neutralization" failed to uncover an NYPD usage that I learned two years ago. A detective told me he was involved in an investigation where "Some guy tried to whack (kill) a cop." As an Assistant District Attorney in the Rackets, Narcotics and Organized Crime Bureau in Queens, I was to hear the term "whack" a few times in that context.

Oscar W. Ruiz
Queens Village, New York

Themeless Pud

Assistant Attorney General Stephen Trott told a "Meet the Press" panel that he was pleased with Israeli promises to cooperate in the investigation of espionage in the United States, but added: "We will take them at their word, but the proof is in the pudding."

The proof is not in the pudding. You could stir around the pudding for hours and never find the proof. The proverb goes: *the proof of the pudding is in the eating.*

The source of that proverb is given in Bartlett's Quotations as Cervantes's *Don Quixote*, but that is based on an English translation in 1700 by Peter Anthony Motteux; an earlier use, dated 1682, is in the Oxford English Dictionary, but the earliest, not in the O.E.D., is in Burton Stevenson's *Home Book of Proverbs, Maxims, and Familiar Phrases.* That underrated work cites William Camden's 1605 history, *Remaines of a Greater Worke Concerning Britaine*, which puts the wisdom in these words: "All the proof of a pudding is in the eating." (Hats off to my language researcher, Jeffrey H. McQuain, who gets a kick out of trumping the O.E.D.)

The point of the proverb is that a pudding may look good, or smell good, or even feel and sound good, but all that is irrelevant and sometimes misleading; the only true test of its success as a pudding is the satisfaction it provides when it is eaten.

The clipping of the proverb to "the proof is in the pudding," stated as flatly as "the saw is in the cake," renders the adage meaningless. I would not ordinarily take a pop at a speaker for making this common error, but I expect the head of the Justice Department's criminal division to be careful about the best-known proverb about proof.

WHAT??? The "best-known proverb about proof" is "The proof of the pudding is in the eating?" Nonsense!! I submit that the best-known must be:

The exception proves the rule.

This, of course, also may be the record-holder for most-misused and misunderstood proverb.

I feel you were somewhat unfair toward Mr. Trott's misquotation of the "pudding" proverb, because it has nothing to do with his area of professional expertise. Both the "pudding" and "rule" proverbs use *proof* in the sense of *test,* not the mathematical or legal sense of *demonstration.* The *test* of the pudding is in the eating, just as an exception *tests* the rule, and there is no reason to expect an attorney to know this. Now if a photographer or an author misused that sense of *proof,* you would have a right to be censorious. For that matter, I have heard rumors that more than one author tends to be all too familiar with *proof* = *test* in the whiskey sense, also.

> John Dierdorf
> Austin, Texas

There, There

"There's no *there* there" was Gertrude Stein's classic slander of the city of Oakland, California. That was the last time a sentence was started successfully with a pronominal, impersonal *there.*

There is an inclination among weak writers to use *there* at the beginning of sentences. Look at the slow-starting agglomeration of words in the previous sentence: it's a wet noodle of a sentence, putting the reader to sleep before coming to life with the word *weak.* Compare that "pronominal there" pap to this vigorous alternative: "Weak writers are inclined to use *there* at the beginning of sentences."

Ah, you say, what about Shakespeare's "There is a tide in the affairs of men. . . ."? Face it: even the Bard had his bad days. If he had a chance, Shakespeare would pick up the phone and say: "Hello, Rewrite? I want to change Brutus's line that begins *There is a tide* to *A tide exists.* . . . No, hold on—make that *Great tides appear.* . . . Yes, same iambic pentameter, and putting the noun up closer to the front gives it a little zing. *There is* is a weak way to start any speech."

Rewrite would say: "But how about the *there* in Hamlet's 'Ay, there's the rub!' That *there* sounds pretty strong to me."

Shakespeare would then patiently point out to Rewrite that *there*, when meaning a place or an intensifier for *that*, is a powerful word. (So *there!*) Moreover, when used to mean "thither" or "yon" (as in "Cassius over there has a lean and hungry look"), *there* has its place. And when meant as "at or to that point," it serves a real purpose. (What is the point of this piece? I'm getting there.) But when used in writing, as a mere "function" word for writers reluctant to bite into the subject without first fiddling around, *there* is a sign of weakness, irresolution and pusillanimity. (Brutus was, deep down, weak; maybe Shakespeare was sending a signal. OK, on that basis, leave the *there is* bit in.)

The linking verb that follows the lazy writer's pronominal impersonal is also weak; sentences that start *There is* stagger to the starting line. Compare the wimpish *There are a couple of reasons I like to hide behind 'there is.'* . . . to the forceful *The reasons I reject 'there is' include.* . . .

Another way not to start a sentence is with a conjunction. (The reader has been euchred into a style piece about ways not to start sentences. We finally got there.) Conjunctions like *and, but* and *because* are intended to join thoughts or to subordinate one idea to another, but when used to start sentences, these conjunctions usually produce a sloppy or choppy effect. This rule can be broken with great effect: Shirley Jackson began a superb short story with "And the first thing they did was segregate me"—but her dramatic purpose in opening with a conjunction was to give the impression of not starting at the beginning. And, yes, to be totally honest, even I have started sentences with *And*—too often, frankly—when I want to give the impression of a sudden afterthought or an admission I dragged out of myself that I had not planned to set forth in my argument.

In starting sentences, you should watch out for *but*, a word that starts a withdrawal from a position. Inside a sentence, where it belongs, *but* is not as specific as *except*—"No alibis except terminal frizzies accepted"—but *but* is a stronger contradiction than *however*. If you want to contradict sharply, use *but* in the same sentence—"She's an intellectual but I like her"—and if you want to slide off a flat statement, introducing a qualification out of fairness or second thought, use *however* after a semicolon or at the start of a new sentence: "She's an intellectual. However, as I am no dummy myself, I like her."

Not every language authority agrees with me on this mild approval of *However* to start a sentence, however. "Strunk and White discourage the use of *however* as a conjunctive adverb at the beginning of a sentence," writes Leslie Brisman, a professor of English at Yale, "(allowing it when it is an adverb meaning 'no matter how'). I and many of my colleagues continue to correct this in our students' writing, but the number of grammar handbooks demonstrating the *however* in the initial position makes us wonder whether there is any ground for continuing to insist on this matter of form."

No grounds; forget it. However many purists insist that the only time *however* may be used to start a sentence is demonstrated at the start of this sentence, the fact is that such a requirement is outdated. More important (meaning "what is more important"—let us continue to resist *more importantly*, which connotes forced significance), we cannot let great old stylebooks dictate today's style.

However, don't use *however* when you mean *in spite of*, which is tougher than the broad-spectrum *but*. If you mean "I know all that, and I am not persuaded" and really want to separate yourself from all that has gone before, you can do much better than *however*. Try *despite*, or if the *spite* turns you off, use the fast-disappearing *nevertheless*. (Remember that song Eddie Fisher used to sing? Hum it on your way to English class.) You can begin a sentence, even a paragraph, with *Nevertheless*; it will have more punch than a paragraph beginning with *However*. (You are the only one reading this paragraph; everyone else skipped it because however-graphs are for timorous State Department speechwriters. Tough speechwriters at State come right out with *On the other hand*.)

We will now rewrite the next-to-last sentence to show how simpering it is to use *Because* at the start. Here's the revision: "Why are you the only one reading this paragraph? *Because* everyone else skipped it. . . ." That use of *Because* at the start creates a sentence fragment and is not as effective as "Why are you the only one reading this paragraph? *The reason is* that everyone else . . ." (If you now ask, "Why is that more effective?" my answer is "Because I'm the Language Maven, that's why, and when I break a rule, as I do in this sentence, I break it wide open—for emphasis.")

Treat your readers to action up front. It's bad enough to dribble off, but it's worse to dribble on. With the tide running to wipe out *There is*, we will next wash away *It is*. (Bor-ing!) Such a tide, taken at the flood, leads on to fortune; omitted, all the cadence of our prose is spent in shallows and in mini-series.

Dear Bill—

There is absolutely nothing wrong with starting a sentence with "There." There are countless circumstances in which it is a natural and rhythmic way to express something. There are countless others in which it is not. There is no point in trying to carry "good writing" rules to such extremes. There is no sense in trying to evaluate the quality of any sentence except in context.

Because I have such great respect for the Language Maven, and enjoy your pieces every week, I feel compelled to register this objection.

> *Kop [Leonard Koppett]*
> *Editor Emeritus*
> *The Peninsula Times Tribune*
> *Palo Alto, California*

There is a tendency among weak writers to think up simple rules like "Don't use *there is*" instead of figuring out how a sentence is to capture and display some piece of reality, as a coat of paint shows up an invisible horse.

Or something. Hell, you know what I mean.

> *Bill Ed Scruggs*
> *Huntington, Connecticut*

The anticipatory expletives *there* and *it* serve to delay the real subject of the sentence and thereby to give it emphasis. "There is a tide" is a hell of a lot more interesting than "Great tides appear . . ."

> *Mark and Maggie Isaacs*
> *Allentown, Pennsylvania*

On "strong" and "weak" sentences—terms that I dislike because the latter carries a pejorative connotation. Too long a series of "strong" sentences affects me very much like music that is relentlessly loud. After a time, either it loses its punch or I recoil from the battering.

There is a place in writing for "soft" sentences, as there is in music for soft sounds. Indeed, the loud can gain emphasis by its contrast with the soft, and a shift from one to the other can bring a piece of writing—or of music—to life. Even journalists and polemicists (I do not equate them), who tend to be addicted to the loud, might benefit from an occasional recourse to a lower, softer tone.

> *Mary McDermott Shideler*
> *Boulder, Colorado*

For the past few years I have increasingly found myself correcting my children's grammar when they line themselves up as pronouns, so to speak, with their friends.

The worst, of course, is "Me, Kim and Ann Marie are going to the mall." "Please put yourself last," I ask, "and it's 'Kim, Ann Marie and I are going to the mall.' "

Sometimes the case is right, but the order, it seemed to me, was still wrong. "Jill asked me and Lori to sleep over." "Lori and me," I corrected. Or thought I corrected. And wondered—don't their teachers hear them speak—not even their English teachers? Do they ever correct them? Does anybody who is supposed to, care? Where are the standard-bearers? Yes, *The New York Times*, I know—and you particularly, of course.

I was reading your however-at-the-beginning-of-a-sentence exploration. Quoting Leslie Brisman, English professor at Yale, you wrote, "I and many of my colleagues continue to correct this [use of "however" as initial word] . . . but wonder whether there is any ground for continuing to insist on this matter of form."

"However" at the beginning of a sentence has annoyed me only slightly over the years, but after reading Professor Brisman's quote I'm left wondering about something else. That is, how much should I insist on "putting yourself last" when you appear in a series? If a Yale professor who cares very much about the position of "however" in a sentence doesn't care, and if you, by your lack of critical comment, put your stamp of approval on it, what's a mother to do?

> *Shirley Snyder Boardman*
> *Wayne, New Jersey*

> "There was a young" something is weak
> And makes lim'ricks less than unique;
> > *In medias res*
> > Is the best starting place
> If mem'rable impact you seek!

> *Donald R. Harkness*
> *Tampa, Florida*

There's evidence to show that writers haven't figured it out yet, else Irving Berlin would have had Ethel Merman singing, "No business exists like show business," and Oscar Hammerstein II's Seabees would have declared that "A dame is that like which nothing is."

> *Sam Meals, M.D.*
> *Long Beach, California*

The Time Has Come

A timely reminder about daylight-saving: Those of us who rely on a mnemonic (pronounce the opening letter *m* as in *pneumonia*, or *gnu*, or *knee-jerk*) murmur, "Spring ahead, fall back," and set our cheap new quartz watches ahead, thereby "saving" an hour of daylight.

The British call this device to put schoolchildren at bus stops in the predawn darkness *summer-time*, hyphenated to differentiate this specific time-juggling from the word that evokes fish jumping and the cotton being high.

Now to the question I am always asked this time of year: does that lurch forward of our method of dividing our day mean we start pushing daylight-*saving* time or daylight-*savings* time? Some people know the difference between *saving*, the noun meaning the money not squandered when a bargain is found, and *savings*, the noun meaning the money you have amassed for a rainy day. ("The saving I'm saving I can add to my savings in the savings bank.") These aficionados of penny-pinching nomenclature will answer confidently: *daylight-saving time*, because *daylight-saving* is the action being taken, and the hyphen may atrophy as hyphens do.

Such a position makes great grammatical sense but is behind the time. Daylight-saving is the action, but the result is neither daylight-saving time nor daylight-savings time. The result should be *daylight time*. (Direct answers are best; avoid equivocation. When asked, "If the sense is *soon*, should you say *presently* or *momentarily*?" I reply, "Say *soon*." This serene decisiveness enrages the Nitpickers' League.)

The *New York Times* stylebook, in its wisdom, also takes that word-saving position, and adds: "Do not capitalize: 9:00 A.M., *Eastern daylight time*. Abbreviation: E.D.T." This dictum is confusing: "Do not capitalize" refers to the *daylight*, not the A.M. At *The Times*, we always capitalize A.M., and not merely out of deference to the executive editor: we stand at ramparts that are being abandoned by many other stylebook writers, who are lowercasing the letters.

Latiniks know that the letters stand for *ante meridiem*, "before midday," as against *post meridiem*, "after noon." (So why do we give Eastern daylight time three capitals, as E.D.T.? Because it would look funny as "E.d.t.," and whenever consistency comes up against looking funny, consistency loses.

Besides, the d.t.'s are short for *delirium tremens*, and punctual people rarely have the shakes.)

With the *saving* saved, we come to the question that keeps getting thrown at the United States Naval Observatory (where they make sure the universe runs on time) by time-servers everywhere: Should noon be referred to as 12 A.M. or 12 P.M.?

This is a matter of dispute that spilled into the political arena when Congress abolished the Synthetic Fuels Corporation and prohibited it from spending money past 12 P.M. on a given day. The White House interpreted that as noon instead of midnight, and blew an extra couple hundred million dollars during that glorious morning; Representative Silvio O. Conte, Republican of Massachusetts, cried: "They're going to try to use any goddam excuse they can to get this goddam thing. They think they've found a loophole."

(In the U.P.I. story on the Synfuels contretemps, Representative Conte's irate adjective was spelled *goddamn*, with an *n* at the end. I explored the variant spellings of this expletive at some length when Frank Sinatra issued a statement saying formally, "William Safire is a god-damn liar," both hyphenating the word and using the *n*. My ruling then, which I maintain today, is that the formal spelling of the adjective is *God-damned*, and the informal spelling is *goddam*, uncapitalized, unhyphenated and with its ending clipped; any other spelling is both inconsistent and looks funny.)

I have been playing for time. Is 12 noon A.M. or P.M.? Again, the answer is neither. Dr. G.M.R. Winkler, director of time service at the Naval Observatory, observes: "A.M. means the time before meridian transit, and P.M. means the time after meridian transit. It is a matter of logic, then, that if noon is exactly the meridian transit, it cannot be either A.M. or P.M."

This logic has at least penetrated the Government Printing Office, which insists in its style manual that noon is to be called "12 M." But that is a mistake in my book, because "12 M." sure looks like "12 *midnight*" to me. What to do?

My observant friend at the time service (where they do not appreciate remarks about bureaucratic time-serving) has a trifurcated, or three-pronged, answer:

"First, we recommend that you use *12 noon* and *12 midnight*, and with midnight, since it is the end of a day, give the dates on either side of it—for example, *12 midnight of April 27–28.*" Too legal-sounding? Try another: "Second, there is the system used by the railroads, which is to avoid noon and midnight—no ambiguity exists between 11:59 A.M. and 12:01 P.M." Sorry—to me, that begs the question of what to designate the mass transit of the meridian. "Third," says the indefatigable Dr. Winkler, "we have the

2400 system, in which midnight is the beginning of a new day: zero hours, zero minutes, zero seconds."

No, thanks; I swore I would stop saying, "Wake me up at 0500," the minute I snatched my discharge. Let the military be military and go by the numbers; let the rest of us fumble with our linguistic ambiguity in a way that communicates precisely without abandoning the traditions of the mother tongue.

Where does that leave us? At 12:00 M? That looks to me like 1,200 thousand, with the M standing for the thousand, and it looks funny so it's out.

My answer: when you mean 12 noon, say or write "12 noon"; when you mean 12 midnight, say "12 midnight" and specify the night unless the tense does it for you. Better still, drop the 12 entirely.

Thus, the Big Spender would say, "How about I cut out the spending at noon?"

"Try that and I'll let go with a torrent of goddams," replies the budget-cutter. "Cut it out at midnight the night before."

That is as much tidying-up as I can do at one sitting. No, I do not know why there is a *high noon* and not a *low midnight*.

In listing a few of your retentions of older usage, you cite *presently* as meaning *soon*. It is much more indefinite—the ideal word for putting off: "I'll do it (or be there) when I'm good and ready."

Jacques [Barzun]
Charles Scribner's Sons, Publishers
New York, New York

You say, ". . . any other spelling *is both* inconsistent *and looks* funny." (My emphasis, of course.)

Say I, it should be either, ". . . is both inconsistent and funny-looking" or "both is inconsistent and looks funny." To me, constructions such as the one of yours that I cite here are flawed to the point of total collapse; yet I see them in the papers all the time. They drive me nuts because they ignore and violate obvious verities of basic structure.

Richard H. Hutzler
Falmouth, Maine

I wish to join the legion of Latiniks who surely wonder why *meridiem* is translated "midday" when preceded by *"ante"* and "after noon" when preceded by *"post."*

As for noon and midnight, we might as well rest our case on technical grounds. A particular day begins some incomprehensibly tiny fraction of a second after midnight. Some twelve hours later, the morning ends with 12:00 noon, properly 12:00 A.M. because it is the very last instant of the morning. The afternoon hours promptly get under way and end with 12:00 midnight, or 12:00 P.M. After all, when counting to ten, we don't begin with zero. Neither do we begin counting the hours with twelve. Congressman Conte be praised!

David Majercik
Williamsburg, Massachusetts

You quote Dr. G.M.R. Winkler of the U.S. Naval Observatory as follows:

"A.M. means the time before meridian transit and P.M. means the time after meridian transit.

What Dr. Winkler says would be true *if* the Equation of Time did not reflect daily changes in the time of meridian crossing and *if* the meridian crossing occurred every day at Noon, Mean Solar Time. The introduction of the concept of transit by such an iffy argument is wholly gratuitous. Ante Meridiem and Post Meridiem mean Before Noon and After Noon as though meridiem acquired the meaning noon just as *Midi* means both Noon and South.

None of this affects the validity of your conclusion since 12 Noon is neither before or after noon and 12 Midnight is both. You just lucked in, or out.

Richard J. Kerry
Manchester, Massachusetts

There is indeed a coherent and compelling reason to define noon as 12 P.M. and midnight as 12 A.M. It has to do with the concept of boundary conditions in the mathematics of continuous curves (in spite of modern physics, we macroscopic beings may still think of time as a continuity).

The idea is to include the endpoint with the rest of the curve of which it is the end. The span of time from 11:59 P.M. all the way back to 12:01 P.M. (the afternoon) indicates that, to be consistent with the 12:xx P.M. range, noon becomes the beginning of P.M., and similarly the minute before 12:01 A.M. must be midnight, 12:00 A.M.

In fact, 12:00 can refer (in practical use) to an entire minute, not only an instantaneous moment, so for that span of time A.M. or P.M. is indeed very well defined. For situations where "##:## X.M." is the required format, we must have a definition (data base developers would flip their bits if you forced some arbitrary "patch" into their systems).

Perhaps you were awake too often around 12:00 A.M. recently—I don't think you really tried that hard on this one.

Dan Krimm
New York, New York

Please, a little logic on the subject of A.M. and P.M.

If A.M. means "ante meridiem" or "before noon" and P.M. means "post meridiem" or "after noon," "meridiem" or "noon" having the same meaning in both phrases, then 1 A.M. means the time that we call eleven o'clock in the morning; which is manifestly not the case.

So we can forget etymology and say, what everybody knows, that A.M. *means* "hours after midnight" and P.M. *means* "hours after noon."

Having settled that issue, we can easily dispose of the question of what to call noon and midnight. Noon is 12 A.M. and also 0 P.M.; and midnight is 12 P.M. and also 0 A.M.

Harry J. Kamack
Newark, Delaware

I am starting this letter not at noon, or 12:00 A.M. or 12:00 P.M., but at "midday," a term I have always used to distinguish it from "midnight."

I am also automatically translating from the French *midi*, the Spanish *mediodia*, and the German *mittag*.

I am uneasy with "noon," since it comes from the Latin *nona* or "ninth" hour after the sunrise.

Anyway, in your fascinating article you referred to your quartz watch as "cheap," when I think you meant "inexpensive." Quartz watches are superb timepieces, but are priced with a fair markup.

My New World Dictionary (Second College Edition) sums up my feelings on these two misused words: "Inexpensive and cheap both mean low in cost or price, but inexpensive simply suggests value comparable to price, and cheap stresses a bargain, with the implication of inferior quality." Its origin is from the French *à bon marché*.

Bern Marcowitz
New York, New York

You refer to the "Nitpickers' League." I question your use of the apostrophe, indicating the possessive. Capitalization of "Nitpickers' League" makes the two words into one entity, a proper noun. "League" is not distinctive and cannot stand on its own merit as a proper noun (as can "Unfinished Symphony" of "Schubert's Unfinished Symphony"). As such, "Nitpickers League" must be considered one entity if a proper noun. Consequently, inference of the possessive is incorrect. "The Nitpickers" do not possess (form) *the* "League"; they possess (form) *a* league, henceforth called the "Nitpickers League" or perhaps the "Nitpicker League."

If a possessive relationship was paramount, then "league" should have appeared in lower case: e.g. Hodgkin's disease. As for "Nitpickers League" as a proper name, I believe I am correct, although theoretically you could spell this proper name any way you wish since you coined it.

Mitchell Goldman
Hollis, New York

To -eur Is Human

"A s a restaurateur," begins a letter from Gregory Dawson, proprietor of the Ballroom, a cabaret-restaurant in New York. That stopped me: shouldn't there be an *n* in *restaurateur?*

No. The word is French, and means more than just "a person who runs a restaurant"; it means "one who restores." But you could lose the National Spelling Bee if you put an *n* in that word.

"What do Ed Koch, Johnny Carson and Jack Klugman have in common?" writes Robert Eck of Chicago, who devotes a portion of his life to tracking down spelling miscreants. "They all assume there is an *n* in *restaurateur*. There ain't. They also assume that *-eur* is correctly said as *-oor*. Not even in Des Moines."

Because most people pronounce *restaurateur* as *rest-uh-ron-toor*, the spelling could vary, as it has with *chaise longue* (now sometimes seen as *chaise lounge*). An *n* may be added, but the *-eur* will remain.

That's because there are twenty-one words in English that have the *-eur* suffix, and they are doing fine the way they are. *Grandeur* was used in Mr. Reagan's rambling summation in debate, as he tootled down a West Coast highway. *Auteur*, which used to mean "author," is now a word for "movie director," used by people who go to *films* rather than *movies*. The modern populist hero is the *entrepreneur*, dressed in shirt sleeves and putting aside all *hauteur*, hoping one day to become a *conglomerateur*. I know a *voyeur* who got into trouble because his *chauffeur* turned out to be an *amateur saboteur*.

"In English," ruminates Sol Steinmetz of Barnhart Books, *"-eur* is not a productive suffix—that is, it does not produce new words in English but is always borrowing from the French. Like *liqueur* in 1729 and *migraineur* in 1971."

What will happen to *restaurateur?* "It will probably pick up an *n* in our dictionaries," he tells us. "The people, not the lexicographers, write the language."

> You probably know that there are, in French, two kinds of "restau-
> rateurs." The ones who "restaure" people and the ones who
> "restaure" objects of art. Their function is the same: putting back into
> shape people or objects which suffer—the objects from old age, the
> people from hunger.
>
> In English, the "restaurateur" of people is still a restaurateur
> whereas the other one is a restorer.
>
> If, as you write it, "the people, not the lexicographers, write the
> language," I do hope that the English restaurateur will become a re-
> storer but not, horror of horrors, a restaurantoor!
>
> > *Jacques Lindon*
> > *Paris, France*

A Toast to White Bread

Describing the effect of softened violence in a movie called *The Dirty Dozen*, John Corry, a *New York Times* television critic, wrote, "It may be a *white bread* war . . ."

Explaining his desire to reach a solid, middle-class audience for his revival of the musical play *The King and I*, Larry Miller of Corinthian Communications said: "We wanted white-bread Middle America. Not necessarily downscale, but not a person who goes to the theater four or five times a year. We wanted people who went once a year. . . ."

This new adjective has puzzled David Cole of Norwalk, Connecticut: "It looks like these fellows are trying to enrich the language. This use of *white bread* (with or without the hyphen) as an adjective suggests some variations: *pita bread politics* in Lebanon; *pumpernickel styling* of a Volkswagen; *unleav-*

ened advice from an attorney. In all seriousness, from whence cometh *white bread* as a modifier?"

Although *whence* means *from where* and does not take a redundant *from*, the question is otherwise well taken. The new adjective was launched in the 1960s, was given special attention in the '70s by *Newsweek* magazine, and is now getting ready to force its way into new dictionaries.

Maclean's magazine, in a 1968 interview with Norman Mailer, quoted the novelist's distaste of a "white-bread mentality" he associated with the baby-care ideas of Dr. Benjamin Spock. In 1977, *Newsweek* described the entertainer Richard Pryor, who is black, as walking off the stage in Las Vegas "fed up with doing 'white bread' humor." A year later, the magazine praised Norman Lear's television series "All in the Family" for going "beyond what the trade called 'white bread and mayonnaise'—and the customers happily lapped it up." In a political context later in 1978, the magazine reported that the former Los Angeles police chief, Ed Davis, once called a California candidate as exciting "as a mashed-potato sandwich on white bread."

The definition of the hyphenated compound adjective *white-bread,* from most of those usages, seems to be "bland." The lexicographer Sol Steinmetz, however, takes it a couple of layers deeper: "Used figuratively and chiefly as an adjective, *white-bread* is one of the most subtle and suggestive terms of disparagement to have appeared in recent years." Emphasizing that its core meaning is "belonging to or reflecting the values of American white society," Mr. Steinmetz points to the way the word suggests the soft, flavorless richness of the supermarket staple. "In slang, *bread* means 'money, affluence,' and *white-bread* is also a pun on *white-bred.*"

The term has an earlier history in waiters' lingo: in a restaurant, *white bread* was long the code reference to the boss. When an employee whispered, "Eighty-six on the free warts—white bread," it meant "Be on your guard; do not dispense extra olives in the martinis—the owner is here." (*Eighty-six* was an American adaptation of cockney rhyming slang, rhyming with *nix,* and *warts* are olives, but I digress.) It may be that this early use of *white bread* originated in black servers about *the man,* or the white owner, but that is speculative.

The compound adjective was immortalized by the singer Billy Joel in his 1983 song "Uptown Girl," part of the *Innocent Man* album. Mr. Joel recently married Christie Brinkley, a model and actress who does not conjure a vision of caraway bagels.

Your column on "white bread" moves me to write, since your definitions only scratched the surface. I have heard the phrase used against me over the past fifteen years or so, always by Jews of Eastern European heritage, and always as an "ethnic" slur. It refers to the alleged life of privilege and ease I led as a Protestant growing up in this nation, as opposed to the multitude of hardships suffered by the speaker, be they real or imagined.

I have never heard the phrase used in a descriptive way only. I am shocked that you and your paper would lend your collective prestige to the advancement of such vulgarisms.

> *Steven T. Flowers*
> *Bryn Mawr, Pennsylvania*

I recall the adjective white-bread as having an additional meaning, which was not specifically mentioned in your column. The term was used to denote an overall quality which was believed to be un-Jewish, i.e. gentile in nature, goyish. In fact, the term was often intended to be pejorative.

> *Denis Murstein*
> *Chicago, Illinois*

I recall my maternal grandmother, black, "self-taught," ex-slave, who, as a very young child, saw Grant's armies entering Richmond, Virginia (our family seat). She told me these stories as a child. I lived with her (off and on) by choice. One of her oft-used expressions involved "white bread," such as: "Boy, you're eatin' your white bread now"; "Oh, Jack, Bill, James, etc., is eatin' his white bread now!" She meant that I, and the others, were "doing well," we had achieved something, i.e., a good job, had a new pair of shoes, new suit, perhaps "hit the numbers"!

It was also an admonition: it also suggested, in an oblique manner, that life would not always permit you to eat "white bread," that from time to time you would have to revert to *corn bread,* which, of course, was the slave diet insofar as "bread" was concerned. This inferred a "bring-down" or "come-down," not being "too uppity."

Finally, my grandmother died in 1945, in her nineties. I was on Okinawa and I couldn't get back for the funeral. Until I read your column, I hadn't thought about "white bread" in years.

> *William H. Staten*
> *Bronx, New York*

I think you've missed part of the point about "white bread" as an adjective. The point is not just Caucasian-ness, or having money; "white bread" to me means outdated orthodoxy of thought and behavior; small-town squareness. People who buy whole wheat bread are nutrition-conscious, thus open to new ideas (such as nutrition consciousness); they are also considered suspiciously liberal by white-bread people, to whom casting aspersions on the healthfulness of Wonder Bread is un-American. Like many liberals, I buy high-fiber or whole-grain breads; I don't think most Republicans would have such food in the house. Many Americans combine ethnicity with bread-eating habits; think of Italian bread (which does not count as "white bread" although it *is* white) or Jewish rye. Wasps very seldom buy rye bread except maybe miniatures for canapes; they do, however, buy raisin bread and other sweetened breads and rolls. White bread people do not buy Pepperidge Farm or Arnold white breads; they buy Wonder Bread. . . . P.F. and A. breads are eaten by the Liberal Establishment.

Camilla C. Hewitt
New York, New York

At the end of World War II when Germany was scraping bottom, it instituted "white bread battalions" into which it impressed Germans who could not eat the coarser regular bread. When a soldier spoke of a "white bread battalion" it assumed a pejorative connotation.

Sidney Rosenfeld
New York, New York

You suggested a solution to our curiosity about the origin of the greeting "Hey, Slice," a term which has gained wide currency among both black and white students during our daughter's past year at Hamilton College. As an extension of the white-bread/white-bred figure, *Slice* carries all the associations of "the soft flavorless richness of the supermarket staple" that Mr. Steinmetz recognizes, and conveys as well intimations of mass production and conformity (as your cartoon suggested).

Yet the friendly universality of the term at Hamilton also illustrates the amelioration of "one of the most suggestive terms of disparagement to have appeared in recent years," as Steinmetz describes *white bread*. In effect, the way that *Slice* is used represents a bleaching out of the enrichment effect referred to by your original correspondent. Of course, the language is indeed enriched by these terms, yet their meaning, as well as the language itself, seems to have a life of its own.

Susan Crowl
Athens, Ohio

You stated that "Eighty-six" came from a cockney rhyme with "nix." I disagree unless you can find me an example of the use of "Eighty-six" before the restaurant Chumley's was in existence.

Chumley's started as a speakeasy during Prohibition in Manhattan. It's located in a courtyard in the Village and to this day has no sign identifying its presence. If you don't know the location by sight, it's very difficult to find.

However, the address for Chumley's is 86 Bedford—the back door. Whenever someone got a little too rowdy, they were thrown out the back door. They were, in essence, Eighty-sixed. I am aware that Peter Hockman of Fiorello's has sent you a copy of my book *(How to Be a Professional Waiter or Waitress,* St. Martin's Press) which includes a chapter on restaurant slang. Although I do not give the origins of slang terms in my book, as far as I know this is the origin of "Eighty-six."

Lishka DeVoss
Long Island City, New York

Towel Pronouns

A rt Buchwald, the itinerant lecturer and columnist, called this morning with a question about grammar. Unlike Casey Stengel, whose stricture was "You could look it up," Mr. Buchwald has an approach to linguistic research that can be characterized as "You could call him up."

"I'm working on a piece and I've run into a problem with pronouns, I think," he said. "What is it when you talk about a person—anybody, man or woman—and then you refer to them again?"

That's definitely a pronoun.

"And what is it when you're talking about one person, and you don't want to say *their?"*

That is a highly desirable refusal to engage in noun-pronoun disagreement.

"But what about when you're stuck with *his,* and you don't want to specify a man, because that leaves out the women. Do you have to say *his or her?* Doesn't that sound like you're pushing it?"

Absolutely; *his or her* sounds legalistic or overly concerned with a need to avoid sexism in speech.

"Yeah, that's it. *His or her* really screws up your sentence. How do you avoid it?"

One of two ways. The easiest way is to remember the phrase "the male embraces the female," and to stick with words like *mankind* rather than the labored *humankind.* On that theory, when you come to a construction like "Every single one should watch *his* pronoun agreement," you are not co-erced into saying "Every single one should watch *his or her* pronoun agree-ment" or being forced into the error of "Every single one should watch *their* pronoun agreement."

The other way, if you happen to be chatting with Betty Friedan, is to recast the sentence: "All of us should watch *our* pronoun agreement." Avoid the *his/her* problem by changing the subject *person* to *people.*

"Oh," said my friend Art, disappointed. "That's pretty boring. I thought I was giving you a good idea for a column." He hung up his or her phone.

Why resist the change in usage that would allow use of the plural pronoun *they* in instances where the gender of the subject is indefinite? To my mind (and to my ear), such noun-pronoun disagreement is the most reasonable, most euphonious resolution of the problem pre-sented by our language's lack of a gender-neutral impersonal pronoun. Using this construction allows one to honor the possibility that an otherwise nondescript "person" could be a woman, while avoiding the awkward *he or she* (and the typographical abomination *s/he),* and while allowing us to retain a degree of precision in language that we give up if we constrain ourselves to talk only in plurals.

Noun-pronoun agreement is an instance of redundancy in language, and although redundancy is necessary and useful in any message, for-going it in this one class of instances seems a small price to pay in order to achieve a nonsexist language.

Certainly the first of the two ways you recommend in your column is no longer acceptable among civilized people. The male no longer embraces the female. I, too, used to think that such locutions as "sewer access cover" for "manhole cover" were awkward and unneces-sary, until I happened to find myself in an environment in which there is widespread use of the *female* indefinite pronoun to stand for the average, everyday person-in-the-street. The experience left me con-vinced that the language we use is important, and that glib assumptions such as yours, which deny the existence of half the human race, should be challenged, examined, and (I have concluded) discarded.

Eric Zencey
Professor of History and Politics
Goddard College
Plainfield, Vermont

I am of the opinion that the only correct pronouns to be used with the antecedent *everybody* are *they, them* and *their*. I maintain that *his, he* and *him* are ungrammatical. Here, briefly, are my reasons:

History: The oldest attestation of *everybody* occurs with the pronoun *their*.

Usage: It sounds ridiculous to say, "Everybody was happy and I rejoiced with him."

Logic: *Everybody,* although it takes a singular verb, is plural in meaning.

Deep structure: *They* is the underlying subject of agentless passives. Thus, *Did they fix the leak?* means the same thing as *Was the leak fixed?* One cannot say *Did he fix the leak?* unless one knows the identity of *he*. *They,* although it takes a plural verb, is unmarked for number in this situation, as it is when it refers to *everybody*.

George Jochnowitz
Professor of Linguistics
College of Staten Island, CUNY
New York, New York

Dear Bill:

In ribbing Art Buchwald for his indolence you raised a question, at least in my mind, about your attribution of "you could look it up" to Casey Stengel. "You Could Look It Up" is the title of a funny short story by James Thurber: a tall tale told by an old-time baseball trainer who, reminiscing, is sure of his facts but hazy about dates. The phrase occurs three times in the text, including the last sentence: "But it'll all be there in the newspapers and record books of thirty, thirty-one year [correctly quoted] ago and, like I was sayin', you could look it up."

Thurber's story was copyrighted by the Curtis Publishing Company in 1941. I looked it up.

John S. Radosta (retired)
Sports Department
The New York Times
New York, New York

Hypersexism and the Feds

Some people take sexism in language very seriously.

It was pointed out here that it was OK to say "Everyone should watch his pronoun agreement," that it was not necessary to say "Everyone should watch his *or her* pronoun agreement." Nor was it required that, in the name of equality, we drop *mankind* and substitute *humankind*; historically, the male usage has embraced the female, and such expressions as "the family of man" is no putdown of women. I don't get worked up over Mother Earth and don't expect women to get worked up over Father Time.

"It seems to me that inequality is so morally unacceptable," writes Iva E. Deutchman, assistant professor of political science at Vassar College, "that one cannot be 'too excited' about inequality." She believes that using the pronoun *their* would be better than *his* in referring back to the singular-construed *everyone*, despite the lack of agreement in number.

"Perhaps, however, you provide an inadvertent autobiographical clue to this," adds Professor Deutchman, "in your empirically incorrect and grossly sexist observation that 'male always embraces the female,' rather than the reverse. Having never known (I surmise) the warmth of a female-initiated embrace, you no doubt came to the astounding conclusion that women were socially and linguistically inferior."

Wow. I have frequently been engaged in *ad hominem* exchanges, but have never before come under *ad mulierien* attack. "Such nonsense as sexism masquerading simply as concern for linguistic purity," snaps the professor, "must stop at once."

My first reaction to that is disappointment that anyone would surmise that I, a lifelong member of the Sadie Hawkins Day committee, have never known the warmth—nay, the all-consuming passion—of a female-initiated embrace. My second reaction is ungrudging admiration: as a professional polemicist who draws vitality from vituperation, I not only respect but also enjoy the sight and sound of a straight, hard shot, delivered with zest and good-natured venom, by an opponent who knows where they stand. (Somehow, the sexless pronoun *they* doesn't sound right as a substitute for *he* or *she* in that sentence, but I'll try anything once.) In my view, the professor goes overboard, but I like the form of her dive.

Academics and journalists can merrily, or even savagely, joust about language: it's a fair field and no favor, with nobody coerced. Not so when a government official enters the fray in his official capacity.

A couple of weeks ago, a seemingly sex-crazed agency that Ronald Reagan long ago promised to abolish—the United States Department of Education—leaned on a university for daring to use such sexist terms as *manmade* in one of its catalogues.

Paul D. Grossman, chief regional attorney for the department's office for civil rights, first called the office of the chancellor of the University of California to report a complaint that the school was using sexist language in course descriptions. When university officials asked him to be specific, the Government lawyer then sent a hit list of words, which Mr. Grossman contended "may be perceived by some persons as subtly discouraging female student interest in the courses to which the phrases pertain." Alongside each word to be deleted by Federal diktat was what the lawyer called "a viable alternative."

I have the departmental hit list. In the business-administration courses, the phrase *manpower development* was deemed outside the pale: in the Government's sexlessspeak, the acceptable version is *human resource development.*

In the education section of the catalogue, the lawyer zeroed in on the colloquial term "grantsmanship" in a course called "The Role of Experts in Social Services." The word *grantsmanship* is an extension of Stephen Potter's *one-upmanship* and *gamesmanship*; it is a mocking coinage, meaning "one who plays the game of getting federal or foundation money." No matter; it has the word *man* in it, and the power of the federal government, wielded by one earnest lawyer, demands that the substitute be *grant acquisition* or *grantwriting*; for no apparent reason, he eschewed *grantpersonship.*

In other courses, the university was directed—"informally," as the lawyer put it—to scrap *mankind*, substituting *the human species, humankind* or *humanity*. In biochemistry, "Of Molecules and Man: A View for the Layman," the school was told to kill the two mentions of "man" and change the course title to "Of Molecules and Human Beings: A View for the Lay Person." In the history department, a reference to *man on horseback*—a phrase about the heroic "solitary horseman" who often led to military rule—was ordered watered down by our Federal bureaucrat to a meaningless *combatant.* (Try this for size: "Gaullists are seeking a new combatant on horseback. . . .")

To its credit, and to the relief of believers in academic freedom, the university told the federal attorney to get lost. Vice Chancellor Roderic B. Park bucked the matter to Professor David Littlejohn of the journalism school, who shrewdly circulated the lawyer's objections to fifteen journalists for comment before answering. Highlights of his report:

On *mankind:* "The argument against the long-accepted universal use of *man* and *mankind* is political, not linguistic or logical. It may be compared to the mandated universal use of *comrade* . . . in 'classless' societies. . . . Pretending, or asserting, that the syllable *man* signifies males exclusively can lead one into such barbarisms as *ombudsperson* or *freshperson.*"

On pronouns: "*His* as the appropriate (and neutral) pronoun to follow *one* or *a person* is an English usage of similar longstanding acceptance, although some writers—especially in state institutions—have lately taken to substituting the cumbersome and unnecessary *his or her.*" (Person-oh-person, are they going to hear from Vassar, which is not even a state institution.)

On hypersensitivity: "In no case should good English words, which are a part of our common history and heritage, simply be legislated in and out of usage according to the whims of persons or groups who suddenly declare themselves 'offended.' " Mr. Littlejohn, who calls himself *chairman* and not *chair,* accepts some changes in the name of clarity, as in changing *workman's compensation* to *worker's compensation.*

On freedom: "In no case should the University accept the idea that the office for civil rights is a better judge of appropriate language in its publications, or descriptions of its courses, than the University itself."

I tried to reach Mr. Grossman, the taxpayer's new Anti-Sexist Language Czar (which includes *czarina*), but was told gruffly that he was "in travel status," which is federalese for junketing or vacationing. The Department of Education's regional director in San Francisco, John Palomino, won't come to the phone: presumably, he has dived under his desk and barricaded himself with blotters until the storm passes.

The Secretary of Education in Washington, William J. Bennett, did return my call: "The minute I saw this story in *The Times,*" he said, referring to Wallace Turner's account of the brouhaha, "I said 'Good grief—I want to know how this happens.' " And how would he characterize the action of his attorney in San Francisco, presently on travel status in Japan? "Intrusive, meddlesome, unwarranted and wrong. My assistant secretary has counseled the regional directors that this should not happen again."

We then discussed the synonymy of his adjectives: *intrusive* implies forcing entrance without right, and *meddlesome* suggests a milder interposition without right; another adjective in this vein is *officious,* connoting authority where none exists. *Unwarranted* is stronger than *unapproved* and both more disapproving than and closer in meaning to *uncalled-for; wrong* imputes a moral or ethical error or, in this case, a big fat mistake. Sexism is *wrong;* the imposition of language change by government fiat, rather than by spirited private debate, is—as the Secretary of Education likes to say—intrusive, meddlesome, unwarranted and wrong.

I'm sure I am not the only girl who had to sit through the grim English class where the bad news was laid on—"when both boys and girls are referred to, use the masculine for both." And I am also sure that I am far from the only little girl who had to endure the smirks of little boys when the class was posed the "clincher question": "Now children, if there are ninety-nine girls and one boy in the room, what do we say?" And the answer caroled forth: "Will everyone open HIS BOOK?" And every little boy's chest swelled with the confidence that ensues from knowing HE outweighed in importance an infinite number of female creatures.

I think that the use of the masculine in mixed-gender situations has a pervasive and subtle effect on both men and women. Women are set off, made to feel that they are "extra," "nonstandard," "special," whatever words that can characterize the "apart from the norm" feeling we often have. I wish some of the grammarians that scoff at these feelings would try and put some of their talents to work to come up with ways to mitigate the problem.

Gail Williams
New York, New York

The push for nonsexist terms such as his/her, mail carrier, chairperson and humanity came as a result of the women's movement together with the beginnings of affirmative action (sex and race) and a general awareness that society was going through various changes. Today sexism, even jokingly, is not tolerated; society and its culture have changed. Why should language lag behind? Why should he/she bother you? Couldn't grantsmanship be re-coined "grant-getting" or "grant-chasing"? Brinkmanship, for example, is also known as brinking or playing chicken; no one seems the worse for having deleted "man" from the term.

Frankly, if you were a woman you would understand. When I, and other professional women, read "men do . . ." or ". . . rational men," we resent it. On the other hand I am truly delighted when I read he/she and similar configurations. I admit it will take time for you to get used to the new usages and terms but believe me it will be worth it. It will ease you into the twenty-first century without a second thought.

Only a person of great courage can admit his/her mistakes. This you have done elegantly, and thus successfully, in the past. You have been completely forgiven before, and no one has ever laughed at you or brought up old foibles. After all, not everyone can be the repented speechwriter of . . .

Mindy Aber
Jerusalem, Israel

I hope you are flooded with letters from ordinary women correcting your sexist attitude in language. I urge you to acquire a small book by Casey Miller and Kate Swift, titled *The Handbook of Nonsexist Writing.* We can all learn.

Dolphna Eggers
Red Bluff, California

You apparently agree with the most frequently used justification for sexist language: "longstanding acceptance." To that kind of lemming-like thinking I say hogwash! In the spirit of scholarly inquiry and exchange, it is always appropriate to question existing theories, practices and philosophies to determine, among other things, whether they continue to make sense. Today, most unbiased, thoughtful people recognize that sexist language is, at the least, exclusionary and inaccurate.

Tracy Dobson
Assistant Professor
College of Business
Michigan State University
East Lansing, Michigan

What I find distressing in your article is your inability to get outside your own ego. It is a problem that I have also, very acutely. This inability is common, I think, among many men, i.e. males. We who have been trained to think of ourselves as above, and separate from, other people, often lack the ability to create relationships, especially relationships of mutual respect, with other persons. When I read your article I was struck by how limited is your ability to relate to people. Your relationships, like mine, have probably focused on control, competition, or domination, which are primitive ways of human interaction.

Speaking from my own experience, it wasn't until I fell in love with a feminist that I began to realize how vast and varied is the terrain of human relationships.

John Hamilton
New Haven, Connecticut

Perhaps our best hope for reconciling sometimes conflicting concerns lies in the creation of new terms, preferably derived from the old, which are not specific to either sex. In written language, some of the terms I have found useful are *s/he* to specify the nominative case, and *hir* to specify the genitive, dative and accusative cases in the third person singular. Of course, whenever the antecedent is known (as with the reference to Professor Deutchman as "they"), the specific term can and should be employed.

Attempts such as these may at first glance seem unduly effortful. I for one believe that they are nevertheless necessary if we are to effect any change, however small, in a linguistic system that both reflects and propagates the long-standing subordination of women in society.

Scott M. Sokol
Baltimore, Maryland

Except for her below-the-belt comment about your prowess with women, Professor Iva E. Deutchman had a most compelling argument in favor of equality in language. Though amusing, her remark is as utterly ridiculous as your statement that "such expressions as 'the family of man' is no putdown of women." That's always been his-story (history).

Joan of Arc rode a horse and was a heroic soldier to boot, but *she* was not a "Man on Horseback" and she was no "solitary horse*man*" either. Mr. Safire, I bet that you would never in a million years consider referring to those "heroic solitary horsemen" as horsewomen, because they simply were not women, or so his-story goes.

Karen Effros
New York, New York

This may sound like a sneaky way out, but at R-E-W-R-I-T-E, our grammar hotline, we advise doing away with the pronoun altogether, which in many cases can be done. In your example, "Everyone should watch his [or her] pronoun agreement," it is possible to substitute, "Everyone should watch pronoun agreement." This *maneuver* is not sleight of hand; it works and often makes for a faster and smoother expression.

Joan Baum
Co-founder, R-E-W-R-I-T-E
York College
Jamaica, New York

My dear fellow ignoramus (= "we are ignorant"):
Be consistent and CORRECT, *bitte.*
Ad virem = to man
Ad hominem = to man/woman
Ad mulierem = to woman (married)
Ad virginem = to celibate woman
"*Ad mulie*rien attack" is not even good pig Latin. From Latin
learned more than forty years ago, I recall that third-declension masc/
fem nouns, singular (to form the accusative—"ad" takes it), add "em"
to the stem (mulier, *mulieris*) after dropping the genitive ending ("is").

John Iannuzzi
Ellicott City, Maryland

Your mistressful disquisition gave those of us in the losing battle for
linguistic sanity a glimmer of hope. However, we note with some dis-
may the sentence: "She believes that using the pronoun *their* would be
better than *his* is referring back to the singular-construed *everyone.* . . ." Come now; hasn't "refer back" been on the proscribed list
since the first edition of Fowler? Why compound good sense and a
pleonasm? Let her/him just plain refer, and leave the looking backwards understood.

D. Anthony English
Somerset, New Jersey

The only trouble with Iva E. Deutchman's remarks to you is that
she doesn't go far enough. Too long have we huperson-beings of the
feperson sex suffered man's inhupersonity to wopersons. Personkind
must rid itself entirely of linguistic sexism. Possibly, strict neutrality
might not apply to a few terms—"seMEN" comes to mind, but that
should be a rare exception. And Ms. Deutchman should immediately
correct her name: Deutchfrau? Deutchesse? Deutchperson?
Come to think of it, even the word "perSON" smacks of machis-
matic impurity. Should not we fepersons refer to ourselves as
feperdaughters?

Anna Lou Klein
San Francisco, California

Uncle Cries "Uncle"

I n a related development (to avoid that cliché, think of it as meaning a
community housing your in-laws), Mr. Reagan was asked in a recent
news conference whether he was advocating the overthrow of the government of Nicaragua. He indicated no, not "if they'd say 'Uncle.' "

My follow-up was directed to Robert Burchfield, editor of the Oxford
English Dictionary, whose new book, The English Language, is the best
short survey of the mother tongue by any of its sons. "Yes, the pages of the
Fourth Supplement of the O.E.D. that include *uncle* have just come from
the printers," the ebullient lexicographer from New Zealand reports. "The
expression is 'to say, holler or cry "Uncle" '—any of those verbs will do—
and we define it as 'to acknowledge defeat, to cry for mercy.' Very current
in America, isn't it?"

Very. The recorded origin is relatively recent, according to Mitford
Mathews in his Dictionary of Americanisms. Mathews's earliest citation for
the expression was the *Chicago Herald-Examiner* of Oct. 1, 1918: "Sic him
Jenny Jinx—make him say 'Uncle.' "

What made the President's use of the kids' street lingo so effective, and so infuriating, was the double meaning of "Uncle." As both the signal for surrender and the short form of "Uncle Sam," the President gave a special emphasis of knuckling under to the United States. I think the double meaning was not intentional; it was delivered in entirely too offhand a way for that.

"What intrigues me is the origin of the term," writes Peggy de Graaff of New York. "Why settle on that particular relative, and for what reason would that imply surrender?"

Nobody knows. Charles Earle Funk, in his *Heavens to Betsy!* book of word origins, tosses out a possibility in the Latin cry *Patrue mi patruissime*— "Uncle, my best of uncles!"—but how that might have made it from the streets of ancient Rome to the playgrounds of America is a mystery. For years, slangymologists have been breaking their heads over the provenance of the term and are about ready to throw in the towel, toss in the sponge, and like that.

About "crying 'Uncle,' " may I offer my family's theory?

When children in my neighborhood wrestled, we used to demand that the child on the bottom *"say you're a monkey's uncle"* to signal surrender.

I remember my mother saying that she thought the expression came from the era of the Scopes trial and the controversy over the theory of evolution. Children's street lingo of that period, she theorized, reflected the issue of the day: that it was humiliating to think of being related to monkeys.

Over time, the expression became shortened to "Say 'uncle.' "

Barbara Coombs Conner
Glens Falls, New York

May I suggest the origin might be in the French language—just as the international distress message is Mayday (not through any significance of the day, but because the sound M'*aidez* is the French for "Help me!").

The French term that sounds closest to "uncle" is *en cul*—a phrase signifying a willingness on the part of the speaker to be sodomized. I would suggest that the ultimate admission of submission in a fight (a situation determining of relative masculinity) is an offer to the other party to manifest his (the winner's) greater masculinity by *en cul*ing the loser.

It is easy to imagine this as a reality in fights in all male situations such as reform schools or prisons. It is also easy to see it moving from being a real offer on the part of the loser to a symbolic statement of submission. (After all, the most likely phrase of one attempting continued resistance would be "screw you!" or words to that effect, so *en cul* becomes the opposite concept.)

The idea that one is using the real term "uncle" seems wholly without merit. There seems no logic to asserting any relationship between the loser and winner of a fight. There is nothing about the relationship of an uncle to a nephew to signify superiority. Moreover, there are problems in squaring the "uncle" phrase in fights involving brothers—a situation which I would suggest would be quite common. The idea of one brother calling another "uncle" makes no sense. But the idea of a losing brother saying *"en cul"* (You've beaten me so soundly you can screw me) makes perfect sense.

Jan R. Harrington
New York, New York

Old Uncle Jim had an enclosure behind his house where he indulged his hobby as amateur aviarist. He had some parrots and lovebirds and canaries and budgies. Everybody called him Uncle Jim and more than anything in the world he wanted his parrot, Napoleon, to learn to say "Uncle Jim." No amount of patience and repetition seemed to sink into Napoleon's head. Uncle Jim would, every single day, spend hours with him saying, "Say Uncle. Say Uncle, Uncle, Uncle. Say Uncle." Nothing. No sign of comprehension. No effort to say it. He just sat there with his head cocked.

One day there was an squawking and screeching like never before. Uncle Jim ran to the enclosure and there was another parrot being held on his back on the ground, screeching. Standing over him with his strong claws holding the parrot was Napoleon and he was yelling down at the other parrot, "Say Uncle, say Uncle, Uncle, say Uncle."

You can tell that only the essence is here, but any good storyteller could make it sound right. I *know* that the thought contained is the origin of the phrase as I heard it for fifty years anyway. But being seventy-six now, I forget some things.

Allie Cassel
Lake Wales, Florida

Unwed Words

How do you break a linguistic taboo?

We all know some words that are not used in what used to be called "polite society." Now that polite society has loosened up considerably, formerly proscribed words are bandied about between people without embarrassment; the vestige of the old ban applies only to words on radio and television, and in your family newspaper. (A "family newspaper" is one that is not primarily aimed at swinging singles; more accurately, "family newspaper" is a phrase used by editors who know that a segment of their audience takes offense at seeing in print words that are used among adults, but are less often used in front of children. If the children are well brought up, they try not to use the words in front of adults.)

We are not talking here about "dirty" words or slang terms for bodily functions, but about standard English words usually associated with sex. *Rape*, for example, only two generations ago, was not a word used in general conversation, certainly not over the air or in the newspaper. The verb *violate* was sometimes substituted, but the preferred euphemism was *attack*; when a woman was said to have been *attacked*, the crime in mind was not an assault, but a rape.

That taboo was broken when the word was used as a metaphor in the Sino-Japanese War of the mid-1930s, as "the rape of Nanking." The word was used in a sense not primarily sexual, which made it printable—besides, it was a city, not a person, getting raped—and the frequency of its use removed some of the taboo from the word's sexual meaning. No longer did we say "unconsenting carnal knowledge"; the word *rape* entered polite society, and has recently been used outspokenly by feminists who believe that the crime deserves more attention.

Bastard is a word in the early stages of breaking its taboo. The word is already acceptable in specialized meanings like "variant from the standard," as in *bastard size,* as well as in verb form for "to debase, make inferior," as in *bastardize.*

However, in its basic meaning—illegitimate offspring, or child born out of wedlock—the noun *bastard* (etymology in dispute) is still looked upon prudishly for its connotation of the result of illicit sex and, more important, is avoided on the air or in print because it is also used as an imprecation. Most often when we call someone a bastard, we do not mean he is a "love child," but we mean he has the characteristics of inferiority that have long been contemptuously and quite unfairly attributed to the product of liaisons not benefited by clergy or city hall. That taboo on the slur spills over to a restriction on the use of the word in its original meaning.

Along comes an event that breaks, or at least reduces, the taboo. In an emotionally stunning interview with Terence Smith, a reporter on "The CBS Morning News," Peter W. Hill, an airline passenger who had been kidnapped and held in Beirut, said bitterly just after his release: "I'm so angry . . . I was just hoping that that plane we saw on the tarmac in Damascus was a B-52, and on the way over, just go in there and wipe out the whole bunch of bastards, OK? That's an irrational thought . . . just because of the anger I feel. . . ." The film clip, including the word *bastards*, led "The CBS Evening News" that night; apparently Dan Rather felt that the usual "bleep" used to censor epithets or profanity would detract from the emotional impact of the statement.

The next morning, *The New York Times* carried a similar quotation on its front page: "There was a definite camaraderie between the original two hijackers and the rest of the bastards."

"I don't believe too many people are really shocked," writes Michael D. Spett of White Plains, New York, "by reading or hearing language they now occasionally use themselves. But Mr. Hill, a fifty-seven-year-old tour guide (for religious groups, no less), may have really started something by the earnestness of his speaking. 'Bristling with Rage' was one of *The Times*'s subheads, and the editor must have felt it imperative to allow the word *bastards* to be printed in order to properly convey the mood."

The taboo has not been wholly removed, but the threshold of its use will be lower next time. The barrier to an angry slur will remain, however; President Harry S Truman's characterization of a columnist as an *s.o.b.* made the initials airable (Drew Pearson promptly formed a club called the Sons of Brotherhood), but it would still be a son-of-a-bitch to get the full phrase on the air, or in this paper, as a slur. (In the specialized form used in the preceding sentence, the phrase means "extremely difficult endeavor" and may thus be used in polite society. It is not the words themselves that carry the taboo, but their meaning, derived from the sense in which they are used.)

Welcome back *bastard*, not as an insult but as a proper English word used in ordinary discourse, not so much meaning "illegitimate" as "unlegitimated." Its breakthrough on the air and on the front page, as an insult, reduces its shock value; as its severity as a slur decreases, its use in its original meaning will increase.

In *King Lear*, Shakespeare allays somewhat the audience's animus toward the villain, Edmund, bastard son of Gloucester, by giving him a soliloquy in which he questions the unfairness of his state:

> . . . *Why bastard? Wherefore base?*
> *When my dimensions are as well compact,*
> *My mind as generous, and my shape as true,*
> *As honest madam's issue?*
> *. . . Fine word "legitimate"!*
> *Well, my legitimate, if this letter speed*
> *And my invention thrive, Edmund the base*
> *Shall top th' legitimate. I grow; I prosper.*
> *Now, gods, stand up for bastards!*

Dear Bill:

I think I may have a source for you for the word "bastard."

I am not sure precisely where this definitive source was first expressed to me, but I believe it was in a class in the freshman year at Columbia Law School taught by the famed legal historian Professor Julius Goebel. The course was called, if memory serves, "Development of Legal Institutions." The derivation of "bastard" was an aside during a lecture about medieval institutions in law.

Apparently, it was the practice in the days of yore for illegitimate sons of noblemen to carry into battle the traditional shield, except that on the left side, where the family crest would normally appear, there appeared a black bar as the illegitimate son was not entitled to carry the family crest. That bar, which identified them as noblemen's sons, was known as the "bar sinister." My belief is that the "sinister" referred to the left-hand side rather than to the present-day usage of that word.

In any event, Professor Goebel insisted that the word "bastard" derived from a bastardization of the phrase "bar sinister."

> Mort [Morton L. Janklow]
> New York, New York

Your discussion of the increasing acceptance of the word "bastard" in general discourse reminded me that the opposite is true for that word in legal terminology. At one time the "key word" (which is a topic heading used in legal research) for the offspring of an unmarried couple was "bastards." At some point (I'm not certain when), the key word for the same topic was changed to "illegitimate children." Still later (again, I'm not sure when), the key word was changed again, this time to "non-marital children." (I suppose this reflects the growing awareness of its being wrong to stigmatize such children for the arguably immoral behavior of their parents.)

Josiah Greenberg
New York, New York

Let me share with you the most expert use of "unwed words" that I've come across. They were spoken by Huey Long in 1934.

The "Imperial Wizard" of the Ku Klux Klan, Hiram Evans, of Stone Mountain, Georgia, threatened to campaign against the Kingfish on grounds he was "un-American." The enraged Long responded by telling the press:

"Quote me as saying that that Imperial bastard will never set foot in Louisiana, and that when I call him a sonofabitch I am not using profanity, but am referring to the circumstances of his birth."

Evans did not go to Louisiana.

Anthony E. Heffernan
Atlanta, Georgia

Upside Risk

Too many editors have degenerated into shovelers.

The etymon of *editor* is the Latin *edere,* "to give out, to publish," and some editors still think of themselves as the people who put out the news. Usually these are people who have the title *the* editor (or editor in chief, executive editor, editor and chief executive officer, etc.). But somewhere in the composing room of language, a specialized meaning was set in type: an editor of copy or film became one who prepared material for publication. *The* editor still grandly gives out; *an* editor, all too often, gives in.

To edit, the verb back-formed from *editor,* is quite different from *to publish,* the verb that led to *publisher; to edit* most often means "to shorten, strengthen, clarify," and an *editor* is supposed to be the person who makes the necessary cuts, checks for accuracy and adds the required qualifiers.

Every editor must be partly copy editor, because news makes words just as words make news, and a great editor is the language's best friend.

At *Forbes* magazine, James W. Michaels is the editor, who is also an editor in the more restricted sense of the term. Recently he told the editors in his shop, in effect, to cut the shoveling, and gave his copy desk the green light to delete business jargon.

Banished from the magazine are such misusages and bromides as *revolution* applied to changes anywhere, such as *an auditing revolution; upscale* when "affluent" is meant (one of these days, *Forbes* may even bring back "rich"); *pricey* for "expensive"; *superstar* ("What's a mere star?"), and *downside risk* ("What's an upside risk?").

Strictly rationed, though not forbidden (to be spooned rather than shoveled out), are such knee-jerking phrases as *Rust Belt, third world, fast track.* He frowns on the grubby grabbers of *hands-on management,* eschews *bells and whistles* and the omnipresent *world class,* and homes in on (not *"hones in on"*) *free fall.* (Have you noticed? *Awash in oil* has been replaced by *free fall in prices.*)

What about verbs to describe the movement of prices of stocks? *Forbes* will not use *soar* or *plummet* on movements of less than 1 percent on the Dow Jones average; I take this to mean if the market jumps 18 points, it *jumps* but does not *soar,* and if it drops 5 or 10 points, it *drops, declines, moves down, retreats, dips, sinks* or *sells off,* but does not *plummet.*

Plummet, for the editor's notebooks, comes from the Latin *plumbum,* the heavy metal known as lead. (I can hear the ancient Roman exercise leader hollering, "Get the lead out, *plumbum!*") In the event of a sudden rise in interest rates or universal profit-taking, nobody would dare use the crass *crash* or *bust;* the tired simile to be avoided on business pages would be *like a ton of bricks.*

Dear Bill:

   There is, I think, a useful distinction between "rich" and "affluent." We would use affluent for anyone who has sufficient income or credit to enable them to live well. Rich we would reserve for those well supplied, not just with spending power, but with a goodly amount of capital. Affluent is flowing. Rich is keeping. Our society has lots of affluent people who are not rich.

Jim [James W. Michaels]
Editor of Forbes
New York, New York

You rhetorically asked "What's an upside risk?," as though that expression were a nonexistent absurdity. I can assure you that is not the case. As an investment adviser and money manager for twenty-seven years, these last few months have presented me with several instances of "upside risk." As you may know, the Dow Jones Industrial Average has climbed 500 points in the last six months while interest rates have declined several hundred basis points. If an investor bought a stock at $10 per share last year, and now sees it selling at $15 in a boiling stock market, the following question might be asked: If I decide to sell this stock at 15 today, and realize a 50 percent profit, what are the chances that it will continue to climb to 20 in the next year (a 33$1/3$ percent appreciation) against earning 6$3/4$ percent interest on the proceeds of the sale? Assuming the current price is not overvaluing these shares, but at the same time they are no longer undervalued, this problem becomes quite real.

So in answer to your question, an "upside risk" is alive and well, and is found all over Wall Street.

Fred Ehrman
New York, New York

Vigilante

I s calling someone a *vigilante* an insult or a compliment? Is the philosophy of the vigilante called *vigilantism* or *vigilante-ism?*

These questions are posed by the issue raised in the New York subway
shooting of four teenagers by Bernhard H. Goetz, who felt menaced when
accosted by them. His act was hailed by many people who feel threatened
by hoodlums and was denounced by many who adhere to the rule of law
even when it falls short. Mr. Goetz was indicted by a grand jury for criminal possession of a gun; only the linguistic case will be considered in this
space.

Vigilante is a noun in English that comes from the Spanish noun for
watchman; the Spanish adjective *vigilante* means "watchful, wide-awake,"
same as the English adjective *vigilant.* The origin of the English noun is in
the Vigilance Committees organized in the South in the 1820s and '30s to
intimidate blacks and abolitionists. "The slave States," said the abolition

leader William Lloyd Garrison in 1835, ". . . have organized Vigilance Committees and Lynch Clubs." The assumption of control of law by citizens not empowered by law was applied more generally as well: "The prevalence of crime in San Francisco," wrote *The Whig Almanac* in 1851, "led to the formation of a voluntary association . . . called the Vigilance Committee."

At first these committees—their members were called *vigilantes,* starting just after the Civil War—were usually considered praiseworthy. Abolitionists called some of their own Underground Railroad organizations by that name, refusing to concede the word to their opponents; the Republican clubs formed to support Lincoln were called "Wide-Awakes." After the war, as the nation expanded westward, "vigilance committee" was the name given to the citizenry that combined to combat lawlessness before the law arrived, or that took charge when the lawmen failed.

But from the start, another meaning grew. "We hate what are called vigilant men; they are a set of suspicious, mean spirited mortals, that dislike fun," wrote *The Missouri Intelligencer* in 1821. Abolitionists equated vigilance with lynching: "As gross a violation of justice," wrote Horace Greeley's *New York Tribune* in 1858, "as vigilance committee or lynching mob was ever guilty of."

Thus, the word comes into modern times with competing senses: good (providing law where there is none) and bad (taking the law into your own hands). When used today in a historical sense, the word looks back at the frontier's rough justice, rather than at the South's repression of blacks, and is usually a compliment. But when applied to modern-day activities, the word *vigilante*—and especially the *-ism* that grows out of it—is usually used to suggest that outdated and unnecessary methods are being employed, and is pejorative.

On National Public Radio, most newscasters say *vigilantism,* though I've heard several say *vigilante-ism;* NBC and CBS agree on *vigilantism.* Which is correct?

I prefer *vigilante-ism,* pronouncing the final *e* in *vigilante.* This *-ism* does not refer merely to "being vigilant"; it has to do with "being a vigilante." Because the *-ism* flows from the noun *vigilante* rather than the adjective *vigilant,* we should logically say *vigilante-ism.*

You think it looks awkward with the hyphen and is hard to say? If you prefer *vigilantism,* then maybe you would like *McCarthism.* Of course not; it's *McCarthyism* and *vigilante-ism.* (Next time I hear an announcer drop the *e,* I'm gonna let him have it.)

Since "vigilante" now is in fashion, I thought you might be interested in an old legal maxim, to wit, *Vigilantibus et non dormientibus jura subveniunt,* which means, "The laws aid those who are vigilant, not those who sleep upon their rights" (Black's Law Dictionary).

Sebastian Destro
Long Island City, New York

Wave Bye-Bye

The *New York Times* financial page headline: " 'New Wave' View of Protectionism." The story dealt with an iconoclastic band of economists who contend that protectionism—a word always used pejoratively— may not always be such a bad thing. "Dubbed 'new wave,' " wrote Nicholas D. Kristof, the reporter, "these findings erode the textbook notion that unrestricted trade is always the best solution."

Meanwhile, in her book, indispensable to corporate clods, *Letitia Baldrige's Complete Guide to Executive Manners*, the sensible etiquettist titles a chapter on teleconferencing: "The Electronic Meeting: The New Wave."

It's the same old new wave. The phrase is from the French *nouvelle vague*, a term coined in the late 1950s to describe film (formerly movie) directors whose work was intimately self-conscious and helped to make the director, or *auteur*, more of a star. After that was translated into English, *New Wave* —usually capitalized—was tacked on to any "different" approach to anything. Before the economists moved in (O Smoot! O Hawley!), the phrase was applied most often to a sophisticated form of punk-rock music, put forward by groups like the Stranglers.

The predecessor phrase may have been *wave of the future*, a title of a 1940 essay by Anne Morrow Lindbergh, widely taken to be an apologia for fascism; Harold Ickes, then Interior Secretary, promptly denounced "the wavers of the future."

I've had it with *new wave*, except as a hairdressing idea, such as the current mousse call. Let's try *neo-wave* next time, if we can't say plain old *new*.

The director is the *metteur en scène*, not *l'auteur*.

Dely Monteser Wardle
Riverdale, New York

What Lie Implies

"I came here to prove that *Time* lied," announced Ariel Sharon after a libel jury had found that a paragraph in a story about him was defamatory and in error. "We were able to prove," the former Israeli defense minister said triumphantly, "that *Time* did lie."

"The jury said not that we lied," countered Henry Grunwald, *Time*'s editor in chief, "but that we made a mistake in good faith, and I just wish Mr. Sharon would stop talking about the jury proving that we 'lied.'" To back up his interpretation, *Time*'s editor pointed to the jury's crucial additional finding that no malice had been proved.

Thus, after the trial ended a new fight broke out over the meaning of the word *lie*. Was a *lie* merely an *untruth*—or was it an *untruth*, or *falsehood*, told with malicious intent?

On "This Week with David Brinkley," the lawyer Floyd Abrams, the great First Amendment expositor, argued that the Sharon jury had carefully distinguished between what it viewed as *Time*'s *mistake* and what it did not view as *Time*'s *lie*.

A few months before, Abrams had taken issue along the same lines with an advocacy advertisement by the Mobil Corporation that asked: "How long will the public support a free press if it is allowed to lie with virtual immunity?'' (The floating *it* in that sentence refers to the press, not the public.)

On the *New York Times* Op-Ed page, Abrams responded: "Not only has the Supreme Court never said the press could lie about public figures and be free of legal responsibility, it has said just the opposite. What the Supreme Court did say was that the press can be liable if it publishes a defamatory and false statement 'with knowledge that it was false, or with reckless disregard of whether it was false or not.' ''

Thus, the central point in libel law affecting celebrated people has to do with intent—was the statement published maliciously, knowing it was wrong or with "reckless disregard" of whether it was inaccurate? Interestingly, the central point in the semantics of the noun *lie* and the verb *to lie* has also to do with intent—is inadvertent or honest error a lie? Do you *lie* when you *make a false statement*, thinking it to be the truth? Or do you merely *misstate the facts*, quite different from a *deliberate distortion*?

Abrams, to whom I will turn if some irate politician seeks to slam me in debtors' prison, has turned to me for semantic counsel on this subject: "Am I not right that a *lie*, fairly understood, is a deliberate untruth?"

The hitch in that query is the phrase "fairly understood," which I take to mean "in common usage, as understood by most people, and not being twisted by interested parties to make their point." Semantics is not like the law; the study of meaning often wallows in the admission of imprecision. Case law gives words specific meaning, neatly differentiating between *burglary* and *robbery*; common usage can give words fuzzy edges.

The Oxford English Dictionary defines the noun as "an act or instance of lying," which doesn't help much, but then gets to the essence of the word as it was defined about a century ago: "a false statement made with intent to deceive; a criminal falsehood." It contrasts this criminal, malicious meaning with *white lie*, which it defines as "a consciously untrue statement which is not considered criminal; a falsehood rendered venial or praiseworthy by its motive." In the O.E.D., the meaning of *lie*, the black variety, is unambiguous: a *lie* is told (originally "made") with conscious, deliberate intent to deceive.

It is tempting to say "Next case!" at this point, but that would be wrong. Not everyone uses the word with that specific malice in mind.

No less an authority than the lexicographer Samuel Johnson preferred a loose construction: "Johnson had accustomed himself to use the word *lie*," wrote Boswell in 1781, "to express a mistake or an errour . . . though the relater did not mean to deceive." That was odd: in Johnson's Dictionary, *lie* is defined as "criminal falsehood," and a quotation is given from the English clergyman Robert South: "A *lye* is properly an outward signification of something contrary to, or at least beside, the inward sense of the mind; so that when one thing is signified or expressed, and the same thing not meant, or intended, that is properly a *lye.*"

However, Johnson also quoted Isaac Watts's *Logick*, which seems to me to give another slant to the word: "The word *lie* . . . implies both the false-hood of the speech, and my reproach and censure of the speaker." In that sense, *lie* is an attack word on the speaker who is in error, and is a charge of lack of moral probity in the speaker rather than a specific description of his intent to deceive.

Perhaps that is why, in Merriam-Webster's Ninth New Collegiate Dictionary, "a charge of lying" is given as one sense of the word, and then in the crucial sense—the "malice" meaning that concerns us here—two different meanings are given: the clear and narrow one of "an assertion . . . believed by the speaker to be untrue with intent to deceive" and the looser usage referred to by Boswell: "an untrue or inaccurate statement that may or may not be believed true by the speaker." Other dictionaries I trust, such as Webster's New World and Random House, also stress the first meaning, including intent to deceive or mislead, and then add another meaning of "to convey a false impression" without necessarily being criminal or deliberately deceitful.

Where does that leave us? Did *"Time* lie," as Sharon holds a jury has decided, or did *Time* not lie, as *Time* says a jury has decided?

My semantic judgment is this: to most people, although not to all, the word *lie* embraces the meaning of "deliberate." I think the jury's understanding of the word is the same as put forward by *Time* and by independent lawyer Abrams: "an untruth told with knowledge of its untruthfulness."

Curiously, a post-trial breakfast with Ariel Sharon leads me to think he agrees: when he says *"Time* lied," he means that he believes *Time* was not merely mistaken in one paragraph about him, but was out to besmear and ruin him. I think Sharon is mistaken (not that he is lying) when he contends that the jury decided that *Time* lied—although I have to admit that some people, including the ghost of Samuel Johnson, use the word in a not necessarily malicious sense.

I hope that helps, although it is not as deliciously determinative as lawyers like language to be. For savage savants who do not wish to be chilled or denied the ability to blast public figures, this advice from the poet William Blake may serve: "A truth that's told with bad intent/Beats all the lies you can invent."

I suggest that the act of lying is but one type of misrepresenting behavior and requires the following conditions to be met:

i. Some "fact" is *asserted* (not implied, entailed, or presupposed)
ii. The speaker *believes* the fact to be untrue (knowledge not req'd)
iii. The assertion is made with *intent to deceive.*

Condition (i) excludes implications such as "I have work to do" which follow from "I have to stay late at the office" from being lies— they are simply inaccurate inferences invited by the speaker. Condition (ii) requires only belief, not knowledge (whatever that is). Thus, uttering "There are ten planets" believing there are but nine could be construed as a lie, even if we find tomorrow that there are ten. Finally, condition (iii) excludes hyperbolic assertions such as "It's so hot outside today you can . . ."

You quote Abrams as saying, "Am I not right that a 'lie,' fairly understood, is a deliberate untruth?" and then appear to relate "fairly understood" to the term "lie." I wonder if this qualification wasn't intended to modify the expression "a deliberate untruth" in this instance. If so, one might examine what this latter expression is taken to mean. (In this regard, John Austin's "Three Ways of Spilling Ink" in *The Philosophical Review,* 1966, 75(427–40) compares acting deliberately, intentionally, and on purpose.)

Finally, Sissela Bok's *Lying: Moral Choice in Public and Private Life,* Pantheon, 1978, provides both historical and current perspective on this issue.

Bruce Fraser
Professor of Linguistics
Boston University
Boston, Massachusetts

What determines a lie is not that what was said fails to correspond to the true state of affairs. Lying is predicated upon what one *believes* to be true or false *about* a state of affairs. I lie when by my utterance I attempt to get you to believe something false about what I believe. This implies that one may lie in a situation in which what was said is true. For example, if I believe that it is not raining, but tell you that it is (perhaps out of a desire to see you inconvenienced by raincoat and umbrella), I have lied even if you are greeted by a downpour at the door.

Raymond Smullyan in his book of logical puzzles, *What Is the Name of This Book?*, offers the following anecdote (page 5):

I read of the following incident in a textbook on abnormal psychology. The doctors in a mental institution were thinking of releasing a certain schizophrenic patient. They decided to give him a lie detector test. One of the questions they asked him was, "Are you Napoleon?" He replied, "No." The machine showed he was lying.

With such instances of lying no legal issue seems to be raised. It's not easy to prosecute someone for telling the truth because he was not truthful in the telling. The examples point out a distinction between the philosophical and the legal notion of lying.

William Kiley
New York, New York

You might be interested in seeing how one of our Roman ancestors wrestled with a similar problem, the distinction between "lying" *(mentiri)* and "speaking a falsehood" *(mendacium dicere)*. The words are those of Nigidius Figulus, a scholar of the first century B.C., as reported by Aulus Gellius (*Attic Nights* Book 11, Chapter 11 [2nd cent. A.D.]):

> There is a difference between speaking a falsehood *(mendacium)* and lying *(mentiri)*. The person who lies is not himself deceived [i.e., he knows the truth], but tries to deceive another; the person who speaks a falsehood is deceived [i.e., does not know the truth] himself . . . [Or to look at it another way:] The liar does deceive, to the best of his ability; but the person who speaks a falsehood does not deceive, to the best of his ability . . . A good man *(vir bonus)* should see to it that he not lie, a cautious and sensible man *(prudens)*, that he not speak a falsehood. . . .

I have to add, though, that Figulus appears to have been swimming against the tide of common usage in attempting his neat distinction: the Oxford Latin Dictionary defines *mendacium* as "a false statement, falsehood, lie," without discrimination between Figulus' more neutral sense and the darker sense of "lie"; and from the passages that the Oxford Latin Dictionary cites, it's clear that the darker sense was very common (perhaps dominant) both before Figulus and after him.

As for Dr. Johnson: notice that, according to Boswell, Johnson "accustomed himself" to use the word in that (rather odd) sense. The phrase suggests the conscious intention of someone to act against a natural or ingrained tendency (as I might say, "I've accustomed myself to arise before dawn" [sc. though I'd naturally rather sleep in]). Boswell's report seems finally to affirm that the ordinary sense of "lie" was clearly not the sense that Johnson (for whatever reason) chose to adopt; the report also seems to show the great lexicographer cast momentarily in the role of Humpty Dumpty (to Alice)—"A word means whatever I choose it to mean" (sorry: quoting from memory here).

Robert A. Kaster
Chicago, Illinois

Your essay probed the word "lie" but did not clarify for me the Time–Sharon controversy. Is it possible that you discussed the wrong word? Had you analyzed "reckless" (as used by the Supreme Court in their phrase "reckless disregard") you would perhaps have helped your readers more.

For example, if the Court used "reckless" to mean "careless" then, had I been a juror, I would have found that Time did indeed evidence careless disregard of their obligation to check in depth the accuracy of the facts reported to them by their correspondent in Israel. I would have attributed their sloppy journalism to a lack of concern for upholding the highest standards of their profession.

On the other hand, if the Court took the meaning of "reckless" to be "utterly heedless," then I would have found in Time's favor. True, I might have believed that their editors had been carelessly incompetent in their handling of the story but I would not have gone so far as to believe that they had acted with utterly heedless disregard for the truth.

The question of course remains as to what the court meant. Is there a hint in the fact that Webster's Second and The Oxford English Dictionary both show "careless" as the first definition?

Jacques H. Isaacs
Greenwich, Connecticut

When Does "Close" Count?

At the end of the year, I do an office-pool column for political junkies. That is one tradition I wish I could shake, because what began as a way of showing off insiderness has become an annual exercise in humility: some nitpicking readers save the columns for a year and send them in with some illuminating comment like "And you call yourself a pundit?"

One reader with the courage of his nitpicking is Daniel J. Buck, a Congressional staff member. He makes his own selections in the multiple-choice test, puts them against mine and sends in both at the end of the year. Neither of us gets a half dozen right out of twenty, but that's OK—these are not Scholastic Aptitude Test scores. Low marks show daring.

On an economics projection (I said we would be recovering from a brief recession this year; he predicted correctly that we would be recession-free), he writes, "I edge you out on No. 6. Hardly hitting on the big one, but close counts in predictions."

That phrase rang a bell; I had just perused an ad for the Dale Carnegie Sales Course headlined "Close Doesn't Count," with a picture of a golf ball lying an inch from the hole. The ad troubled me because it seemed to misstate a delicious piece of American folklore.

The inadequacy of propinquity—or, to draw closer, the impotence of proximity—used to be expressed as "A miss is as good as a mile," but that, as we know, has atrophied because it is sexist. Derision at closeness to victory—specifically, sneering at claims of the virtue of running second—was made famous by Jody Powell, Jimmy Carter's press secretary. He put down the claims of the Kennedy camp in 1980 that the Senator's second-place showing in the Maine Democratic caucuses against the President had been better than expected and augured well for the loser. "Where I come from," said the aide, a Georgian, "when you win, you win, and when you lose, you lose." He then added the word-picture that made his comment memorable: "And close counts in horseshoes."

Reporting this for a European audience, Reuters adjusted the quotation to make it more understandable: "Close only counts in pitching horseshoes." (Unfortunately, the news service inserted its clarifying *only* in the wrong place: strictly speaking, the fixed-up phrase should have read, "Close counts *only* in pitching horseshoes.")

The game of *quoits*—tossing rings at a stake—was called *horseshoes* in northern English dialect in the early nineteenth century, because the game was played with them there, as in rural Georgia whence Mr. Powell came. In that game, a side scores three points for a *ringer*—when the horseshoe thrown encircles the stake—but scores a point when its horseshoe comes closer than one thrown just before by the opponent. Thus, in the game, closeness counts; the phrase "close counts" means "being close, or coming close, counts."

The Powell formulation was later taken up by the political columnist Mark Shields, who wrote of a possible weakness in candidate Ronald Reagan's debating style: "In horseshoes, unlike most competitive sports, close really does count. On more than a couple of occasions, Reagan has adopted the horseshoes approach to issues. If his facts or figures are questioned or corrected, the Californian is quicker to apologize than to bristle."

The adage has now found a permanent place in American politics. Early in the evening of Election Day, a losing candidate puts forward the brave Berra-ism, "It's not over till it's over," but later, when he claims a moral victory in nearly making it, the campaign manager for the other side is expected to mutter ungraciously, "Close counts in horseshoes."

Two words have been added recently, giving the proverb a grisly connotation. "Norfolk housewife Claire Mathis moans that she was only one number away," wrote Art Harris in the *Washington Post* last May, reporting on a bingo game, "so close. 'But close,' she says, 'only counts with horseshoes and hand grenades.' " There's a ringer.

The problem, Safire, is that you have never been exposed to the actual world of politics, nor yet the life of politicians. Any who have would know that the correct answer after winning a squeaker is "The only things where close counts is horse shoes *and hand grenades.*" (Suggest manliness, active duty combat service, non wimpishness. Also infantry/Army. No Navy la-di-da and clean sheets.) Southerners elide the l in only as in "on'y." The verb is always singular lest you look snooty *and* victorious which don't go over good. You are a good academic word watcher but you need to pay more attention to people like me.

Daniel P. Moynihan
United States Senate
Washington, D.C.

Whose Oxymoron Is Gored?

One of the language's great tropes is on the ropes. Something must be done to save the *oxymoron.*

"Oxymoron in Moscow" is the headline of a *Wall Street Journal* editorial that points to the Kremlin's announcement of changes in the Russian economic system. Such capitalist incentives as profit sharing are being put forward tentatively, along with the use of price changes to stimulate innovation. The editorial compares this loosening of some controls to being half pregnant—"Over the long haul, you can't have an economy that's half free"—and concludes that this is a good time to remind ourselves "of just what an oxymoron is really represented by the notion of a free communist economy."

The political point is well taken but the word's piquancy of meaning is being watered down. An *oxymoron* is not a mere *contradiction in terms.*

I'm not knocking the surge of interest in the *contradiction in terms,* both intended and unintended. When Senator Edward M. Kennedy recently denounced a Republican action as "a *transparent cover-up,*" that was widely noted as a delicious example of the unintended contradiction (especially from someone with *high negatives*). Similarly, a sign in a delicatessen window advertised a *Chicken Hero.* CBS touted its George Washington shows as an *epic miniseries,* which verged on the internally contradictory, though not as blatantly as ABC's description of its yearlong coverage of the Iranian hostage crisis as *nightly specials;* the ultimate television contradiction in terms is the now-enshrined *guest host.* Harry F. Themal of Wilmington's *News-Journal* sent me a clip of a new-car ad that states "automatic transmission is a *mandatory option.*" Consider, too, this statement by Prime Minister Shimon Peres of Israel: "My job is to worry about the *future history* of Israel."

Those unintentionally jarring juxtapositions of words caused a cottage industry to spring up among social "derisionaries," who now delight in finding phrases that can be construed as unwitting contradictions—not real mistakes, but seeming mistakes. Randy Cohen of New York points to *military intelligence, educational television, athletic scholarship* and *Congressional ethics,* holding jocularly that the words are in inherent conflict; Don Menchel of New York does the same with *jumbo shrimp, plastic glasses* and *original print.* In the same way, an Op-Ed piece by Senator Daniel Patrick Moynihan was titled "*Budget Process* Is an Oxymoron," in which he also took a lick at the irony now in the phrase *senatorial courtesy.*

In my book, none of those contradictions are oxymorons. Lester Silbernagel of Pine Bluff, Arkansas, calls our attention to the confusion among contradiction buffs by citing an item in *Winners and Sinners,* the Gotcha! Gang's favorite newsletter. A writer had misused the word *peruse* in this way: "that generation of writers whose names . . . flashed like a red signal to the casual peruser of cartoons and ads." The correction was: "*Casual peruser* is an oxymoron; *peruse* means 'to inspect minutely,' not 'to browse.' "

Right about the meaning of *peruse,* though repeated error is changing that once-precise verb's meaning, but wrong about *oxymoron*. Here we come to the point at last: an oxymoron is never the result of accident or error but is in essence always a carefully thought-through creation by an inspired writer.

That opinion (presented here as immutable fact, because that is what mavenism requires, but it's only my opinion, well-informed and defensible) will meet with furious objection from Lexicographic Irregulars who have dictionaries that do not make such a distinction.

First, the etymology: the *oxy* in *oxymoron*, like the same letters in *oxygen*, comes from the Greek *oxys*, meaning "sharp, keen, pungent, acid"; the *moron*, as any dope knows, is from *moros*, "foolish." The ancient Greeks put the words together as *oxymoros*, "pointedly foolish": there is method to the madness.

That *oxy* means the incongruous words are put together for a purpose, by a "wise fool," to use an oxymoron that, in Greek, comes out *sophomore*. Seemingly incongruous words are put together to achieve a dramatic, poetic or epigrammatic effect: the most frequently used examples are *cruel kindness, thunderous silence* and *deliberate speed* (the last an adaptation of Shakespeare's "with all convenient speed"). The sobriquet of Stephen Douglas, "The Little Giant," shows how it can be applied to an individual.

Not too many real oxymorons are being coined these days. The play title *Alone Together* was effective. *Open secret* has been around for some time, and *genuine phony* (with its variant about authentic Hollywood living, *real tinsel*) is not new. *Haughty humility* is fresher, and Richard Schickel's remarkable new book about the culture of celebrity offers a genuine oxymoron in its title: *Intimate Strangers.*

Do not allow this glorious device to be undermined by association with all other contradictions in terms. Fight oxymoronic pollution. Oxymorons must be calculated, not stumbled into, to produce harmonious contradiction.

I was struck by your description of Shimon Peres' phrase "future history" as "jarring"; the phrase has long been in use among readers of science fiction to describe a collection of stories or novels having mutually consistent settings, which together elaborate the development—political, technological, cultural, religious, and so on—of a place, population, or society. Heinlein, Blish, Piper, Niven, and Cherryh have all created future histories.

Scott E. Cooper
Marblehead, Massachusetts

Re oxymorons, one of my recent crossword puzzles in *New York* had oxymorons as its theme and title. To my surprise, my mail indicated that not many people knew what an oxymoron was.

I was also interested to note that none of the oxymorons I included appeared in your column. So here they are, with the definitions that appeared in the puzzle, if you wish to pursue it further:

PRETTY UGLY Not very comely
FRESH FROZEN Quickly preserved
CONSTANT CHANGE Continual progress
FREE SLAVES Slogan of 1861
OUT AT HOME Base runner's failure
STUDENT TEACHER Would-be educator
LOOSE TIGHTS Anorexic's clothing problem
LONG SHORTS Bermudas
FIRST FINAL Start of the end-term ordeal
FUTURE PRIOR Ambitious monk

Do these qualify as *calculated* oxymorons? Please say yes and make me proud we're on the same wavelength.

> *Maura B. Jacobson*
> *New York, New York*

Shame on you. The plural is *oxymora*.

I too collect oxymora: student athlete, domestic tranquillity new retreads.

> *John E. Lorz*
> *Great Bend, Pennsylvania*

I liked the remark about "peruse." It might be interesting to compile a list of words that people routinely use to mean something that the word doesn't really (i.e. historically) mean. Such as "decimate," "mayhem," "flay" . . .

> *Richard Sharvy*
> *Coral Gables, Florida*

Wines Without Caps

L ess and less *veritas* appears in the punctuation of *vino*. Today, we will dissociate ourselves from the roundheels of descriptivism and lay down "Winespell, Safire's Rigid Rules for the Clarity of Capitalization in Wines."

Here is how the need for an authoritative ukase became known. Editing his novel about the gushing intrigues in the American wine industry, *A Day Without Sunshine*, Les Whitten found himself cultivating a vineyard of confusion:

"There is no rule that makes any sense," the novelist and sometime sleuthlike reporter says. "*Cabernet* is uppercase, *zinfandel* is lower; *Pinot* is up, *port* down. To make matters worse, an American 'chablis' is not a Chablis, but an American Tokay is a Tokay. Help! It has led me to drink, during the proofreading process."

We can shoot this viticultural gap by acknowledging at the start that great dictionaries differ on the handling of the names of wines. At Webster's New World, where David Guralnik enjoys a glass of *Burgundy* at lunch, the word is capitalized and a notation is made that it is "occasionally" spelled with a small *b*; at Merriam-Webster, Fred Mish prefers his *burgundy* with a small *b*, taking cognizance that the word is "often capitalized."

In the same way, New World Guralnik of Cleveland, Ohio, lifts his glass of *Chardonnay*, while Merriam-Webster Mish of Springfield, Massachusetts, clinks back with *chardonnay*. By the time we get to the Cabernet Sauvignon, the eminent lexicographers are ready to heave bottles at each other. (David capitalizes, Fred does not.)

Once more into the breach, my friends. When experts wrangle, that old jazz great Pops Grammarian can call the tune. I may not know Lafitte from rotgut, but I am a palate-clearing, bowl-swirling, snifter-sniffing connoisseur of punctuation. As Jimmy Durante used to say, "Da Nose knows."

Rule 1: *When a wine is named for a place, and actually comes from that place, capitalize its name.* Thus, the wine from the Burgundy and Bordeaux regions of France, as well as bubbly from Champagne and brandy from Cognac— all real places, shipping booze as if there were no tomorrow—the first letter is uppercased. *(Uppercase* is a newer verb, elbowing out *capitalize;* you do not uppercase a word, only a letter, but you capitalize a word by beginning with a capital letter. Printers once kept letters in a pair of cases; the upper case held capitals, and the lower case held small letters. Have another drink.)

Rule 2: *When a wine is named for a place but does not come from that place, do not capitalize.* Thus, we have burgundy made in California, chablis from New York State, you name it—but keep it lowercased. You like Chianti? Fine, capitalize if it's from somewhere near that place in Italy, but not if it's California chianti, or if it is Sicilian chianti. For you white-winos, if the chardonnay does not come from Chardonnay in Burgundy, leave it lowercased and try it with a shot of seltzer.

Rule 3: *When a wine is named after a grape, do not capitalize—unless the grape is named after a place and the wine comes from that place.* Now we're getting into deep water, or profound wine. *Cabernet Sauvignon* originated in Bordeaux, and if the wine comes from there, capitalize; *cabernet* is the name of the grape, not a city, and deserves no capital. Neither is *pinot noir* named after a town; its French name derives partially from "pine cone," which describes the shape of the grape cluster, and the wine's name is not capitalized. Wine carrying the name *tokay* is named after a grape that is named after a town in Hungary, so the only time to capitalize a tokay is when the wine comes from around that town in Hungary. Similarly, the *concord* grape was developed in Concord, Massachusetts, and concord grape wine from outside of that part of Massachusetts I would lowercase. (The dictionaries disagree with me on the way I decapitate *tokay* and *concord* wines, but the dictionaries are merely doing their duty by describing the present confusion; follow me to wine-punctuation clarity. When wine novelists are parched for guidance, prescriptivism lives.)

Rule 4: *If the wine is named after a place and comes from that place, but the name has changed slightly in transmission from place to wine, do not capitalize.* Thus (we're big on *thus* today—steer clear of *thusly),* the wine called *sherry* is never capitalized, even when it comes from Jerez, originally Xeres, in Spain. In the same way, forget about capitalizing *port,* because Oporto suffered a clip.

Rule 5: *If the law calls for a certain spelling, for the purpose of identifying the point of origin to the consumer, obey the law.* I generally resist language-by-fiat, but am willing to go along on a ukase-by-ukase basis with those legislative requirements limiting the name Cognac to the brandy distilled from wine produced in that area, and calling all other brandy merely brandy, or *grappa,* or *marc,* or *weinbrand.* Rory Callahan, spokesman for the Wine Institute, representing California wines, points out that the American version of French *Sauternes* must not be spelled with the final *s*, to distinguish it from the French product: it's American *sauterne*.

Why should we work ourselves up over this? Isn't it in the nature of wine to loosen our tongues? Certainly the drift in this, as in any specialized lingo, is to knock down capitals as did the Visigoths of old—in that case, why should we not go with the flow of contradictions, saying OK to Tokay or OK to tokay? Answer: The purpose of language, of which capitalization is a part, is to differentiate and specify. If we can generally agree on certain signals to inform the buyer quickly and reliably about the product, we contribute to precision in purchasing. Think up before you drink up.

Hubris in hand, I am ready to consider emendations and challenges from all the well-lubricated but seldom lubricious lexicographers. However, for all those who have been ready to pop their corks at capitalistic confusion in alcohol proofreading, these Five Rules should provide cool, soothing relief.

On that score, the question is sure to come: Is *cooler* ever capitalized? Wine cooler, a blend of booze and fruit juices with half the alcohol content of wine, is now slaking the thirst of the country. Designed to be swilled rather than sipped, wine coolers currently account for nearly 15 percent of United States wine sales, and that is driving the mavens of Madeira (capitalized when from that Portuguese island) right up the wall.

Wine coolers—containers for chilling wine by immersing it in ice—have been around since at least 1815, but the drink with that name is much more recent, says Jack E. Daniels, executive director of the Society of Wine Educators. The word from Jack Daniels: "*Wine cooler* is a generic name that several companies use. It was just applied to the drink about six years ago, and as a generic name, *cooler* wouldn't be capitalized." According to my sure-fire system, however, if there were a city in the United States named Cooler, and the wine were bottled there, then—and only then—would we capitalize "wine Cooler."

Thank you so much for your article. This is a subject that has bothered me for a number of years, and I think you have clarified it perfectly. Quite a number of the French magazines have been uncapitalizing everything, which I feel is an insult to the wine and silly.

I shall from now on follow with confidence your five rules.

From a grateful and faithful reader,

Julia Child
Cambridge, Massachusetts

At *The Wine Spectator*, we deal with the capitalization problem in nearly every piece we edit. After considering all the possibilities, we settled on the following rule:

> Capitalize wine names when referring to a specific wine, grape variety or proprietary name. Cabernet Sauvignon, Chardonnay, Chenin Blanc, etc., are always up. Burgundy and Chablis are up when referring to a specific wine, but down when referring to a generic type, as in "I had a glass of jug chablis at the bar." It's Robert Mondavi Chardonnay, Kenwood Vintage Red, Paul Masson Emerald Dry, J. Moreau Chablis, etc.

Our reasoning is that grape varieties should be capitalized, the same as Golden Delicious, Winesap or Pippin (capitalized) varieties of apples (not capitalized). That's why your dictionaries capitalize Tokay and Concord. They are specific varieties of grapes.

Most American wine types are named after grape varieties. They would be capitalized anyway when used in reference to a specific wine (being the proper name of the wine, such as Louis M. Martini Cabernet Sauvignon 1978). Most European wines are named after places, which requires capitalization no matter how you look at it. To avoid confusion, it makes sense to capitalize all proper wine names.

"The purpose of language," you write, "is to differentiate and specify." I concur. No useful purpose is gained by making distinctions between cabernet sauvignon wines and the Cabernet Sauvignon grapes used to make them. There is, however, a valid distinction to be made between Burgundy wine from the Burgundy region of France and generic burgundy wine from elsewhere. That is why we choose to capitalize the real thing and lowercase the knock-off.

Moreover, *The Wine Spectator* style has the advantage over yours: It solves in one rule what yours does in five.

Harvey Steiman
Managing Editor
The Wine Spectator
San Francisco, California

I think your capitalization rules are excellent, and "Cognac" should indeed be reserved for brandy distilled from wine produced in the Cognac region. However, though all other brandy may properly be called "brandy" or *weinbrand,* as you suggest (if ordering in Germany), it should not be called *marc* or *grappa. Marc* is the French term for the spirit distilled from the mash of skins and other residue of grapes after the pressing for wine. *Grappa* is the Italian term for *marc.* Brandy is the spirit distilled from the wine itself. If you wish to order a non-Cognac brandy in France, try *eau de vie de vin* or simply *fine*.

Jon O. Newman
United States Circuit Judge
Hartford, Connecticut

You state that if a wine is named for a grape, do not capitalize unless the name of the grape derives from a place name and the wine comes from that place. But then you contradict yourself by capitalizing cabernet sauvignon. To my knowledge, neither cabernet nor cabernet sauvignon is the name of a town either in the Bordeaux district or in the rest of France. Neither is it the name of a province, department or other region. Consequently, following your rule, I see no reason why it should be capitalized. In any event, you will never find a "Cabernet Sauvignon" wine emanating from Bordeaux or anywhere else in France for the simple reason that cabernet sauvignon is not an approved appellation. It is a grape, which in combination with other grapes (cabernet franc and merlot) constitutes the blend (*cépage*) which then, depending on the level of quality, is sold as Bordeaux, Médoc, Haut Médoc or any of the other higher appellations.

Stanley A. Bowker
New York, New York

Your point concerning cabernet sauvignon is completely off the mark. Bordeaux is correctly capitalized, following the logic of Rule #1. Cabernet sauvignon, either as a grape or as a wine, should fall under other rules. By my lights, I would capitalize it only when identifying a specific wine, such as the Louis Martini 1974 Cabernet Sauvignon.

What is actually at issue in Rule #3 is a botanical concept. Wines whose names derive from the grape from which they are made (or varietal wines) deserve capitalization no more than the term "vinifera," the species of which the variety is a subcategory. I think we perpetuate the confusion when we choose to consider the point of origin, or more precisely, the point of naming of a particular grape. As a variety of grape, it makes sense to leave concord, tokay, and napa gamay without caps.

If we thus elect to assume that the names of grape varieties are not capitalized, unless used to refer to a varietal wine produced by a specific company (i.e., a brand name), many difficulties are resolved.

For example, there is the delicate problem of johannisberg riesling. By your rules, wines emanating from Johannisberg in West Germany would be Johannisberg Riesling while wines of the same variety from

California or New York would be johannisberg riesling. Or would they be Johannisberg riesling, since Johannisberg is indeed a proper name which normally would require capitalization? And what about wines from South Africa of the same variety? Must the consumer really be expected to know the origin of the grape variety in order to establish the authenticity of a wine? Would it not be less confusing to simply state that grape varieties are not capitalized? The example of tokay vs. Tokay rightly falls under Rule #1, not Rule #3.

Elizabeth A. Schwartz
Lodi, New York

In general, you were on the right track. As a former contributing editor (or Contributing Editor) of *Food & Wine* magazine, may I offer my own rules for capitalization of wine names?

1) All place names, being proper nouns, must be capitalized, as Napa Valley, Finger Lakes Region, Medoc, Pomerol, Burgundy, Celares, Tokay etc.

2) The use of a specific place name of one wine in a generic way to describe similar or dissimilar wines from other places is to be avoided out of politeness. If that's impossible, then at least do not capitalize. I like Napa Valley sparkling wine, California red wine and white; in a pinch I'll have some California champagne or a glass of Gallo chablis or burgundy.

3) Grape variety names are always capitalized by ampelographers. I'd suggest capitalizing when one is talking about specific wines— Ridge Zinfandel, Mondavi Chardonnay, Heitz Cabernet Sauvignon—and leaving the first letter lowercased when speaking of the grapes themselves—riesling, furmint, concord grapes. Many wine lovers would, however, insist on capitalizing all grape varietal names as proper nouns; and they may be right.

4) Never capitalize sherry, port or madeira, even if the wines come from Jerez, Oporto or Madeira. Do capitalize the various types of wines from those places, as Fino, Amontillado, Ruby, Tawny, Sercial, Malmsey etc.

5) When a wine is named neither for a place nor a grape variety, capitalize, e.g. Est! Est! Est!, Lacrima Christi, etc.

In a future column, you might take a look at the unfortunate Californian (a tautology, I know) drift toward abbreviating varietal names.

Out there, wine folk now compare zins and cabs and gewurtzes all the time.

Carl Desens
New York, New York

Rule number 2 has formed a dark cloud over a manuscript I am just now completing. Rule 2, recall, was "When a wine is named for a place but does not come from that place, do not capitalize." If I generalize from your specific, the subject of my book will change from a *Panama* hat to a *panama* hat. Much to the chagrin of Ecuadorians, in whose country the straw hats are hand-made, the name is a misnomer, and one which is unlikely to change.

(Briefly: The Isthmus of Panama was the main trading center for South American goods destined for the United States and Europe in the nineteenth century, Ecuadorian straw hats among them; when gold rushers passed through to and from California, they bought the lightweight straw hats and named them for their point of sale rather than country of origin. When Canal builders and then Theodore Roosevelt wore the hats, the name became indelible.)

My question is—did Edward VII, Al Capone, and Truman Capote all wear Panama hats or panama hats? (And if the latter, must we speak of idaho trout, philadelphia lawyers, and ripon Republicans when the noun originates outside the jurisdiction of the adjective?)

Tom Miller
Tucson, Arizona

The Big O of Oporto is a ringer; and the legitimate entry is a lowercase o, the Portuguese definite article, pronounced oo, not oh, standing ahead of, but separate from, the traditional name of the home of the ruby and tawny tipples: Porto, with an uppercase P. The Portuguese very commonly call it *o Porto*; and *vinho do* [= *de* + *o*] *Porto* is their name for the wine we call port.

The English, with their fine disdain for the speech of other people (who else could call Livorno Leghorn?) have mispronounced the o and have attached it to the name of the city, making two words into one: Oporto. An early stage of this process, dated 1692 in the O.E.D., is two words, both capitalized (even one-letter words can be): "An English vessell . . . with O Porto wine and some passengers on board."

With a lowercase p, *porto* simply means port or harbor, an appropriate name for a city at the mouth of the Douro River. The ancient ancestor of Porto, possibly on the other bank of the river, was first named Cale, then called Portus Cale (from which comes the name of

Portugal). So the name Porto has been on the scene for some two thousand years.

How, or indeed if, the final o of Porto got clipped is anybody's guess, because anything can happen to words transported to England, witness Bedlam from Bethlehem. But just maybe it is not a coincidence that the English word for the wine and the Portuguese name for the city can mean the same thing; and the English vintners at the mouth of the Douro have been bilingual for many generations: they can think in two languages simultaneously.

> *Raymond S. Willis*
> *Princeton, New Jersey*

Once more:
"Once more UNTO the breach, dear friends, once more . . ."
If it was meant to have anything to do with K. Henry V.
Appreciatively, if there is such a word,

> *Joe Hanson*
> *Wilmington, Delaware*

While reading your article, I was struck by your use of the word "punctuation" in regard to capitalization. My understanding of the word was that it refers only to commas, periods, and the like, and not to the actual letters in words. My American Heritage defines it as "The use of standard marks . . . in order to clarify meaning." Since clarification of meaning was the whole point of the essay, then I guess I must concede the point.

> *Edmund DeWan*
> *Urbana, Illinois*

Words of the Right

A generation ago, people on the political right did not mind being called *right-wingers*. We kind of resented *lunatic fringe*, the great coinage of Theodore Roosevelt, and *little old ladies in tennis shoes* was known to be a knock, but *right wing* had a sassy connotation—even the "moderate" among us counted ourselves as part of a hardy band of conservatives, murmuring "I'd rather be right" as we consigned ourselves, legs bowed but heads unbowed, to the clubbiness of permanent-minority status. We could not understand why our counterparts on the liberal side winced when we called them *left-wingers*.

Then everybody got into the conservative act. Some of us resented having to share our resentments, but nobody could dispute that the political center of gravity shifted in both parties. Suddenly most right-wingers started calling themselves *rightists* or *neo-cons*, short for *neo-conservatives*, and a few Kemp followers even put forward *New Populists*. At the same time, *right-winger* lost its appeal to right-wingers: it became the term used by those on the left to attack us, and instead of reveling in that attention, we took umbrage. At a conclave of conservatives from around the world, Richard V. Allen, President Reagan's former national security adviser, told reporters, "Don't call us right-wingers—that's a slander."

The problem is in the *wing*, or on the wing. When *left* was predominant (Franklin Delano Roosevelt's self-description was "a little left of center"), the *left-winger* label was resented because it smacked of radicalism, beyond left to *pinko* and *fellow traveler*. In the same way, when the right became predominant, *right-winger* ceased to be acceptable. Many on the right became self-conscious, eager to dissociate from the *nuts and kooks, troglodytes, Neanderthals* and *nuke-'em-back-to-the-Stone Age* extremists.

Some who are called the "far" right (by those who no longer want to be called "left") prefer to change the metaphor, calling themselves the "hard" right, thereby distinguishing themselves from the softies near the center; many more of these prefer "the New Right," conferring immediate old-fogy status on the not-new right.

The political right, hard and soft, old and new, is sensitive to the use of language by ideological opponents. Neo-con Daniel Patrick Moynihan, a soft-right, near-left Democrat, objected years ago to the Communist assumption of such words as *people's, democratic, peace-loving* and *liberation*, and launched a counterattack in the United Nations and in the United States Senate to recapture *democracy* from totalitarians and *peace* from the bellicose. *Imperialist* was tacked on to Soviet moves, and *liberation* was liberated to be used liberally on our liberators. No longer did we concede vocabulary victory to the other side; even *free world* regained its proud ring.

That was satisfying, but now a new and more subtle phase of the right's language awakening is under way. The linguistic battleground is no longer merely between East and West; the new target for rightists is the leftists' hitherto-unchallenged lingo. (Note the clipping of both *wings* and the assumption of the suffix *ist*, as in *centrist*. The *center-winger* has not yet appeared.)

Defense Secretary Caspar W. Weinberger, in a speech to Margaret

Thatcher and other members of the International Democrat Union assembled by the right-winger Richard Allen (go ahead, sue me), launched the linguistic counteroffensive last month. The name of the game being exposed is *moral equivalence*, sometimes called *moral symmetry*; those are attack phrases on the position of those who loftily try to put the Good Guys and the Bad Guys in the same bag.

An inversion of the meaning of words, says Cap (whose Pentagonese has often been ridiculed here and who is entitled to a break when he comes up with a good speech), is "the connotation that is always assigned to the term *arms race.*" "It's flatly false," because "it clouds the distinction between the reasons why we arm and the reasons the Soviets arm. *Arms race* doesn't focus on the difference between arming for aggressive, offensive military action and intimidation and, on the other hand, building defenses to protect the freedoms we have." This "rather flip diminishment"—the phrase, *arms race*—"implies that our efforts to counter the military threats that we face are really devoid of philosophical impulse, empty of any broader significance than a sporting event."

Let's think about that: ask anybody "Are you for an arms race?" and the answer is "No." Change that to "Must we counter the Soviet buildup?" and the answer is "Yes." That suggests that *arms race* is an effective pejorative characterization of the defense efforts of both superpowers. You never hear righties using the phrase *arms race*; it's a term used by anti-hardliners, which includes neutralists, doves, leftists, and the group denounced by the right-minded with the mouthfilling derogation *unilateral disarmers.*

Superpower is another word that turns off our Defense Secretary: "It's become widespread practice, especially in Western Europe, to refer to the United States and the Soviet Union together as *superpowers.*" That's OK if the word is used as shorthand for the militarily strong, but "its frequent repetition implies that the Great Divide in international affairs is between superpowers and all the other nations, rather than between democrats and totalitarians."

That catchall term *superpower*, says Mr. Weinberger, "implies that the essential characteristic of the United States is its military power rather than the political and economic freedom of its people. . . ." Here's the point: "In lumping together the United States and the Soviet Union in that single term *superpower*, one promotes the debilitating and essentially false notion of . . . moral symmetry between East and West."

Moral symmetry and *moral equivalence* (the phrase is from "The Moral Equivalent of War," a 1910 essay by the pragmatic William James), is the rightist's description of a position that superficially equates the United States and the Soviet Union. For example, when a critic of United States policy in Central America compares our pressure against Nicaragua to the Soviet invasion of Afghanistan, or when the Israeli attack on the Palestine Liberation Organization in Lebanon is equated with the PLO's campaign of terror in the last decade, many on the political right call that the practice of falsely asserting *moral equivalence:* although fighting is fighting, to ignore the moral chasm between fighting to achieve freedom and fighting to impose tyranny is to pretend no difference exists between right and wrong.

Of course, the Pentagon's targeting of the lump-together tone of *superpower* is not going to obliterate one of the great coinages of Cold War II. The word can be found in the early 1920s to mean the electric-power requirements of the zone between Boston and Washington (now called Bosnywash); and D. H. Lawrence, in his 1922 novel *Aaron's Rod,* described a character "newly flushed with his own male super-power." Those citations do not do us a whole lot of good.

"The earliest citation for the meaning you have in mind," reports superlexicographer Robert Burchfield of Oxford, whose end-of-the-alphabet last volume of his monumental Supplement to the O.E.D. is nearing completion, "which is 'a nation or state having a dominant position in world affairs,' and usually refers to the United States and the Union of Soviet Socialist Republics, is a 1944 book by William T. R. Fox entitled *The Super-Powers.*"

Mr. Fox is a professor of political science at Columbia University who is finally getting credit for his major contribution to our current vocabulary, and for causing our Defense Secretary to lose sleep. His classic line: "There will be 'world powers' and 'regional powers.' These world powers we shall call 'super-powers' in order to distinguish them from the other powers . . . whose interests are great in only a single theater of power conflict."

Great word, Fox; now, who came up with the *arms race?*

You seriously distort James's meaning and render him in effect a moral idiot. He knew as well as any of us that no activity is in *moral symmetry* with the making of war. He was fully aware that the making of war is the ultimate immorality. What he was seeking was a moral (good) equivalent to war which he believed to be bad (immoral) in that it resulted in deaths and other disasters. He was hardly pointing out any *moral symmetry* between war and some other activity. The case is quite the contrary.

James believed that there is in human beings a competitive, bellicose need. This need had traditionally been satisfied by the immoral activity of making war. James was seeking a *moral* equivalent, *equivalent* in the sense of equally satisfying bellicose and competitive needs, *moral* in that death and disaster do not result. He suggested international athletic competitions such as soccer games.

It is really a slander on James to suggest that he saw a *moral symmetry* between soccer games and war, particularly as he had no way of foretelling the behavior of contemporary British spectators.

David Kornbluh
Yonkers, New York

While you are cogitating the esoteric or cosmic designations such as *arms race, moral symmetry,* or moral *equivalent,* ordinary mortals such as the undersigned concern ourselves with words of grass-roots coinage —such as *spondulicks* or *spizzerinctum. Spondulicks* is cash, wherewithal; *spizzerinctum* is the equivalent of *élan vital.*

Karl Kohrs
Port Chester, New York

Yes, the World Is Lit

Students of oratory were interested in President Reagan's use of *yes* in his Second Inaugural Address. Not since Molly Bloom, in James Joyce's *Ulysses*, punctuated her stream of consciousness with *yes* to register passion has this technique been used so variously.

When the President puts *yes* before a word, it can mean "even," as in "I remember a time when people of different race, creed or ethnic origin found hatred and prejudice installed in social custom and, *yes*, in law."

Or it can mean "lastly," as after a series of "when" clauses, he concluded with "And, *yes*, the years when America . . . turned the tide of history. . . ."

Or it can be "the defiant yes," a characteristic of Mr. Reagan's style, often accompanied by a tightening of the mouth and a ducking of the head. It uses "yes" to mean "and I know some of you won't like this, but I'm going to say it anyway." Example: "A society . . . where the old and infirm are cared for, the young and, *yes*, the unborn protected. . . ."

Those who search for literary allusions in presidential speeches hit pay dirt in his peroration: "My friends, we live in a world that's lit by lightning."

Henry Hanson of *Chicago* magazine promptly turned to his copy of Tennessee Williams's 1944 play *The Glass Menagerie* and the memorable "I didn't go to the moon" curtain speech, in which Tom tells his crippled sister, Laura, who believes in the magic of candlelight on little glass animals, that he has been searching for "anything that can blow your candles out! . . . for nowadays the world is lit by lightning."

Did the President, or any of his writers, know of this allusion? Did he mean, as Williams's character did, to contrast gentle candlelight with fierce lightning? That is for the orator to know and for us to guess.

You Not Tarzan, Me Not Jane

America's relationship with New Zealand, a nice country with a democratic tradition, ain't what it used to be. Wellington doesn't want our nuclear-armed vessels visiting its ports, and Washington thinks a military alliance must be a two-way street. Seeking to capture the new feeling between Yanks and Kiwis in a phrase, I hit upon a song that Russ Columbo made famous, recalling its title as "Friends, Lovers No More."

Not quite right. As a large detachment from the Nitpickers' League reminded me, the correct title of that 1931 song is "Just Friends." (The Nitpickers' League uses an apostrophe outside the plural word; an offshoot of the league, which styles itself the Nitpicker's League, places its apostrophe before the possessive *s* and refuses to have anything to do with the parent body. That must have been some convention.)

I am not the only person who gets things almost, but not quite, right. "As a pianist," writes Irving Joseph of New York, "I have been asked to play songs like 'Someday He'll Come Along,' 'Sometimes I Wonder,' or 'Kiss Today Goodbye,' which, decoded, are the opening lines to 'The Man I Love,' 'Stardust,' and 'What I Did for Love.' "

That strikes a responsive lost chord. For many years, my favorite song was "Come, Come, I Love You On-Uh-Ly," and not until recently did I learn that its title is "My Hero," now the name of a sexist sandwich.

How many other near-misses afflict people who like to be accurate in their language? (The apostrophe-on-the-outside gang objects to *near-miss*,

insisting that the compound noun denotes "a preteen-age girl" and preferring *near-hit* as a synonym for "collision" or "slight inaccuracy." To each
his own.) Try, for example, writing "Play it again, Sam," thinking you are
calling up the words said by Humphrey Bogart to Dooley Wilson in *Casablanca*. A herd of insomniacs will bear down on you with tapes and scripts
proving the line to be "Play it!"—no "again, Sam."

Same goes in politics: Herbert Hoover never promised "a chicken in
every pot"; that was a canard, not a chicken, helped along by Al Smith,
who derided a 1928 Republican campaign flier with that title, which
quickly became a "quotation" directly attributed to his opponent. (It was
French King Henry IV who was *le Roi de la poule au pot*.) Nor did Marie
Antoinette say "Let 'em eat cake"; nor did Richard M. Nixon ever say the
words "I have a secret plan to end the war," as George Romney's 1968
supporters contended that he did.

The obsession for absolute accuracy in recollection was driven home to
me again by Judge Jon O. Newman of the United States Court of Appeals
for the Second Circuit, in Hartford. In a recent piece, I used a line from an
early Tarzan movie that has become part of the language: you know the
one, "Me Tarzan, you Jane."

"This is perhaps the most widely used quotation of a nonexistent line
from movie dialogue," writes Judge Newman, "exceeding in frequency even
the well known and equally nonexistent line 'Play it again, Sam.'

"Three years ago a case in our court brought to our attention the exact
lines from the original 1932 film *Tarzan, the Ape Man*. We took the occasion to set the historical record straight." Here's the judge with a copy of
the pertinent page of the court's opinion, written by his colleague, Judge
Amalya Lyle Kearse, setting out the correct dialogue in footnote 20:

*Contrary to popular belief, the line "Me Tarzan, you Jane" (or, as it is some-
times quoted, "You Tarzan, me Jane") does not appear in the 1932 film. The
actual dialogue is as follows:*

(Tarzan causes an ape that has frightened Jane to leave her alone)
JANE: Thank you for protecting *(pointing to herself)* me.
TARZAN: *(tapping her on the chest)* Me.
JANE: No. *(pointing to herself)* I'm only me for *me*.
TARZAN: *(tapping her)* Me!
JANE: No. *(pointing to him)* To *you* I'm *you*.
TARZAN: *(tapping himself on the chest)* You?
JANE: No. *(pause)* I'm Jane Parker. Understand? Jane.
TARZAN: *(tapping her)* Jane.

TOGETHER: *(Tarzan taps her)* Jane.

TARZAN: *(tapping her)* Jane.

JANE: *(nodding)* Yes, Jane.

JANE: *(pointing to him)* You? *(Tarzan does not respond; she points to herself)* Jane.

TARZAN: *(tapping her)* Jane.

JANE: *(pointing to him)* And you? You?

TARZAN: *(tapping himself)* Tarzan. Tarzan.

JANE: *(slowly)* Tarzan.

TARZAN: *(alternately tapping her and himself, harder and harder each time)* Jane. Tarzan. Jane. Tarzan. Jane. Tarzan. Jane. Tarzan. Jane. Tarzan. Jane. Tarzan. Jane. . . .

JANE: *(exasperated)* Oh, please stop. Let me go. I can't bear this. *(realizing he cannot understand)* Oh, what's the use?

The use—the purpose in widely disseminating this obscure but significant judicial footnote—is not merely to show the difficulty of teaching language to ape men, but to provide irrefutable proof that a phrase our society has come to believe was once said was not said. It is a superb specimen of "near-miss quotation," and we are all indebted to the federal bench's record-straightening Second Circuit. (You appellate judge; me language maven.)

Dear Bill:

"You played it for her. You can play it for me. Play it!" Said to whom? Astonishing the number of people who say, "Fats Waller" or, if they're jazz-cum-movie buffs, "Hoagy Carmichael." 'Twas indeed none other than Dooley Wilson, a member of the Houseman-Welles Federal Theatre company, who achieved his finest hour by singing Herman Hupfeld's 1931 non-hit, "As Time Goes By," in *Casablanca* (1943), thereby making the forgotten number into a hit, through the reissue of Rudy Vallee's old and unsuccessful recording. Why did they not record Wilson himself, or have Sinatra, say, put out a new record? Because the American Federation of Musicians was at the time, and for most of a year, effectively exercising a ban against all recordings. (N.B. It would be incorrect to say that old Dooley *played* as well as sang the number. He could not play a note, and the piano accompaniment was dubbed.)

Alistair [Cooke]
Founder Member-SANPICKLE
(Safire Nit Pickers' League)

At the very moment you were busily driving stakes through several famous phrases that in fact were never said, your next-door neighbor Russell Baker was hard at work giving new life to such a phrase.

Mr. Baker wrote that Henry Ford more or less said that customers could have a car in any color they wanted, "so long as the color they wanted was black."

This legendary remark (usually cited as referring to Mr. Ford's Model T) is, in my opinion, just that—a legend. In 1949 and 1950, I was attempting to restore a 1923 Model T roadster. Before planning the paint job for my car, I wrote the public relations office of the Ford Motor Company, which sent me a list of factory colors and combinations used on the Model T's. I was amazed at the time to find the variety of colors available, since I too had thought black body (with red wheel spokes) was about the only color. I selected light blue for the roadster body, with white spokes.

Ralph W. Richardson
New Castle, Delaware

You might add to your list of famous unspoken words the phrase "Elementary, my dear Watson," so often attributed to Sherlock Holmes. The great detective never uttered those words in any of Doyle's original stories. He did use the word "elementary" in that context (probably only once, in "The Crooked Man" memoir) and, of course, he often addressed his friend as "my dear Watson," but never in the now famous conjunction.

José Toro
Old San Juan, Puerto Rico

Zing 'em with Zugzwang

You cannot write about world affairs without a *Weltanschauung*; you cannot practice literary criticism without an understanding of *Zeitgeist*; you cannot nibble your nails properly without *Angst*, and you cannot report on turmoil anywhere without *Sturm und Drang*.

Let us suppose you already have a world view *(Weltanschauung)*, dig the spirit of the age *(Zeitgeist)*, are suffering anguish to the point of depression *(Angst)*, and can thus clearsightedly observe the storm and stress of a thundering confusion *(Sturm und Drang)*. What is it that you need?

You need *Zugzwang*.

I used this word in a column about a world-championship chess match, defining it as "forced to move but doomed by moving." Then a reader wrote to say, "Safire doesn't seem to understand the concept of *Zugzwang*." (Both the reader and I had failed to capitalize the German word. Remember the rule: when in Deutsch, capitalize. Mnemonic: *Ubermensch* is uppercase.)

For guidance in chess (and, en passant, the words used in its play), I am a pawn in the hand of Arthur Bisguier, *grandmaster* (the best title around, higher than *all-pro*, more believable than *Imperial Wizard*) and technical adviser to *Chess Life* magazine. I turned to him: have I embarrassed myself with my *Zugzwang* gambit?

"You have used a word," replied the grandmaster, "for a position in which each player would obtain a worse result if it were his turn to move than if it were not. It occurs only in endgame situations or in composed problems."

Frankly, Arthur, I would use *was* rather than *were* in that construction, because the contrary-to-fact state is unclear, and I suspect an "endgame situation" is the same as an "endgame," but the game you are a grandmaster in is chess, not language, and it's still your move.

"It might be a whoever-moves-loses situation," he explains. "Briefly stated, the onus of moving causes a worse result than would otherwise occur."

How might *Zugzwang*—with its guitar-strumming sound, similar to Wang Chung, the rock group—be used in a non-chess situation, or what Gary Kasparov might call real life?

"When standing in a traffic island, with cars going in both directions, one is most assuredly in *Zugzwang.*"

I was right. The slogan of people in *Zugzwang* is "Don't just do something, stand there." ("Traffic Island," by the way, is part of the archipelago that includes "Self-Serve Island" and "Full-Serve Island.") The noun *Zugzwang* cannot be translated into a single English word; in this characteristic, it is similar to *Gemütlichkeit* (which means more than "camaraderie") and *Schadenfreude* (the guiltily pleasurable thrill some people get when a friend is in trouble, the way most of the Soviet grandmasters felt about former champ Karpov).

Plop a little dumpling of a German word into your language soup for flavor or even for affectation's sake. But choose with care; for this sort of thing, you have to have what Hildegarde Merrill Mahoney, rubbing the sensitive tip of her thumb against her other fingertips, calls *Fingerspitzengefühl.*

I talked to my father on the phone today. Boy, is he mad at you for daring to pick on his card and chess crony Arthur Bisguier. According to my dad, you are dead wrong even to suspect that "an 'end game situation' is the same as an endgame," because there is really no such thing as an endgame all by itself. No one, he says, plays an end game; the game one plays is chess. The *Zugzwang* gambit is indeed the situation that can happen at the end of a chess game—or the "end game

situation," for short. As they say in the Ave J poolhall, chalk one up
for Bisguier.

Lawrence K. Grossman
President, News Division
National Broadcasting Company
New York, New York

Arguing with Arthur Bisguier on the meaning of *Zugzwang* might be
like taking issue with the Pope on Original Sin. Nevertheless I will
reject the case of the person standing on a traffic island with traffic
going by in both directions as being in Zugzwang, because he (or she)
doesn't *have to move* at that instant. If, on the other hand, a heavy
rain, with thunder and lightning, was pushing him (or her) to get out
of there, he (or she) would really be in Zugzwang.

Let me give you a real example of Zugzwang in a chess situation.
(Bisguier might like this one. He might even have known the man I
will mention.)

Back in the '30s I had a young friend named Donald MacMurray,
who was a marvelous (and ranked) chess player. Once in a while he
would play me, a real *Patzer*, by omitting his queen—giving me
queen's odds. On that basis I *once* won a game from him. Now comes
the Zugzwang.

He played me a game in which he said he would force me to
checkmate him. Naturally I put all my pieces *en prise* early on. To my
surprise he took them. But finally I found myself, as a result of a series
of checks, in a position in which the only legal move I had indeed
checkmated Meckele, as some of his chess friends used to call him.
That was a *real* Zugzwang.

Arthur J. Morgan
New York, New York

Well, you really covered yourself with it this time. Allow me to make
the following observations:

1. Arthur Bisguier may be a former U.S. chess champion and my
   undisputed better at the play of the game, but his definition of
   zugzwang is wrong. *Zug* is the word used in German for a chess
   move (literally a stroke or blow); *Zwang* means force or compulsion (related to the English word *thong*, originally meaning a restraint). Thus *zugzwang* simply means "the compulsion to move,"
   which alternates from one player to the other throughout the
   course of a chess game.

2. It is true that the word has come to refer specifically to a situation in which the necessity of moving works to a player's disadvantage; but it is *not* necessary for both players to find themselves simultaneously in this unenviable predicament. It is perfectly acceptable chess usage to say, for example, that "Black is in zugzwang." Certainly, as Bisguier correctly notes, there are endgames and composed positions in which either player will lose if compelled to move—but even in these cases, only one player actually *is* so compelled.

3. Your zugzwang slogan, "Don't just do something, stand there," misses the point. In zugzwang you *have* to do something; you *can't* just stand there; the rules won't allow you to pass your move.

4. Webster's Third New International lists *zugzwang* in lower case, as well as all your other examples (weltanschauung, zeitgeist, angst, sturm und drang). It seems to me that Webster's is right on this one and you're wrong: words such as these should be lowercased when used as English common nouns, capped only when set in italic as a foreign term. (I'm not so sure about *Sturm und Drang*, though.)

5. In any case, your general rule, "when in Deutsch, capitalize," is misleading. It's only the *nouns* that get capitalized in German. (Yes, all your examples happen to be nouns, but that doesn't justify the overgeneralization.)

6. Yes, you have embarrassed yourself by referring to your original usage of the term *zugzwang* as a "gambit." A gambit is a specific type of strategic maneuver, entailing the sacrifice of material (usually a pawn) for an advantage in position.

7. You let Bisguier badly dangle a modifier and get away with it ("Briefly stated, the onus of moving causes a worse result than would otherwise occur.") The onus of moving is not, of course, being briefly stated; what Arthur meant was, "To state it briefly, the onus of moving . . ." This reminds me of the increasingly common "simply put" construction, which sets my teeth on edge every time I hear it.

In the face of such a devastating catalog of misdeeds, may I suggest that your only honorable course would be to turn over your king and resign?

Stephen Chernicoff
Berkeley, California

Let us imagine two people playing Russian roulette, not by spinning the barrel but by firing the revolver in sequence; and let us further imagine they had reached the fifth of six chambers unharmed. The player whose turn it is knows that he has a fifty-fifty chance of blowing his brains out. In desperation he decides he will simply point the gun at his opponent and pull the trigger. At that moment he reflects: If I play the game fairly, I could be dead; if I shoot my opponent, I could be convicted of murder; if I fire at my opponent and the chamber is empty, he will have full warrant for shooting me with the cartridge we will then *know* to be in the next chamber. *Zugzwang.*

Paul A. Lacey
Richmond, Indiana

You state: "Mnemonic: *Ubermensch* is uppercase." Alas, you've misspelled the word. The *u* requires an umlaut. If the *Times* house style specifies that diacriticals should be omitted from capital letters, then *"Übermensch"* should be rendered as *"Uebermensch."*

Stephen Calvert
New York, New York

Acknowledgments

A *maven* is a self-proclaimed connoisseur, an enthusiastic expert, an affectionate aficionado of some usually recondite subject. This great Yiddishism has now gained a foothold in standard dictionaries, and if you have steadfastly plowed through this tome, you can confidently call yourself a language maven and award yourself the secret ring and give the secret handshake.

In our fellowship of mavenhood, you will find the kind of people who helped in my strip-expertise. These include lexicographers like Robert Barnhart and Sol Steinmetz of Barnhart Books, Robert Burchfield of the O.E.D., Frederic Cassidy and Joan Hall of the Dictionary of American Regional English, Stuart Berg Flexner of Random House, Victoria Neufeldt at Webster's New World, Frederick Mish at Merriam-Webster, and Anne Soukhanov at the American Heritage Dictionary.

On usage, Jacques Barzun keeps me on the straight and narrow when he can. Among the great phrasedicks, quotation anthologists James Simpson, Justin Kaplan of Bartlett's, and my brother Len Safir are always helpful, as is Jeanne Smith at the Library of Congress.

At the *New York Times* bureau in Washington, D.C., my research associate Jeffrey McQuain—now a language columnist in his own right—and my assistant Ann Elise Rubin knock themselves out to keep these columns from the primrose path of dalliance. Barclay Walsh, our chief librarian, Monica Borkowski, and Marjorie Goldsborough will lend a hand, knowing that they can get a language fix at any time in my roomful of word books. Earl Smith saves my life and work when systems crash. For help at Doubleday, I'm grateful to Nancy Evans, senior editor Sally Arteseros, and copy editor Chaucy Bennetts.

For errors, misjudgments, egregious sins of syntax, blame everyone mentioned herein, not me. To all the members of the Nitpickers' League, including the shock troops of the Gotcha! Gang, I say: you've got the wrong man. I am headed for the hills in the arms of Norma Loquendi.

Index